FOUNDATION PRESS

ENVIRONMENTAL LAW STORIES

Edited By

RICHARD J. LAZARUS

Professor of Law
Georgetown University

OLIVER A. HOUCK

Professor of Law
Tulane University

FOUNDATION PRESS
New York, New York
2005

THOMSON
—★—™
WEST

Cover photograph by Rick Rickman.

Foundation Press, of Thomson/West, has created this publication to provide you with
accurate and authoritative information concerning the subject matter covered. However,
this publication was not necessarily prepared by persons licensed to practice law in a
particular jurisdiction. Foundation Press is not engaged in rendering legal or other
professional advice, and this publication is not a substitute for the advice of an attorney. If
you require legal or other expert advice, you should seek the services of a competent
attorney or other professional.

© 2005 By FOUNDATION PRESS
       395 Hudson Street
       New York, NY 10014
       Phone Toll Free 1–877–888–1330
       Fax (212) 367–6799
       fdpress.com
Printed in the United States of America

ISBN 1–58778–728–8

TEXT IS PRINTED ON 10% POST
CONSUMER RECYCLED PAPER

This book is dedicated to the hundreds of environmental lawyers who, often at considerable financial, professional, and even personal risk, have dedicated their lives to the making of the nation's environmental protection laws.

*

ENVIRONMENTAL LAW STORIES

*

FOUNDATION PRESS

ENVIRONMENTAL
LAW STORIES

*

Introduction

Oliver A. Houck
Richard J. Lazarus

The Story of Environmental Law

We all enjoy a good story. The story of environmental law is a particularly rich one, improbable and unpredictable, and has been driven forward by lawsuits large and small. It is also a story about which your editors care deeply and in which, by way of disclaimer, we have been frequently involved.[1] Like many of our colleagues, the development of environmental law has dominated, even defined, much of our professional and personal lives. It continues to do so: while no longer new, environmental law remains very much a work in progress.

The story format is especially rewarding here. Those who study and practice environmental law soon find themselves buried in the detail of statutes the size of telephone directories, bookshelves of regulations and a constant stream of cases that clarify, interpret and, yes, confuse. As a federal court recently described one of the less dense pollution control statutes: "The Clean Water Act is an enigmatical piece of legislation. Filled with more sesquipedalian jargon than a year's subscription to any trade journal and a Byzantine system of cross references, its intricacies are virtually indecipherable."[2] An earlier court, interpreting the Coastal

---

1. We have each served as counsel or amici in several of the cases discussed in this book and have also written about them. Oliver A. Houck, *The Secret Opinions of the United States Supreme Court on Leading Cases in Environmental Law, Never Before Published*, 73 U. Colo. L. Rev. 459 (1994); Oliver A. Houck, *The Water, the Trees and the Land: Three Nearly Forgotten Cases That Changed the American Landscape*, 70 Tul. L. Rev 2279 (1995); Oliver A. Houck, *Unfinished Stories*, 73 U Colo L Rev 867 (2002); Oliver A. Houck, *More Unfinished Stories: Lucas, Atlanta Coalition and Palila/Sweet Home*, 75 U. Colo. L. Rev. 331 (2004); Richard J. Lazarus, *The Making of Environmental Law* (2004); Richard J. Lazarus, *Restoring What's Environmental about Environmental Law in the Supreme Court*, 47 U.C.L.A. L. Rev. 703 (2000); Richard J. Lazarus, *Putting the Correct "Spin" on Lucas*, 45 Stan. L. Rev. 1411 (1993). Those were reasons, we decided, to look beyond ourselves as possible chapter authors and to tap instead into the insights offered by others in the academy.

2. Citizens Coal Council v. U.S. EPA, 385 F.3d 969, 971 (6th Cir. 2004).

Zone Management Act, reasoned that "the federal bureaucracy is legally permitted to execute the congressional mandate with a high degree of befuddlement as long as it acts no more befuddled than the Congress must reasonably have anticipated."[3] Understanding environmental law is not for the faint of heart.

Within this complexity, it is easy, if not inevitable, to lose sight of the extraordinary events and personalities that made environmental law happen, and then made it work. The field itself was not a given. Environmental protection laws are by their nature radically redistributive. They express a dramatic reorientation of priorities and values in terms of the relationship of humankind to the natural environment and of the present to the future. They impose substantial costs on some for the benefit of others, especially future generations, and preservation values that wield little clout in the market place or ballot box. Indeed, for just this reason, political scientists and economists long asserted that a new field of of environmental protection laws would not happen.[4] At least in theory, it should not be possible to enact statutes and promulgate regulations that impose significant costs on the economically and politically powerful on behalf of interests far less so because of their noneconomic character and diffusion over space and time.

The story of environmental law is, accordingly, a remarkable story of defiance and persistence. The enactment during the second half of the twentieth century of a series of aspirational and breathtakingly ambitious environmental protection laws defied the oddsmakers. When, moreover, environmental law's obituary was repeatedly written, first in the 1970s with the OPEC oil embargo, next in the 1980s with the election of Ronald Reagan, and finally in the 1990s with the Contract with America, environmental law persevered and rebounded. To be sure, serious inequities and significant gaps in coverage remain, impeding the ability of these laws to achieve their full promise and statutory goals. But it cannot be gainsaid that the nation's environmental laws have succeeded in preventing in the United States the kind of widespread ecological damage witnessed in other industrialized nations of the world during the same time period. Meanwhile, nay-sayers notwithstanding, the American economy boomed.

What is also remarkable about environmental law is the extent to which its statutory programs were advanced, indeed at times mandated, in all cases heavily impacted, by lawsuits. Some sought to compel

---

3.   American Petroleum Institute v. Knecht, 456 F. Supp. 889, 931 (C.D. Cal. 1978).

4.   *See* Mancur Olson, *The Logic of Collective Action: Public Goods and the Theory of Groups* (1965); Daniel A. Farber, *Politics and Procedure in Environmental Law*, 8 J. L. Econ. & Org. 59, 60–61 (1992); Christopher H. Schroeder, *The Political Origins of Modern Environmental Law: Rational Choice Vs. Republican Moment—Explanations for Environmental Laws 1969–73*, 9 Duke J. Envt'l L & Policy Forum 29, 29–31 (1998).

government action, others to restrain it, yet others aimed directly against an offending activity, all pieces of the frame. They were started by those who at times went on to greater things and at other times by people who, once their fifteen minutes had expired, simply faded away. Sometimes they lost their case, but went on to prevail in another forum. Sometimes they won, but went on to lose their war. In almost no case did the reported decision terminate the issue. The stories go on. There is nothing static about environmental law. It is a game in motion.

Environmental Law Stories seeks to describe this motion, where these cases came from and where they have led. The challenge was to select only ten decisions from the thousands that make up the field. Some we have chosen are historic because they affirm radically new environmental programs. Others are significant because they present leading statutes and concepts at their crossroads, and still others because of their conflicts with other statutory and constitutional issues including commerce clause powers, takings jurisprudence, and standing to sue. In the end, we decided to concentrate primarily on pollution control rather than natural resources law, which has its own unique and considerably longer history. Slighting the importance of no case, this book inclines towards students and practitioners dealing with the more typical environmental statutes and introductory courses. But you will find, and enjoy, some rich exceptions to this rule.

The ten cases that we have selected feature characters as diverse as community activists, small farmers, big businesses, dedicated scientists, skilled lawyers, strong-willed judges, and Presidents of the United States. In a field dominated by statutes, the precedents they set accrete like common law and stand like navigation markers for the next set of actors to steer by or avoid. Within this spectrum, we have selected four marker cases that established environmental law, three others that went on to refine it, and, as noted, a final three that have sought to limit its effectiveness and reach. This selection mirrors, as well, the development of the field of environmental law itself, from the first, heady days of its creation to its current conflicts with other laws and values, including some embedded in the Constitution.

Setting the baseline for environmental law. Professor Daniel Farber leads off in Chapter 1 with a discussion of one of the most famous cases in several fields of law, *Boomer v Atlantic Cement Company*. Arising from modest origins, emissions from a cement plant onto a neighboring auto repair shop, this action in nuisance previewed many of the statutory issues to come in benefit-cost analysis, risk assessment, technology-forcing remedies and the institutional competence of the judiciary in environmental lawmaking. Environmental law came from many places, but one of the first was *Boomer* and the clashing impact of a major new industry in an old town in upstate New York.

Professor John Applegate follows in Chapter 2 with *Reserve Mining Co. v Environmental Protection Agency*, involving a major old industry and newly-discovered contamination that threatened Lake Superior and potable water for communities the size of Duluth, Minnesota. Spawning more than twenty judicial opinions, it took an early stand on the haunting issues of scientific uncertainty, toxic substances and precautionary principles. It also featured some of the most intemperate war-within-the-war conflicts among industry, local communities and even presiding judges. No one connected with *Reserve Mining* would want to go through it again. Like *Boomer*, however, it drew a line in the sand and established a strong, judicial role.

Calvert Cliffs Coordinating Committee v US Atomic Energy Commission, authored here by Professor Daniel Tarlock, presents in Chapter 3 our first look at statutory environmental law in the case that could fairly be said, and is often said, to have put environmental law on the map. The National Environmental Policy Act of 1969 (NEPA), the nation's first comprehensive environmental statute, was written in a few brief paragraphs and in language of uncertain enforceability. In a time of acute energy shortage, environmentalists invoked NEPA to challenge the licensing of a nuclear power plant, an agency of enormous prestige, and an industry with two decades of momentum virtually unchecked by the law. The outcome was by no means foreordained. What emerged, however, was an opinion that converted NEPA into one of the nation's strongest procedural requirements, and the courts into supervisory agents for this process and other laws. From *Calvert Cliffs* forward, courts were an integral part of administrative environmental law.

Professor Holly Doremus describes in Chapter 4 *Tennessee Valley Authority v Hill*, perhaps the high-water mark for any environmental statute in the United States Supreme Court. The case pitted a lowly, endangered minnow against an agency that was a legend and the driving force for economic development in the Appalachian region, another outcome by no means predictable for environmental concerns. By the time the case reached the Court, the dam was largely constructed, presenting the justices with the unpalatable choice of accepting the inevitable or enjoining it on the basis of a statute that seemed to ignore development interests and other equities: the Endangered Species Act simply required the protection of endangered species. The discussion here reveals many of the paradoxes at work in environmental law, including the competing roles of federal agencies and, at bottom, what winning and losing really mean. Whatever else they mean, *TVA v Hill* put the Supreme Court strongly on record in favor of enforcing the literal terms of environmental statutes.

Refining the baseline. Professor Thomas McGarity presents in Chapter 5 *Industrial Union Department, AFL–CIO v American Petro-*

leum Institute, which took the questions of *Reserve Mining* to a new level of sophistication, and to the Supreme Court. Better known as "the Benzene decision," the case arose under worker safety law but raised the challenge of regulating human health risks by chemicals known to be toxic at low levels, indeed carcinogenic at levels too low to measure, and the related issue of benefits and costs. It also questioned the competence of agencies and courts themselves to deal with issues of complex and indeterminate science. The Court's treatment of these issues, in widely-split opinions, presents even today a serious challenge for workplace safety and environmental health regulation.

Chevron Inc v Natural Resources Defense Council raises in Chapter 6 a companion issue of agency competence, and the deference due to agency interpretation of facts and law. Professor Jody Freeman is, by background, an expert in administrative law and it is no happenstance that she treats *Chevron* because, like most recent headliners in her field, it arose from environmental law, in this case the Clean Air Act. On a primary level, the case was about whether the Environmental Protection Agency could, in a reversal of policy, interpret the Act in a way to delay pollution abatement in areas already designated as unsafe for human health and the environment. In a larger sense, however, the case turned on how courts should treat administrative interpretations of law, a question of critical importance to environmental statutes that rely broadly on administrative rulemaking, and on administrations and philosophies that can change dramatically within short periods of time.

Professor William Buzbee describes in Chapter 7 the war over environmental enforcement in *Friends of the Earth v Laidlaw Environmental Services*, which arose over multiple, to put it mildly, violations of the Clean Water Act. Environmental law is nearly unique in its reliance on the innovative strategy of citizen suit enforcement, a strategy intended by Congress to advance statutory programs over the sometimes reluctant efforts of governmental agencies. Early in the 1970s, the Supreme Court had pronounced itself in favor of liberal standing rules that facilitated citizen suits, but by the time that Laidlaw came before the Court a more recent line of cases had begun to impose significant hurdles and limit the field. *Laidlaw* was viewed, by all sides, as the case that would forecast the future of citizen enforcement not only for the Water Act but all environmental law. Processor Buzbee treats these issues, and the story behind the story, in deserving detail.

Setting the limits. In Chapter 8, Professor Carol Rose presents *Lucas v South Carolina Coastal Council*, a leading case in both property and environmental law. It presents the conflict between public values and private property rights in the excruciating context of high-end coastal development, high-probability storm losses, and the high-value natural resources of the coastal zone. The issue was stark: under the

Fifth Amendment of the Constitution would the state have to compensate landowners for regulations reducing property values in high-hazard coastal areas? The case became the darling of property rights advocates, and a potential nightmare for environmentalists and coastal management agencies. The final opinion, the outcome of the development, and the consequences of this case are all somewhat surprising. And well worth this read.

Solid Waste Agency of Northern Cook County v US Army Corps of Engineers (SWANCC) is treated here by Professor Thomas Merrill in Chapter 9 and raises, obliquely by the Supreme Court but with obvious intention, another constitutional issue central to all federal environmental programs: the reach of the Commerce Clause on which nearly all of these programs are founded. On one level, it reflects the increasing skepticism that the Court expresses towards federal environmental statutes and its intent to return at least the more peripheral applications of these programs to state control. Underneath, however, the story also reveals the near chaos of conflicting agendas among environmental groups, communities and state and federal agencies. Whatever you knew and thought about *SWANCC* previously, this treatment will open your mind, and perhaps change it.

Professor Christopher Schroeder completes this series in Chapter 10 with *Whitman v American Trucking Association*, a case perhaps best described as the limit that did not happen, the bomb that did not go off. It returns the reader to the Clean Air Act, with its now-familiar questions of costs and benefits and insufficient information, and adds a new one that the regulated industry wanted very much to win: whether in the absence of precise, statutory limits, the EPA had authority to set clean air standards at all. The tactics behind these arguments are a lesson in lawyering, and the new industry litigation offensive described here is a lesson in the practice and dynamics of contemporary environmental law.

These stories done, we as editors are left only with the regret that we could not offer ten more. But please be assured, the cases presented here are at the top of one of the most dynamic, challenging and important fields of law on earth. Be also assured that the authors who have researched these cases, taught them, published on them, and deal with their issues on an almost daily basis, are among the best voices from whom to hear these stories and, perhaps for the first time, really understand them. Each of these stories is a gift, and for their work we are extremely grateful.*

* We would like to thank Meredith Byers, Tulane Law School Class of 2006, Randi Wallach, Georgetown University Law Center Class of 2005, and Kate Mayer, Georgetown University Law Center Class of 2004, for their outstanding assistance.

1

Daniel A. Farber

The Story of *Boomer*: Pollution and the Common Law

Boomer v. Atlantic Cement Co.[1] has become an established part of the legal canon. It looms large, not just in environmental law, but also in property, remedies, and torts. Its lasting fame is reflected in a law review symposium on the case some twenty years after the decision. The introductory article to the symposium observed that "for many years the case was taught in three first year courses—Property, Torts, and Civil Procedure–and in two upper class courses–Remedies and Environmental Law."[2] On this basis, *Boomer* was called "the great fertile crescent of the first year curriculum, and it seems that the whole first semester of law school could be taught out of that one case."[3] It is now fifteen years after that symposium, making this *Boomer*'s thirty-fifth birthday. But the case remains a staple of the law school curriculum and a constant preoccupation of legal scholars.

The staying power of the case may be partly due to historical accident, but probably owes more to the powerful simplicity of its facts. On the one hand, we have a multimillion-dollar cement plant, on the other, neighbors suffering from air pollution. These simple facts raise questions of enduring interest: Should the neighbors get an injunction, shutting down the plant? Or should they only receive damages for the decreased value of their land? Should the court simply try to resolve this as a dispute between neighbors? Or should it expand its focus to include broader public interests: the value of the cement plant to the local community or the harmful health effects of the pollution in the region?

---

1. 257 N.E.2d 870 (N.Y. 1970).

2. Joel C. Dobris, Boomer *Twenty Years Later: An Introduction, with Some Footnotes about "Theory,"* 54 Alb. L. Rev. 171, 171 (1990).

3. *Id.*

Does the common law have anything to contribute to environmental protection, or has it been supplanted by more sophisticated regulatory regimes?

As is often true of famous cases, the facts in *Boomer* were more complicated than the casebooks would suggest, and the issues correspondingly more complex. We will begin with a look at how the case arose and its progress through the New York courts. Then we will examine *Boomer* from three different perspectives. The first perspective involves the issue of damages versus injunctive relief and examines that issue through the lens of economic analysis. The second perspective relates to the extent of judicial discretion in remedying environmental harms. How freely should courts balance economic and environmental values? The final perspective asks about the continuing vitality of the common law in an age of statutes, and seeks to probe the complex relationship between these two sources of law. Is the common law of nuisance a living fossil in the modern age of environmental regulation or does it continue to have a vital role to play?

Each of the three perspectives has engaged the attention of courts and scholars. *Boomer*'s continuing vitality is due in no small part to the ability of such a short, simple opinion to raise such weighty and sophisticated questions. Like a small but multifaceted crystal, *Boomer* reflected light in several directions, each of which remains relevant today.

I. The Boomer *Litigation*

The Court of Appeals' opinion gives only the most cursory version of the facts, leaving the impression that the plaintiffs were suffering more or less routine damage from air pollution. In fact, the air pollution was far from routine, and the plaintiffs also suffered from other serious impacts. Nor was the Court of Appeals' opinion the final word in the case. Viewing the opinion without considering what happened on remand also gives a misleading impression of the outcome. In this section, we will attempt to remedy those failings.

A. The Cement Company and its Neighbors[4]

Atlantic Cement was formed in 1959 under the name "Burwill Realty Company," but the name was changed just before construction began. Presumably, the original name was meant to avoid cuing sellers that their land might have special value to the buyer for a large

---

4.   Unless otherwise indicated, the information in this section is drawn from Daniel A. Farber, *Reassessing* Boomer: *Justice, Efficiency, and Nuisance Law, in* Peter Hay & Michael H. Hoeflich eds., *Property Law and Legal Education: Essays in Honor of John E. Cribbet* 7(1988).

industrial venture. Atlantic had assembled a large tract of land: a later tax appraisal lists it as 3260 acres.[5]

Atlantic was a joint venture of two mining companies.[6] This was the joint venture's only plant, but it had distribution centers all along the East Coast, served either by rail or barge. (Thus, calling it the "Atlantic" cement company was quite appropriate.) The plant employed about four hundred people, and its assessed value was about half of the total assessed value of the entire township. The Albany area had other cement plants, being rich in the necessary raw materials, with a handy source of river transportation provided by the Hudson.

Cement is composed of various minerals that are quarried, heated in a kiln, and ground into a fine powder. The primary environmental impacts are air pollution (especially particulates) and vibration from the quarrying. A significant amount of solid waste is also generated.

When construction of the Atlantic cement plant began in 1961, the area was unzoned. The plant was located about a mile from the village of Ravena and was composed of small houses and businesses such as the auto junkyard and body shop owned by Oscar and June Boomer. The locale sounds typical of the fringe areas found on highways on the outskirts of towns all over the country: junkyards, inexpensive houses, roadside taverns, and so on. Thus, it is unlikely that anyone with any political influence was in the area. In any event, the company seemed to have had no trouble with the planning authorities. Soon after the construction began, the site was zoned "heavy industrial" by the town board.

Atlantic invested more than $40 million in the plant, which incorporated what was then state-of-the-art pollution control. There is no indication of how much of this sum covered land acquisition, whether the plant machinery could have been removed and used at another site, or what value the land would have had if used for other purposes. So far as the record shows, Atlantic did what it could to mitigate the environmental impact of its operations. The $2 million dust collection equipment was allegedly considered the best in the country. Before the litigation was over, the company had spent an additional $1.6 million installing a spray system, a fiberglass bag collector, and converting from coal to oil.

Despite its mitigation efforts, Atlantic had drastic effects on its neighbors, partly due to its quarrying operation rather than the cement manufacturing operation. The quarrying operation caused severe vibra-

---

5. *See* Blue Circle Inc. v. Schermerhorn, 652 N.Y.S. 2d 817 (1997). There is no indication of a major expansion in the intervening years between *Boomer* and *Blue Circle*.

6. *See* Michael A. Mogill, *Dialing for Discourse: The Search for the "Ever After,"* 36 Willamette L. Rev. 1, 9 (2000).

tion. Using what was called the "millisecond delay" method, a series of blasts would be used to remove layers sequentially, so a new blast would go off just as the previous layer of rock was falling away. Thus, a sequence of explosions would continue for some period of time, seriously affecting neighboring landowners. For example, the Millious couple lived in a ranch house about half a mile from the quarry. The blasting caused large cracks in the wells, ceiling, and even exterior of their house. Air pollution added to the troubles of the Milliouses and other neighbors. Fine dust from the cement operation coated the interior with what the Milliouses described at trial as a "plastic-like coating." Mr. Millious also recalls today that he had to scrape the cement dust off of his windshield with a razor blade and that the gutters on his house filled with so much dust that they fell off the house.[7] Similar harm was reported by the Venturas, who lived about the same distance from the plant and the conveyer.

The noise from the blasting was also a serious problem, causing major vibrations and sometime panicking small children who lived in the area. One woman's testimony vividly portrays the effects of the blasting:

> Well, we were sitting on the floor in the living room, playing a game when they had this awful tremble, and to me the house seemed like the whole house was rocking, and I would see the lamp shades vibrating and it just scared the children. That was one of the times that they just got up and started to run for the basement.

In short, the neighbors had all the disadvantages of living right on top of the San Andreas fault, without the California climate as compensation!

According to Mr. Boomer, he tried numerous times to reach some agreement with the company prior to bringing suit. He recalls that they wanted to shut his business down and have him come work for the company as a machinist. But Mr. Boomer said, he did not trust them "as far as he could throw them." Mr. Millious recalls that the company denied that the dust was even coming from the plant, blaming it on a source across the river. Even today, he sounds agitated when he discusses the company's response to his complaints.[8]

B. Background on the Law of Nuisance

In an effort to remedy this situation, the plaintiffs filed a common law action known as a nuisance suit. A brief detour to explain this cause of action is therefore in order. Unfortunately, providing a crisp description of nuisance law is not easy. While the general concept of nuisance liability is reasonably clear, the details quickly become fuzzy. The law of

---

7. This information is based on interviews conducted by Sky Stanfield with Boomer and Millious in early September of 2004.

8. *Id.*

nuisance has an ancient history and, according to some, an equally inscrutable one. As the leading Torts hornbook says,

> There is perhaps no more impenetrable jungle in the entire law than that which surrounds the word "nuisance." It has meant all things to all people, and has been applied indiscriminately to everything from an alarming advertisement to a cockroach baked in a pie. There is general agreement that it is incapable of any exact or comprehensive definition.[9]

The doctrine dates back to seven centuries, and was well-established by the time of Edward III, apparently gathering complexity and difficulty as it went along.[10]

One source of confusion is the distinction between public and private nuisances. A private nuisance is an ordinary tort. A public nuisance is an interference with a public right—for example, in the early cases, interference with a public road.[11] Today, public nuisances are often defined by statute. Normally, the government brings actions to abate a public nuisance. But a private citizen who suffers "special damage" from a public nuisance also has standing to abate the nuisance. The same conduct can constitute a public nuisance and a private one, and sometimes actions are brought by the same plaintiff under both theories. It's easy to understand the reasons for confusion between a private nuisance suit and a public nuisance suit brought by a plaintiff with special damages. Fortunately, we will focus only on private nuisance. With the exception of a single case discussed later (*Spur Industries*), the discussion will only be concerned with private nuisances.

The crux of a private nuisance is an unreasonable and substantial interference with the use of land.[12] Even if the defendant's conduct was reasonable, according to some authorities, liability can be found where the defendant interfered with the use of plaintiff's land to the extent that justice requires compensation.[13] "Unreasonable interference" sounds like a straightforward concept. Still, there is considerable confu-

---

9. W. Page Keeton ET AL., *Prosser and Keeton on the Law of Torts* 616 (5th ed. 1984).

10. *Id.* at 617; Jeff L. Lewin, *Boomer and the American Law of Nuisance: Past, Present, and Future*, 54 Alb. L. Rev. 189–206 (1990). Notably, the English courts were not receptive to defenses based on the social value of the offending activity. *See* H. Marlow Green, *Common Law, Property Rights and the Environment: A Comparative Analysis of Historical Developments in the United States and England and a Model for the Future*, 30 Cornell Int'l L.J. 541, 546, 563 (1997).

11. *See* Robert Abrams & Val Washington, *The Misunderstood Law of Public Nuisance: A Comparison with Private Nuisance Twenty Years After* Boomer, 54 Alb. L. Rev. 359 (1990) (discussing public nuisance doctrine in detail).

12. Keeton, *supra* note 10, at 623, 625.

13. *Id.* at 629.

sion about whether to focus on the reasonableness of the defendant's conduct or the unreasonableness of the impact on the plaintiff, about whether the utility of the defendant's activity is relevant to liability or only to remedy, and about how important that factor might be in either context.

Once a private nuisance has been found, the question of remedy arises. Because land is considered unique and irreplaceable, the typical remedy in real estate disputes is an injunction. In the nuisance context, however, courts have been concerned about the possible adverse effects of injunctive relief. The fear is that an injunction may suppress an activity important to society, though burdensome to neighbors. For this reason, many courts will "balance the equities" in determining whether an injunction will issue.[14] This is said to have become the prevailing view by 1940.[15] But other courts adhered to the view that an injunction is mandatory when a nuisance exists and damages fail to provide an adequate remedy.[16] New York was generally considered to adhere to this second school of thought. (As we will see, however, the New York rule may not have actually been quite this rigid even before *Boomer*.) Whether to balance the equities was, of course, a key issue in *Boomer*.

The Second Restatement of Torts made a strong effort to bring order out of this somewhat unsettled area of doctrine. (Restatements are summaries of the law by a widely respected professional body, the American Law Institute.) The Restatement defines an interference as unreasonable if "the gravity of the harm outweighs the utility of the actor's conduct."[17] An injunction would seem appropriate in those cases. But even where the balancing test is not met, the Restatement allows damages when "the harm caused by the conduct is serious and financial burden of compensating of this and similar harm to others would not make the continuation of the conduct not feasible."[18] Restatements are not official legal documents, but they are often followed by courts.

The extent to which the Restatement's view of nuisance has been followed by the courts, however, is unclear. In particular, the question of how the utility of the defendant's conduct enters into the analysis has not been settled. As of 1990, about eight states had adopted the Restatement's approach completely; seven had adopted the balance of utilities test without expressly considering the proviso allowing compensation for serious harm; and the remaining states were happy to roll all of the relevant factors into a general "reasonableness" test, with little indica-

---

14.   *Id.* at 631.

15.   *See,* Levin *supra* note 11, at 206.

16.   Keeton, *supra* note 10, at 632, 640.

17.   *Restatement (Second) of Torts* § 826(a).

18.   *Id.* § 826(b).

tion of the weight carried by any individual factor such as the social utility of the defendant's conduct.[19] By and large, then, nuisance doctrine is still a bit muddy, if not quite the horrendous quagmire portrayed by some commentators.

Thus, when the plaintiffs filed suit in *Boomer*, they were walking into a contested area of doctrine. The economic interest of the defendant, a major corporation, obviously was much greater than the market value of the plaintiffs' few acres of commercially marginal land. The key issue in the *Boomer* litigation was whether this factor should enter into a determination of liability or the choice of remedy.

C. The Road to the Court of Appeals

The liability issue was settled at a fairly early state of the litigation, leaving the focus on remedial interests. The trial judge found that the plaintiffs had established the existence of a nuisance:

> Although the evidence in this case establishes that Atlantic took every available and possible precaution to protect the plaintiffs from dust, nevertheless, I find that the plaintiffs have sustained the burden of proof that Atlantic in the operation of its cement plant . . . created a nuisance insofar as the lands of the plaintiffs are concerned. The discharge of large quantities of dust upon each of the properties and excessive vibration from blasting deprived each party of the reasonable use of his property and thereby prevented his enjoyment of life and liberty therein.[20]

Note that the trial court's analysis focused on the impact of the plant on the neighbors, rather than trying to determine whether that impact was justified by the social utility of the plant.

Although they were vindicated in this liability finding, the plaintiffs were not so lucky when it came to the remedy. Here, the social utility of the plant loomed large. The trial judge refused to issue an injunction because of Atlantic's "immense investment in the Hudson River Valley, its contribution to the Capital District's economy and its immediate help to the education of children in the Town of Coeymans through the payment of substantial sums in school and property taxes."[21] Consequently, the trial judge refused to enter an injunction and merely awarded damages instead. Nor was the damage award generous. The trial judge awarded the plaintiffs a total of $535 per month in damages for past losses but suggested that the parties settle the case for the

---

19. *See*, Levin *supra* note 11, at 234. The Restatement approach has been more popular in cases involving diversion of surface waters. *See id*. at 230–233.

20. Boomer v. Atlantic Cement Co., 287 N.Y.S.2d 112, 113–114 (1967).

21. *Id*. at 113–14.

amount of the permanent loss of market value, which he calculated as $185,000 for all the plaintiffs combined.[22]

Not surprisingly, the plaintiffs appealed. The appellate division (an intermediate appeals court in the New York state system) affirmed in a brief opinion.[23] It found no abuse of discretion in the denial of injunctive relief, taking into account "the zoning of the area, the large number of persons employed by the defendant, its extensive business operations and substantial investment in plant and equipment, its use of the most modern and efficient devices to prevent offensive emissions and discharges, and its payment of substantial sums of real property and schools taxes." Remaining dissatisfied, the plaintiffs appealed again, setting the stage for the Court of Appeal's famous opinion in the case.

D. The *Boomer* Decision

The plaintiffs took the case to the New York Court of Appeals (the highest court in the state). They launched a battery of challenges to the lower courts' rulings. The first half of their argument focused on the injunction issue:

> I.   The trial court, as well as the Appellate Division, erred as a matter of law by depriving plaintiffs of their property rights when the courts failed to grant an injunction against the nuisances created by the Atlantic Cement Company, Inc. II. The trial court and Appellate Division in our instant cases have devised a new "economic utility doctrine," which if left unchallenged will leave in jeopardy the rights of small property owners throughout the State of New York.[24]

The injunction was not, however, the only focus of the plaintiffs' attack. The second half of their argument focused on the question of how to measure damages:

> III.   The trial court and the Appellate Division erred in their decision by leaving plaintiffs with an inadequate remedy at law, which results in a multiplicity of suits ... V. The temporary damages granted by the trial court to plaintiffs were inadequate. VI. The reasonable market value of the real property of plaintiffs and of the business known as the Coach House Restaurant as well as the permanent damage found by the trial court were grossly inadequate as a matter of law.[25]

---

22.   *See id.* at 115–116.

23.   Boomer v. Atlantic Cement Co., 294 N.Y.S.2d 452 (1968).

24.   These "points of counsel" are quoted in the official reporter, 26 N.Y.2d 219, 220 (1970)(citations omitted).

25.   *Id.*

It is notable how much the plaintiffs emphasized the issue of damages in their argument. As it turned out, the damage issue received less attention from the Court of Appeals in this round of the litigation but then dominated the proceedings on remand.

1. *The Opinion*

The case was argued on October 31, 1969, and decided on March 4, 1970. This was a period of great interest in environmental law in general and air pollution in particular, as demonstrated by the passage of the federal Clean Air Act of 1970. The majority opinion was written by Judge Francis Bergan. He was a career judge, who had been born in 1902 and was elected as a city judge in 1929, only five years after passing the bar Judge Bergan's majority opinion begins by putting the public interest in environmental quality to the side:

> [T]here is now before the court private litigation in which individual property owners have sought specific relief from a single plant operation. The threshold question raised by the division of view on this appeal is whether the court should resolve the litigation between the parties now before it as equitably as seems possible; or whether, seeking promotion of the general public welfare, it should channel private litigation into broad public objectives.

> A court performs its essential function when it decides the rights of parties before it. Its decision of private controversies may sometimes greatly affect public issues. Large questions of law are often resolved by the manner in which private litigation is decided. But this is normally an incident to the court's main function to settle controversy. It is a rare exercise of judicial power to use a decision in private litigation as a purposeful mechanism to achieve direct public objectives greatly beyond the rights and interests before the court.

> Effective control of air pollution is a problem presently far from solution even with the full public and financial powers of government.... This is an area beyond the circumference of one private lawsuit. It is a direct responsibility for government and should not thus be undertaken as an incident to solving a dispute between property owners and a single cement plant—one of many—in the Hudson River valley.[26]

Thus, the court carved away the larger public issues raised by the case, and trimmed it down to a dispute between neighbors, not much different in kind from a quarrel between homeowners about an overhanging tree-limb.

---

26. *Id.* at 223.

Having eliminated the public interest aspect of the case, the court observed that there was a large economic disparity between the stakes of the parties but stated that the injunction could not be denied on this basis without overruling a line of previous New York decisions.[27] (As we will see, this may have been an over-reading of the precedents.) Nor was the majority attracted to the idea of a delayed shut-down order to allow the defendant to abate the nuisance, which it thought would only put pressure on the defendant to settle without doing anything to improve pollution control at the plant. The court observed that the "parties could settle this private litigation at any time if defendant paid enough money and the imminent threat of moving the plant would build up the pressure on the defendant."[28] The court was skeptical that the defendant, as a single company in a large industry, could do much to accelerate the technological advances needed for effective control of the problem.

In contrast, the court said, "to grant the injunction unless defendant pays plaintiffs such permanent damages as may be fixed by the court seems to do justice between the contending parties."[29] To ensure against later litigation between the parties or future owners of the property involved, the court required the judgment to contain a term providing that "the payment by defendant and the acceptance by plaintiffs of permanent damages found by the court shall be in compensation for a servitude on the land."[30] Without specifically addressing the measure of damages, the court remarked that the lower court "should be entirely free to re-examine this subject."[31]

Judge Matthew Jasen alone dissented. (Jasen's sparse court biography indicates little, beyond the facts that he attended the "Harvard University Civil Affairs School" rather than law school, and that he had served as a military judge in occupied Germany and as a state trial judge before joining the Court of Appeals.) Judge Jason stressed the seriousness of the air pollution problem and the contribution of dust from cement plants to that problem. He also argued that the majority was "in effect, licensing a continuing wrong"—"It is the same as saying to the cement company, you may continue to do harm to your neighbors so long as you pay a fee for it."[32] He also argued that giving the cement company an easement was essentially allowing it to exercise the power of eminent

---

27. *Id.* at 224.

28. *Id.* at 225.

29. *Id.* at 226.

30. *Id.* at 228.

31. *Id.*

32. *Id* at 230 (Jasen, J., dissenting).

domain, but for its one private benefit rather than for public use.[33] Having been well aware of the plaintiffs' presence when it opened the plant, the company should have the burden of coming up with a technological solution within eighteen months.[34]

Quite apart from the question of whether it reached the right result, the majority opinion was less than a model of judicial craftsmanship. The *Boomer* court's treatment of precedent was quite unsatisfactory and received little correction from the dissent. The main point on which the majority and dissent agreed was that prior New York law would have entitled the plaintiffs to an injunction against operation of the plant. But this actually was not completely clear. The majority cited *Whalen v. Union Bag & Paper Co.*[35] as the authority for the "rule that had been followed in this court with marked consistency."—that rule being that "whenever the damage resulting from a nuisance is found not 'insubstantial,' viz $100 a year, injunction would follow."[36] But the case law was not so unequivocal as this language from *Whalen* would suggest.[37] Even in *Whalen* itself, the court said that "[i]t is not safe to attempt to lay down any hard and fast rule for the guidance of courts of equity in determining when an injunction will issue."[38]

The court cited three other cases as following the *Whalen* rule. Those cases uphold the issuance of injunctions, but they gave little indication that an injunction would be required when the effect would be to render a large industrial facility worthless. Instead, the earlier opinions had made it clear that nothing so drastic was involved in those cases.

The first of the three earlier cases, *McCarty v. Natural Carbonic Gas Company*, involved a plant discharging sulfur dioxide fumes, and the court did hold that injunctive relief was warranted despite the expense of compliance by the defendant.[39] But the injunction, as modified by the court of appeals, did not involve an undue burden on the defendant:

---

33. *Id.* at 231.

34. *Id.* at 232.

35. 101 N.E. 805 (1913).

36. *Boomer*, 26 N.Y.2d at 224.

37. *See* Louis A. Halper, *Nuisance, Court and Markets in the New York Court of Appeal, 850–1915*, 54 ALB. L. REV. 301, 301 (1990) (arguing that a survey of earlier New York case law concludes that *Boomer's* preference for damages had "centenarian ancestors in the New York Court of Appeals".).

38. *Whalen*, 101 N.E. at 805. The *Whalen* court quoted language from an Indiana case to the effect that, before locating a plant where it would discharge large amounts of pollutants into a small stream, the defendant should have taken into account the rights of downstream owners. *Id.* at 806.

39. McCarty v. Natural Carbonic Gas Co., 189 N.Y. 40 (1907).

> This is not a case where the defendant cannot carry on its business
> without injury to neighboring property, for all damage can be
> avoided by the use of hard coal, as is done by one of its competitors
> in the same kind of business in the same locality, or perhaps by the
> use of some modern appliance such as a smoke consumer, although
> either would involve an increase in expense. It is better, however,
> that profits should be somewhat reduced than to compel a house-
> holder to abandon his home, especially when he did not "come to the
> nuisance," but was there before.[40]

Requiring the defendant to use available methods of pollution reduction,
which were apparently already in use by competitors, can hardly be
considered so harsh as to call for any judicial relief.

The second case cited by the *Boomer* court, *Strobel v. Kerr Salt
Company*, involved massive pollution of a stream by a salt manufacturer.[41] But again, the relief was not a shut-down order:

> It does not follow from these views that, if upon another trial the
> facts are unchanged, the defendant and the other salt manufacturers
> will be compelled to make such terms as they can, for a court of
> equity, with its plastic powers, can require, as a condition of with-
> holding a permanent injunction, the construction of a reservoir on
> the upper sources of the stream, to accumulate water when it is
> plentiful for use in times of scarcity, and thus neutralize the
> diminution caused by the manufacture of salt. The court may also
> require, on the like condition, greater care in preventing the escape
> of salt water and salt substances into the stream, as the defendant
> attempted to do during the trial, and thus prevent or minimize the
> pollution.[42]

In modern terms, what both of these decisions require is that the
defendant use the best available technology (BAT), not that the plant be
shut down.

The third case, *Campbell v. Seaman*, involved a brick kiln that killed
hundreds of a neighbor's trees because of its sulfuric acid fumes.[43] The
court held that an injunction was warranted, even though the trees were
merely ornamental rather than having commercial value. But the circumstances were a far cry from *Boomer*:

> We know that material for brick making exists in all parts of our
> State, and particularly at various points along the Hudson river. An
> injunction need not therefore destroy defendant's business or inter-

---

40. *McCarty*, 81 N.E. at 551.

41. 164 N.Y. at 303 (1900).

42. *Strobel*, 164 N.Y. at 323.

43. Campbell v. Seaman, 63 N.Y. 568 (1875).

fere materially with the useful and necessary trade of brick making. It does not appear how valuable defendant's land is for a brick-yard, nor how expensive are his erections for brick-making. I think we may infer that they are not expensive. For ought that appears, his land may be put to other use just as profitable to him. It does not appear that defendant's damage from an abatement of the nuisance will be as great as plaintiffs' damages from its continuance.[44]

"Hence," the court said, "this is not a case within any authority to which our attention has been called, where an injunction should be denied on account of the serious consequences to the defendant."[45] Thus, while the injunction would regard discontinuing the current use of the property (unlike the other two cases), it would not have an especially harsh economic impact on the defendant.

Fairly read, these cases stand for the proposition that the default remedy in a nuisance case is injunctive. These cases also make it clear that an injunction may be appropriate even if the monetary benefit to the plaintiff is smaller than the monetary cost to the defendant. But they do not seem to foreclose the possibility that, in extreme cases, hardship to the defendant or the public might justify denial of an injunction in a nuisance case.[46] The *Boomer* court should not have leaped to the conclusion that these cases stood in its way.

Thus, the *Boomer* opinion's analysis of precedent was clumsy at best. Moreover, it is not completely clear how the outcome in *Boomer* itself was supposed to relate these earlier cases. On a first reading of the opinion, the impression is that *Boomer* is overruling the *Whalen* rule in favor of a damage remedy for nuisance.

But on a closer reading, *Boomer* seems to leave *Whalen* generally intact. The court says that the action of the lower courts was "a departure from a rule that has become settled; but to follow the rule literally in these cases would be to close down the plant at once."[47] The court then discusses two alternatives to avoiding this result: postponing the injunction or conditioning it on the defendant's failure to pay damages. The ultimate relief granted was "to grant an injunction which shall be vacated upon payment by defendant of such amounts of permanent damage to the respective plaintiffs as shall for this purpose be

---

44. *Id.* at 586.

45. *Id.*

46. *See* Halper, *supra* note 37, at 353–354 "It is simply not possible to read New York nuisance law as having internalized a general view that large-scale industry is liable to be shut down at the behest of a smallholder, which required modification through balancing tests that became ever more incoherent until the rescue of nuisance doctrine by *Boomer*."

47. Boomer v. Atlantic Cement Co., 257 N.E. 2d 870, 873 (1970).

determined by the court.''[48] The court could have remitted the plaintiffs to their remedy at law, a damage action, but instead seemed to feel compelled to play at least lip service to the *Whalen* rule that the plaintiffs were entitled to some form of injunctive relief. Nowhere does the court explicitly state that it is overruling *Whalen* or any other prior opinion. Thus, one tenable reading is that *Boomer* merely placed a gloss on the *Whalen* rule: the plaintiff is always *prima facie* entitled to an injunction, but in the case of highly disproportionate harm to the defendant or the public, the injunction can be made defeasible by a damage payment.

The *Boomer* court's opinion is also cursory in its discussion of the balancing of the equities. It refers to one third-party interest favoring the defendant—the number of employees at the plant—but ignores the third-party interest favoring the plaintiff, the regional impact of the defendant's air pollution. This seems like an obvious inconsistency. Moreover, the majority opinion fails to consider the possibility of equitable relief that would mitigate the harm to the plaintiffs, such as a lower level of operation, changes in the scheduling of blasting, construction of barriers between the plaintiffs' land and the plant, and so forth. Presumably, the court assumed that none of these remedies would be feasible or effective, yet nothing in the opinion indicates that these alternatives were even considered. The court's disposition also left the lower courts somewhat at large about how to handle the remand. The court of appeals invited a further consideration of damages on remand but with no explanation of why the previous determination was unsatisfactory or what standards should be used on remand.

The sloppiness of the opinion suggests that the court did not view the case as particularly important; if so, the amount of attention given the case by scholars must have come as something of a surprise. But perhaps, as one commentator suggests, the shortcomings of the opinion actually made the case more attractive to teachers and scholars: ''The opacity of the court's opinion leaves room for provocative questioning and dialogue in the classroom and for more refined analysis in academic journals, especially by the economically-oriented commentators....''[49]

---

48. *Id.* at 875.

49. Lewin, *supra* note 11, at 221. Those who consider *Boomer* insensitive to environmental concerns should consider a later Idaho decision, *Carpenter v. Double R Cattle Company, Inc.*, 701 P.2d 222 (Idaho 1985). The Idaho court held that no remedy—not even the payment of damages—is available if the utility of the defendant's activity outweighs the harm to the plaintiff. It observed that ''Idaho is sparsely populated and its economy depends largely upon the benefits of agriculture, lumber, mining and industrial development.'' *Id.* at 228. To make damages available would ''place an unreasonable burden upon those industries.'' *Id.* The dissenting judge *only* observed that ''[i]f humans are such a rare item in this state, maybe there is all the more reason to protect them from the discharge of industry.'' *Id.* at 229. At least *Boomer* offered the plaintiffs a damage award, though the

2. *The Aftermath*

As it turns out, the proceedings on remand suggest that the Court of Appeals decision was actually more favorable in its ultimate effect on the plaintiffs than one might have expected. Taking advantage of the Court of Appeals' open-ended invitation to reconsider damages, the lower courts were generous in their appraisal of the plaintiffs' claims.

On remand, the trial judge agreed with the plaintiffs that damages would not be limited to the decrease in fair market value. On the other hand, he also rejected their theory that damages should be set at the level that the plaintiffs would have demanded before they would have agreed to lift a permanent injunction. He considered this unduly punitive. In setting damages, he appeared to seek a middle ground. He considered the above-market prices that Atlantic had spent in acquiring other property in the neighborhood, as well as the conflicting expert testimony about market value. All but one of the cases settled before the judge fixed the amount of damages. In the one remaining case, he found the decline in market value to be $140,000 and awarded $175,000 in damages.[50]

The appellate division upheld this amount as a reasonable estimate of loss of market value due to the servitude.[51] Interestingly, all five of the judges joined a concurring opinion by Judge Herlihy,[52] arguing that the defendant should have to pay more than an independent third-party would have been willing to pay for the land:

> The present record contains proof offered by the plaintiff of a sale which demonstrated the ability of a seller to obtain the price of $32,500 for a small parcel of land which only the year before had been purchased for $3,438 when the buy was an adjoining landowner needing the land for business expansion purposes. While such sales are sometime referred to in a derogatory manner as "holdups," there is nothing which would seem immoral or illegal in assessing value as between private citizens upon a consideration of business facts. The plaintiffs have not created the situation which required the necessity for the defendant to obtain a a legal interest in the fee simple absolute title of the plaintiffs' premises. While the public interest may dictate that the defendant be offered an opportu-

---

stingy estimate of damages by the trial court left some doubt about the significance of this "consolation prize."

50. Boomer v. Atlantic Cement Co., 72 Misc.2d 834, 340 N.Y.S.2d 97 (1972).

51. Kinley v. Atlantic Cement Co., 42 A.D.2d 496, 349 N.Y.S.2d 199 (1973).

52. It seems odd that a *unanimous* "concurrence" was filed, but the answer is presumably that another judge was assigned to write the opinion (perhaps, as in some courts, in advance of the oral argument), but that Herlihy felt more strongly about the case and was willing to contribute a more involved analysis, which the other judges then joined.

nity to acquire a servitude, there is no apparent reason to assume that the purchase is being either made by or on behalf of the public, and accordingly the value of the servitude should reflect the private interests of the parties to the lawsuit.[53]

Although it has not received much attention from commentators, the damage determination is intriguing. The question is how to calculate the value of the land absent the nuisance, which constitutes the baseline for establishing the damages. The most obvious possibility is the amount that the plaintiffs could have gotten if they had put their property on the market before Atlantic was on the scene—the amount they could have obtained at that earlier point by selling to another homeowner or small business. But this measure of damages in effect would provide no incentive for the defendant to seek voluntary transactions with its neighbors. In effect, this stingy measure of damages would give a neighboring landowner the option of acquiring the plaintiff's land at market without making any effort to buy it first. A second measure of damages would be the amount that Atlantic would have been willing to pay to lift the injunction. But if that was supposed to be the measure of damages, the courts might just as well have given the plaintiffs an unconditional injunction and left Atlantic to bargain with them on its own. Thus, the trial court seems to have been right to reject both of these possible measures of damages.

The measure that the lower courts adopted was more nuanced. It seems to have been based on the premise that Atlantic should have purchased a buffer zone for its operations; as in establishing any large package of real estate, Atlantic would have had to pay a premium to get the land it needed. If Atlantic had merely been required to pay what an ordinary buyer would have been willing to pay, it would be unjustly enriched in the amount of the premium it would otherwise have had to pay for the buffer zone. Thus, the damage award can be considered a form of restitution, putting the parties in the same position that they would have been in if Atlantic had done the right thing in the first place and purchased a buffer zone.[54]

---

53. *Kinley*, 349 N.Y.S.2d at 202.

54. *See* James Gordley, *The Purpose of Awarding Restitutionary Damages: A Reply to Professor Weinrib*, 1 Theoretical Inquiries 39 (2000) (enumerating some consideration, that might support restitution in this case). Gordley mentions *Boomer*, but not surprisingly, seems unaware of the restitutionary nature of the damages that were ultimately assessed in the lower courts. *Id.* Gordley mentions an interesting English case, involving violation of a covenant rather than a nuisance, where the court awarded such damages as "might reasonably have been demanded by plaintiff" if the defendant had tried to obtain advance permission. *Id.* Gordley aptly refers to these damages as a "pragmatic effort to deal with the problem" while avoiding windfall profits to the plaintiff or giving the defendant a bargain-basement price for the plaintiff's acquiescence. Much the same seems to be true of the damages awarded in *Boomer*.

The plaintiffs were not completely satisfied with the outcome. To this day, Boomer and Millious believe that the judge should have shut the plant down entirely. Millious complains that he ended up with a smaller house on less land with a bigger mortgage. Even though he now lives four or five miles from the plant, there is still occasionally dust in the air. Boomer sold his land to the company at a price negotiated by his lawyer. He then moved his business a few miles away. He still believes that the judge should have "taken the bull by the horns" and issued the injunction.[55]

In contrast, David Duncan, the lawyer who represented all but one of the plaintiffs, is more favorable in his assessment of the outcome of the case. He feels that "upon reflection, it was fair." Overall, he thinks "virtually all of the plaintiffs got very good settlements for the value of their land." He was particularly happy with the outcome for one family, the Kenleys, who were able to get nearly the entire value of their house in exchange for an equitable easement that was never properly filed by the company. His recollection is that the case actually led the state to pursue an enforcement action against the company that resulted in some improvements in pollution control.[56]

After the damage award, Atlantic became involved in litigation with its insurance company over whether the damages were covered by its policy. Fourteen years after the Court of Appeals' initial decision, the same court ruled in Atlantic's favor in the insurance litigation.[57] Atlantic had paid out a total of $710,000 in damages and settlements, about four times more than the damage estimate mentioned in the first Court of Appeals decision.[58]

According to the long-time Technical Manager of the plant, Atlantic itself would not have moved even if an injunction had been issued.[59] Instead, if anyone relocated, it was the plaintiffs. Atlantic belatedly purchased most of the plaintiffs' properties to create a buffer zone. Several of the plaintiffs moved away after receiving damages. But at age 80, Mr. Boomer himself still runs a business in the area.

As part of a settlement with the insurance company, Atlantic agreed to sell the insurance company some of the property that Atlantic had received in settlements with some of the plaintiffs. Atlantic agreed to convey quitclaim deeds and easements. But the parties were unable to do

---

55. This information is taken from interviews conducted by Sky Stanfield in early September 2004.

56. Interview with Sky Stanfield, Sept. 15, 2004.

57. Atlantic Cement Co. v. Fidelity & Casualty Co., 471 N.E.2d 142 (N.Y. 1984).

58. *See* Atlantic Cement v. Fidelity & Casualty Co., 459 N.Y.S.2d 425, 427 (1983).

59. *See* Mogill, *supra* note 7, at 9–10.

so on the language of the easements. Fidelity was ultimately able to get a court order eliminating some of the language from the easements which would have authorized Atlantic to "render the Premises uninhabitable, unmarketable and not useable for any purpose."[60] (Thus, the *Boomer* court seems to have been wrong if it assumed that the nature of the easements would be self-explanatory.) Thus, in 1989, some twenty years after the Boomers originally filed suit, the litigation over the property finally came to an end.

In the meantime, the Atlantic Cement Company itself went through some changes. In 1973, Atlantic was sold to the Newmount Mining Company.[61] In turn, Newmount sold the operation to a British company, Blue Circle Industries, for $145 million.[62] By 2001, the facility had been sold again, to Lafarge S.A.[63]

On one point the Court of Appeals was indubitably right: the solution to Atlantic's environmental problems was not going to be found within eighteen months. On the contrary, like many other pollution problems, this one dragged on with some improvement but no real solution. EPA embarked on a complex series of rule-making dealing with the cement industry. EPA's first set of standards was remanded by the D.C. Circuit in 1973,[64] but EPA succeeded in getting its standards approved two years later.[65] Later, the focus shifted to hazardous air pollutants emitted by cement plants such as hydrochloric acid, dioxins, and metals. In 2000, the D.C. Circuit upheld standards requiring the industry to use the "maximum achievable control technology" for these hazardous pollutants.[66] The Fact Sheet accompanying the rule says that it will reduce particular emissions by 5200 tons per year, and hydrocarbons by 220 tons per year, at an initial capital cost of $108 million and a recurring annual cost of 37 million.[67] Later revisions of the rule stretched into 2002.[68]

---

60. Atlantic Cement Co. v. Fidelity & Casualty Co. of New York, 547 N.Y.S.2d 287, 289 (1989).

61. N.Y. TIMES, May 5, 1973, at 45.

62. *Blue Circle Buys Major U.S. Concrete Supplier,* FIN. TIMES (London), Oct. 4, 1985, at 26.

63. Steven Prokopy, *LaFarge Corp. to Manage Blue Circle Assets*, CEMENT AMERICAS, Sept./Oct. 2001.

64. Portland Cement Ass'n v. Ruckelshaus, 486 F.2d 375 (D.C. Cir. 1973), *cert. denied*, 417 U.S. 921 (1974).

65. Portland Cement Ass'n v. Train, 513 F.2d 506 (1975).

66. National Lime Ass'n v. EPA, 233 F.3d 625 (D.C. Cir. 2000).

67. *See* Fact Sheet—Final Air Toxics Rule for Portland Cement Manufacturing Plants, http://epa.gov.ttn/atw/pcem/portf_fs.html.

68. *See* the EPA's docket page, http://www.epa.gov/ttn/atw/pcem/pcempg.html.

In the early 1990s, Blue Circle did introduce new technology to control dust emissions.[69] Nevertheless, throughout the 1990s, the plant was the focus of scrutiny by groups assessing pollution, and it often appeared near the top of lists of regional polluters.[70] According to a 1997 report, Blue Circle's operation emitted ten thousand tons of sulfur dioxide (the seventh-highest in the state of New York), another ten thousand tons of nitrogen oxide (the highest in the state), and it ranked third for particulate matter at 954 tons.[71]

What about the situation today? The plant remains the second largest cement facility in the United States.[72] The plant's most recent TRI report lists 142,000 pounds of hydrochloric acid, 29 pounds of lead, 37 pounds of mercury compounds, and small amounts of dioxins in 2002.[73] In 2000, the state environmental agency said it was investigating complaints by local residents about dust deposits and respiratory problems, although the agency had previously issued small fines against the company for high levels of dust emissions and other violations.[74] The present-day equivalents of Oscar and June Boomer, Jill Sampson and her husband Lott Charles, live less than a mile from the plant. Lott Charles complained of their daughters' year-long "deep, barking cough, which is really alarming.... There is a peculiar dust that coats things around here. It ate the finish off my porch chairs."[75]

II. The Three Faces of Boomer

Part of *Boomer*'s fame is due to its dramatic facts and its influence on other courts. But *Boomer* has also attracted so much attention because it raises deep doctrinal and theoretical issues. We will focus on three of those issue here.

---

69. See *LINKman Improves Quality at Raven; LINKman Process Control and Optimization System at Blue Circle Cement's Ravena Plant*, World Cement, Jan. 1992, at 34.

70. See, e.g., Sarah Metzgar, *Three Local Firms Listed Among Worst Polluters in State*, Times Union (Albany, N.Y.), May 30, 1997, at B2.

71. See *Id.*

72. See EPA Fact Sheet, *supra* note 66.

73. http://www.epa.gov/cgi-bin/broker?zipcode=12143 & _service=oiaa & _program=xp_tri.sasmacr.tristart.macro & trilib=TRIQ0 & view=ZPFA & tab_rpt=1 & sort=_VIEW_ & fld=E1 & fld=E2 & fld=AIRLBY & fld=RELLBY & fld=TSFDSP & fld=RE_TOLBY & fld=TRIID & sort_fmt=1 & industry=ALL & chemical=_ALL_ & year=2002

74. *Ravena DEC Acts on Neighbors' Complaints about Air quality*, Times Union (Albany, NY), November 3, 2000, at 89.

75. *Id.* Currently, LaFarge is proposing to burn millions of tons of tires as fuel in its cement kilns. See Matt Pacenza, *Tire Burning Plan Draws Critics; Kinderhook Residents Downwind of Proposed Site Raise Health, Habitat Concerns*, Times Union (Albany, N.Y.), February 8, 2004, at D1.

The first issue relates to remedies for environmental violations. The question *Boomer* raises is whether "balancing the equities" is limited to common law cases, or whether that process applies to all environmental injunctions. Nuisance actions are only the tip of the iceberg in terms of environmental litigation. Can courts use their equitable discretion to postpone or exempt polluters from statutory requirements? Or do environmental concerns trump economic interests in framing remedies against polluters? Obviously, this is a question of some importance in an era when so many environmental statutes authorize injunctions as a remedy against violators.

The second issue is whether the *Boomer* court was right to favor damages over an injunction on economic grounds. Legal scholars have devoted considerable ingenuity to analyzing the economic implications of remedies, and *Boomer* has figured prominently as an example. At first blush, given the disparity in economic interests between the *Boomer* plaintiffs and the defendant, the economic answer to the case may seem obvious. It turns out, however, that the economic analysis is considerably more involved, and the conclusions are less clear.

The final issue is whether the common law continues to have any relevance in today's environmental law, given the predominance of environmental statutes. *Boomer* was decided at the very beginning of what some consider to be the "golden age" of environmental law, when almost all of today's complex regulatory schemes were enacted. The *Boomer* court cut back on the scope of its inquiries in deference to the state's statutory pollution scheme. A few years later, the U.S. Supreme Court abolished the federal common law of nuisance in favor of a purely statutory approach. Environmental law courses focus almost exclusively on statutory regulation, with the common law getting much scanter attention. How much room, one might well wonder, is left for the common law today? Was the *Boomer* court right in thinking that the common law has no further contribution to make to environmental policy?

A. *Boomer* and Equitable Discretion

We begin with the first of these three issues, examining *Boomer* through the lens of remedies law. *Boomer* is a notable affirmation of the discretionary nature of equitable remedies and the judge's power to "balance the equities" in crafting a remedy. This approach to the issuance of injunctions originated in cases where courts were the source not only of the relief but of the underlying legal rule. But today, environmental law is largely based on statute. Often, these statutes authorize courts to issue injunctions against violators. How should the

Boomer tradition of equitable discretion operate in this new setting?[76] Should traditional canons of equitable discretion apply to statutory injunctions, or should *Boomer* be limited to the common law context?

This issue was presented to the Supreme Court in dramatic form in *TVA v. Hill*, the famous snail darter case discussed in a later chapter.[77] Having found that completion of a multimillion dollar dam would threaten an endangered species. Chief Justice Burger's opinion for the Court observes that a judge "is not mechanically obligated to grant an injunction for every violation of law."[78] That statement calls to mind the traditional doctrine of equitable balancing, and seems to signal that the Court was going to deny the injunction in *Boomer*-like terms because of the huge investment in the dam. But then the opinion takes a different turn:

> But these principles take a court only so far. Our system of government is, after all, a tripartite one, with each branch having certain defined function. . . . [It is] the exclusive province of the Congress not only to formulate legislative policies and mandate programs and projects, but also to establish their relative priority for the Nation. Once Congress, exercising its delegated powers, has decided the order of priorities in a given area, it is for the Executive to administer the laws and for the courts to enforce them when enforcement is sought.[79]

Because Congress had spoken "in the plainest of words, making it abundantly clear that the balance has been struck in favor of affording endangered species the highest of priorities," the Court declined the request to shape a "reasonable" remedy.[80] Thus, *Boomer* seemed to have been excluded from the statutory sphere.

TVA v. Hill seemed to establish a firm rule in favor of statutory injunctions. But the Court soon muddied the picture in a Clean Water Act decision, *Weinberger v. Romero–Barcelo*.[81] The facts were somewhat offbeat compared to the normal pollution case, which is one of the reasons the case is hard to interpret. In *Weinberger*, the district court held (probably correctly) that the Navy needed to obtain a Clean Water Act permit before conducting exercises on the coast of Puerto Rico. The

---

76. *See* Peter Shane, *Rights, Remedies and Restraint*, 64 Chi.-Kent L. Rev. 531 (1988); Daniel A. Farber, *Equitable Discretion, Legal Duties, and Environmental Injunctions*, 45 U. Pitt. L. Rev. 513 (1984); Zygmunt Plater, *Statutory Violations and Equitable Discretion*, 70 Cal. L. Rev. 524 (1982).

77. 437 U.S. 153 (1978).

78. *Id.* at 193.

79. *Id.* at 194.

80. *Id.*

81. 456 U.S. 305 (1982).

theory was that by foreseeably (and sometimes intentionally) releasing ordinance into the sea, the Navy was discharging from point sources (muzzles and bomb bays), thereby triggering the permit requirement. The trial judge refused to issue an injunction, however, viewing the violation as purely a technical one with no adverse environmental impact. The question before the Court was whether the judge had discretion to deny the injunction while the Navy applied for a permit, or whether *TVA v. Hill* required that the statutory violation be halted.

Justice White's opinion for the Court began with reminders of the broad discretion of equity courts.[82] He distinguished *TVA v. Hill* as an exceptional case in which only an immediate injunction could vindicate the goals of the statute.[83] In contrast, he viewed such an injunction as unnecessary to vindicate the goals of the Clean Water Act. After all, the purpose of the statute was clean water, not the issuance of permits for their own sake. And unlike the Endangered Species Act, the Clean Water Act displays a concern about feasibility and practicality in many of its provisions, making it more legitimate for a court to consider these factors in issuing an injunction.[84] The sole dissenter, Justice Stevens, criticized the Court for granting "an open-ended license to federal judges to carve gaping holes" in the statutory scheme.[85]

Weinberger may look like a revival of *Boomer*ism in the statutory context. The court emphasized the parallel with traditional nuisance law "where courts have fully exercised their equitable discretion and ingenuity in ordering remedies."[86] What did the Court cite as examples? *Boomer* and *Spur Industries*! It was little wonder that the dissent accused the majority of reducing the statute to "little more than a codification of the common law of nuisance."[87]

But does *Weinberger* really transfer *Boomer* to the statutory context? This would seem an odd transplant, if indeed it was what Justice White had in mind. It would be peculiar if the only effect of violating the Clean Water Act was to allow the government to bring a nuisance suit, leaving it up to the trial judge to decide whether compliance with the statutory requirements was really worthwhile. Of course, the Clean Water Act contains other sanctions, which might not be equally discretionary. Still, it seems peculiar for a court to second-guess Congress about whether a defendant should comply with statutes.

---

82. *See Id*. at 311–13.

83. *See Id*. at 313–14.

84. *See Id*. at 317–318.

85. *Id*. at 323.

86. *Id*. at 314 n.7.

87. *Id*. at 330 (Stevens, J., dissenting)(citing the majority's references to *Boomer* and *Spur*).

Despite its approving citation of *Boomer*, the *Weinberger* Court probably did not mean to endorse open-ended judicial discretion. One clue is the Court's disposition of the case. Notably, the Court did not affirm the district court's exercise of equitable discretion, as Justice Powell urged in a separate opinion.[88] If pure *Boomer*-type balancing were involved, Justice Powell's proposed disposition would have made complete sense. Under *Boomer*, it seems obvious that an injunction should not issue. Instead, the Court held that the question was whether the district court had abused its discretion, and remanded for the court of appeals to consider that question.[89]

Moreover, *Boomer*-style balancing would substantially undermine the statutory scheme. Although it is true that the Clean Water Act is attentive to issues of feasibility, it does set deadlines, and the legislative history makes it clear that Congress wanted to be "swift and direct."[90] Even those who, like Justice Scalia, do not believe in consulting legislative history, ought to be able to discern the same seriousness about enforcement from the statute itself. (Consider, for example, the extensive civil and criminal sanctions against violators, and the direct review of regulations in the court of appeals, clearly designed to expedite implementation.) Furthermore, a *Boomer*-type holding would have been most unwelcome to the party resisting the injunction in *Weinberger*, which was the federal government. Of course, in its capacity as a defendant in that case, the government would have welcomed broad equitable discretion, but in its far more frequent capacity as an enforcer, such discretion would have been a great hindrance. Thus, the government was seeking circumscribed discretion for trial courts, not a blank check for judges to balance at will.

Unfortunately, the Supreme Court has done little to clarify the availability of environmental injunctions in the twenty years since *Weinberger*, so we still cannot be completely positive about the extent to which *Boomer* carries over to statutory injunctions.[91] Probably the most enlightening recent decision about equitable discretion and statutory injunctions is a non-environmental case, *United States v. Oakland Cannabis Buyers' Co–Op*.[92] In *Oakland Co–Op*, the Court held that the lower court had discretion when issuing an injunction to enforce the Controlled

88. *See Id.* at 321–22 (Powell, J., concurring).

89. *See Id.* at 320.

90. S. REP. No. 92–414, at 64, 68, 80 (1971).

91. *See, e.g.*, Amoco Production Co. v. Village of Gambell, 480 U.S. 531 (1987), holding that procedural violations do not necessarily constitute the irreparable injury needed for a preliminary injunction, but that an environmental injury would normally do so.

92. 532 U.S. 483 (2001).

Substance Act. Nevertheless, the Court held that it could not use that discretion to exempt medically necessary use of marijuana from the injunction, because Congress had made a contrary policy determination. Equitable discretion, according to the Court, applied only to choices between injunctions and other enforcement methods, not to non-enforcement of the statute.[93] Although it did not arise in an environmental context, *Oakland Co–Op* suggests by analogy that equitable discretion cannot be used to excuse statutory violations in environmental cases. But of course the statute in question was quite different from environmental regulation, making the decision's environmental implications unclear.

In any event, the lower courts have not read *Weinberger* as giving them carte blanche to excuse or postpone compliance with environmental statutes. In a thoughtful recent opinion in an SWDA enforcement case, the First Circuit remarked:

> Under the SWDA, it should be a rare case in which a violation of regulatory standards does not lead to an injunction if the responsible enforcement agency requests one.... Expressions by Congress of this sort, once identified, must be respected by courts, lest equitable discretion become the judiciary's preferred method of reshaping policy determinations made by other branches of government that are better equipped to make them.[94]

The court contrasted this situation with that presented in common law cases such as *Boomer*:

> Courts asked to issue an injunction must ordinarily assume the role of a court of chancery—a role that requires them to determine whether the equities of the case favor, and whether the public interest would be served by, the granting of injunctive relief.... But in the context of statutory injunctions, the court's freedom to make an independent assessment of the equities and the public interest is circumscribed to the extent that Congress has already made such assessment with respect to the type of case before the court.[95]

Thus, injunctions seemingly remain the default remedy for environmental violations, and *Boomer* is probably limited to common law cases.[96]

---

93. *See Oakland Co–Op*, 532 U.S. at 495–498.

94. United States v. Massachusetts Water Resources Authority, 256 F.3d 36, 58 (1st Cir. 2001).

95. *Id.* at 47. The district court concluded that the case before it was just such a "rare case," and the court of appeals affirmed, rejecting the argument that it was in effect allowing a permanent exemption from a statutory requirement. *See Id.*

96. *See also* United States v. Wheeling–Pittsburgh Steel Corp., 818 F.2d 1077 (3d Cir. 1987)(refusing to delay compliance with Clean Air Act requirements on basis of hardship.) *Cf.* Little Joseph Realty v. Town of Babylon, 41 N.Y.2d 738, 363 N.E.2d 1163 (1977)(stating

But, given the Court's invocation of *Boomer* in *Weinberger*, it may still turn out to have ripple effects even in statutory cases.

B. *Boomer* and Economic Analysis

Another aspect of *Boomer*, and one which has loomed large in legal scholarship, has involved the economics of the decision. Recall that the plaintiffs in *Boomer* warned against the adoption of a new "economic utility doctrine." Their warning was prescient. The case was decided at the start of the Law and Economics movement in legal scholarship, which would re-conceptualize wide areas of the law in terms of economic utility. *Boomer* (often in conjunction with *Spur Industries*) became a standard citation in this new area of scholarship. In short, events were to prove that economic utility and *Boomer* were indeed deeply connected.

Boomer owes some of its fame among legal scholars to an equally famous law review article published two year's later. In 1972, Guido Calabresi and A. Douglas Melamed published a piece entitled, "Property Rules, Liability Rules, and Inalienability: One View of the Cathedral."[97] The subtitle was a reference to a series of paintings by Monet showing the same cathedral in a variety of lighting and weather, the implication being that the article also was offering only one among many perspectives.[98] (Monet produced a number of such series of paintings, but presumably it would have been less dignified to have subtitled the article "another view of the haystacks" or "another view of the lily pond.") Despite the modest implications of the subtitle, the goal of the article was ambitious: to provide a unified perspective of tort and property law.[99] *Boomer* was one of the cases on the minds of the authors. They offer *Boomer* as an example of the choice between tort-like rules (damages) and property-like rules (injunctions),[100] and the final portion of the article is devoted to analysis of a stylized pollution problem with two neighbors,[101] which seems to be loosely based on *Boomer*.

Calabresi and Melamed discuss four remedial regimes that might apply to the holder of an entitlement.[102] It may be helpful to list the remedies, with a brief description.

Boomer does not apply to injunctions enforcing a zoning ordinance, where balancing of equities is impermissible.)

97. 86 Harv. L. Rev. 1089 (1972).

98. *See Id.* at 1089 n.2.

99. *See Id.* at 1090.

100. *See Id.* at 1106 n. 34.

101. *See* Calabresi & Melamed, *supra* note 98, at 1115–1128.

102. *See Id.* at 1118–1125.

- The first possibility is that no remedy exists. Thus, victims receive no assistance from courts. Their only option is to negotiate with the polluter to abate the nuisance. Although this is referred to as a "remedial" option, what it really means is that for all practical purposes the victims have no rights.

- A second possibility is a "liability rule," under which victims receive compensation for the harm they suffer, but no injunctive relief is possible. In other words, invading the entitlement is a tort. Under a liability rule, there is some sense in which the entitlement is not a full-fledged right. It is permissible to invade the entitlement at will, so long as you pay for any resulting harm. That's why the dissenters in *Boomer* and *Spur* were worried that the neighbor's rights were being undermined by a damage remedy.

- The third possibility is a "property rule." Victims have the right to abate the nuisance. This time it is the polluter whose only remedy is to "bribe" the other party by acquiring an easement or by settling the lawsuit with a cash payment.

- The final option discussed in victims may obtain an injunction abating the nuisance, but must compensate the polluter for the losses caused by the injunction. By coincidence, *Spur Industries,* the one significant case supporting this remedy was decided at the same time as the Calabresi and Melamed article.

The fourth option may seem peculiar, but it was utilized by the Arizona Supreme Court in a decision a couple of years after *Boomer.* That case has received great attention from law-and-economics scholars, and is often taught and discussed in conjunction with *Boomer.* At the risk of a brief digression, a quick look at that case may help make the Calabresi and Melamed proposal more understandable.

Spur Industries, Inv. v. Del E. Webb Development Co.[103] involved two activities that even today present important environmental issues, leap-frog urban development and animal feedlots. Del Webb, a real estate development company, brought suit against Spur, which operated a feedlot. The feedlot was there first, but had greatly expanded its operations. In the meantime, Del Webb had created Sun City, which steadily grew in the direction of the feedlot. The two activities were destined to collide. By bringing the "populous" to the "nuisance," Spur had converted what would otherwise have been a private nuisance in a sparsely populated area, which would not have been subject to injunction, into a public nuisance for the people of the new city. In a sense, then, much of the fault was Spur's for unexpectedly transforming the surroundings of

---

103.   494 P.2d 700 (Ariz. 1972).

the feedlot in an urban area, but the court nevertheless allowed a permanent injunction against the feedlot as a public nuisance.[104]

This led the court to a bold remedial innovation. The court both granted the injunction against the feedlot and awarded damages against the plaintiff to the feedlot. On these facts, the court concluded, "[i]t does not seem harsh to require a developer, who has taken advantage of the lesser land values in a rural area as well as the availability of large tracts of land on which to build and develop a new town or city in the area, to indemnify those who are forced to leave as a result."[105] But unlike *Boomer*, with which it is often paired, *Spur Industries* seems to have been a unique response to unusual circumstances rather than a doctrinal milestone.[106] Still, it does show that Calabresi and Melamed's "compensated injunction" option is more than just an academic's pipe-dream.

The other remedies are more familiar, but Calabresi and Melamed proved a new economic perspective on them. Some simple examples may help to sort out these remedies and their economic implications. Consider two scenarios. In both, to simplify the analysis, imagine that there are only two parties, Atlantic and Boomer, and that the only options are either to shut down the cement factory or leave it in its present state of operation.

In one scenario, which we could call the *excess harm* scenario, the harm to Boomer from pollution is greater than the benefit to Atlantic from keeping the plant open. To make this concrete, assume Atlantic's profits are $500,000, but the harm to Boomer is $1,000,000. In this scenario, a cost-benefit analysis would tell us to shut down the cement plant, since its harm outweighs its benefits. This will clearly happen with a property rule (Boomer gets an injunction) or under a liability rule (Atlantic will chose to close rather than pay the damages, which are large enough to wipe out the plant's profits.) At least some of the other

---

104. *See Spur Industries*, 494 P.2d at 706.

105. *Id.* at 708.

106. In another part of the litigation, a dissenting judge argued that if "these Spur cases are adhered to by this Court in the future, every operator of a nuisance which sends smoke, fumes, dust, stench, etc. onto his neighbors may be guaranteed economic protection should anyone be annoyed or harassed enough to try and stop the wrongful activity by court action." Spur Feeding Co. v. Superior Court of Maricopa County, 109 Ariz. 105, 505 P.2d 1377, 1380 (1973)(Holohan, J., dissenting). This alarm turned out to unjustified in relation to *Spur Industries*. The decision has been read narrowly by later Arizona courts, which have never found occasion to provide similar relief. *See* Salt River Valley Water Users' Association v. Giglio, 549 P.2d 162 (Ariz. 1976); Brenteson Wholesale, Inc. v. Arizona Public Serv. Co., 803 P.2d 930 (Ariz. Ct. App. 1990). Elsewhere, the decision does not seem to have fared even that well. As of 1990, *Spur* was said to be the "only reported decision in which a court has held a ... compensated injunction to be the appropriate remedy in civil litigation." Lewin, *supra* note 11, at 248–249. I have not located any more recent cases, and *Spur Industries* is rarely cited at all.

rules—for example, the "no liability" rule under which Boomer has no legal rights—would seem to lead to the contrary outcome in which the plant stays open even though it flunks a cost-benefit test. Calabresi and Melamed took the analysis one step further, however, by asking how other rules might shape negotiations between the parties.

Potentially, negotiations could produce the same outcome as the injunction rule (i.e., a plant shutdown) even under the other legal rules. For instance, the plant may end up being closed under a "no liability" rule—at least if we're willing to assume that everyone behaves rationally and there are no barriers to negotiation. Rather than suffer $1,000,000 in damages, Boomer can bribe Atlantic $500,001 to shut down. That's a good deal for both sides: it increases Atlantic's profits (though only slightly) and saves Boomer from a $1 million in harm at the cost of a $500,001 bribe. For similar reasons, the plant would also be shut down under the compensated injunction rule. Boomer would be willing to get a compensated injunction, closing the plant at the cost of $500,000 to themselves but eliminating a $1,000,000 worth of damages. (Note that these outcomes are "the same" as the injunction rule in terms of whether the plant closes down, but depending on the legal rule, one side or the other may be better off financially. Economists tend not to be interested in the question of who benefits so long as the total benefit to society is the same.)

We can contrast the excess harm scenario with another scenario, in which a cost-benefit analysis would favor keeping the plant open. In this, the *excess benefit* scenario, the benefit to Atlantic from operating the plan is greater than the harm to Boomer from the pollution. Again, to be specific, assume Atlantic's profits are $1,000,000 and Boomer's harm is only $500,000. Clearly, a cost-benefit analysis would say to keep the plant open—its benefit to Atlantic outweighs its harm to Boomer. The plant would clearly stay open under a liability rule, because it would pay Atlantic to pay the damages and keep operating. Under the no liability rule or the compensated damage rule, Boomer would have to pay $1,000,000 to get Atlantic to agree to shut the plant, but he would not be willing to do so because his own damages are only $500,000. The final remedy is the property rule, under which Boomer can get a cost-free injunction. This would seem to result in shutting down the plant, but once again we have to consider the possibility of negotiations. In the actual *Boomer* case, the New York court forecast that an injunction would result in a monetary settlement, under which the plant would stay open after Atlantic made a sufficiently large payment to Boomer. Thus, as was true in the excess harm scenario, under ideal conditions the outcome (in terms of the extent of pollution) does not depend on the legal rule: if the benefit to Atlantic is greater than the harm to Boomer, the plant stays open regardless of which legal rule is in effect.

The key word in the last sentence, of course, was "ideal." Under ideal circumstances, it makes no economic difference (in terms of the level of pollution and the level of cement production) which rule applies. What that means is that from an economic point of view, the choice of rule will be dictated by the ways in which a circumstances fall short of the ideal. In an ideal world, litigation is instantaneous, cost-free, and infallible, which is hardly the world in which lawyers actually operate. The extent to which these conditions fail to hold has a direct impact on remedies. For example, a liability rule requires that a court be able to accurately calculate Boomer's damages, but this may not always be possible. Similarly, a court may not be able to accurately calculate how much an injunction will harm Atlantic, which is necessary for the compensated injunction remedy. Or the litigation costs may be different for various remedies.

Also, in several of the situations discussed in the previous two paragraphs, reaching the economically optimum outcome depends on negotiations between the parties. In reality these negotiations may be impossible for various reasons: the parties are two angry to negotiate at all, or there are multiple victims of pollution who cannot coordinate their negotiations, or the parties end up in a stalemate as a result of destructive negotiating tactics. Thus, when a legal rule leads to inefficient results, negotiation might not be available as a solution. If so, the choice of legal rule become decisive. A no-liability rule might result in the plant remaining open, even in the first (undue harm) scenario, whereas a property rule might result in an injunction and a plant closure even in the second (excess profits) scenario.

Because of the various imperfections in the litigation and bargaining processes, the choice of legal rule does matter. The question is what rule to adopt for nuisance cases. Calabresi and Melamed lean toward a liability rule for nuisance cases, or at least most nuisance cases:

> The case of nuisance seems different, however. There the polluter knows what he will do and, often, whom it will hurt. But ... freeloader or holdout problems may often preclude any successful negotiations between the polluter and the victims of pollution; additionally, we are often uncertain who is the cheapest avoider of pollution costs. In these circumstances a liability rule, which at least allowed the economic efficiency of a proposed transfer of property to be tested, seemed appropriate, even though it permitted the nonaccidental and unconsented taking of an entitlement. It should be emphasized, however, that where transaction costs do not bar negotiations between polluter and victim, or where we are sufficiently certain who the cheapest cost avoider is, there are not efficiency

reasons for allowing intentional takings, and property rules, supported by injunctions or criminal sanctions, are appropriate.[107] Thus, they would favor a liability rule, except where there are a small number of pollution victims (making negotiations more feasible) or the victims' damages are highly subjective, making it hard for the polluter to take them into account. This seems to be a stronger preference for a damage remedy over an injunction than was expressed in *Boomer* itself, where the court selected damages because of the dramatic disparity in the impact of an injunction on the plaintiffs and the defendants.

The Calabresi and Melamed article turned out to be highly influential. A citation study concluded that in fact the article's influence has probably increased over time, which seems to be quite unusual for legal scholarship.[108] Some of the ideas in the article had roots in earlier work by others (as is always the case with even the most innovative scholarship). But what particularly distinguished the work was "its rigorous and systematic approach to topics that before had been handled rather haphazardly, if at all."[109] This analytic framework was rendered more understandable by the authors' use of a paradigm case—a case that has become familiar to most law students and teachers. That same case has loomed large in other scholarship. As with the "cathedral" article itself, in many of the later works, "a particular explanatory example looms in the foreground," that being "an instance of environmental pollution, grounded on a classic nuisance case, *Boomer v. Atlantic Cement Co.*"[110] In short, at least partly because of Calabresi and Melamed, *Boomer* has become a law-and-economics classic.

Calabresi and Malamed seemed to provide shape and clarity to the notoriously confused field of nuisance law. But there is continuing dispute among economists over the relative merits of property and liability rules.[111] Thus, the law and economics literature on nuisance has been most useful, not in providing a solution to the problems of nuisance law, but in clarifying those problems. In particular, the economic analy-

---

107. Calabresi and Melamed, *supra* note 98, at 1127. By "cheapest cost avoider", Calabresi and Melamed mean the party who is in a "better position to balance the costs of polluting against the costs of not polluting." *Id.* at 1118.

108. *See* James E. Krier and Stewart J. Schwab, *The Cathedral at Twenty–Five: Citations and Impressions*, 106 Yale L.J. 2121, 2130 (1997).

109. *Id.* at 2135.

110. Carol M. Rose, *The Shadow of the Cathedral*, 106 Yale L.J. 2175, 2175–2176 (1997).

111. *See* Henry E. Smith, *Exclusion and Property Rules in the Law of Nuisance*, 90 Va. L. Rev. 965 (2004); Richard R.W. Brooks, 97 Nw. U. L. Rev. 267 (2002); Ian Ayres and Eric Talley, *Legal Entitlements as Auctions: Property Rules, Liability Rules, and Beyond*, 106 Yale L.J. 703 (1996); Ian Ayres and Eric Talley, *Solomonic Bargaining: Dividing a Legal Entitlement to Facilitate Coasean Trade*, 104 Yale L.J. 1027 (1995).

sis focuses attention on transaction costs of various kinds, especially the costs of bargaining between the parties at various points in their interactions and the costs of obtaining accurate valuation information in order to assess damages. Higher costs of bargaining favor liability rules, whereas valuation difficulties by the court make liability rules less feasible.

C. *Boomer* and the Common Law Tradition

We have examined *Boomer* through the lenses of remedies law and economic analysis. It can also be usefully examined through a jurisprudential lens. Jurisprudentially, the question the case raises is what role the common law should continue to play in an "age of statutes."

The idea behind the economic analysis is that we should establish legal rules that, perhaps after some bargaining by the parties, will result in the optimal use of society's resources. In the nuisance case, this means resolving the conflicting interests of neighboring owners in the way most useful to society as a whole. Yet nuisance law is only one mechanism for controlling pollution. We do not, by and large, rely on nuisance law to control conflicting land uses or to control spillover effects. Instead, we have a complex body of environmental and land use statutes. One of the key arguments in *Boomer* was that the court should ignore the larger issues of pollution control presented by the case, leaving those issues to regulatory agencies. Academic discussion of the case has tended to by-pass the jurisprudential issues raised by the court's refusal to use the common law to address widespread pollution problems.

Yet, the question of how to coordinate the common law and modern regulatory regimes is pervasive, not merely in state courts but at the federal level.[112] Indeed, at roughly the same time that *Boomer* was decided, the United States Supreme Court had claimed a large role for the federal common law of nuisance in addressing pollution issues. Only a few years later, the Court retreated and seemed to call for a complete withdrawal by the federal courts, only to qualify its ruling a few years later and leave those courts a continuing role.

The origins of the federal common law of nuisance date back to the early years of the last century. In *Georgia v. Tennessee Copper Co.*,[113] the state of Georgia filed suit against an out-of-state smelter whose pollution was causing widespread damage in Georgia and elsewhere. (The Su-

---

112. For discussion of this issue, see Daniel A. Farber and Philip P. Frickey, *In the Shadow of the Legislature: The Common Law in the Age of the New Public Law*, 89 Mich. L. Rev. 875 (1991); Peter L. Strauss, *Courts or Tribunals? Federal Courts and Common Law*, 53 Ala. L. Rev. 891 (2002).

113. 206 U.S. 230 (1907).

preme Court had original jurisdiction over this suit, without any previous proceeding being held in a lower court, because it was filed by a state government against a noncitizen.) The Court held that the state was entitled to a federal forum because "[w]hen the States by their union made the forcible abatement of outside nuisances impossible to each, they did not thereby agree to submit to whatever might be done."[114]

Seeking to take advantage of this right to file suit in the Supreme Court, the state of Illinois filed a nuisance complaint against the city of Milwaukee, because Milwaukee was discharging 200 million gallons of raw sewage into Lake Michigan on a daily basis. In *Illinois v. City of Milwaukee [Milwaukee I]*,[115] the Court unanimously dismissed this case on the ground that Illinois had an adequate remedy in federal district court because its nuisance claim "arose under" federal law—namely, the federal common law of nuisance. The Court argued that use of federal common law was justified because of the quasi-sovereign nature of the state's interest, the need for a uniform rule governing nuisance in interstate waters, and strong congressional concern over water pollution.[116] Ironically, it was the very strength of that congressional concern that later convinced the Court to overrule *Milwaukee I*.

On remand, the lower federal courts attempted to harmonize common law remedies with the newly enacted Clean Water Act. In contrast to *Boomer*, the Seventh Circuit took a more constructive view of the relation between pollution statutes and the common law, rather than seeing the pollution statute as eliminating the common law's ability to respond to the public interest in pollution cases. Judge Tone's opinion for the Seventh Circuit repeatedly turned to the federal regulatory scheme as a source of guidance. In Judge Tone's view, the Act implied the undesirability of discharging untreated sewage, and the EPA regulations indicated a presumptive balance between cost and water quality needs. In short, he viewed the statute as informing the application of the common law, not as displacing it.[117]

The Supreme Court disagreed and overruled *Milwaukee I*.[118] In *Milwaukee II*, the Court emphasized that the federal courts, unlike state courts, are not courts of general jurisdiction and that the creation of a federal rule of decision is generally the job of Congress. Hence, federal law is the exception, rather than the rule. The Court concluded that the new Clean Water Act displaced the "often vague and indeterminate

---

114. *Tennessee Copper,* 206 U.S. at 237.

115. 406 U.S. 91 (1972).

116. *See Milwaukee I,* 406 U.S. at 101–102, 104–107.

117. *See* Illinois v. City of Milwaukee, 599 F.2d 151, 170–175 (7th Cir. 1979).

118. *See* City of Milwaukee v. Illinois & Michigan [Milwaukee II], 451 U.S. 304 (1981).

nuisance concepts and maxims of equity jurisdiction" embodied in the federal common law of nuisance.[119] "It would be quite inconsistent" with the Clean Water Act, the Court said, "if federal courts were in effect to 'write their own ticket' under the guise of federal common law after permits have already been issued and permittees have been planning and operating in reliance on them."[120] Thus, the ruling seemed to be based primarily on jurisprudential concerns about the relationship between statutes and federal common law, rather than on any specific feature of the statutes.

Justice Blackmun wrote a strong dissent, joined by Justices Marshall and Stevens.[121] The dissent demonstrates convincingly that the result in *Milwaukee II* was not contemplated by Congress. In particular, Justice Blackmun relied on the text of section 505(e) of the Clean Water Act, which provides that "[n]othing in this section shall restrict any right which any person (or class of persons) may have under any statute or common law ... to seek any other relief" to infer Congress's preservation of the federal common law of nuisance.[122] As Justice Blackmun pointed out, the legislative history of this section provides further evidence that Congress meant to leave common law remedies intact. The Senate Report on section 505(e) says that "the section would specifically preserve any rights or remedies, under any other law"—and the Report adds that "[c]ompliance with requirements under this Act would not be a defense to a common law action for pollution damages."[123] Moreover, EPA and the Justice Department had consistently taken the view that the federal common law remained effective despite the statute.[124] But these arguments were to no avail.

Milwaukee II might give the impression that the nuisance law has been completely displaced by federal regulation. A few years later, however, the Court made it clear that this conclusion was too hasty, even in connection with federal courts. In *International Paper Co. v. Ouellette*,[125] the Court allowed a diversity action in federal court against an interstate polluter based on *state* nuisance law. (Unlike *Milwaukee II*, the basis for bringing the case in federal court was not that it involved federal law such as the federal common law of nuisance, but that the case involved entities from different states.) The Court held that the Clean Water Act preempts the federal common law and the nuisance law

---

119. *Milwaukee II,* 451 U.S. at 312, 317, 319–326.

120. *Id.* at 326.

121. *See Id.* at 332 (Blackmun, J., dissenting).

122. *Id.* at 339 (Blackmun, J., dissenting).

123. *Milwaukee II*, 451 U.S. at 343.

124. *See Id.* at 346.

125. 479 U.S. 481 (1987).

of downstream states, but not the nuisance law of the state where the discharge took place. Finding complete preemption of state nuisance law would have flown in the face of the Clean Water Act's powerful savings clause:

> Except as expressly provided in this chapter, nothing in this chapter shall (1) preclude or deny the right of any State or political subdivision thereof or interstate agency to adopt or enforce (A) any standard or limitation respecting discharges of pollutants, or (B) any requirement respecting control or abatement of pollution [unless it is less stringent than federal requirements] or (2) be construed as impairing or in any way affecting any right or jurisdiction of the States with respect to the waters (including boundary waters) of such States.[126]

A contrary ruling in *Ouellette* would also have left pollution victims without any damage remedy. The Clean Water Act does allow citizen suits for injunctions and other relief, but damages for pollution-caused injuries are not an available remedy.

Since state law created the remedy, and the district court had jurisdiction under its diversity jurisdiction (because the parties came from different states), the case could be brought in the federal district court located in the downstream state. Thus, we seem to have come almost full circle: *Milwaukee I* preempted state law in favor of the federal common law of nuisance, *Milwaukee II* preempted the federal common law of nuisance, and *Oullette* reinstated state law. Given what the *Milwaukee II* Court had to say about the vagueness of nuisance law, replacing federal common law with state common law probably makes limited practical difference: either way, the federal judge hearing the case has a great deal of discretion to impose requirements on sources that exceed the Clean Water Act. In short, after hanging by its fingernails from a cliff in *Milwaukee II*, the common law came roaring back in the final episode.

The Supreme Court's ultimate decision in *Oullette* to preserve common law remedies is consistent with the pattern among the states.[127] Only a few states limit nuisance suits under their environmental statutes. Alaska and probably New Jersey allow suit only if a source is not complying with its permits. There is no clear statutory or judicial guidance in North Dakota, Oregon, and Rhode Island. In the remaining forty-five states, the nuisance action is available regardless of permit

---

126.   Clean Water Act, 33 U.S.C. § 1370.

127.   *See, e.g.*, Andrew Jackson Heimert, *Keeping Pigs Out of Parlos: Using Nuisance Law to Affect the Location of Pollution*, 27 Envtl. L. 403 (1997) (detailing state-by-state information on the preservation of common law remedies).

compliance.[128] Thus, the nuisance tort remains available as a backstop to pollution statutes.[129]

One might wonder whether the continued availability of nuisance actions has practical significance, given the existence of statutory remedies. How often is this backup to statutory regulation used? Historical statistics show a large increase in the number of common law environmental suits brought in state and federal court beginning at around the time of *Boomer*.[130] After expanding rapidly, the number of state court cases tapered off over the the next twenty years, but part of the slack was taken up by the federal courts (presumably, after *Milwaukee II*, state law claims brought in federal court.) Thus, in 1994, there were twenty-three reported state decisions (about half of the peak year, 1973), and thirty-three reported federal decisions of common law environmental cases.[131] By contrast, in the year when *Boomer* was decided, there had been twenty-five reported state cases but only four federal cases.[132]

Perhaps more importantly than these traditional nuisance suits, the common law is not merely a supplement to modern statutes but has also been given a role within those statutes. For example, RCRA's imminent hazard provision authorizes injunctive relief but gives little guidance about the form of that relief. The courts have relied on the common law tradition of broad equitable discretion in crafting remedies.[133] Similarly, court have turned to the common law to resolve liability issues under CERCLA, particularly those involving joint liability and contribution.[134] Thus, the common law has continued to play a role in environmental law, even in this pervasively statutory era. Announcements of the demise of the common law in the modern regulatory state apparently have proved exaggerated. To the extent that *Boomer* might be thought to signal the irrelevance of the common law to the larger social issues raised by environmental law, that signal has turned out to be misleading.

---

128. *See Id.* at 435–536 nn. 207 & 210.

129. In addition, some states have recognized a related cause of action, for abnormally dangerous activities, in the case of hazardous waste sites. *See* State v. Ventron Corp., 468 A.2d 150 (N.J. 1983).

130. *See* H. Marlow Green, *Can the Common Law Survive in the Modern Statutory Environment?*, 8 Cornell J. L. & Pub. Pol'y 89, 100 (1998).

131. *See id.* at 98–99. It should be noted that the rest of the civil docket expanded more quickly, so that common law environmental cases accounted for a diminishing percentage of litigation.

132. *See Id.*

133. *See, e.g.,* United States v. Waste Industries, Inc., 734 F.2d 159 (4th Cir. 1984).

134. *See, e.g.,* United States v. Monsanto Co., 858 F.2d 160 (4th Cir. 1988), *cert. denied*, 490 U.S. 1106 (1989).

Conclusion

It is unfortunate that only the Court of Appeals opinion has attracted the attention of scholars and law students. The appellate court's decision on damages, with its pragmatic effort at fairness, is equally intriguing. Taking the litigation as a whole, the New York courts seem to have done a creditable job of blending economic concerns, which dominated the resolution of the injunction issue, with fairness to victims, which dominated the damage phase. The final outcome was more balanced than most scholars and students realize. But perhaps a deeper understanding of the case would have deprived it of dramatic impact and diminished its academic appeal.

Boomer survives in the law schools in part because the New York Court of Appeals opinion is such a great teaching tool. *Boomer* has a drama that is deeply appealing. Generations of law students have wondered whether, in this battle between David and Goliath, Goliath should walk away so apparently unscathed, leaving a battered David with nothing but a few coins for his trouble. (And of course, as one *Boomer* afficionado put it, "We must not forget that *Boomer* is about cement. It is a very concrete problem, if you will."[135]) Another part of the opinion's appeal is its apparent simplicity, which ironically is due in large part to the court's failure to discuss adequately either the facts or the New York precedents, not to mention the measure of damages. This simplicity is a great asset in the classroom, and a stark contrast with the immense complexity of many statutory environmental cases.

Part of the *Boomer*'s fame is also due to timing. It was decided at the beginning of the modern environmental era, but it presaged what would turn out to be continuing remedial, economic, and jurisprudential issues: the scope of judicial discretion, the tradeoffs between environmental values and economic costs, and the role of the common law in an age of statutes. *Boomer* was also decided at the beginning of the modern Law and Economics movement, and it became a paradigm case for discussing the economics of entitlements and remedies. Thus, *Boomer* was emblematic of the issues that would preoccupy a whole generation of legal thinkers, and that continue to shape environmental debate today. It is likely to remain a prominent case so long as those issues continue to perplex scholars, students, and policymakers.*

---

135. Dobris, *supra* note 3, at 172 n. 13.

* I would like to thank Sky Stanfield for her research assistance, and Professor David McGowan for his valuable comments.

2

John S. Applegate

The Story of *Reserve Mining*: Managing Scientific Uncertainty in Environmental Regulation

U.S. Environmental Protection Agency v. Reserve Mining Co.,[1] is in every respect a big case. Physically, the Reserve Mining Company operated a factory on the heroic scale of the heavy American industries of the mid-twentieth century. From 1955 to 1980, Reserve's factory yearly produced 10,700,000 tons of iron pellets and *daily* dumped 67,000 tons of mining waste into Lake Superior, the largest, deepest, and most pristine of the Great Lakes. It discolored the lake's water for fifty miles southwest toward Duluth, Minnesota, and it formed a delta of tailings large enough to be characterized as "a major geological event" in the history of Lake Superior.[2] Temporally, Reserve obtained its first permit to discharge tailings into Lake Superior in 1947, it became the object of serious regulatory attention in about 1965, and from 1968 to 1978 it was the focus of nearly constant attention from federal and state administrative and judicial authorities. The federal litigation alone lasted over five years; the federal trial took 139 days, heard over 100 witnesses, saw over 1500 exhibits, and covered 18,000 pages of transcript. Institutionally, Reserve Mining's operations were investigated by state agencies in two states, several Minnesota courts, and three federal courts. Depending on how you count, it generated twenty published judicial opinions, in addition to the en banc decision of the Eighth Circuit that is the centerpiece of this story. Each major opinion fills dozens of pages in the reporter. Politically, Reserve and environmental groups lobbied, were

---

1. 514 F.2d 492 (8th Cir. 1975) (en banc).

2. Quoted in Lisa Heinzerling, Book Review, *Pragmatists and Environmentalists*, 113 Harv. L. Rev. 1421, 1422 (2000) (reviewing Daniel A. Farber, *Eco-Pragmatism: Making Sensible Environmental Decisions in an Uncertain World* (1999)).

lobbied against, found supporters, and battled detractors in the Minnesota state government, both houses of the U.S. Congress, the White House, and in the national and regional news media. Environmentally, the case is a virtual issue-spotter for themes in modern environmental law, from scientific uncertainty, to the management of complex litigation, to the selection of equitable remedies, to the inability of state and local governments to protect even their most treasured natural resources without federal help. Historiographically, the case has been the subject of seven books[3] and many more articles, and it is a leading case in most environmental law texts.

Reserve Mining remains the archetype for the regulation of chemical threats to human health, because the central problem for the court was the management of scientific uncertainty, the salient characteristic of this area of environmental law and policy. The facts of *Reserve Mining* posed the problem of uncertainty in a particularly stark way: the inhalation hazards of asbestos were well known, but what was the danger from ingestion of asbestos fibers in drinking water? To decide the case, the court had to analyze the parties' scientific disagreement in detail, and it had to determine whether the applicable law was remedial and based on proven harm, or precautionary and seeking to avoid harms

---

3. Three of the books are comprehensive: Thomas F. Bastow, *"This Vast Pollution . . . ": United States of America v. Reserve Mining Company* (1986); Robert Bartlett, *The Reserve Mining Controversy: Science, Technology, And Environmental Quality* (1980); Frank D. Schaumburg, *Judgment Reserved: A Landmark Environmental Case* (1976). Bartlett is by far the most thorough and analytical. It is extensively researched, drawing on both primary and secondary sources, and it seeks to place *Reserve Mining* in its broadest social and political context. Bastow was EPA's chief lawyer in the litigation. He was a true insider, he had access to an enormous amount of information in government files, and he interviewed dozens of participants (only Reserve's counsel and employees refused his requests for interviews), but he could not be called a disinterested observer. Bastow is very clear about his loyalties, but Schaumberg is another matter altogether. While the book does not disclose any financial connection with Reserve, it subsequently developed that Reserve's public relations firm had recruited Schaumberg and that Reserve had a financial arrangement with the publisher. Bartlett, *supra*, at 225–26. Schaumberg denied any influence, but contemporaries were dismissive of the work, and one is struck on several occasions by the parallelism between Schaumberg's arguments and those of Reserve's lawyers. This book, in other words, must be approached with great caution. Two contemporaneous books—Wendy Wriston Adamson, *Saving Lake Superior: A Story of Environmental Action* (2d ed. 1976); Stanley Ulrich et al., *Superior Polluter* (1972)—are highly polemical but give valuable insights into the environmental opposition to Reserve. In addition, *Reserve Mining* is an extended case study in Farber, *supra* note 2, (and also Daniel A. Farber, *Risk Regulation in Perspective*: Reserve Mining *Revisited*, 21 Envtl. L. 1321 (1991)), and David M. O'Brien, *What Process Is Due? Courts And Science–Policy Disputes* (1987). All of these books all cover a common core of operative facts, and so they are not individually cited, except where one source provides a unique perspective or particularly detailed information. For an overview of the legally relevant facts, one cannot do better than the trial court's opinion, *U.S. v. Reserve Mining Co.*, 380 F. Supp. 11, 29–54 (D. Minn. 1974).

before they are realized or even fully understood. The Eighth Circuit took up this challenge in *Reserve Mining*, and the result was a landmark of environmental law whose science-based, precautionary approach continues to influence the regulation of toxic threats to human health and the environment.

I. Social and Legal Background

Lake Superior is a natural marvel, the Grand Canyon of lakes. It is the largest, deepest, coldest, and clearest of the Great Lakes.[4] While it is known for the power of its waters, especially in storms, it is also, paradoxically, the most fragile of the Great Lakes. Superior's geological age is the same as the other Great Lakes, but its depth and exceptionally cold temperature make it a young lake (oligotrophic) in biological terms. Eutrophication, the aging process by which algae and bacteria gradually turn a lake from water to wetland to land, has made little progress in the chilly waters of Lake Superior, which accounts for their astounding clarity and deep blue color. The early explorers reported being able to see a hundred feet through the water to the bottom of the lake. In consequence, the lake is particularly vulnerable to the addition of materials that would encourage the growth of algae and bacteria. Moreover, Lake Superior has a very low hydraulic flushing rate, because it is the receiving basin for a surprisingly small watershed and drains slowly into the lower Great Lakes–St. Lawrence River System. The water in the lake is not entirely replaced for 500 years, so anything added to the lake's water cannot be counted on to leave for five centuries. Most additions, of course, quickly disappear in the vastness of the water volume (nearly 3000 cubic miles), but pollution that is particularly eutrophic or toxic or large is for all practical purposes irreversible.

Taconite. In addition to its beauty, Lake Superior was (and is) a major economic resource. It supported a commercial fishery and provided a transportation corridor for the region's natural resources, first furs, then timber, and finally iron ore. Iron deposits were discovered in Minnesota in 1865, and the Mesabi Range in northeastern Minnesota proved to be one of the greatest iron ore deposits ever found. The ore fell into high-and low-grade categories: hematite, which is about 70% iron and constituted about 5% of the ore; and taconite, which is about 20% iron and constituted 95% of the ore body. Taconite is a very hard and brittle, silica-rich rock, throughout which magnetite (another high-grade iron ore) particles are distributed. The silicate matrix is comprised predominantly of a mineral called cummingtonite-grunerite.

---

4. Its surface area is nearly 32,000 square miles; it is about 350 miles long and 160 wide; its maximum and average depths are 1333 and 475 feet, respectively. Bartlett, *supra* note 3, at 41.

The Mesabi deposit was so large that for nearly a century there was no reason to resort to the low-grade taconite ore. Hematite was mined in Minnesota and shipped directly, via Lake Superior, to the great steel-making centers of Indiana, Ohio, and Pennsylvania. However, as the supply of hematite began to dwindle in the early twentieth century—accelerated by the demands of World War I—interest began to focus on taconite. Taconite was no commercial match for hematite without fur-ther processing, and so, in 1913, one of the early investors in Mesabi Range property approached the University of Minnesota School of Mines to explore processes that might economically produce a high-grade feed-stock from the low-grade ore. The task fell to E.W. Davis, a new mathematics instructor at the Mines Experiment Station, and Davis began his life-long commitment to the perfection and promotion of taconite ore.[5]

The process of deriving a feedstock with a high iron content from ore with a low iron content is known in the mining industry as "beneficiating" the ore. It is the conceptually simple process of extract-ing the iron in the ore from the rest of the rock. In practice, it is far more difficult, and Davis worked on the process for years. The taconite was mined from open pits and crushed into progressively smaller pieces. These were mixed with large volumes of water to make a slurry, and then further ground until it was roughly the consistency of powder.[6] At a number of points in the process, the slurry was passed over huge drum magnets to separate out the iron-rich fraction. The separated fraction was then dewatered through a filtration process, and the filter cake was mixed with bentonite clay and rolled into small pellets for easy handling. The pellets, containing about 65% usable iron, were baked in rotary kilns and shipped. For each ton of iron pellets, the Davis process consumed 3 tons of ore and 71 tons of water, and it yielded, in addition to the pellets, 2.3 tons of wet, unused rock, called tailings, which had to be disposed.

Davis was able to make commercially viable taconite ore by 1918, based on the demands of World War I. It could not compete in a peacetime market, though, and taconite beneficiating operations ceased in 1924. Despite the lack of a current market for the ore, Oglebay Norton & Co. organized the Reserve Mining Company in 1939 on behalf of four steel manufacturers[7] literally as a *reserve* supply of ore for their

---

5. *See* E.W. Davis, *Pioneering with Taconite* (1964). Reserve's plant in Silver Bay—the subject of this litigation—was aptly named the E.W. Davis Works.

6. Photographs of the process and equipment can be found at http://www.cleveland-cliffs.com/GeneralInformation/ (last visited July 8, 2004), and at http://www.cleveland-cliffs.com/MiningOperations & Technology/Default.htm (last visited July 8, 2004). *See also Reserve Mining,* 380 F. Supp. at 30–31.

7. They were American Rolling Mill (Armco Steel Corp.), Wheeling Steel Corp., Montreal Mining Co., and Cleveland–Cliffs Iron Co.

furnaces. World War II brought hematite supplies still closer to exhaustion, and serious plans began in 1944 to create a taconite industry. Reserve would excavate a huge open-pit mine at Babbitt, Minnesota, build a company town there for its workers, transport the ore 47 miles to Lake Superior on its own railroad, construct a beneficiating plant on the north shore of the lake, and build the company town of Silver Bay to service the plant.

The captains of the steel industry were not the only ones concerned about the exhaustion of hematite supplies. Thousands of Minnesotans and their state and local governments, economically dependent on iron ore, feared the demise of this extremely important industry. When Reserve announced its plans to build, the company was regarded as a local hero, not least by the Minnesota's progressive Democratic–Farmer–Labor (DFL) Party. Reserve made the most of its status as savior of the economy of northeastern Minnesota. It claimed to be operating at the very edge of profitability and in need of state subsidies to be economically viable.

Minnesota responded. To encourage taconite mining, in 1941 the state had changed its tax laws to replace a property tax on taconite holdings with a production tax on iron shipment, eliminating much of the financial risk of going into the business of taconite beneficiation. Minnesota also supported Reserve with permits. The shore of Lake Superior was an economically ideal location for the beneficiating plant, and, despite the fact that six other taconite processors operated in the interior, using recycled process water and on-land disposal of tailings,[8] Minnesota in 1947 permitted Reserve to dispose of its tailings in the lake. The permits, therefore, were another kind of subsidy, one which allowed a single private entity (and not its competitors) to consume a valuable and unique public resource at no cost.[9] And in 1964, Reserve sought and received one more subsidy. It had begun work on its plant in

---

8. Bastow, *supra* note 3, at 8; Bartlett, *supra* note 3, at 23.

9. At a late stage in the *Reserve Mining* litigation, a state court judge was moved to observe:

[E]ven in 1947 the State Conservation Department was limiting the use which landowners bordering along lakes and streams could make of their property, and by the 1950's it was extremely difficult for a cottage owner to even get a permit to place some sand on his beach, even one truckload. Yet Reserve was permitted to dump 67,000 tons of waste, amounting to thousands of truckloads, into the king of fresh waters each and every day. Lake Superior was sold 30 years ago, bartered away for dollars and jobs, albeit hundreds of millions of dollars and thousands of jobs.

Reserve Mining Co. v. Herbst, 256 N.W.2d 808, 849–50 (Minn. 1977) (Yetka, J., concurring specially). *See also* Richard A. Epstein, Book Review, *Too Pragmatic by Half: Eco-Pragmatism: Making Sensible Environmental Decisions in an Uncertain World*, 109 Yale L.J. 1639, 1652–53 (2000) (reviewing Farber, *supra* note 2) ("so matters got off on the wrong foot when Reserve Mining received its sweetheart deal in 1947").

1951 and produced its first pellets on October 10, 1955, by which time Reserve employed thousands of Minnesotans. Reserve's activities remained so popular and its influence in Minnesota so great that a "Taconite Amendment" to the Minnesota constitution, assuring Reserve no increase beyond the current production tax for 25 years, passed by a 7–1 margin.

Emerging environmentalism. Even as Minnesota was amending its constitution to subsidize Reserve, a different trend was developing. Since at least Theodore Roosevelt's designation of Yellowstone and Yosemite as the world's first national parks, Americans have been acutely aware of the unique beauty of their country. A body of water like Lake Superior is valued not only for its commercial fishing and transportation possibilities, but also as a recreational destination for sailing, canoeing, bathing (not for the faint of heart), and viewing. The threat that industrialization and other aspects of modern society brought to America's landscape was crystallized by Lady Bird Johnson's "Keep America Beautiful" campaign of the early 1960s, culminating in the White House Conference on Scenic Beauty in May 1965. In the same period, Rachel Carson's *Silent Spring*[10] tied these aesthetic concerns to toxic threats to human health and the environment.

Water pollution was an obvious threat to the appreciation of natural beauty, and Reserve's earliest opponents were motivated by the aesthetic harm to Lake Superior. Arlene (Harvell) Lehto had grown up on the shores of the lake and remembered being able to see far down into the water to the boulders that lined its bed. She left in 1957, and when she returned in 1968 she was devastated that her son could no longer enjoy the clear water.[11] Grant Merritt, a lawyer and local DFL officer, was a scion of one of the founders of the Minnesota iron industry, but he too had come to believe that it was wrong to sacrifice the lake for the iron industry. And Verna Mize, though she lived in Washington, D.C., was an annual summer visitor to the lake. Between 1967 and 1969, Lehto formed the Save Lake Superior Association (SLSA) in communities around the western end of Lake Superior, Merritt formed the Minnesota Environmental Control Citizens Association (MECCA) in the Minneapolis–St. Paul area, and Mize began to act as an unofficial federal lobbyist for both.

The emerging conflict in values is exemplified by the public career of John A. Blatnik. After a successful career as a DFL state legislator, Blatnik in 1946 was elected to Congress from a district that included

---

10.   Rachel Carson, *Silent Spring* (1962).

11.   http://news.minnesota.publicradio.org/features/2003/09/29_hemp-hills_reservehistory/ (last visited July 8, 2004) [hereinafter Minn.Pub. Radio] (interview of Lehto).

Duluth and Reserve's operations. In Congress, he was a champion for taconite mining and for Reserve. Indeed, he and the congressman from the neighboring district were known—not altogether admiringly, but not inaccurately—as the "Taconite Twins." Blatnik was a strong supporter of the Taconite Amendment, and yet, as a representative from the region, he could hardly be oblivious to the extraordinary qualities of Lake Superior. In Washington, he earned himself a reputation as "Mr. Water Pollution" by sponsoring several pollution control measures, leading up to the Water Quality Act of 1965.[12] The 1965 act created the Federal Water Pollution Control Administration (FWPCA)[13] and, for the first time, required the states to establish water quality standards and to have the standards approved by the federal government in accordance with federal water quality criteria.[14] Moreover, it strengthened the weak federal enforcement mechanism by making the state standards enforceable by the federal government, though only after holding an "enforcement conference" with the pollution control authorities of the affected states.[15] The act also included a pork-barrel project for its sponsor, a National Water Quality Laboratory (NWQL) in Duluth. The conflict between taconite and water pollution control was perhaps not apparent in 1965, but for Blatnik the contradiction became irony when Reserve became the subject of an enforcement conference under the act, which recommended a federal abatement action against Reserve, based in large part on the work of the Duluth NWQL.

II. Factual Background

The permits. In 1947, Reserve applied for operating permits from the state of Minnesota and from the U.S. Army Corps of Engineers. The Corps permit was of little importance at this point because it focused entirely on obstacles to navigation; to the extent that pollution was an issue, the Corps left it to Minnesota, and Minnesota was extremely supportive of Reserve. At Minnesota's hearings on the permits, Reserve claimed that its tailings would have a minimal effect on Lake Superior, because the larger particles would form a delta by the side of the lake,[16]

---

12. For a general history of the enforcement provisions of the pre–1972 Clean Water Act, *see* Frank J. Barry, *The Evolution of the Enforcement Provisions of the Federal Water Pollution Control Act: A Study of the Difficulty in Developing Effective Legislation*, 68 Mich. L. Rev. 1103 (1970).

13. The FWPCA was originally part of the Department of Health, Education, and Welfare (predecessor of Health and Human Services), but it was moved a year later to the Department of the Interior.

14. 33 U.S.C. § 1160(c) (1970). The FWPCA developed "guidelines" for state standards. Key guidelines can be found in Barry, *supra* note 12, at 1122–23.

15. 33 U.S.C. § 1160(c)(5), (d), (g) (1970).

16. Remarkably, filling part of the lake with a delta was apparently not regarded as harm to the lake *as such*.

and that the fine tailings were like sand, insoluble and biologically inert. Moreover, the fine tailings, which might otherwise be expected to disperse and cloud the water, would be carried by a "density current" (created by the weight of the tailings-bearing slurry) down the face of the tailings delta to the depths of Superior's Great Trough, from which they could not escape due to the temperature layering (thermoclines) of the lake water. Reserve predicted that the tailings would cover a disposal zone of nine square miles of the lake's deep bottom, with no cloudiness (turbidity) outside of the immediate mixing zone.

Opponents were few, and Minnesota issued a permit that tracked exactly what Reserve claimed to be able to do. The tailings could contain no material quantities of water-soluble matter; deposits would be limited to the zone of discharge; and there could be no material clouding of water outside the discharge zone, no material effects on fish life or public water supplies, and no material interference with navigation. The repeated qualification "material" in the permit promised that, even if conditions were not as Reserve promised, enforcement would be a nightmare of measuring degrees and increments. Moreover, Minnesota placed no time limitation on its permits. Reserve could discharge its tailings into Lake Superior until it violated the permit's vague terms or the taconite ran out, whichever came first.

Reserve announced final plans to build the plant in 1951, though it still ostentatiously worried about the profitability of the operation. (Reserve had mastered the art of playing hard to get.) By 1955 it produced the first pellets and in 1956 first shipped the pellets out of the Silver Bay harbor. By April 10, 1956, production exceeded one million tons a year, and permits to draw more water and discharge more tailings were issued. And it turned out that Reserve needn't have worried about profitability. In 1950 Armco and Republic Steel had bought out the other owners of Reserve, each becoming a 50% owner of the company. Reserve returned a strong profit to its parents and expanded two more times, in 1963 and 1965, until it produced 10.7 million tons of pellets—and 25 million tons of tailings—each year. By 1967, Reserve was shipping 12% of all of the iron mined in the United States.

The Water Quality Act. From the beginning of operations, however, it became apparent that Reserve's operations were not as benign as promised. In 1956, commercial fishermen in the vicinity of the plant complained of gray slimes on their nets, and they found that they needed to be at least seven miles from shore to catch fish.[17] They also began to notice that the normally clear blue water appeared to be a milky green along the lake shore between Silver Bay and Duluth. The Minnesota Department of Health investigated in 1956 and 1957, and it found that

---

17. Minn. Pub. Radio, *supra* note 11.

the slimes were composed of iron-fixing bacteria, algae, and cummingtonite-grunerite, *i.e.*, Reserve's tailings. It also confirmed that the "green water" extended over 35 miles southwest from Silver Bay. Upon analysis, the green water was found to contain increased suspended solids consisting of cummingtonite-grunerite. The department's report, however, was not released to the public, and Reserve continued to operate and expand.

The 1965 Water Quality Act set into motion, albeit indirectly, three events that precipitated the *Reserve Mining* litigation. First, in 1966 a scientist named Louis Williams was transferred to the new NWQL in Duluth. He became curious about the green water phenomenon after hearing complaints from local commercial fishermen. Taking samples around the western end of Lake Superior, he found taconite tailings in the open waters of the lake, around Wisconsin's Apostle Islands, and in the Duluth drinking water intake. Like the Minnesota report a decade earlier, however, Williams' findings were suppressed. In frustration, Williams wrote to Senator Gaylord Nelson of Wisconsin, who had been expressing concern about the effect of Reserve's discharge on Wisconsin waters for some years, and he wrote an article for the magazine *Bioscience*. The letter and the article encouraged Nelson and others to advocate federal action against Reserve.

Second, the Department of the Interior had begun, pursuant to the 1965 act, the process of approving Minnesota's water quality standards. Secretary Stewart Udall promulgated *Guidelines for Establishing Water Quality Standards for Interstate Waters*, including one which required state standards to include an anti-degradation clause.[18] The clause was not qualified by "material," as Reserve's permits were, and it overrode previous permit terms. The Minnesota water pollution control regulations (WPC 15) that were approved on November 26, 1969, included an anti-degradation clause.

Third, President Lyndon Johnson issued an executive order that required elements of the federal government to consult with the FWPCA before taking action that might affect water quality. When Reserve asked the Corps for an indefinite extension of its permit in late 1969, Interior was called upon to coordinate the federal response with an eye to water quality issues. Interior created a "Taconite Study Group" under Charles Stoddard, a career federal land manager who was Interior's regional coordinator for the western Great Lakes area. Until the asbestos issue arose four and a half years later, the so-called Stoddard Report comprehensively defined the terms of the debate over Reserve's discharges. The report began by emphasizing the sheer volume of the tailings. In twelve

18. *See* Barry, *supra* note 12, at 1123 n. 115 ("In no case will standards providing for less than existing water quality be acceptable.").

days, Reserve's discharge equaled the combined sediment discharged from all of Lake Superior's tributaries in one *year*. The report went on to challenge the factual basis for the granting of the 1947 permits, point by point. The tailings did not, in fact, stay put. Less than half of the tailings were in the delta, and much of the remainder dispersed into the lake. There was a southwest current in the lake, as the fishermen had long claimed, and it kept smaller particles in suspension for long distances. Moreover, the tailings were not inert. They reduced bottom fauna (the foundation of the lake's food chain) up to 15 miles from the plant, and they leached iron, lead, copper, zinc, and cadmium to an extent that violated water quality standards and guidelines. Finally, on-land disposal methods were technically and economically feasible. The report suggested a disposal site at Lax Lake, a few miles inland from the Silver Bay plant.

III. Prior Proceedings

The enforcement conference—part 1. When Stoddard circulated his report in draft form to Reserve and to his superiors in Washington on December 31, 1968, he was met with a storm of criticism. Following the pattern set in 1947, Reserve's first reaction was an economic threat: "Thousands of jobs, two communities and a major business enterprise have been placed in jeopardy by this erroneous paper."[19] With the powerful assistance of Congressman Blatnik, Reserve put enormous pressure on Secretary Udall to suppress the report—as had happened with the Minnesota report of 1957 and the Williams report of 1967—and Udall acquiesced. Stoddard feared that the report would disappear forever when the Nixon administration took office on January 20, 1969, so he leaked the report to the Minnesota press on January 15.[20] On January 16, the story ran under the headline, "U.S. Study Finds Taconite Tailings Pollute Superior," and it generated opposing pressure on Udall from Senator Nelson and environmental groups. As a result, while still maintaining that the Stoddard Report was a "preliminary staff report" and "unofficial," Udall convened a Lake Superior Enforcement Conference under the terms of the Water Quality Act just before leaving office.

Stoddard's fears that the new administration would be hostile to the environment were confirmed when he was summarily fired and his office locks changed on January 20. However, Nixon's Secretary of the Interior, Walter Hickel, did not countermand Udall's order to hold an enforcement conference, probably because enforcement conferences were designed to obtain cooperation by persuasion and publicity, not to apply legal coercion. Reserve would not be required to do anything that

---

19. Quoted in Bartlett, *supra* note 3, at 60; *see also* Ulrich, *supra* note 3, at 40.

20. *See* Minn. Star–Tribune (Dec. 30, 1977) (obituary of Stoddard); Bastow, *supra* note 3, at 18–21.

Minnesota did not agree to—and Minnesota had, as Bartlett puts it, a substantial and growing investment in the Reserve Mining Company.[21]

The enforcement conference convened on May 13, 1969, with representatives of the federal government, Minnesota, Wisconsin, and Michigan in attendance. In many ways, the conference went just as Reserve would have hoped. Congressman Blatnik was an active participant in the proceedings and to a large degree ran the show behind the scenes.[22] Charles Stoddard testified, but the director of the NWQL, Donald Mount, was highly critical of Stoddard's report on technical grounds. The Minnesota Pollution Control Agency (MPCA), too, asserted that it had no evidence of violation of the 1947 permits,[23] and Reserve used the opportunity to present its own detailed rebuttal of the Stoddard Report.

The conference did, however, exhibit some early warning signs of trouble for Reserve. Borrowing tactics from the Civil Rights and growing anti-war movements, Arlene Lehto and Grant Merritt saw the conference as their opportunity to put public pressure on Reserve to stop dumping in the lake and on the government to take action against Reserve. The conferees were met by about 600 demonstrators, and the hotel ballroom where it was held was packed. SLSA, MECCA, and an umbrella group called the Northern Environmental Council made a very strong showing at the conference, both in their numbers and in the anecdotal and technical testimony they offered.[24]

The enforcement conference met again in September, and a new, science-driven process began to emerge. While not part of the official record, the Stoddard Report had as a practical matter defined the issues for the conference by bringing together a number of different sciences into a coherent narrative. Reserve's chief lawyer, Edward Fride, and its scientific consultant, G. Fred Lee, orchestrated a detailed counter-narrative with their own group of experts. The conference in turn began to look to scientists to answer the question whether Reserve's discharges were "polluting" Lake Superior.[25] The views of Donald Mount, as director of the NWQL, became the particular focus of the conference.

---

21. Bartlett, *supra* note 3, at 30.

22. For example, when environmental groups learned that the director of the NWQL, Donald Mount, had sampled Wisconsin waters and found cummingtonite-grunerite, Blatnik prevailed on Mount and David Dominick, the Commissioner of the FWPCA, who was chairing the conference at that point, to insist that the results were inconclusive. Blatnik's influence was discovered by an enterprising reporter who hid in what appeared to Blatnik, Dominick, and Mount to be an empty hotel ballroom, while the three talked. Bastow, *supra* note 3, at 36.

23. Schaumberg, *supra* note 3, at 70–75; Bastow, *supra* note 3, at 32–36.

24. Adamson, *supra* note 3, at 46–53.

25. Bartlett, *supra* note 3, at 79–80.

Mount had assigned another scientist at the laboratory, Gary Glass, to spend the summer conducting sampling and other studies designed to provide the supporting evidence (or not) for Stoddard's report.[26] By September, Mount and Glass had confirmed many of Stoddard's findings,[27] though Mount was equivocal in his testimony to the conference.[28] Faced with conflicting conclusions on the science, the conference resorted to a technical solution. It issued a request to Reserve to present a plan within six months for reducing tailings discharge to the "maximum practicable extent." Instead of developing a plan, however, Reserve swung into political action. It hired former Secretary of Defense Clark Clifford to arrange private meetings between Reserve officials, Congressman Blatnik, and senior Corps of Engineers officials in a successful attempt to forestall action to limit the permit.

The state trial. Before the enforcement conference met in September 1969, the Sierra Club had filed suit in Hennepin County (Minneapolis) to obtain a writ of mandamus to require the Minnesota Pollution Control Agency (MPCA) to enforce its regulations against Reserve.[29] The Sierra Club obtained an order requiring MPCA to hold hearings on the question of violation, but on Christmas Eve Reserve filed suit in Two Harbors, a few miles from Silver Bay and firmly in the taconite region, challenging the validity of WPC 15. Reserve's case drew Judge C. Luther Eckman, and he conducted a full trial on the merits between June 22 and August 5, 1970.[30] Reserve opened, as usual, by threatening to shut down if it

---

26.   Bastow, *supra* note 3, at 77–87 (describing Glass's work).

27.   They concluded "beyond doubt" that Reserve's tailings were found in the west end of the lake and in Wisconsin waters. They had also found tailings at the bottom of toilet tanks in Duluth, proving that they were in Duluth's drinking water. Bartlett, *supra* note 3, at 67–77; Bastow, *supra* note 3, at 32–36.

28.   He asserted, for example, that there was a "clear endangerment of the use of the lake" from eutrophication, Bastow, *supra* note 3, at 45, but nevertheless opined that the case was really about "the Lake's appearance rather than the toxic effects on fish and fish food organisms, or endangering water supplies." Yet he also warned that, given the low flush rate of Lake Superior, any effects—including the ecological ones—were "irreversible and cumulative."

29.   WPC 15 included several provisions applicable to Reserve's operations. It provided that waters of naturally high quality could not be degraded ((a)(4)); prohibited the discharge of wastes that cause nuisance conditions or have "offensive or harmful effects" ((c)(2)); limiting the allowable suspended solid content of discharges ((c)(6)); controlled the discharge of substances that make waters unfit to drink even after chemical treatment ((d)(1)); it incorporated the Minnesota statutory definition of pollution at Minn. Stat. Ann § 115.01(5).

30.   Eckman's first action was to overrule the mandamus issued by the Hennepin county courts, a rather astonishing move, since he was not a higher court. The Hennepin county courts reluctantly acceded, however, and Minnesota, finally goaded into action, counterclaimed that Reserve was violating WPC 15.

lost.[31] Eckman himself never betrayed any real understanding of the technical issues—he said as much in his opinion—but he was shaken by the extent of the green water in Lake Superior.[32] His decision found "no measurable adverse or deleterious effects upon the water quality or use of Lake Superior," and it ruled that WPC 15 was arbitrary as applied to Reserve.[33] Nevertheless, Eckman ordered Reserve to submit plans to the court by May 15, 1971, for a new disposal system that would assure that the tailings did not disperse into the lake.[34] The Minnesota Supreme Court eventually handed Reserve a more complete victory by affirming Judge Eckman's ruling on the invalidity of WPC 15 and reversing his order to Reserve to negotiate to a different disposal method,[35] but by then (August 18, 1972) the dispute was in federal court and events had overtaken it.

The enforcement conference—part 2. While the litigation in Judge Eckman's courtroom was proceeding, the Lake Superior Enforcement Conference held sessions in April and August 1970 and January 1971. By now, it was clear that the enforcement conference would not be the innocuous proceeding that Reserve and Hickel had expected. Wisconsin's new governor, Patrick Lucey, was a friend of Charles Stoddard and a protégé of Senator Nelson. Even worse from Reserve's point of view, Wendell Anderson, Minnesota's new governor, appointed Grant Merritt as the executive director of MPCA. Furthermore, the newly created U.S. Environmental Protection Agency now chaired the enforcement conference, and the agency's Administrator was William Ruckelshaus, an experienced official well known for his commitment to the agency's mission and to vigorous enforcement of the law. While Mount continued to act as *de facto* scientific arbiter for the conferees, his concerns about the effects of the tailings were also increasing and, following his lead, the conferees were beginning to change their minds.[36] At the August meeting, the conference adopted the conclusion that there was evidence that

31. Ulrich, *supra* note 3, at 113.

32. The state arranged to have him flown in a state police helicopter over a particularly long patch of green water. Upon his return, he told Reserve's counsel, "It looked pretty bad out there today, Ed." Bastow, *supra* note 3, at 49.

33. Reserve Mining Co. v. Minn. Pollution Control Agency, 1 ELR 20073 (Dist. Ct. Minn., Dec. 15, 1970).

34. Eckman's opinion incorporated a disposal plan that Reserve first introduced in the litigation, the so-called deep pipe plan, discussed below.

35. Reserve Mining Co. v. Minn. Pollution Control Agency, 200 N.W.2d 142, 147–48 (Minn. 1972).

36. The Michigan representative remarked: "I, for one, would not like the record to stand that as conferees we are waiting for a dead body to be floating in Wisconsin waters." Bastow, *supra* note 3, at 40.

the tailings endangered the health and welfare of persons in states other than Minnesota, and thus laying the foundation for federal jurisdiction.

At the January 1971 meeting—no doubt influenced by the accession of Governors Anderson and Lucey and Administrator Ruckelshaus– Reserve proposed the so-called deep pipe plan. Reserve's existing disposal mechanism ran the tailings out to the delta in large open troughs called "launders." The launders stopped before the end of the delta, allowing the larger particles to settle on (and extend) the delta, and the smaller, still suspended particles to flow off the edge, riding the density current to the bottom. The deep pipe plan would thicken the effluent by adding a chemical flocculant, and then pipe it underwater directly to the bottom of the lake, avoiding the problem of tailings stripping off the density current and being spread by the lake currents.[37] Reserve's offer to begin work on the deep pipe plan met with no enthusiasm whatsoever. Opponents questioned both the technical feasibility of the mechanism and the effect of adding large volumes of a new chemical (the flocculant) to the discharge. Whatever Reserve might say about the inertness of the tailings, it could not say the same about the flocculant. The conferees closed the second session by appointing a technical committee to study the deep pipe plan, and in March the committee reported back that it was technically infeasible and would not, in any event, eliminate the green water problem.[38]

The enforcement conference met for its final session on April 22 and 23, 1971. David Dominick, the commissioner of the FWPCA, chaired the meeting.[39] After some further wrangling on the first day, on the second day Dominick announced his intention to recommend to Administrator Ruckelshaus that he give Reserve the required 180–day notice before asking the Department of Justice to file an abatement action. Wisconsin's representative objected to the peremptory nature of Dominick's announcement, but voted to support it. Merritt (representing Minnesota) and Michigan's representative were enthusiastically supportive.[40]

From one perspective, the conference could be seen as a great victory for environmental interests, and, indeed, it succeeded in harden-

---

37. This was of course completely inconsistent with its original positions that the existing method of lake disposal was the only technically or economically feasible way of handling its tailings and that the density current carried all of the tailings to the bottom of the lake.

38. Schaumberg, *supra* note 3, at 142.

39. According to Bastow, Dominick had particularly smarted from his characterization as a political hack at the time of his appointment (his major qualification for the post appeared to be the patronage of his uncle, a powerful Colorado senator). The criticism rankled and ultimately gave Dominick an incentive to prove his independence. Bastow, *supra* note 3, at 23–24.

40. The conference also unanimously adopted a finding that the deep pipe plan was unacceptable and recommending on-land disposal.

ing the position of the states (especially Minnesota) and federal government against the dumping.[41] On the other hand, it demonstrated, better
than anything else could, the weakness of the enforcement conference
mechanism. In two years of deliberations, six long meetings, hundreds of
witnesses, and thousands of exhibits, the conference was utterly stymied
by Reserve's intransigence. Thomas Bastow, EPA's lawyer in the subsequent litigation, put it this way: "In effect, the Federal–State enforcement conference declared bankruptcy and called in a receiver."[42] As it
turned out, however, Judge Lord was not your ordinary receiver.

The federal trial—health issues. Ruckelshaus duly issued the 180–
day notice on April 28, 1971, and there followed what can best be
described as a phony war. Litigation was threatened and deadlines
issued, but the parties spent their time in intensive lobbying efforts
throughout the federal government. Reserve achieved some delay, but
the Justice Department filed suit in federal district court on February
17, 1972, alleging that Reserve's discharges into the air and into Lake
Superior violated the Rivers and Harbors (Refuse) Act,[43] the Clean Water
Act,[44] Minnesota WPC 15 and 26,[45] Minnesota air pollution regulations,
federal common law nuisance,[46] and state common law nuisance.[47]

The case was assigned to Judge Miles Lord. Lord's judicial approach
and temperament were modeled on his judicial hero, Justice William O.
Douglas—only more so. Professor Daniel Farber observes that by comparison to Lord, Douglas "was a hair-splitting legalist."[48] Like Douglas,

---

41. Bartlett, *supra* note 3, at 115.

42. Bastow, *supra* note 3, at 61.

43. 33 U.S.C. § 407.

44. 33 U.S.C. § 1160(c)(5) (1970). The United States was authorized to seek abatement of such violations in § 1160(g)(1)-(2). This section of the Clean Water Act was
repealed and replaced by the 1972 amendments to the act. The legislative history of the
1972 amendments makes it abundantly clear that the amendments did not affect the
validity of actions filed before their enactment, and no one seriously challenged the
applicability of § 1160. *See* Robert V. Percival, *The Clean Water Act And The Demise Of
The Federal Common Law Of Interstate Nuisance*, 55 Ala. L. Rev. 717, 763 (2004).

45. The relevant parts of WPC 15 are summarized in note 29, *supra*. WPC 26 was a
general effluent standard for Lake Superior, which incorporated the standards in WPC 15.

46. The federal common law of interstate nuisance was in flux at the time. The
Supreme Court first recognized such a cause of action in 1972 in *Illinois v. Milwaukee (I)*,
406 U.S. 91 (1972), though it later ruled that *Milwaukee I* had been superseded by the 1972
Clean Water Act amendments. *Milwaukee v. Illinois (II)*, 451 U.S. 304 (1981).

47. The suit also alleged violation of Minnesota air pollution regulations, APC 1, 5, 6,
and 17, and state common law nuisance for air emissions. For reasons that will become
apparent, these causes of action created fewer conceptual problems.

48. Farber, *supra* note 2, at 20. Among the bar, he was sometimes called "Miles the
Lord." *Id.*

Lord came from humble roots—in Lord's case, Minnesota iron miners—
and he had worked his way through college and law school in a variety of
laborer's jobs. He was elected state attorney general on the DFL ticket,
President Kennedy appointed him U.S. Attorney for Minnesota, and
President Johnson elevated him to the federal bench. It was therefore
hardly surprising—though inauspicious for the government—that Lord
opened the proceedings by gratuitously assuring unions and local governments that he had no intention of forcing the closure of Reserve
Mining.[49]

The trial of the case appeared to be little more than a replay of the
arguments that had defined the dispute since the Stoddard Report, when
something entirely unexpected happened. On December 7, 1972, while
trial preparations were underway but well before the trial began, Arlene
Lehto attended a meeting of the International Joint Commission (IJC), a
venerable U.S.-Canadian institution that seeks to resolve boundary water issues between the two countries,[50] to make a presentation on
Reserve's pollution of Lake Superior. At the conference, a geologist at
the University of Wisconsin–Superior handed her an article that tied the
unusually high rate of stomach cancer in Japan to the practice of mixing
rice with talc that contained asbestos-like material. The asbestos-like
material was cummingtonite-grunerite. It occurred to the geologist that
it was the mineral in taconite, and it occurred to Lehto that "we're
drinking it." She explained this to the IJC, more or less as an after-
thought to her aesthetic concerns, and it made no impact on the IJC at
all. Her argument did, however, make an impact on an NWQL scientist
in the audience, Phillip Cook. Cook began to test Duluth drinking water
for traces of cummingtonite-grunerite and began to research asbestos
and its relationship to gastrointestinal cancer.

"Asbestos" is a generic name for a number of crystalline minerals
that have a high degree of resistance to heat or impart that quality to
materials of which they are part. There are two basic types: chrysotile,
which particularly lends itself to being woven into fabrics, and amphibole. There are several amphibole types of asbestos, one of which is
commonly called amosite and is composed of the mineral cummingtonite-
grunerite.[51] Asbestos fibers cause cancer when they are inhaled. The

---

49. Bastow, *supra* note 3, at 75.

50. It is, in fact, a model of international cooperation and has taken an increasingly
aggressive role in combating pollution in the Great Lakes. For a recent and interesting
history of the IJC and its relationship to environmental issues, *see* Gordon Durnil, *The
Making of a Conservative Environmentalist* (1995).

51. For a history of the use of asbestos and a taxonomy of its types, *see* James E.
Alleman & Brooke T. Mossman, *Asbestos Revisited*, 227(1) Scientific American p. 70 (July
1997); B.T. Mossman et al., *Asbestos: Scientific Developments and Implications for Public*

exact mechanism is uncertain—it is thought that when the fibers lodge in the lung and surrounding tissues, they cause a particular type of irritation that results in cancer[52]—but there is no doubt of asbestos' connection with lung cancer and mesothelioma, a particularly aggressive cancer of the lining of the chest cavity. There is also a strong statistical connection between inhaled asbestos and gastrointestinal cancer. The typical latency period between exposure to asbestos and cancer diagnosis extends to 30 years and is not known to be less than 15 years. Nothing can be done to prevent cancer after exposure.

Remarkably, Lehto and her geologist acquaintance were the first people to make the connection between taconite and asbestos, and Cook was the first person to pursue it systematically. When Cook first reported this connection to Gary Glass, Glass was dismissive. However, as if to confirm the "Eureka!" theory of scientific discovery, Glass had a dream on the night of May 20, 1973, in which Duluth's residents were killed by asbestos in their drinking water. When he went to the office the next day, he and Cook set to work on the scientific literature on ingestion of asbestos. By the end of the day, they had found an article on the extreme carcinogenicity of amosite asbestos by Irving Selikoff, a physician at the Sloan–Kettering cancer center in New York and the country's leading expert on asbestos-induced cancer, and they had confirmed that amosite is another name for cummingtonite-grunerite.

A cascade of activity within the federal trial team followed,[53] and on June 11, 1973, John Hills, the government's chief lawyer, presented a witness statement from Dr. Selikoff to Judge Lord and counsel for Reserve at a pre-trial conference. Immediately recognizing the implications of Selikoff's statement and the potential for public panic, Judge Lord during the week of June 11 held a series of closed hearings on the danger from asbestos. The claim that the tailings presented a health risk involved many factual steps, none greater than the difference between ingestion and inhalation. Trying to assess the seriousness of the problem, Lord received little guidance from EPA, which declined to ask for a preliminary injunction.[54] The scientists, too were troubled by the uncertainties. Finally, Lord asked Mount whether he was still drinking Duluth

---

Policy, 247 Science 294 (1990); *see also* letters in response to Mossman *et al.*, 248 Science 795 (1990).

52. The mechanism appears to involve both mechanical and chemical impacts on the cell's genetic material. ASTDR, *Toxicological Profile for Asbestos* (Sept. 2001) at 57 http:www.atsdr.cdc.gov/toxprofiles/tp61.html (last visited July 8, 2004). The chemical impacts may include iron content, which would be highly relevant to taconite. Mossman et al., *supra* note 51, at 297–98; ATSDR, *supra*. EPA's resources on asbestos can be found at http://www.epa.gov/oppt/asbestos/ (last visited July 8, 2004).

53. This is described in detail in Bastow, *supra* note 3, at 98–105.

54. *Id.* at 105–10.

water, and Mount had to say that he was not.[55] By the end of the week, then, the judge was convinced that a public health problem existed. EPA issued a public announcement mildly advising against using Duluth drinking water for "very young children," and Judge Lord did not issue an injunction, because, as he told the parties at the time, he recognized that such an injunction would require closure of the Silver Bay plant.

Mass panic, therefore, did not ensue, but the ecological case was now all but forgotten. The first phase of the trial, from August 1973 to January 1974, was entirely taken up with the health case. Selikoff proved a powerful, if somewhat unpredictable, witness. Reserve grew increasingly concerned that it had not been able to locate anyone of equivalent stature who would rebut Selikoff, and so Reserve asked Judge Lord to appoint a neutral consultant to the court. At the Mayo Clinic, Lord found Dr. Arnold L. Brown, chairman of the department of pathology and anatomy. Lord had Brown attend all of the medical testimony, sometimes sitting in the jury box and sometimes on the bench to help with questions. Lord came to rely very heavily on Brown's view of the case, much as the enforcement conference had come to rely on Mount's views.

The government's case on the health question had several steps, virtually all of which were debatable. The first step was to show that Reserve's tailings were in fact present in Duluth's water supply.[56] The second was to demonstrate that cummingtonite-grunerite was asbestos or its functional equivalent in shape and size.[57] Third, while the carcinogenicity of inhaled asbestos was well known, the effects of the ingestion of asbestos were unknown. Lacking direct evidence, the government sought to infer a hazard from epidemiological studies of asbestos workers,[58] animal studies on the movement of fibers within mammalian

---

55. *Id.* at 112.

56. To do this, the government used cummingtonite-grunerite as a "tracer." It was undisputed that cummingtonite-grunerite was contained in the tailings, but Reserve maintained that other tributaries of the lake were also sources of the mineral. Reserve's claim in this regard had little substance.

57. While cummingtonite-grunerite is among the amphibole class of minerals, and the variety of amphibole asbestos known as amosite asbestos is made up of cummingtonite-grunerite, Reserve maintained that the particular species of cummingtonite-grunerite in its tailings was not fibrous like asbestos. Dueling experts on the morphology of cummingtonite-grunerite and the tailings offered differing opinions on this question. Fiber size was also thought to have some relation to the dangerousness of the fibers. Even assuming that the pieces of cummingtonite-grunerite could be considered fibers, Reserve contended that they were too short (<5 microns) to be comparable to the asbestos known to cause cancer.

58. These showed that they had higher rates of gastrointestinal cancer, which suggested that the fibers had malign effects on those tissues, as well as on the lungs and pleura. There were, however, other theories to explain how the fibers reached the GI tract, which discounted the dangers of drinking water as a route of exposure.

bodies, and a study of numbers of fibers found in residents of Duluth as compared with a control group.[59] Epidemiological studies of gastrointestinal cancer among Duluth residents did not show a higher than expected rate; however, given the long latency of the disease, the worst effects could have been yet to come.[60] Finally, the government had to show that there were enough asbestos fibers in Duluth's water to have toxic effects. Theoretically, there is no known threshold below which asbestos no longer has carcinogenic effects, and so the government argued, with Dr. Selikoff, that *any* exposure posed risks. Reserve argued, to the contrary, that it was not clear that a toxic dose had even been reached.[61]

On February 5, 1974, Judge Lord ruled that EPA had made out a prima facie case of a health risk and that Reserve had failed to rebut the government's health evidence. Just as the Stoddard Report, Judge Eckman, and the enforcement conference had done before him, Judge Lord, having concluded that the tailings should not be in the lake (though this time for human health, rather than ecological, reasons), sought to resolve the case through an investigation of disposal alternatives.

The federal trial—disposal issues. Judge Lord had understood from the beginning that remedy would be the critical issue. He repeatedly said that he wanted to find a way to abate the pollution without closing the plant, and yet he increasingly found that Reserve was unwilling to engage candidly on this subject.[62] Instead, Reserve offered the deep pipe

---

59. Judge Lord ordered Dr. Brown to carry out a study of tissues from deceased residents of Duluth compared to another city (Houston, as it turned out). The study found no more asbestos fibers in the GI tracts of Duluth residents than Houston, but an electron microscope has an extremely small field of view, and the fibers would have been easy to miss. (On cross-examination, a Reserve witness conceded that it would take 9000 years, 24 hours a day, 7 days a week, to go through 1 cm^3 of tissue with an electron microscope. Bastow, *supra* note 3, at 116.)

60. Latency, indeed, hung like a sword of Damocles over the whole proceeding. Adamson, *supra* note 3, at 60–62; Bastow, *supra* note 3, at 120–24. As one government witness put it, "If we wait to see bodies in the street, we would then be certain that there would be another thirty or forty years of mortality . . . before us. We would have built up a backlog of disease over which we have little control." Quoted in Bastow, *supra* note 3, at 116.

61. As a practical matter, it was extremely difficult to count fibers, and estimates ranged over at least an order of magnitude.

62. His first frustration was the "shell game" of Reserve's corporate ownership. Reserve was what is known as a "stock company," that is, its stock was owned entirely by two other corporations, Armco and Republic. Its board consisted of Armco and Republic officers, plus one officer of Reserve itself. All of its product went to Armco and Republic, as did all profits, expenses, and losses. To engage the real decisionmakers, therefore, on January 4, 1974, Lord ordered the joinder of Armco and Republic as defendants. Armco and Republic immediately took an interlocutory appeal to the Eighth Circuit, which ruled that Lord had acted prematurely. Though the court left the door open to later joinder, Armco Steel Corp. v. United States, 490 F.2d 688, 691 (8th Cir. 1974), this early skirmish

plan. It impressed Judge Lord, like his predecessors, not at all, and he repeatedly pressed Reserve's lawyers and officers for alternative plans. It seemed incredible to Lord that Reserve had no Plan B, and he became increasingly suspicious that he was not being told everything. In late February, he sent one of his law clerks to suggest to the government attorneys that they subpoena Armco and Reserve for relevant documents.[63]

When the subpoenas were returned on March 1, 1974, Judge Lord and the government learned that the central claims of Reserve's case for in-lake disposal were lies. The documents revealed that the initial choice to dispose of wastes in the lake instead of at the mine site was based on economic convenience and not engineering infeasibility. Moreover, Reserve's parents had long before rejected the deep pipe plan as technically unworkable. Reserve had in fact undertaken numerous studies of on-land disposal, and the studies had found that the costs were far lower than the $250 million that Reserve had repeatedly cited to the court. In fact, a recycled-water system would have actually *improved* the quality of the iron pellets, increasing their value and offsetting some of the increased cost. Even worse, Reserve's main witness on the infeasibility of on-land disposal had chaired the meetings of the on-land study group, and Reserve's chief trial counsel, who had repeatedly made contrary representations to the court, had been present at the meetings. Fride offered the improbable excuse that he had not understood the government or court to have previously asked for this information (a position Reserve maintained ever after), but he also offered, for the first time, to negotiate disposal.

The rest of March was taken up by ultimately fruitless negotiations over disposal options. Exasperated once again with Reserve's intransigence, Lord again involuntarily joined Armco and Republic as defendants. Reserve then proposed on-land disposal at Palisades Creek, in a wilderness area near the lake shore. This location was entirely unacceptable to the federal government and Minnesota, so EPA finally moved for an injunction against Reserve's discharge. This brought Reserve's lawyers to agree to recommend Palisades Creek to their clients, but Armco's and Republic's boards rejected what Reserve had initially proposed. Lord concluded that the defendants were not negotiating in good faith and ordered the presidents of Armco and Republic to appear as witnesses in his courtroom on the morning of Saturday, April 20.

Lord began, "I have stated fairly consistently that I would do everything I could to prevent the closing of the plant," but he had found

---

established the appellate court's general attitude, which would become more pronounced over time, of suspicion toward Lord's zealousness and solicitude toward Reserve's economic status.

63. Bastow, *supra* note 3, at 147–48.

Reserve to be simply playing for time. William Verity, the chairman of Armco, was unmoved by this admonishment, so Lord dismissed him from the witness stand and told him to return from lunch with Reserve's last best offer. That afternoon, Verity began by reminding Lord of Reserve's economic significance. He then said that the defendants would again recommend to their boards that they adopt the Palisades Creek plan (itself a non-starter for the plaintiffs, of course), but only on several transparently unacceptable conditions.[64] As one reporter put it: "Verity's reading of that statement was the most amazing display of arrogance I've ever seen. I'm no fan of Miles Lord, but it was like Armco and Republic were giving him the finger right in his face."[65]

Lord returned to his chambers, put the finishing touches on his order, and delivered it later that afternoon. He had from the beginning made clear his intention to keep the plant open, and he never wavered from that position. The lengthy opinion that describes his reasoning is a model of organization and logical analysis.[66] His discussion of the medical testimony is balanced, clearly acknowledging the strengths and weaknesses of the government's case, and it relies most heavily on the independent expert whom Reserve had asked him to appoint. The forceful language and draconian order were aimed entirely at the behavior of the three corporate defendants.[67] As of 12:01 a.m., on Sunday, April 21, 1974, Reserve was to cease all discharges into Lake Superior.

The Eighth Circuit's stays. The following Monday, Judge Lord told the defendants that he would take "every reasonable step within [the court's] power to help you to reopen that plant."[68] Reserve's lawyers responded by asking for a stay of the order (which Lord denied), though they had already applied to the Eighth Circuit for a stay without even informing government counsel. As it happened, the Eighth Circuit judges were all at a conference in Springfield, Missouri, on April 22, and the government's lawyers eventually found Reserve's lawyers there. A hastily convened panel held court in a hotel meeting room, very informally. The panel was comprised of Judges William H. Webster, Myron H. Bright, and Donald R. Ross, all former corporate lawyers. Their attitude

---

64. Specifically, Reserve would not meet the Minnesota air pollution standards; it would have five years (not three) to build the on-land facility; the court would require Minnesota to issue the required permits (a constitutional impossibility); the court would make "satisfactory resolution" of—*i.e.*, dismiss—the health claims; and, last but not least, the state and federal governments would offer financial assistance to Reserve.

65. Bastow, *supra* note 3, at 159.

66. United States v. Reserve Mining Co., 380 F. Supp. 11 (D. Minn. 1974), *rev'd*, 514 F.2d 492.

67. *Id.* at 20–21 (footnote omitted).

68. Bastow, *supra* note 3, at 157.

from the beginning was skeptical, if not hostile, to Lord's order. They accepted without argument Reserve's claims of dire economic harm (to the whole nation, no less), and they put the government—the non-moving party—on the defensive. "Show me one individual that's being harmed by this. Show me one dead body," said Judge Ross.[69] After fifteen minutes of deliberation, the judges issued a one-month stay. A month later, in St. Louis, the panel's approach was much the same, and it extended the stay for 70 days. Most important, it found that Reserve was likely to succeed on the merits of the government's health claims.[70] And yet, the panel also said that it was inclined to find that there was some pollution, and it ordered Reserve to come back to Judge Lord with an acceptable disposal plan.

This of course has the feel of what Yogi Berra called "déjà vu all over again." It is exactly what Judge Eckman found and ordered, exactly what the enforcement conference sought to accomplish, and exactly where Judge Lord was going until Verity gave him the final brush-off. Health effects or not, the enormity of the dumping into Lake Superior deeply impressed all of the tribunals, and all of them wanted Reserve to find a way to stop it. Indeed, the appellate panel, in one of the more unusual aspects of this litigation, itself became deeply involved in efforts to settle the case, and for several months through the summer of 1974, negotiations in the form of hearings continued in front of Judge Lord and the Eighth Circuit panel.[71]

The negotiations made some progress. Reserve and Minnesota Governor Anderson agreed to consider two adjacent on-land sites, at Lax Lake, where the Stoddard Report had recommended disposal five and a half years earlier, and at Milepost 7 (counting from the lake along Reserve's rail line). To the federal government and the state agencies, however, the negotiations had all of the earmarks of Reserve's familiar delaying tactics. Minnesota sought Supreme Court review of the Eighth Circuit's stay order after that court's second stay, but the Court denied review, Justice Douglas dissenting.[72] When, at the end of the summer, the appellate court once again continued its stay without ruling on Judge Lord's actual findings of fact and conclusions of law, the United States joined the states in seeking Supreme Court review. On the same day,

---

69. *Id.* at 166.

70. The court, however, seemed to get basic concepts backwards. It focused on the lack of demonstrable harm with no apparent understanding that *latent* illness was the problem, and it inverted the concept of threshold to suggest that it called into question the reality of *high*-dose effects. Reserve Mining Co. v. United States, 498 F.2d 1073, 1082 (8th Cir.1974).

71. This clearly was Reserve's strategy. Judge Lord had seen the defendants' duplicity at first hand and Reserve no longer had any credibility with him. The Eighth Circuit judges, however, were much more kindly disposed to Reserve.

72. Minnesota v. Reserve Mining Co., 418 U.S. 911 (1974).

perhaps to forestall the Court's intervention, the Eighth Circuit granted an en banc hearing. The Supreme Court again denied review, but this time four justices (*i.e.*, enough to grant certiorari) indicated that they would accept the case if the Eighth Circuit failed to rule definitively by January 31, 1975.[73] Justice Douglas wrote a brief, scathing dissent.[74] The court of appeals had its orders, and a week later Judge Lord issued his final opinion in the case.[75] The stage was set.

IV. *The Eighth Circuit's En Banc Decision*

The Eighth Circuit finally issued its en banc opinion, written by Judge Bright, a member of the original panel, on March 14, 1975. The court concluded that, while not free from doubt, the cummingtonite-grunerite was sufficiently close in size and shape to asbestos to present a danger, and it had no difficulty concluding that Reserve's "asbestiform" tailings were in fact present in Duluth's drinking water. Even though the fiber levels were far less than the occupational exposures that had been studied epidemiologically, the court had come to understand that the absence of a known threshold for asbestos suggested a risk at *low* levels of exposure. The court quoted Dr. Brown: "Until I know what the safe level is, I therefore could not, as a physician, consider with equanimity the fact that they are being exposed to a human carcinogen."[76] He continued, "the presence of a known human carcinogen, sir, is in my view cause for concern, and if there are means of removing that human carcinogen from the environment, that should then be done."[77] The tailings, the court determined, created a potential health hazard.

---

73. Specifically, the Court stated: "Four Justices, however, state explicitly that these denials are without prejudice to the applicants' renewal of their applications to vacate if the litigation has not been finally decided by the Court of Appeals by January 31, 1975." Minnesota v. Reserve Mining Co., 419 U.S. 802 (1974).

74. He wrote:

If, as the Court of Appeals indicates, there is doubt, it should be resolved in favor of humanity, lest in the end our judicial system be part and parcel of a regime that makes people, the sovereign power in this Nation, the victims of the great God Progress which is behind the stay permitting this vast pollution of Lake Superior and its environs. I am not aware of a constitutional principle that allows either private or public enterprises to despoil any part of the domain that belongs to all of the people. Our guiding principle should be Mr. Justice Holmes' dictum that our waterways, great and small, are treasures, not garbage dumps or cesspools.

Id. (citation omitted).

75. This is also reported at 380 F. Supp. 11. He found Reserve in violation of the Refuse Act and Minnesota air pollution control regulations, and that it lacked permits for a number of other sources of discharge. He dismissed Reserve's counterclaims alleging the invalidity of Minnesota's regulations.

76. Reserve Mining Co., 514 F.2d 492, 513 (1975).

77. *Id.* This part of the opinion actually addressed the air pollution issues in the case. The court used its consideration of air pollution to link the tailings with asbestos, because

The opinion then turned to the most difficult question, whether ingested asbestos is a health risk. Judge Bright's opinion carefully analyzed the indirect evidence upon which the government necessarily relied. The tissue study showed no increase in the asbestos fibers in Duluth as compared to Houston residents; however, it "cannot be deemed conclusive in exonerating the ingestion" hypothesis,[78] because the negative result could well have been a *false* negative. The animal studies designed to show whether asbestos fibers could cross the gastrointestinal mucosa and lodge in other parts of the body, causing cancer, were contradictory and equivocal. Here, too, the danger could not be entirely discounted. Finally, the epidemiological studies of excess gastrointestinal cancer among occupationally exposed individuals could be explained in ways other than direct ingestion, but ingestion could not be ruled out as an explanation. The evidence of danger, therefore, while equivocal, was not nothing, and the potential consequences were severe.

The question of level of exposure was problematic because of the difficulties in coming up with a reliable estimate. Nonetheless, the court concluded that "the possibility of a future excess incidence of cancer attributable to the discharge cannot be ignored."[79] Note in particular the concern with "future" excess cancer. Like the threshold problem, the latency issue—the backlog of mortality, in Dr. Nicholson's words—had at last become clear in the judges' minds. The court responded by adopting Dr. Brown's precautionary "medical" standard of proof over a "scientific" one, quoting Brown's testimony:

> Well, science requires a level of proof which is pretty high. . . . [However, a]s a medical person, sir, I think that I have to err, if err I do, on the side of what is best for the greatest number. And having concluded or having come to the conclusions that I have given you, [concerning] the carcinogenicity of asbestos, I can come to no conclusion, sir, other than that the fibers should not be present in the drinking water of the people of the North Shore.[80]

This standard, the court recognized, clearly differs from the ordinary standard of proof that applies in civil cases:

> In assessing probabilities in this case, it cannot be said that the probability of harm is more likely than not. Moreover, the level of probability does not readily convert into a prediction of consequences. On this record it cannot be forecast that the rates of cancer will increase from drinking Lake Superior water or breathing Silver

---

the inhalation effects of asbestos were well known. The court found no federal common law nuisance based on air pollution, but did find violations of Minnesota law.

   78. *Id.* at 515.

   79. *Id.* at 517.

   80. *Id.* at 519.

Bay air. The best that can be said is that the existence of this asbestos contaminant in air and water gives rise to a reasonable medical concern for the public health. The public's exposure to asbestos fibers in air and water creates some health risk. Such a contaminant should be removed.[81]

The full court, including the members of the original panel, had come a long way from Judge Ross's "show me one dead body" view of the risks of asbestos. While they were perhaps more cautious than Judge Lord in interpreting the data and more fastidious in their assessment of the magnitude of the risk, they were nevertheless convinced on reflection that some kind of danger existed and that, under existing law, it should be abated.

To justify the adoption of the "medical" over the "scientific" standard, the court emphasized the goals of the statute. It relied heavily on two recent D.C. Circuit opinions, which spoke of the need for caution "on the frontiers of scientific knowledge"[82] and of the preventive goals of environmental regulation in the face of uncertainty.[83] Confronted with scientific uncertainty, the court justified taking action based on—

> an acceptable but unproved medical theory. . . . We sustain the district court's determination that Reserve's discharge into Lake Superior constitutes pollution of waters "endangering the health or welfare of persons" within the terms of §§ 1160(c)(5) and (g)(1) of the Federal Water Pollution Control Act and is subject to abatement.[84]

The situation therefore "justifie[d] an injunction decree requiring abatement of the health hazard on reasonable terms as a *precautionary and preventive measure* to protect the public health."[85]

To this point, the en banc court had consistently agreed with Judge Lord. Its only substantial disagreement was on the remedy, to which the court turned last. Following the equitable model, in which the court itself makes the remedial choice, the opinion explicitly used a gentler remedy to counterbalance its very broad interpretation of the relevant law:

> we believe that Congress used the term "endangering" in a precautionary or preventive sense, and, therefore, evidence of potential harm as well as actual harm comes within the purview of that term.

---

81. *Id.* at 520.

82. Industrial Union Dept., AFL–CIO v. Hodgson, 499 F.2d 467, 474 (1974).

83. Ethyl Corp. v. EPA, 541 F.2d 1, 19–20 (D.C. Cir. 1976) (en banc), *cert. denied*, 426 U.S. 941 (1976).

84. Reserve Mining Co. v. EPA, 514 F.2d 492, 529 (1975) (footnote omitted).

85. *Id.* at 520 (emphasis added).

We are fortified in this view by the flexible provisions for injunctive relief.[86]

To justify immediate closure, therefore, it was not enough for the district court to speak of a "substantial" risk. Moreover, the court recognized the relevance of countervailing benefits of Reserve's operations (employment, the services of a company town, etc.) and countervailing risks of a shut-down (unemployment as a physical and mental stressor). The pollution was to be abated "on reasonable terms," and Reserve was to have a "reasonable time" in which to stop discharging its wastes.

The problem of finding a suitable on-land disposal location was turned over to Minnesota with instructions to act expeditiously. The court gave very little guidance on a "reasonable time" (its supplemental opinion suggested three years), but it expressed great confidence in Reserve's eagerness to find an acceptable on-land solution. The government lawyers saw the Eighth Circuit's opinion as a *non sequitur*—how could the court find pollution but take no action to abate it?[87]—but they might have recognized the by now familiar compromise. In any event, EPA, perhaps as the result of political pressure,[88] chose to regard the case as an important substantive precedent and to ignore the weak remedy. It did not ask the Justice Department to appeal.

V. The Aftermath of the Eighth Circuit's Decision

The en banc opinion did not bring resolution to the case. It did not even end Judge Lord's anger or Reserve's intransigence. On the day following the issuance of the en banc opinion, March 15, 1975, Lord summoned the parties to a hearing, the gist of which was his bitter observation that apparently Reserve could do no wrong in the Eighth Circuit's eyes. He urged the governor and legislature of Minnesota to involve themselves directly in the case so that they might identify a suitable on-land disposal site and prohibit dumping in Lake Superior. This was hasty, to say the least, and in an addendum to its published opinion the Eighth Circuit chastised Lord for his intemperate and arguably insubordinate behavior.[89]

Negotiations between Reserve and Minnesota made little progress, however, and on November 14 and 15, 1975, Lord held an "educational hearing" to which not only the parties, but also government officials and school administrators were commanded to appear. He criticized local governments and schools for their "almost total failure" to provide filtered water to Duluth residents, and he excoriated Reserve: "In every

---

86. *Id.* at 528.

87. Bastow, *supra* note 3, at 182.

88. *Id.* at 182–85.

89. Judge Lord's written opinion on remand can be found at 380 F. Supp. at 71–91.

instance and under every circumstance Reserve Mining Company hid the evidence, misrepresented, delayed and frustrated the ultimate conclusions which had to be arrived at.''[90] Unabashed and unrepentant, Reserve sought Lord's removal from the case. Probably unwisely but certainly characteristically, Lord represented himself at the hearing before the Eighth Circuit. If it had been Reserve's lawyers' strategy to get Lord so angry that he impugned his own credibility (as trial lawyers sometimes do in cross-examination), they had taken the correct measure of Miles Lord. The appellate court directed the chief judge of the District of Minnesota, Edward D. Devitt, to appoint a new trial judge,[91] and Devitt assumed the responsibility himself.

As it turned out, the difference between Lord and Devitt was more one of style than substance. Devitt, a former Republican congressman who had been appointed by President Eisenhower, was fairly conservative, but he was known mainly as "a brisk, no-nonsense judge" with "more of a reputation for briskness than for ideology."[92] This characteristic did not bode well for tactics of deceit and delay, and over the next few months Devitt confirmed virtually everything that Lord had done. He charged Reserve over $1,300,000 in water filtration costs,[93] fines for permit violations,[94] and sanctions for misconduct in discovery.[95] In July, Devitt ordered Reserve to stop all discharges one year hence, by July 7, 1977.[96] The Eighth Circuit upheld each and every one of Judge Devitt's orders.[97]

Throughout this period, Reserve continued to negotiate with Minnesota, as the Eighth Circuit instructed, over a permit to construct an on-land disposal facility at Milepost 7. Minnesota's environmental agencies took the position that a site at Milepost 20, farther from the lake, was more appropriate, and MPCA denied the Milepost 7 application.[98] Re-

---

90. Quoted in O'Brien, *supra* note 3, at 100.

91. Reserve Mining Co. v. Lord, 529 F.2d 181 (8th Cir. 1976). Lord's irascibility and zealousness for the underdog continued to bring him into conflict with the Eighth Circuit. He retired from the federal bench in 1985 and is currently a plaintiffs' lawyer in Minnesota. He can be found at www.mileslord.com, or call 612–333–LORD. Farber, *supra* note 2, at 31.

92. "Pollution; Shake-up in Court," The Economist, Jan. 24, 1976, at 57.

93. United States v. Reserve Mining Co., 408 F. Supp. 1212 (D. Minn. 1976); 412 F. Supp. 705, 710–12 (D. Minn. 1976).

94. *Reserve Mining Co.*, 412 F. Supp. at 709 ("It is reasonable to conclude that some of those profits are attributable to operations made less costly by discharging tailings in Lake Superior rather than on land, as is done by its competitors.").

95. *Id.* at 710–12.

96. United States v. Reserve Mining Co., 417 F. Supp. 789 (D. Minn. 1976).

97. United States v. Reserve Mining Co., 543 F.2d 1210 (8th Cir. 1976).

98. For discussion of these hearings, *see* Bartlett, *supra* note 3, at 183–93.

serve appealed to a three-judge Minnesota district court in Lake County, whose panel included the familiar (and, to Reserve, welcome) face of Judge Eckman. On January 28, 1977, the district court ordered MPCA to grant the permit, and the Minnesota Supreme Court upheld the district court on April 28.[99] Two months later, MPCA issued the Milepost 7 permit, as ordered, but with several important conditions attached. Reserve again appealed, again the district court ruled for Reserve, but this time the Minnesota Supreme Court reversed the district court and upheld the permit conditions.[100] In the meantime, Judge Devitt had extended his deadline until April 15, 1980.[101] All of the pieces were in place for a final resolution of the case. Nevertheless, Reserve waited two months, supposedly considering whether it could afford to build at Milepost 7 despite the conditions, before announcing that it would remain open and meet the 1980 deadline.

Reserve's dumping in Lake Superior ended on March 16, 1980—five years (almost to the day) after the Eighth Circuit's en banc opinion, six years after Judge Lord's initial injunction, seven years after the announcement that asbestos fibers were in Duluth's drinking water supply, nine years after the enforcement conference concluded its work, and *eleven and a half years* after the Stoddard Report recommended disposal at essentially the same location. Intransigence, in the end, bought Reserve eleven years of continued pollution and continued profits.

The epilogue is cruelly ironic. Over the years, from the original permit hearings to Milepost 7, Reserve had maintained that an end to dumping in the lake would be an end to its operations. In fact, Reserve profitably shifted to on-land disposal in 1980—only to shut down two years later in the general economic downturn of 1982. Reserve reopened, but in 1986 LTV Steel, which succeeded Republic as the co-owner of Reserve, declared bankruptcy and withdrew from the Reserve partnership. In 1988, the Armco subsidiary that was operating Reserve declared bankruptcy, and the Silver Bay plant closed on July 31, 1988. It was sold in bankruptcy to Cyprus Minerals Company in 1989, which reopened the facility at half capacity as Northshore Mining Company. Northshore is now a wholly owned subsidiary of Cleveland–Cliffs, coincidentally one of the original owners of Reserve.

VI. *The Continuing Importance of* Reserve Mining

The immediate legal significance of *Reserve Mining* was muted because the case was decided on the basis of a superseded section of the

---

99. It issued a brief opinion on April 28 and a longer one on May 27. Reserve Mining Co. v. Herbst, 256 N.W.2d 808 (Minn. 1977).

100. Reserve Mining Co. v. Minn. Pollution Control Agency, 267 N.W.2d 720 (Minn. 1978).

101. U.S. v. Reserve Mining Co., 431 F. Supp. 1248 (D. Minn. 1977).

Clean Water Act. The court's interpretation of "endanger" has been adopted for other statutes that use the same term.[102] However, Congress took a different route in its overhaul of the Clean Water Act in 1972. While Congress, in amending the statute in 1972, made sure not to derail the then just-begun *Reserve Mining* litigation, it showed no interest in imitating the Byzantine enforcement conference process that led up to the litigation. Congress instead established directly federally enforceable, quantitative, technology-based water quality standards. *Reserve Mining*'s protracted litigation and extended denouement can only be regarded as confirmation of the basic wisdom of this course of action.[103]

Pollution control and public health. Reserve Mining's longer-term significance lies in the fundamental shift in public attitudes toward pollution that the decision represents. The government's trial lawyers called EPA's decision not to appeal the en banc opinion "the craven crawl,"[104] but in the longer view, EPA was correct to see in *Reserve Mining* an important and favorable precedent. The court rejected the idea that Lake Superior was a free sink for industrial wastes, and it said No to a major industrial polluter. This was clearly the significance of the case for the authors of the five books devoted entirely to it. The stark contrast between the uniqueness and beauty of Lake Superior and the enormity of Reserve's discharge—in Thomas Powers' words, "sacrificing what is scarce and unique for what is common and cheap"[105]—brought into focus the growing environmental awareness in the United States. The threat of cancer from the tailings in drinking water, and in particular the fear of its long latency period, also marked a shift in the focus of environmental law from concern for the aesthetic and ecological, to

---

102. *Reserve Mining* became the specific precedent for an expansive reading of "endanger" in judicial abatement actions in the Resource Conservation and Recovery Act, *see* U.S. v. Vertac Chemical Corp., 489 F. Supp. 870, 880–81, 885 (D. Ark. 1980) (interpreting 42 U.S.C. § 6973 and 33 U.S.C. § 1364); *see also* U.S. v. Valentine, 856 F. Supp. 627, 632 (D. Wyo. 1994) (holding that endangerment need not be immediate or tantamount to an emergency, and circumstantial evidence and inference (risk assessment) are sufficient); Barry J. Trilling, *"Potential for Harm" As the Enforcement Standard for Section 7003 of the Resource Conservation and Recovery Act*, 2 UCLA J. Envtl. L. & Policy 43, 52–59 (1981), and Superfund (CERCLA), U.S. v. Conservation Chemical Co., 619 F. Supp. 162, 194 (W.D. Mo. 1985).

103. *See* William L. Andreen, *Water Quality Today—Has the Clean Water Act Been a Success?*, 55 Ala. L. Rev. 537, 592 (2004). For discussion of the technology-based approach generally, *see* Wendy E. Wagner, *The Triumph of Technology–Based Standards*, 2000 U. Ill. L. Rev. 83; Sidney A. Shapiro & Thomas O. McGarity, *Not So Paradoxical: The Rationale for Technology–Based Regulation*, 1991 Duke L.J. 729.

104. Bastow, *supra* note 3, at 183.

105. Thomas Power, *Lost Landscapes and Failed Economics: The Search for Value of Place* 237 (1996), *quoted in* Farber, *supra* note 2, at 33.

concern for subtle (or sinister, to use a favorite Carson term) effects on human health.[106]

At the same time that the Eighth Circuit was considering how to deal with the uncertain science of asbestos ingestion and human health under the abatement provision of the 1965 Water Quality Act, the D.C. Circuit was considering how to deal with the uncertain science underlying EPA's rulemaking that phased out lead in gasoline under the Clean Air Act. *Ethyl Corp. v. EPA*[107] was *Reserve Mining*'s doppelganger among agency review cases.[108] The essential point of the courts' agreement was what the D.C. Circuit called "the precautionary nature of 'will endanger' "[109]:

> ... The [*Reserve Mining*] court thus allowed regulation of the effluent on only a "reasonable" or "potential" showing of danger, hardly the "probable" finding urged by Ethyl as the proper reading of the "endanger" language in Section 211 [of the Clean Air Act]. The reason this relatively slight showing of probability of risk justified regulation is clear: the harm to be avoided, cancer, was particularly great.[110]

In upholding EPA's power to assess risks in deciding whether and how to regulate, the court described its approach as follows:

> Where a statute is precautionary in nature, the evidence difficult to come by, uncertain, or conflicting because it is on the frontiers of scientific knowledge, the regulations designed to protect the public health, and the decision that of an expert administrator, we will not demand rigorous step-by-step proof of cause and effect. Such proof may be impossible to obtain if the precautionary purpose of the statute is to be served.[111]

---

106. *See generally* Samuel P. Hays, *Three Decades of Environmental Politics: The Historical Context, in Government and Environmental Politics* 21–37 (Michael J. Lacy ed., 1998) 21–37.

107. 541 F.2d 1 (D.C. Cir. 1976) (en banc), *cert. denied*, 426 U.S. 941 (1976). *Ethyl Corp.* was originally decided against EPA by a panel of the D.C. Circuit, with Judge J. Skelly Wright dissenting. On rehearing en banc, however, the court decided for EPA, and Wright wrote the majority opinion in the landmark case. In leapfrog fashion, Judge Bright's en banc opinion in *Reserve Mining* cited Wright's panel dissent with approval, and Wright returned the favor by relying heavily on *Reserve Mining* in his opinion for the en banc majority. 541 F.2d at 18–19.

108. That is, *Ethyl* involved review of a duly promulgated agency regulation, whereas the agency appeared as a mere litigant in *Reserve*. *See* Joel Yellin, *Papers from the Yale Law Journal Symposium on the Legacy of the New Deal: Problems and Possibilities in the Administrative State*, 92 Yale L.J. 1300, 1313–15 (1983).

109. *Ethyl Corp.*, 541 F.2d at 13.

110. *Id.* at 19.

111. *Id.* at 28 (citations and footnotes omitted).

Science and precaution. From the beginning of the Reserve Mining controversy, the opponents of dumping gravitated toward scientific inquiry to determine whether Lake Superior was being "polluted" and whether there was a danger to human health.[112] The enforcement conference increasingly turned to Dr. Mount as it proceeded, Judge Lord increasingly turned to Dr. Brown, and both Lord and the Eighth Circuit relied heavily on Brown's medical approach to determine the appropriate legal standard. *Reserve Mining* brought to maturity the scientific orientation that currently dominates environmental law and especially the regulation of toxic chemicals. As happens today, the tribunals were really asking legal and policy questions—the acceptable level of human health risk, the appropriate cost of the remedy—and not purely scientific ones,[113] but the authority of science offered an apparently objective basis for resolving these difficult issues.[114]

Having turned to science, the parties were bound to science and, in particular, to scientific uncertainty. The most dramatic uncertainty, of course, was ingestion *versus* inhalation, but the questions of threshold, dose, and fiber size meant that scientific uncertainty pervaded the case. This in turn imposed enormous information demands on the opponents of the pollution and on the decisionmaker. Reserve's opponents could not simply point to the dumping and say, "This is an outrage; stop it," because Reserve could always claim insufficient evidence, as it repeatedly did. Science, as Dr. Brown said, sets a very high bar for action, and the party who bears the burden of proof must orchestrate a complex yet coherent narrative that combines many sciences. This remains the defining characteristic of the environmental regulation of pollutants and toxic chemicals.

The government's case in *Reserve Mining* was indeed scientifically tenuous, but rather than accept inaction in the face of danger, the court found in federal environmental law a precautionary approach to scientific uncertainty. This is the great legacy of the case and the outstanding principle for which it stands today. Substantively, precaution meant sharply distinguishing preventive regulation from tort law. The court accepted *risk*, instead of actually demonstrated or more-likely-than-not harm, as the basis for environmental regulation.[115] Procedurally, the Eighth Circuit sitting en banc concluded (as did the D.C. Circuit in *Ethyl*, also sitting en banc) that the burden of uncertainty must lie with

---

112. *Id.* at 79–80.

113. Bartlett, *supra* note 3, at 2, 79–80.

114. *See* Wendy E. Wagner, *The Science Charade In Toxic Risk Regulation*, 95 Colum. L. Rev. 1613 (1995); Donald T. Hornstein, *Reclaiming Environmental Law: A Normative Critique of Comparative Risk Analysis*, 92 Colum. L. Rev. 562 (1992).

115. *See* John S. Applegate, *Introduction, in The International Library of Essays in Environmental Law: Environmental Risk* xiii-xix (2004) (John S. Applegate ed., 2004).

the risk-creator. Otherwise, uncertainty would be a virtually insurmountable barrier to the environmentally protective action that Congress clearly intended.

The foregoing are also the central tenets of the Precautionary Principle, a concept that has gained broad acceptance in international environmental law. Its most common formulation echoes *Reserve Mining*,[116] and it, too, identifies scientific uncertainty as the central problem in environmental regulation.[117] Like *Reserve Mining*, the Precautionary Principle requires a firm scientific basis for concern and a serious harm in prospect, and it permits regulatory action *before* the uncertainty has been resolved. That is clearly the gist of Dr. Brown's statement, quoted by the court, "As a medical person, sir, I think that I have to err, if err I do, on the side of what is best for the greatest number."[118]

In considering this approach, it is worth noting that the general view in the public health community today is that ingestion of asbestos fibers in drinking water is not a significant hazard to human health. EPA shows no interest in this route of exposure (it remains extremely interested in inhalation, however),[119] and the Agency for Toxic Substances and Disease Registry, a part of the Centers for Disease Control, is dismissive of the danger.[120] Does that mean that the Reserve Mining Company was right all along, and that EPA, the states, and the courts were wrong? Not at all. Under a precautionary approach, it is permitted (if not required) to take preventive action in the face of uncertainty. The parties and the tribunals in *Reserve Mining* faced true scientific uncertainty. No epidemiological studies could be expected to give definitive answers, and the indirect evidence was at best equivocal—yet there was "cause for medical concern." The precautionary approach adopted by *Reserve Mining* tells us that under these circumstances, it is better to err on the side of avoiding the harm if reasonably possible. The Precautionary Principle also requires that the regulatory response be proportionate

---

116. "Where there are threats of serious or irreversible damage, lack of full scientific certainty shall not be used as a reason for postponing cost-effective measures to prevent environmental degradation." Rio Declaration of the United Nations Conference on Environment and Development (UNCED), June 14, 1992, 31 I.L.M. 874.

117. *See* John S. Applegate, *The Taming of the Precautionary Principle*, 27 Wm. & M. Envtl. L. & Policy Rev. 13 (2002).

118. Reserve Mining Co. v. EPA, 514 F.2d 492, 519 (8th Cir.1975).

119. EPA's resources on asbestos can be found at http://www.epa.gov/oppt/asbestos/ (last visited July 8, 2004).

120. ATSDR, Toxicological Profile for Asbestos (Sept. 2001) at 57 ("Studies in humans and animals indicate that ingestion of asbestos causes little or no risk of carcinogenic injury."). It may be found at http://www.atsdr.cdc.gov/toxprofiles/tp61.html (last visited July 8, 2004). *See also* Jill Burcum et. al., *Despite Assurances, Taconite Fears Remain,* Minneapolis Star Tribune, Feb. 20, 2003, at 3B (summarizing the results of several, mainly industry sponsored, studies of asbestos ingestion).

to the danger, which is precisely how the Eighth Circuit determined the proper remedy.[121]

As we shall see in a later chapter, the Supreme Court in the *Benzene* case[122] accepted risk as a legitimate basis for governmental intervention to protect human health and the environment, but it demanded a more quantified and evidentially based showing to support risk-based regulation. Moreover, it placed a traditional burden of proof squarely on the governmental proponent of the regulation. Nevertheless, *Reserve Mining* (with *Ethyl*) established a protective and preventive approach that remains the baseline for environmental regulation of chemical hazards to human health.

Conclusion

In any legal system that is built on the accumulation of case holdings, an individual case comes to have at least two meanings: its meaning as precedent for subsequent cases, and its meaning as the specific resolution of a dispute between particular parties.[123] As precedent, *Reserve Mining* confronted scientific uncertainty in a particularly stark way, and the principle for which *Reserve Mining* came to stand was its precautionary approach to environmental regulation.

As the resolution of a particular dispute, the meaning of *Reserve Mining* is revealed by looking beyond the courts' words to what they actually *did*. Every tribunal that considered Reserve's pollution of Lake Superior—Stoddard's Taconite Study Group, Judge Eckman, the Lake Superior Enforcement Conference, Judge Lord, the Eighth Circuit, Chief Judge Devitt, and finally the Minnesota pollution and natural resources agencies—came to the conclusion that Reserve's continued despoliation of Lake Superior's pristine waters was unacceptable, but none was able to define the acceptable level of pollution and health hazard in purely scientific terms. Therefore, every one of these tribunals ended up trying to prescribe (or, more precisely, trying to get the parties to agree on) the best available technology for on-land disposal of the tailings. The first session and the final session of the enforcement conference ordered Reserve to come up with plans for on-land disposal. Judge Eckman and the Eighth Circuit panel found no violation of the law, but ordered or encouraged an end to dumping anyway. Conversely, the enforcement

---

121. Reserve Mining Co., 514 F.2d at 537. *See also* Applegate, *supra* note 115, at xiii-xix (stating that risk defines the environmental problem and disciplines the regulatory response).

122. Industrial Union Dep't, AFL–CIO v. American Petroleum Inst., 448 U.S. 607 (1980).

123. In Noonan's masterful interpretation, Cardozo's majority opinion in the *Palsgraf* case epitomizes this disjunction. *See* John T. Noonan, Jr., *Persons and Masks of the Law: Cardozo, Holmes, Jefferson, and Wythe as Makers of the Masks* (1976).

conference, Judge Lord, and the en banc appellate court found Reserve in violation of the law, but demanded or urged a technical solution ("abatement on reasonable terms"). And the final negotiations between Reserve and Minnesota were aimed at resolving which technology—in this case, which disposal site—was the best, and Minnesota blinked first.

This should come as no surprise. Professor Oliver Houck has observed that science-based programs "eat up heroic amounts of money, remain information-starved, feature shameless manipulation of the data, face crippling political pressure, and produce little abatement."[124] As he has written of EPA's efforts to regulate another toxic water pollutant (dioxin)—

> The near-routine predictions of layoffs, plant closings, and economic ruin notwithstanding, when the paper industry has had, at last, to convert to a less polluting process, it has done so. At bottom, the struggle is not over the ability not to pollute, but over lead time and competitiveness.[125]

This is *Reserve Mining*. Science and health concerns constituted the terms of discussion. However, what was truly unacceptable was the "outrageous river of pollution [and the] greedy and dishonest defendant"[126] dumping 67,000 tons of tailings a day into the spectacularly clear lake, and what was truly at issue was the best technology for stopping the dumping and the amount of time that Reserve would have to implement that technology. From Judge Eckman on, *no one* (except Reserve Mining itself) seriously suggested that the lake dumping should continue: the question was when and how to stop it.*

---

124. Oliver A. Houck, *Tales from a Troubled Marriage: Science and Law in Environmental Policy*, 17 Tul. Envtl. L.J. 163, 169–70 (2003).

125. Oliver A. Houck, *The Regulation Of Toxic Pollutants Under The Clean Water Act*, 21 Envtl. L. Rep. (Envtl. L. Inst.) 10528, 10554 (1991). Feasibility analysis has had a renaissance of support. *See, e.g.,* David M. Driesen, *Distributing The Costs Of Environmental, Health, And Safety Protection: The Feasibility Principle, Cost–Benefit Analysis, And Regulatory Reform*, 32 B.C. Envtl. Affs. L. Rev. ___ (2004); Sidney A. Shapiro & Robert L. Glicksman, *Risk Regulation At Risk: Restoring A Pragmatic Approach* (2003); Wendy E. Wagner, *The Triumph Of Technology–Based Standards*, 2000 U. Ill. L. Rev. 83.

126. Heinzerling, *supra* note 2, at 1426.

* I would like to credit with gratitude the research assistance of Greg Arnett.

3

A. Dan Tarlock, **Distinguished Professor of Law**
Chicago–Kent College of Law

The Story of *Calvert Cliffs*: A Court Construes the National Environmental Policy Act to Create a Powerful Cause of Action

I. The Social and Legal Background

Calvert Cliffs' Coordinating Committee, Inc. v. United States Atomic Energy Commission (*Calvert Cliffs'*)[1] played a pivotal role in creating modern environmental law by providing an effective environmental cause of action to challenge a wide range of federal activities. Both the case and statute that made it possible, the National Environmental Policy Act of 1969[2] (NEPA), are the products of a moment in time, 1968–1972, which has long passed. The political consensus that produced the statutory foundations of modern environmental law no longer exists, and our naive faith in the ability of science to provide simple, objective environmental quality criteria and decision standards has long given way to a much more wickedly complex view of environmental protection. However, the statutes and judicial glosses on them produced by this moment of time live on in an increasingly contested environment.

Calvert Cliffs' challenged the then powerful Atomic Energy Commission's (AEC) recently adopted NEPA compliance rules. Judge J. Skelly Wright's opinion invalidated parts of the rules and announced in ringing tones that courts must ensure that agencies strictly comply with NEPA's

---

1. 449 F.2d 1109 (D.C. Cir. 1971).

2. National Environmental Policy Act of 1969, Pub. L. No. 91–190, 83 Stat. 852 (1970) (codified as amended at 42 U.S.C. §§ 4321–4370f (2000)).

environmental impact assessment duties at all stages of decisionmaking. Not only did the opponents of nuclear energy score a rare, tactical victory in the fight to slow down and eventually turn the energy industry away from the nuclear option, but the decision launched the law of environmental impact assessment (EIA)[3] and institutionalized NEPA compliance within the federal bureaucracy. Whether *Calvert Cliffs'* contributed to making NEPA an effective, long-term source of substantive environmental policy, as its drafters hoped, is a more complicated question.

There are two stories of *Calvert Cliffs'*. The first is how a small group of young lawyers used a moment in time to produce new, radical legal ideas about our relationship to nature. The decision gave life to a new fundamental idea—advance environmental impact assessment— which has transcended both NEPA's statutory context as well as the immediate litigation to become one of the foundational principles of domestic and international environmental law.[4] The second story is more sobering because it is about the limits of courts to change the decisions we make about our relationship to the natural world. *Calvert Cliffs'* launched a powerful principle, but the agency practice that it induced ultimately became progressively divorced both from the transformative ethical vision of the drafters' of NEPA and the Court of Appeals for the District of Columbia Circuit's understanding of the Act. As a result, the NEPA process has come under increasing criticism and political attack from a wide variety of perspectives as a formal, costly, and ineffective one which often fails to advance the larger substantive goals of environmentalism.

---

3. The law has its own treatise. Daniel R. Mandelker, *NEPA Law and Litigation* (2d ed. 1992), and the preparation of environmental impact assessments has become an academic subject, e.g., Larry W. Canter, *Environmental Impact Assessment* (2d ed. 1996).

4. United States experience after *Calvert Cliffs'* helped to spread the concept of advance environmental impact assessment to the states and then throughout the world. Some seventeen states have adopted little NEPAs, Daniel R. Mandelker, *NEPA Law and Litigation* § 12.01 (2d ed. 1992), as has the European Union, Council Directive 85/337, 1985 O.J. (L 175) 40–48. Over 100 countries and federal states, developed and developing, have some form of EIA legislation or administrative regulations. International legal scholars have speculated that the duty to prepare an environmental impact statement for activities with substantial potential adverse cross-border environmental impacts may be a customary international law duty. Patricia W. Birnie & Alan E. Boyle, *International Law and the Environment* 130–35 (2d ed. 2002). A separate opinion of an International Court of Justice case asserts that all countries have a continuing duty of environmental assessment for major projects with potential adverse environmental impacts: "EIA, being a specific application of the larger principle of caution, embodies the obligation of continuing watchfulness and anticipation." Case Concerning the Gabcikovo–Nagymaros Project (*Hung. v. Slovk.*), 1997 I.C.J. 7, 112 (Sept. 25) (separate opinion of Vice–President Weeramantry).

A.   The Case: A Product of the Two "60s"

Calvert Cliffs' construed the recently enacted NEPA, but the decision ultimately reflects the convergence of three ideas contributed by the environmental movement which emerged in the late 1960s. One of the many ironies of the case is that it is a marriage of the two parts of the now mythic 1960s. Although formulated and enacted at the height of one of the most turbulent periods of twentieth century social unrest,[5] NEPA, the statute, is actually a product of the more optimistic, technocratic, and decidedly non radical early 1960s. NEPA, the practice area, is the product of the more familiar, radical 60s. NEPA was formulated at the end of the Kennedy and Johnson administrations, 1960–1968, which laid the foundation for the burst of important environmental legislation enacted between 1969 and 1973.[6] Led by Secretary of the Interior Stewart Udall,[7] the Congress and the two Democratic administrations undertook many important legislative and administrative environmental protection efforts. In contrast, Judge Wright's opinion reflects the growing skepticism, triggered by the racial and social unrest of the late 1960s, of the ability of the state to address modern social and technological problems and more generally of the idea of *a* public interest articulated by "expert" administrative agencies. Among its many legacies, the radical 60s, which lasted until about 1973, produced a fundamental power shift by allowing non-governmental organizations (NGOs) to participate in regulatory processes which had previously been a closed conversation between the regulators and the regulated community.

Calvert Cliffs' grew out of challenges to nuclear power plants in 1960s. Opponents and those challenging other federal licensing and construction decisions faced a fundamental problem: environmental consciousness was rapidly increasing but no viable "environmental" cause of action existed. Congress had not yet enacted the bulk of the statutes that would permit citizen suits. *Calvert Cliffs'* construed NEPA to create the missing cause of action.

---

5.   The worldwide political protests over the Vietnam war, racial and gender discrimination and repressive governments and authority generally have been well documented. *E.g.,* Todd Gitlin, *The Sixties: Years of Hope, Days of Rage* (1987); Arthur Marwick, *The Sixties: Cultural Revolution in Britain, France, Italy, and the United States, 1958–1974* (1998).

6.   This moment has been characterized as a "republican moment" because both Republicans and Democrats cooperated to promote environmental protection. The contrast between 1969–1973 and the political gridlock that has characterized environmental politics since 1980 is explored in Richard J. Lazarus, *A Different Kind of "Republican Moment" in Environmental Law*, 87 Minn. L. Rev. 999 (2003).

7.   Stewart L. Udall, *The Quiet Crisis* (1963) played a major role in putting environmental degradation on the political agenda in the Johnson Administration.

Calvert Cliffs' has its immediate origins in the concern of Johns Hopkins University scientists that the discharge of heated cooling water from the power plant would be detrimental to a crucial element of the Chesapeake Bay ecosystem, the Bay's famed blue crabs.[8] This concern reflected two seminal ideas of environmentalism. The first was that the "environment," which was understood primarily as the protection of ecosystems and the reduction of visible pollution, was a suitable public policy focus, and the second was that ecosystems should be protected qua ecosystems. Modern environmentalism inherited the early twentieth century preservation movement's idea that sacred and spectacular nature should not be disturbed by human intervention and gave it a scientific cast by making the presumed inherently stable ecosystem the focus of protection.[9]

The second idea turned the still dominant New Deal State on its head by venerating guerilla legal warfare and strategic law suits seeking aggressive judicial review of administrative action.[10] The environmental movement, along with the women's movement and the civil rights movement, is one of the lasting legacies of the 1960s. They all adopted guerilla litigation out of necessity.[11] In brief, the environmental movement fused diverse public health fears with a growing concern about the rate of loss of the natural landscape. Concern about radiation had been building since the 1950s, visible pollution became a political issue after smog was linked to the internal combustion engine, and the 1969 Santa Barbara oil spill focused national attention on the dangers of inadequate

---

8. Oliver Houck, *Unfinished Stories*, 73 U. Colo. L. Rev. 867, 885 (2002).

9. Richard N. L. Andrews, *Managing The Environment, Managing Ourselves: A History of American Environmental Policy 202* (1999), observes, "[t]he most revolutionary element of this new public consciousness was a powerful new awareness of the environment as a living system—a 'web of life,' or *ecosystem*—rather than just a storehouse of commodities to be extracted or a physical or chemical machine to be manipulated."

10. Two lawyers led the way. David Sive, a New York lawyer and Sierra Club member, successfully obtained the first remand of an administrative decision for environmental reasons. See David Sive, *The Litigation Process in the Development of Environmental Law*, 13 Pace Envtl. L. Rev. 1 (1995) *reprinted in* 19 Pace Envtl. L. Rev. 727 (2003). The extraordinarily creative mind of Professor Joseph L. Sax, who quickly established himself as the leading environmental law scholar, provided the theory for this strategy in his book, *Defending the Environment: A Strategy for Citizen Action* (1971).

11. Many historians emphasize the post World War II roots of modern environmentalism such as leisure and the dissemination of information about the negative effects of the fruits of war research, pesticides and atomic power. Samuel P. Hays, *Beauty, Health and Permanence: Environmental Politics in the United States, 1955–1985* (1987) and Richard N. L. Andrews, *Managing The Environment, Managing Ourselves: A History of American Environmental Policy 201–202* (1999). *Environmental Quality—1979: The Tenth Annual Report of the Council on Environmental Quality* 10 (1979) noted that "[t]he environmental outlook, with its opposition to careless impersonal use of technology in a way that destroys life rather than conserving it, had strong spiritual ties with the peace movement and the ethical climate of the 1960s."

pollution control technology.[12] These concerns were ultimately folded into some of the energy of the anti-Vietnam War movement. The net result was that faith in technological progress and the ability of the expert New Deal state to control technology and to adapt to new values was severely undermined. All three ideas were captured in Rachel Carson's best-selling brief against synthetic organic pesticides, *Silent Spring*. Secretary of the Interior Stuart L. Udall later wrote of the book, "it spurred new lines of thought about resources and the limits of technology that began to alter the thinking of my generation" and "it is undeniable that Rachel Carson's concepts inspired . . . the enactment of a National Environmental Policy Act."[13]

In the late 1960s, litigation was not a promising means of channeling these concerns, but lawyers turned to it because administrative agencies seemed unresponsive to environmental degradation and few could imagine how quickly Congress would take up the issue in the early 1970s. Litigation to contest government actions that caused environmental damage was daunting because New Deal administrative law immunized almost all agency exercises of discretion allocating natural resources from judicial review.[14] The immunization started with the law of standing which precluded NGO public interest suits.[15] Constitutional and

---

12. James E. Krier & Edmund Ursin, *Pollution & Policy: A Case Essay on California and Federal Experience With Motor Vehicle Air Pollution 1940–1975* 263–77 (1977), discusses the relationship between pollution crises and new pollution control legislation.

13. Stewart L. Udall, *The Quiet Crisis and the Next Generation* 195, 202–03 (1988). Udall defended *Silent Spring* in a 1964 Saturday Review of Literature review at a time when the chemical industry was spending large amounts of book money to discredit the book. Secretary Udall, among others, imported one the Carson's basic lessons into the legislative history of NEPA. During the July 17, 1968 Joint House–Senate Colloquium to discuss a national policy for the environment, Secretary Udall stated as his first principle for a national environmental policy: "We must begin to work with, not against, the laws of the planet on which we live, rejecting once and for all the false notion that man can impose his will on nature. This requires that we begin to obey the dictates of ecology, giving this master science a new and central position in the Federal scientific establishment." *Joint House–Senate Colloquium to Discuss a National Policy for the Environment: Hearings Before the Senate Comm. on Interior and Insular Affairs, and the House Comm. on Science and Astronautics*, 90th Cong., 2d Sess., 17 (1968) (testimony of Secretary of the Interior Stewart Udall).

14. Oliver A. Houck, *More Unfinished Stories: Lucas, Atlanta Coalition, and Palila/Sweet Home*, 75 U. Colo. L. Rev. 331, 375–76 (2004) describes the "unexpected" middle class rebellion against the location of interstate highways through parks and "good" neighborhoods, and the frustrations that highway location opponents faced bringing judicial challenges.

15. Anyone who participated in the development of environmental law will emphasize the importance of the liberalization of the law of standing. Standing historically limited access to courts to challenge administrative action to those who had suffered a common law, constitutional or statutory injury. In short, standing was directly tied to the merits of the plaintiff's claim. Section 10 of the Administrative Procedure Act, 5 U.S.C. § 702,

common law challenges were equally unpromising. The idea of direct constitutional challenges enjoyed a brief flurry of interest, but the idea died because no express or implied Constitutional right to a decent or healthy environment exists. Attempts to characterize as nuisance the impact of a project such as a power plant on the landscape floundered because the common law does not recognize aesthetic injuries and was loath to enjoin activities in advance of demonstrated harm.

B. NEPA

The passage of NEPA made *Calvert Cliffs'* possible, but Judge Wright's construction of NEPA was far from inevitable. There are at least three stories of NEPA relevant to *Calvert Cliffs'*. The first is the most conventional. NEPA was intended as a simple, effective way to rationalize the federal bureaucracy's protection of the environment. Its sponsors, primarily Senator Henry Jackson of Washington State, considered themselves heirs to the New Deal tradition of a strong, caring federal government and sought only to adapt the federal bureaucracy to cope with the newly emerging environmental consciousness. The second, which follows from the first, is that courts would play a limited role in this process because Congress and the Office of Management and Budget (OMB) would be the chief enforcers.[16] In this scenario, the goals of the

---

granted standing to those who suffered a "legal wrong." In 1968, the Supreme Court detached standing from the merits and interpreted the Act to allow a person who was "injured in fact" to obtain standing. Association of Data Processing Serv. Orgs., Inc. v. Camp, 397 U.S. 150 (1970). Even before this case, the Second Circuit granted standing to an NGO to raise aesthetic objections to a Federal Power Commission license. *See* Scenic Hudson Pres. Conference v. Federal Power Comm'n, 354 F.2d 608 (2d Cir. 1965), *cert. denied sub nom.* Consolidated Edison Co. of New York v. Scenic Hudson Pres. Conference, 384 U.S. 941 (1966). Courts never adopted the theory any NGO could become a private attorney general and challenge administrative action, but one year after *Calvert Cliffs'*, the Supreme Court created a factitious private attorney theory by allowing an NGO to obtain standing by pleadings that its members used the impacted area. *See* Sierra Club v. Morton, 405 U.S. 727 (1972). The Supreme Court has since taken a narrow, formalist view of standing, see *Lujan v. Defenders of Wildlife*, 504 U.S. 555 (1992), but it has not overruled the core principle that an NGO may obtain standing by alleging that an illegal action interferes with its use of a resource. See Chapter 7 of this volume on *Friends of the Earth v. Laidlaw Environmental Service*, 528 U.S. 167 (2000).

   16. One of the most authoritative analyses of the contemplated judicial role is an article co-authored by one of the two principal drafters of Section 102. Daniel A. Dreyfus & Helen M. Ingram, *The National Environmental Policy Act: A View of Intent and Practice*, 16 Nat. Resources J. 243 (1976). The authors note that one of the drafters, William J. Van Ness, Jr., was a lawyer, and the other, Daniel A. Dreyfus, a "student of administration and practitioner of bureaucratic infighting" and therefore that "[t]here [was] no question that the original drafters of Senate Bill 1075 contemplated a role for the courts." *Id.* at 254–55. They were aware of the landmark 1965 Second Circuit decision, *Scenic Hudson Pres. Conference*, 354 F.2d at 608, which remanded a federal power license for inadequate consideration of environmental impacts. However, no one foresaw the "hundreds of cases involving matters of purely regional or even local concern." *Id.* at 257.

statute rather than the preparation of environmental assessments and impact statements, which is NEPA today, were the core of the Act. Senator Jackson's biographer reports that the Senator was vexed by the vast inflation of the impact statement because "[h]e had intended it to be a short document laying out the costs and benefits of a given project, rather than a labyrinthian process involving mountains of detail" to block projects.[17] The third story is that NEPA was intended as a vehicle to transform fundamentally our nation's values and relationship to nature but this objective has been frustrated by Congress, the executive and the courts.

1. A Brief History of NEPA

NEPA is a relatively unique statute which makes it both easy and difficult to approach through the various standards of statutory interpretation. NEPA legislated major, new ideas—an explicit federal environmental policy enforced in part by advance environmental impact assessment[18]—which were not completely formed. It was not the typical, hard-fought legislative compromise among powerful competing interests.[19] Senator Jackson had to make some crucial compromises with other Senators, notably Edmund Muskie of Maine,[20] but the basic idea behind the statute survived from start to finish and the entire process took place out of the public eye.

It was possible for Congress to pass a statute such as NEPA because

---

17. Robert G. Kaufman, *Henry M. Jackson: A Life in Politics* 208 (2000). This view was confirmed by Jerry T. Verkler. *See* Interview by Donald A. Ritchie with Jerry T. Verkler, Staff Director of the Senate Interior and Insular Affairs Comm., Interview #2: Scoop Jackson and the Interior Committee 75 (Jan. 30, 1992), *available at* http://www.senate.gov/artandhistory/history/resources/pdf/verkler_interview_2.pdf (relaying that "[o]ne of Senator Jackson's contributions, which he felt has gone beyond what we had in mind was the passage of the National Environmental Policy Act in 1969.")

18. Justice Thurgood Marshall, one of the most environmentally conscious justices to sit on the Court, wrote that "[e]arly consideration of environmental consequences is the whole point of NEPA." Kleppe v. Sierra Club, 427 U.S. 390, 417 (1976). Professor William H. Rodgers, Jr. ranks Section 102 of NEPA as the fifth most influential of seven statutory provisions of United States environmental law. *The Seven Statutory Wonders of U.S. Environmental Law: Origins and Morphology*, 27 Loy. L.A. L. Rev. 1009 (1994).

19. *Richard A. Liroff, A National Policy for the Environment: NEPA and Its Aftermath* 10–11 (1976). Rodgers, Jr., *supra* note 18, identifies three components of NEPA's enactment, strong leadership, an inspirational and radical message and growth and "sleeper" potential, as general characteristics of successful environmental laws.

20. Like Senator Jackson, Senator Edmund Muskie, the father of the Clean Air and Water Acts, came from a mill town, but Senator Muskie's experience as a Maine state legislator, governor and later Senator underscore his life long interest in environmental protection. See Robert F. Blomquist. *In search of Themes: Toward the Meaning of the Ideal Legislator—Senator Edmund S. Muskie and the Early Development of Modern American Environmental Law, 1965–1968*, 28 Wm. & Mary Envtl. L. & Pol'y Rev. 539 (2004).

environmental protection was still viewed as a nonpartisan issue.[21] Protection was seen as a logical extension of the long-standing federal stewardship over natural resources that began in the Progressive Conservation Era.[22] Thus, the best way to interpret the statute is to understand the problems that it attempted to address, the manner it chose to do so and the problems it did not address rather than to parse its specific language.

NEPA was enacted just as the idea of environmental protection was making the transition from a public policy problem identified and defined by elites to a mass political issue that demanded a swift Congressional and Executive response. During the 1950s and early 1960s, no general concept of environmental protection existed within the federal agencies that developed or regulated natural resources from public lands to wetlands. The failure of the two Roosevelt administrations to develop a coordinated federal conservation policy and comprehensive resource planning process left a legal landscape of federal agencies with narrow statutory mandates. When an agency action was challenged as environmentally harmful, the agency's response was either that it had no power to consider environmental values, or, if it had power to consider them, the agency also had virtually unlimited discretion to trade them off against developmental ones.[23]

NEPA was the creation of a collaboration between Senator Henry Jackson and Lynton K. Caldwell, a political scientist at Indiana University, Bloomington. The legislation was signed by a Republican president because the growing environmental movement created pressure for more

---

21. Leon G. Billings, the staff director of the Senate Pollution Control Committee when the Clean Air and Water Acts were passed has observed that "[m]embers of Congress developed today's national environmental policy behind closed doors before Congress opened up its processes to the public and to the media. . . . But, as the person charged with the responsibility to write the legislation and the legislative history . . . I can report . . . [that] [t]he debate was vigorous, sharp, sometimes humorous, sometimes acrimonious, but always constructive and never partisan." Leon G. Billings, Keynote Address at the 75th Annual Meeting of the Missouri Water Environment Association (Mar. 22, 2004), *available at* http://www.muskiefoundation.org/leon.missouri.html.

22. See *Future Environments of North America* (F. Fraser Darling & John P. Milton eds., 1966) for an example of the efforts of the "old" conservation community to address the emerging new issues such as ecosystem and habitat conservation.

23. During a 1968 Joint House–Senate Colloquium to discuss a national policy for the environment, Secretary of the Interior Stewart Udall testified that when he pointed out to Tennessee Valley Authority officials that the agency's coal contracts were destroying the hills of Eastern Kentucky, "their very blunt and direct answer was that their mission was to produce electric power as cheaply as possible . . . and that if this destroyed resources, rivers and hillsides, and ruined parts of the country outside the TVA area for all time, this was none of their business." *Joint House–Senate Colloquium to Discuss a National Policy for the Environment: Hearings Before the Senate Comm. on Interior and Insular Affairs, and the House Comm. on Science and Astronautics*, 90th Cong., 2d Sess., 15 (1968) (testimony of Secretary of the Interior Stewart Udall).

comprehensive government responses to the perceived "crisis," and the new Nixon Administration did not want to be outflanked on what it considered an important issue in key states such as California, Florida and New York.[24]

Henry Jackson, the son of Norwegian immigrants, was elected to the Senate in 1952, bucking the Eisenhower landslide. He became the chairman of the Senate Interior and Insular Affairs Committee in 1963 and pursued an aggressive pre-environmental decade conservation agenda which included passage of the Wilderness Act of 1964, major extensions of the National Park system, the Wild and Scenic Rivers Act, as well as major water resources development and planning legislation. Jackson's major concern was not pollution but out of control mission agencies who were destroying scenic natural resources. Opposition to the interstate highway program, begun in the mid–1950s, was growing as highways began to encroach on urban parklands, older low income neighborhoods and scenic mountain areas. The United States Army Corps of Engineers was building dams, channelizing streams and turning inland areas into ports as fiscal and environmental criticisms of the programs mounted. The AEC was a cheerleader for nuclear power plants on large lakes, rivers and bays. Jackson, however, cannot be described as a modern environmentalist; he remained a "Teddy" Roosevelt conservationist who saw no incompatibility between the selective preservation of nature and its rational, regulated exploitation.[25]

NEPA was enacted to address agency indifference or hostility in a transformative, across the board manner by sending a Congressional directive to the federal mission agencies to assess the environmental consequences of their activities, to presume sufficient authority to protect the environment unless Congress had expressly withheld the authority, and to coordinate more effectively their activities with each other. The original version had no environmental impact statement requirement; it only authorized the Secretary of Interior to conduct ecological research,[26] and created a Council on Environmental Quality. The bill met

---

24. President Nixon signed NEPA on January 1, 1970. The biggest news story of the day was whether Texas, which defeated of Notre Dame in the Cotton Bowl, or Penn State, which downed Missouri in the Orange Bowl, should be the national football champion. J. Brooks Flippen, *Nixon and the Environment* 3–53 (2000) details the largely unsuccessful early efforts of the administration to confront the rising popularity of environmentalism, which culminated in the massive Earth Day demonstrations on April 22, 1970. He argues that President Nixon decided to make NEPA, especially the Council on Environmental Quality, the centerpiece of an administration environmental offensive, in part, to counter the growing national popularity of Senators Henry Jackson and Edmund Muskie, both of whom subsequently ran for president.

25. Kaufman, *supra* note 17, at 164.

26. Senator Jackson's faith in the Department of Interior was a tribute to Secretary of the Interior Stewart L. Udall (1961–1968) who was greatly influenced by Aldo Leopold's

with general public indifference, even within the small conservation community, although there was initial opposition from the new administration of Richard M. Nixon and a few members of Congress. The opposition was more jurisdictional. Senator Jackson adroitly maneuvered around this opposition, but in the process NEPA was both strengthened and weakened. A provision recognizing a right to a healthful environment was dropped, but the "action-forcing" EIS requirement was added.

2. The Birth of the "Action–Forcing" Environmental Impact Statement

The change in NEPA was the addition of the "action-forcing" requirements of Section 102. "Action Forcing" was the brainchild of Professor Caldwell,[27] who had been asked by the Senate Interior and Insular Affairs staff to strengthen the bill.[28] In the mid–1960s, one of the major environmental NGOs was the Conservation Foundation, which primarily acquired open space, but it was also the center of nascent environmental thinking in Washington, D.C. It had a small advisory board and Caldwell was one of its members. At the request of the staff of the Senate Interior Committee, the Foundation funded a consultancy for Caldwell to work with the committee.[29]

Caldwell was the first political scientist to use the word "environment" as opposed to conservation and to propose it as an overarching public policy concept. He developed his ideas of environmental protection in two stages. The first stage was a critique of the way in which the country was beginning to deal with the problems caused by the exploitation of resources with little heed to the environmental costs. If environ-

---

A Sand County Almanac (1949) and later by Rachel Carson's *Silent Spring* (1962), sought to synthesize the utilitarian and preservation strains of the old conservation movement to create a new conservation movement.

    27. William H. Rodgers, Jr. reports that Professor Caldwell developed the idea looking at a sunset upon Hong Kong Harbor. *The Most Creative Moments in the History of Environmental Law: The Whos*, 39 Washburn L.J. 1, 12 (1999). I remember a less poetic explanation. I taught at Indiana University Bloomington from 1968–1982, and Professor Caldwell told me in 1969 that he did not want NEPA to suffer the fate of the Full Employment Act of 1946: a good policy with no implementation mechanism.

    28. Richard A. Liroff, *A National Policy for the Environment: NEPA and Its Aftermath 16 (1976)*.

    29. Oral History Interview by Dr. Michael Gorn with Russell E. Train, first Chairman of the Council on Environmental Quality, Washington, D.C. (May 5, 1992) *available at* http://www.epa.gov/history/publications/train/index.htm. Train noted that "I don't think this is a story and an association that has been particularly well-known." I met Professor Caldwell in 1969, during my first year teaching at Indiana University, Bloomington, and remember him telling me how jealous some of his political science colleagues were of his increasing public recognition. In typical academic back-biting, they criticized his lack of traditional scholarship, although he has produced a great deal of that. I remember him proudly telling me, "I now publish in the Congressional Record."

mental degradation was being addressed at all, it was done in a segment-
ed manner as opposed to a holistic, forward-looking manner. Reflecting
the then prevailing faith in comprehensive rationality (the ability to
evaluate a wide range of options systematically), Caldwell argued in 1963
that environmental protection should be a public policy objective because
it "will provide a common denominator among differing values and
interests."[30]

The question was how to enlighten the federal bureaucracy. In a
major piece of Senate Interior testimony that preceded his more famous
"action-forcing" proposal, Caldwell framed the issue as the most effective governmental structure for the development of environmental policy. He came down in favor of a general policy which would apply to all
government agencies, enforced by an agency like the Council on Economic Advisors. He and the other proponents of NEPA thought that environmental impact issues would be a closed dialogue between the United
States Congress and the "mission" administrative agencies moderated
by the OMB.[31] This approach led directly to the need for an "action-
forcing" mechanism. In his widely cited testimony, Caldwell argued that
it was essential that federal agencies, especially the mission agencies, be
required "in submitting proposals, to contain within the proposals an
evaluation of the effect of these proposals upon the state of the environment" to insure that the policy declarations did not remain unimple-
mented.[32] Today we have forgotten that the action that NEPA was
intended to force was not the detailed EIS churned out by government
agencies and consultants but the disclosure of "bad" projects that should
be nipped in the bud.[33] Professor Caldwell later wrote:

> [T]he procedural requirements of NEPA are intended to force atten-
> tion to the policies declared in the Statement of Purpose (Section 2)
> and in Title I (Section 101) of the Act. The purpose is to write
> impact statements. To regard the action-forcing provision of Section
> 102 (the so-called NEPA Process) as the essence of the Act is to

30. Lynton K. Caldwell, *Environment: A New Focus for Public Policy*, 23 Pub. Admin.
Rev. 132, 138 (1963);*see also* Lynton K. Caldwell, *Administrative Possibilities for Environ-
mental Control, in Future Environments of North America* 648, 666–67 (F. Darling & J.
Milton eds., 1966).

31. The drafters of NEPA envisioned that the executive OMB would control the
preparation of impact statements. Frederick R. Anderson, *NEPA in the Courts: A Legal
Analysis of the National Environmental Policy Act* 11 (1973). Professor Caldwell has
written extensively about NEPA, *e.g.*, Lynton Keith Caldwell, *The National Environmental
Policy Act: An Agenda for the Future* (1998).

32. *National Environmental Policy Act, Hearing on S. 1075, S. 237 and S. 1752
Before the Senate Comm. on Interior and Insular Affairs*, 91st Cong., 1st Sess., 116 (1969)
(statement of Dr. Lynton K. Caldwell, professor of government, University of Indiana).

33. Matthew J. Lindstrom & Zachary A. Smith, *The National Environmental Policy
Act: Judicial Misconstruction, Legislative Indifference, & Executive Neglect* 39 (2001).

misinterpret its purpose—the substance of which had been under consideration in the Congress for at least a decade before the concept of the environmental impact statement (EIS) was introduced in 1969. Impact analysis is an important aspect of planning and decisionmaking and has been applied to a wide range of policy determinations—but it ought not be substituted for the declared policies which it is intended to activate.[34]

II. Factual Background

Calvert Cliffs' was one of the many efforts to stop nuclear power plants, or at least site them in safer and more environmentally suitable locations, in a regulatory environment structured to ignore these problems.[35] Concern about military and civilian use of nuclear power had been building since the 1950s after the initially reluctant[36] public utility industry joined "the Great Bandwagon Market for nuclear power."[37] The AEC was one of the early bete noirs of the environmental movement because of its political power, its determination to use it to promote nuclear power, and its insistence that environmental protection was not part of its statutory mission. By the mid–1960s, concern about the environmental impact of cooling towers joined concerns of reactor safety and radiation leaks.[38] The various citizen groups springing up around the

---

34. Lynton Keith Caldwell, *The National Environmental Policy: An Agenda for the Future* xvi–xvii (1998).

35. The history of this campaign is told in Constance Ewing Cook, *Nuclear Power and Legal Advocacy* (1980). Nuclear energy is a bi-product of the development of the atomic bomb during World War II. The first nuclear power plant came on line in 1957. Utilities were initially reluctant to invest in nuclear power generation but improvements in plant technology, rising energy demand and strong promotion of the nuclear option by the AEC resulted in a large number of new plant orders in the late 1960s, especially in the Midwest and the East. Fred Bosselman, Jim Rossi & Jacqueline Lang Weaver, *Energy, Economics and the Environment: Cases and Materials* 944 (2000).

36. Ralph Nader & John Abbotts, *The Menace of Atomic Energy* 26–29 (1977) summarizes the initial difficulties that the AEC had in convincing the electric utility industry to "go nuclear." Daniel Ford, *The Cult of the Atom: The Secret Papers of the Atomic Energy Commission* (1982) argues that the AEC consistently suppressed doubts of reactor safety to promote nuclear power. The *Calvert Cliffs'* plaintiff's lawyers, Anthony Roisman and Myron Cherry, contributed information to the book.

37. Boyd Norton, *A Brief History: The Early Years, in Nuclear Power: Both Sides* 15, 20 (Michio Kaku & Jennifer Trainer eds., 1982). In 1954, Lewis L. Strauss, the chairman of the AEC, uttered a much quoted prophecy that "our children will enjoy ... electrical energy too cheap to meter." Ford, *supra* note 36, at 50 (quoting Lewis L. Strauss, Address to the National Association of Science Writers (Sept. 1954)).

38. *Thermal Pollution—1968, Hearings Before the Senate Subcomm. on Air and Water Pollution of the Comm. on Public Works*, 90th Cong., 2d Sess. (1968). A nuclear plant is basically a large tea kettle supplied by large amounts of fresh or salt water. Two types of reactors are in widespread use. Boiling water reactors boil water within the reactor itself. Pressured water reactors remove heat by water flowing in a closed pressurized loop and

country to question nuclear power plants faced a kind of comedy of the absurd, starting with the calculation of future energy demand, and ending in a Kafkaesque regulatory structure riddled with gaps. There were many regulatory checks on a nuclear plant, but each stage addressed only a limited issue,[39] and the only searching evaluation was the two-tier AEC licensing process. The commission required separate construction and operating licenses, but AEC jurisdiction was still partial as its authority was shared with state and local governments.

Nuclear power plants were industrial facilities and had to obtain local zoning approval, but this was perfunctory; approval was often obtained after the siting decision had been made. Power plants were seen by many small communities as an ideal guest; they paid high taxes but required few services. The decision to site and build Calvert Cliffs followed this pattern. Baltimore Gas and Electric Company purchased land for the plant in 1966, quickly applied for a rezoning which was granted, and ordered the first two turbines in December of 1966. The utility did not publicly announce its plan to build a plant at Calvert Cliffs until May of 1967,[40] and construction started the next year.

State public utility commission approval was required, but these bodies generally did not question a utility's demand projections or evaluate the environmental impacts of the plant.[41] In the 1960s, energy regulatory agencies and the industry used a simple time basis projection

transfer the heat to a second water loop through a heat exchanger. The lower pressure in the second loop causes the water to boil. Nuclear fission heats the intake water to over 500 degrees and converts it to steam to drive the turbines that produce electricity. Additional water must be used to cool the condensed steam, and in the 1960s, this water was discharged directly into the lake, river or bay from which it was taken. Nuclear plants have a thirty-three percent thermal efficiency rate, compared to forty percent for fossil fuel plants and therefore, they need 60 percent more cooling water compared to coal-fired fuel plants. Nuclear plants must also heat cooling water to temperatures greater than twenty percent of the later. Report of the Association of the Bar of the City of New York Special Committee on Electric Power and the Environment, *Electricity and the Environment: The Reform of Legal Institutions* 39 (1972). There was great concern that these large discharges of heated water or thermal pollution would impair fish and shell fish production in many systems, especially in warmer receiving waters. Calvert Cliffs' two units each required 1.2 million gallons per minute.

39. Report of the Association of the Bar of the City of New York Special Committee on Electric Power and the Environment, *supra* note 38, surveys the difficulties of incorporating issues such as energy demand and environmental impact into the then existing structure of power plant regulation.

40. Daniel A. Bronstein, *The AEC Decision–Making Process and the Environment: A Case Study of the Calvert Cliffs Nuclear Power Plant*, 1 Ecology L. Q. 689, 700–01 (1971).

41. Maryland's Public Service Commission was one of the first to take environmental impacts seriously. It issued Baltimore Gas and Electric a certificate of public convenience and necessity on January 19, 1971 and conditioned it on the utility backfitting the plant to provide the technology which would reasonably protect public health and safety and the environment. Brief of Petitioners', *Calvert Cliffs' Coordinating Comm.* (No. 24,871).

to estimate future demand; past growth in electric demand was projected into the future. This method produced projections of incrementally rising demand leading to a potential capacity "crisis" by the then distant target year of 1980. For example, the cover of the Federal Power Commission's[42] 1970 *National Power Survey* summarized a widespread consensus that many new power plants were urgently needed with a graphic which featured a steep upward sloping demand curve formed by the words *"Guidelines for Growth of the Electric Power Industry."*[43]

Calvert Cliffs' quickly morphed from a challenge to the specific plant into a test case to challenge the AEC's post-NEPA rules for the consideration of the environmental impacts of power plants in licensing proceedings. Calvert Cliffs' Coordinating Committee was picked over other groups challenging plants in the East and Midwest as the lead plaintiff because the site was well known to the small environmental law community in Washington and their standing to bring the suit seemed easy to establish should it be contested. Many members of organizations such as the Sierra Club or the Conservation Foundation had homes on Maryland's western shore or sailed in the area. The Committee was an ad hoc group formed in response to a study by a group of John Hopkins University scientists, now deceased, about the potential adverse impacts of radiological emissions and thermal discharges from the proposed plant on the Chesapeake Bay's ecosystem. After the study was made public, Jess W. Malcolm, the executive director of the recently founded Chesapeake Bay Foundation,[44] founded the Coordinating Committee to serve as an umbrella for all groups protesting the plant.[45] Their representation of all but one of the groups that had participated in the AEC licensing proceedings allowed them to challenge the AEC's NEPA rules, as an

---

42. In the 1960s, the Federal Power Commission (FPC) had jurisdiction over the siting of hydroelectric plants on navigable rivers and the interstate transmission of electricity and natural gas. The AEC had jurisdiction over nuclear plants. In 1974, the AEC's promotional functions were given to the newly created Department of Energy and the regulatory functions combined with the FPC's in a new agency, the Federal Energy Regulatory Commission (FERC).

43. Federal Power Comm'n, *National Power Survey, 1970: Report* (U.S. Gov't Printing Office 1971).

44. The group was founded between 1964 and 1967 by a group of Baltimore businessmen who sailed, fished and hunted on the bay and were concerned with the growing stresses on the bay from increased boating, industrial discharges and urban development. Congressman and soon to be Secretary of the Interior Rodgers Morton encouraged them to form an organization that would organize public and private support to address the Bay's problems. The group has been a major force in galvanizing federal and state action to protect the entire watershed and now has over 116,600 members. The Chesapeake Bay Foundation at a Glance, *at* www.cbf.org/site/PageServer?pagename=about_index (last visited Jan. 29, 2005).

45. Bronstein, *supra* note 40, at 711.

agency aggrieved party, directly in the D.C. Circuit.[46]

Originally, the Committee approached James Moorman, a young lawyer practicing in a small nonprofit NGO, the newly created Center for Law and Social Policy, who later served as the Assistant Attorney General for Lands and Natural Resources during the Carter Administration. Moorman, who was one of the first lawyers to practice what we now call environmental law, took on the case on behalf of the Sierra Club and National Wildlife Federation. Moorman prepared a memo which outlined a wide range of possible federal and common law theories of relief in anticipation of a federal district court case.[47] However, an overworked Moorman quickly gave the case to another small recently formed for profit public interest law firm,[48] Berlin, Kessler and Roisman.[49] Tony Roisman had been drawn into environmental law through the efforts of Malcolm Baldwin, the Senior Legal Associate at the Conservation Foundation and a major strategic thinker about the need for an environmental law (theories that could be used to sue government agencies and polluters) which did not then exist.[50] Another plaintiff's lawyer, Myron

---

46. The court's jurisdiction was based on 28 U.S.C. § 2342, and the court apparently concluded without discussion that Calvert Cliffs' was an aggrieved party entitled to challenge a final AEC order.

47. Telephone Interview with James Moorman (Aug. 10, 2004). Moorman recalls being very busy at the time with the litigation to cancel DDT's registration and to challenge the Trans–Alaska Pipeline and thus did not devote a great deal of time to the case.

48. Moorman recalls trying to shift cases which had potential paying clients to lawyers in more traditional practice so that the Center for Law and Social Policy could concentrate on pure public interest litigation. Telephone Interview with James Moorman (Aug. 10, 2004).

49. Mr. Roisman, now an environmental attorney in New Hampshire, was an IRS tax attorney who formed a small firm for-profit public interest firm in January of 1969 with Edward Berlin, an Assistant General Counsel of the Federal Power Commission, and Gladys Kessler, who had worked in Congress and is now a federal district judge in Washington, D.C. Judge Kessler has issued a number of major, high profile decisions. In July of 2003, she issued an injunction against the U.S. Army Corps of Engineers to reduce water levels in the Missouri River below South Dakota to protect the habitat of two endangered species. The three attorneys initially thought that they would do FPC consumer work, lobbying and offering tax advice to the growing number of public interest firms. They each took home $1,300.00 their first year. Telephone Interview with Anthony Z. Roisman (Aug. 5, 2004).

50. In the late 1960s, a small number of young lawyers who had either large firm or high level government experience began to join small public interest firms in Washington, D.C., which the foundations were beginning to fund. Mr. Baldwin brought these lawyers together for regular luncheons. He also played a major role, along with David Sive, in the development of environmental law by organizing a conference of academics, lawyers and politicians, who were trying to create a new area out of whole cloth, on Law and the Environment at Airlie House in Northern, Virginia in September of 1969. Those of us who were there date the birth of environmental law as a formal legal sub-specialty from that

Cherry, was the leader of a then largely unsuccessful campaign of legal and political guerilla warfare against the AEC and public utilities to stop the licensing of a number of newly planned nuclear power plants.[51]

Roisman changed the case from a potentially long federal district court trial to a direct appellate review of an agency rulemaking because he thought the case would be a perfect vehicle to put teeth into the recently enacted NEPA. He basically put aside the Moorman memo and began to prepare for a NEPA suit.[52] To do so, he began to appear in various individual AEC licensing proceedings to make an administrative record to support his challenge to the AEC's NEPA rules. Roisman wanted the AEC to be the first major NEPA case because, unlike most

conference. The field was given form by the newly founded Environmental law Institute's decision to publish the Environmental Law Reporter. The conference papers were published as *Law and the Environment* (Malcolm F. Baldwin & James K. Page, Jr. eds., 1970). All three members of Berlin, Kessler and Roisman, and James Moorman, attended the conference.

   51. Mr. Cherry, then a young lawyer in Chicago, has been described as perhaps the most important anti-nuclear lawyer in the 1970s. His career has been recorded on film and in books. *E.g.*, Cook, *supra* note 35; *see also* Frank Graham, Jr., *The Outrageous Mr. Cherry and the Underachieving Nukes*, 79 Audubon 50 (1977); John R. Emshwiller, *Nuclear Nemesis: Using the Law's Delay, Myron Cherry Attacks Nuclear Power Projects,* Wall St. J., Mar. 10, 1978, at A1. Mr. Cherry's route to environmental law was even more fortuitous than those of the other young lawyers. In the mid–1960s, he was a partner at a large Chicago tax law firm which was retained by the president of Upjohn Pharmaceutical to ask questions about the Palisades nuclear power plant in Michigan. Wealthy Chicago and Michigan businessmen with second homes along the shore of Lake Michigan were becoming concerned about the impact of existing and proposed nuclear plants on the lake. The president of Upjohn took the lead after his general counsel's sailboat was damaged by debris from the Palisades plant's recently constructed discharge pipe permitted by the U.S. Army Corps of Engineers. With the help of another leading lawyer in an anti-nuclear crusade, the late David Comey of the Chicago public interest organization Businessmen for the Public Interest, and the legendary Lake Michigan activist, Lee Botts, Mr. Cherry was able to mount a multi-front war on the nuclear industry. It was so successful that the Chicago banks financing the industry put pressure on his firm to fire him. While pressure was mounting, Mr. Cherry was invited by Harold Graves, General Counsel of Consumer Power of Michigan, to the Gull Lake Inn near Battle Creek, Michigan. Correctly anticipating a bribe, Mr. Cherry had a houseplant next to their table wired and the offer was broadcast live on the radio. The general counsel lost his job, and Mr. Cherry soon left the firm and founded his own, initially partially supported by foundation grants. Mr. Cherry remains a leading Chicago lawyer and active Democratic Party fund raiser. In addition to helping Mr. Roisman with the Calvert Cliffs brief, Mr. Cherry made an earlier crucial, direct contribution to the litigation. When NEPA was being considered in Congress, he approached Senator Jackson's staff and asked them to include an express right to sue to compel the preparation of an EIS. The staff refused but allowed him to draft some of the "legislative history" on which Judge Wright relied to reach the same result. *See Calvert Cliffs' Coordinating Comm.*, 449 F.2d at 1114–15. Telephone interview with Myron Cherry (Sept. 14, 2004).

   52. Mr. Moorman agreed with this strategy. Telephone Interview with James Moorman (Aug. 10, 2004).

other federal agencies, it had considerable environmental science expertise in the national laboratories that Congress had created to support the civilian use of nuclear power. As a former Internal Revenue Service lawyer, he was much more comfortable with appellate work and understood the arguments necessary to convince a court of appeals to remand an administrative rulemaking.

The AEC helped Roisman's case by issuing NEPA compliance rules which shifted most of the burden of environmental reviews to the staff and utilities. After the Act's passage, the agency instituted a notice and comment rulemaking proceeding,[53] and at the end of 1970 issued Appendix D to its licensing rules.[54] Appendix D required all applicants for a construction permit to submit an "environmental report." When the applicant applied for an operating license, a second report noting any changed factors had to be submitted. The Commission's regulatory staff had to use the reports to prepare a detailed statement of the environmental costs, benefits and alternatives of the plant. However, the environmental factors raised by this process did not have to be considered by the hearing board which made the ultimate license recommendations to the full Commission. Hearing boards had to conduct an independent review of all staff recommendations except environmental ones. An independent review was *only* required if outside parties or a staff member affirmatively raised an environmental issue.[55]

Roisman thought that it was clear that NEPA imposed affirmative duties on all federal agencies.[56] The trick would be to convince the D.C. Circuit that the AEC's compliance efforts fell short of these duties because NEPA required a full consideration of the environmental impacts of each individual nuclear plant early in the licensing process and

53. Licensing of Production and Utilization Facilities, 35 Fed. Reg. 8594 (AEC June 3, 1970). The Commission had earlier issued only a policy statement of the implementation of NEPA's procedural requirements. Licensing of Production and Utilization Facilities, 35 Fed. Reg. 5463 (AEC Apr. 2, 1970).

54. Licensing of Production and Utilization Facilities, 35 Fed. Reg. 18,469 (AEC Dec. 4, 1970) (formerly codified at 10 C.F.R. pt. 50, App.D 246–50).

55. 10 C.F.R pt. 50 App.D at 249 provided: If "no party to such a proceeding . . . raise[s] any [environmental] issue . . . those issues would not be considered by the atomic safety and licensing board. Under such circumstances, although the Applicant's Environmental Report, comments thereon, and the Detailed Statement will accompany the application through the Commission's review processes, they will not be received in evidence, and the Commission's responsibilities under the National Environmental Policy Act of 1969 will be carried out in toto outside the hearing process."

56. Justice William O. Douglas, the most committed environmentalist to sit on the Supreme Court, had characterized NEPA as follows in a dissent from a highway location controversy. "Congress has said that ecology has become paramount and that nothing must be done by federal agencies which does ecological harm when there are alternative albeit more expensive, ways of achieving the result." *San Antonio Conservation Society v. Texas Highway Dep't*, 400 U.S. 968, 978 (1970) (Douglas, J., dissenting from denial of certiorari).

that NEPA created a cause of action for NGOs. The winning strategy was to identify four specific instances of noncompliance.[57] Two were challenges to the AEC's decision to limit the rules to proceedings commenced before the statute took effect.[58] However, the real targets were the provisions that excused the hearing board from analyzing environmental issues considered by the staff unless either outside members or the staff affirmatively raised them and the rules exempting the Commission from an independent evaluation and balancing of environmental factors if "other responsible agencies" had certified that their environmental standards were satisfied, i.e., state agency certification that the plant's discharges complied with applicable water quality standards.

III. The D.C. Circuit Decision

Calvert Cliffs' was not the first NEPA case, but it was the first to make it clear that the courts should enforce the statute against the entire federal bureaucracy. Lawyers litigating environmental claims immediately perceived the importance of NEPA, but the first cases either used NEPA as an additional reason to construe a statute,[59] or dealt with issues such as party standing,[60] or the retroactivity of the statute.[61] Good lawyering and a "dream panel"[62] allowed the *Calvert Cliffs'* plaintiffs to

---

57. The court's identification of the four deficiencies in Appendix D tracks the petitioners' brief. Brief of Petitioners' at 9–25, *Calvert Cliffs' Coordinating Comm.* (No. 24,871).

58. Parties were prohibited from raising non-radiological environmental issues for any hearings noticed before March 4, 1970 and the Commission refused to consider environmental factors for plants which had a construction permit before NEPA compliance was required even though no operating license had been issued.

59. One of the first major environmental cases, *Zabel v. Tabb*, 430 F.2d 199 (5th Cir. 1970), cited NEPA in the course of holding that Section 10 of the Rivers and Harbors Act of 1899 gave the United States Army Corps of Engineers the power to deny a dredge and fill permit soley for environmental reasons.

60. In the first major environmental decision, *Scenic Hudson Pres. Council, Inc. v. FPC*, 354 F.2d 608 (2d Cir. 1965), *cert. denied sub nom. Consolidated Edison Co. Of New York v. Scenic Hudson Pres. Council*, 384 U.S. 941 (1966) the Second Circuit allowed an environmental organization to sue to vindicate primarily aesthetic interests

61. *Compare* Investment Syndicates, Inc. v. Richmond, 318 F. Supp. 1038 (D. Or. 1970) (holding that NEPA does not apply to project where planning was substantially completed prior to enactment of statute) *with* Envtl. Def. Fund, Inc. v. Corps of Eng'rs of the U.S. Army, 325 F. Supp. 749 (D. Ark. 1971) (holding that NEPA applies to on-going reservoir construction project).

62. Judge J. Skelly Wright authored the unanimous opinion. The other two panel members, Edward Allen Tamm and Spottswood William Robinson, were both nominated by President Lyndon Baines Johnson. Judge Robinson was the first African–American member of the District of Columbia Circuit Court of Appeals. He had been part of the NAACP legal team in *Brown v. Board of Education* and was serving as Dean of Howard Law School when President John F. Kennedy nominated him to federal district court.

influence the future of environmental law worldwide by creating a duty of strict compliance with NEPA's "procedural" duties.

The opinion was authored by Judge J. Shelly Wright, whose background and close observation of federal agencies made him very receptive to the plaintiff's arguments. Judge Wright was appointed by President Truman to the Eastern District of Louisiana and distinguished himself by strictly enforcing *Brown v. Board of Education* and other anti-discrimination Supreme Court precedents in a hostile environment.[63] When one of the leaders of southern resistance to segregation, Senator James Eastland of Mississippi, blocked Wright's nomination to the Fifth Circuit, President John F. Kennedy appointed him to the D.C. Circuit. Judge Wright's Louisiana experience made him a firm believer in the need for judicial protection for those excluded from political power.[64] Environmental protection has never precisely fit this model because environmentalists have never lacked access to political power and are not an insular minority. However, in the late 1960s and early 1970s, the idea of the need for institutionalized environmental protection was just becoming recognized and few could foresee the breath and depth of the laws passed by Congress in the 1970s. Environmentalists felt themselves to be a small, embattled minority facing powerful, entrenched government agencies whose missions seemed to be to change irrevocably the natural landscape for the worse and to endanger public health. There was much talk of agency "capture" by the "regulated community" in those days.

Judge Wright shared the then-growing skepticism about the federal bureaucracy's ability to adapt to these values given their entrenched missions.[65] Federal courts were beginning to abandon the cardinal principle of New Deal Administrative Law—extreme deference to agency expertise—and adopting more probing standards of judicial review as a reaction to the narrowness of agency decisions. The expert agency model was being replaced with one of the agency as forum for resolving

---

63. Jack Bass, *Unlikely Heroes: The Dramatic Story of the Southern Judges of the Fifth Circuit Who Translated the Supreme Court's Brown Decision into a Revolution of Equality* 112–35 (1981) recounts Judge Wright's courageous role in implementing *Brown* by issuing the first date certain desegregation order for New Orleans public schools.

64. *E.g.,* Javins v. First Nat'l Realty Corp., 428 F.2d 1071 (D.C. Cir. 1970) (holding that residential tenancies are subject to implied warranties of habitability); *see also* J. Skelly Wright, *No Matter How Small*, 2 Hum. Rts. 115 (1972).

65. See Arthur Selwyn Miller, *A "Capacity for Outrage": The Judicial Odyssey of J. Skelly Wright* 110 (1984). Judge Wright had vigorously defended the judicial activism of the Warren Court in the face of legislative unwillingness to act. J. Skelly Wright, *The Role of the Supreme Court in a Democratic Society—Judicial Activism or Restraint?*, 54 Cornell L. Rev. 1, 5–6 (1968).

conflicts among competing interests or, in contemporary terms, stake-holders.[66]

The plaintiff's primary argument was that the AEC's rules did not comply with NEPA because they did not require early and independent agency evaluation of all environmental impacts of nuclear power plants. To counter this, the AEC and the public utility interveners tried to convince the court that NEPA compliance duties were "flexible," and that even though the agency accepted that NEPA expanded its jurisdiction, Appendix D constituted sufficient compliance with the Act.[67] The government's primary defense was that NEPA permitted, if not required, the agency to defer to state and federal water quality agencies and that this was good policy as the AEC was "without developed competence" in all environmental areas.[68] To support the flexibility argument, the Commission and the interveners relied on scattered statements in early district court decisions that NEPA duties were flexible, i.e. discretionary.[69] Ultimately, the case raised two fundamental, hard questions in addition to those raised by the AEC rules. Did NEPA create judicially enforceable duties and if so, what was the standard of compliance?

There is no doubt that the drafters of NEPA intended that it would have substantive consequences. Section 101 declares a set of far-reaching aspirational policies that all federal agencies must apply and implement. However, judicial enforcement of these substantive policies does not follow from Section 101. Section 101's breath caused a problem for lawyers and judges because it did not easily yield a consistent set of standards. Courts require that a statute contain some ordering of competing, inconsistent interests before they will use a statute to control agency action.[70] One scholar speculates that Senator Jackson did not

66. The classic articulation of this theory is Richard B. Stewart, *The Reformation of American Administrative Law* 88 Harv. L. Rev. 1669 (1975). The Supreme Court adopted the "hard look" doctrine for judicial review of informal agency action the same year that *Calvert Cliffs'* was decided. *See* Citizens to Pres. Overton Park, Inc. v. Volpe, 401 U.S. 402 (1971).

67. Prior to 1970, the AEC relied on *State of New Hampshire v. Atomic Energy Commission*, 406 F.2d 170 (1st Cir.), *cert. denied*, 395 U.S. 962 (1969) for the proposition that it did not have jurisdiction over thermal pollution, but it conceded that NEPA had expanded its jurisdiction. Brief of Respondents' at 13, *Calvert Cliffs' Coordinating Comm.* (No. 24,871).

68. Brief of Respondents' at 28, *Calvert Cliffs' Coordinating Comm.* (No. 24,871).

69. The AEC and the intervenors cited *Pennsylvania Envtl. Council, Inc. v. Barlett*, 315 F. Supp. 238 (M.D. Pa. 1970) and *Bucklein v. Volpe*, 1 Envtl. L. Rep. 20043 (N.D. Cal. 1970).

70. Another towering judge on the District of Columbia Circuit Court of Appeals said of *Calvert Cliffs'*: "The new student who comes to *Calvert Cliffs'* after having read *Overton Park*, 401 U.S. 402 (1971) (construing Section 4(f) of the Federal Highway Act), may not develop a detailed legislative record on the assessment process that might have structured judicial enforcement because he viewed the EIS process as a management tool, "largely internal to the federal bureaucracy" as agencies transformed themselves and, ironically in light of *Calvert Cliffs'*, because "environmental lawyers had not [yet] become a significant force in administrative politics."[71] Judge Wright recognized the difficulty of deriving consistent standards from NEPA and dealt with it by a familiar dichotomy which has dominated NEPA jurisprudence.

His opinion styled Section 101 as substantive and thus soft,[72] and Section 102 as procedural and hard. Although Judge Wright fundamentally shifted the focus of NEPA from the substantive to the procedural, he held out the tantalizing possibility that the Act was also substantive in the rare case where "the actual balance of costs and benefits that was struck was arbitrary."[73] Judge Wright was therefore able to answer the first hard question with a resounding "yes" in the ringing tones of an Old Testament prophet and thus launched environmental law.[74] He asserted the need for a strong judicial role to enforce "the commitment of the Government to control, at long last, the destructive engine of material 'progress'"[75] and that "[o]ur duty . . . is to see that important legislative purposes, heralded in the halls of Congress, are not lost or misdirected in the vast hallways of the federal bureaucracy."[76] Thus he

---

fully capture its drama and significance. Whereas the statutory provision construed in *Overton Park* gives environmental values dominant significance under certain circumstances, NEPA does not assign a relative weight to environmental concerns and therefore leads the courts to recognize much broader governmental discretion in deciding whether or not those concerns should prevail in a given case." Harold Leventhal, *Environmental Decisionmaking and the Role of the Courts*, 122 U. Pa. L. Rev. 509, 520 (1974).

71. Richard A. Liroff, *A National Policy for the Environment: NEPA and Its Aftermath* 32 (1976).

72. The declaration of policies was characterized as a "flexible one. . . . [which] leaves room for a responsible exercise of discretion and may not require particular substantive results." *Calvert Cliffs' Coordinating Comm.*, 449 F.2d at 1112.

73. *Id.* at 1115.

74. Oliver A. Houck, *The Secret Opinions of the United States Supreme Court on Leading Cases in Environmental Law, Never Before Published!*, 65 U Colo. L. Rev. 459, 463 (1994).

75. *Calvert Cliffs' Coordinating Comm.*, 449 F.2d at 1111.

76. *Id.* at 1111. Mr. Roisman suggested that the AEC Solicitor was responsible for the tone. One of the AEC's key arguments was that the Commission did not need to make an independent determination of the environmental impacts of thermal discharges because the then federal water pollution control acts permitted the AEC to rely on a state certification that a plant complied with applicable water quality standards. When Judge Wright asked the AEC solicitor arguing the case, Marcus A. Rowden, to cite the specific section that excused further AEC consideration, Mr. Rowden reached for a copy of the United States Code Annotated and responded, "let us parse the statute together." Roisman remembers Judge Wright immediately stiffening. Telephone interview with Anthony Z.

created a cause of action in the face of legislative history that was
ambiguous at best.[77]

This duty was primarily found in the language of Section 102(c)
which provides that all agencies of the federal government shall:

[I]nclude in every recommendation or report on proposals for legislation and other major Federal actions significantly affecting the
quality of the human environment, a detailed statement by the
responsible official on—

(i) the environmental impact of the proposed action,

(ii) any adverse environmental effects which cannot be avoided
should the proposal be implemented,

(iii) alternatives to the proposed action,

(iv) the relationship between local short-term uses of man's
environment and the maintenance and enhancement of long-
term productivity, and

(v) any irreversible and irretrievable commitments of resources
which would be involved in the proposed action should it be

Roisman (Aug. 5, 2004). The response is a classic appellate mistake, especially since
existing federal water pollution control legislation was a rather weak program that relied
on state water quality standards to prevent pollution and did not deal at all with the
relationship between compliance with state standards and AEC licensing. The AEC's brief
relied both on Section 104 of NEPA, 42 U.S.C § 4334, and Section 21(b) of the 1970 Water
Quality Improvement Act. Section 104 reinforces the authority of pollution control agencies
(the EPA had not yet been created) to enforce their standards regardless of the outcome of
the EIS process. Section 21(b), the origin of Section 401, 33 U.S.C. § 1341(a), of the Clean
Water Act, prohibited a federal agency from a licensing project that did not comply with
applicable state or interstate water quality standards. The brief did not reply on the
language of the statute alone and in fact placed the greatest weight on the legislative
history of both NEPA and the Water Quality Improvement Act. Brief of Respondents' at
23–39, *Calvert Cliffs' Coordinating Comm.* (No. 24,871). The Petitioners' reply brief had
argued that neither the Federal Water Pollution Act nor any state standard involved "the
exhaustive case by case review and balancing of factors required by NEPA." Reply Br. of
Petitioners' at 15–16, *Calvert Cliffs' Coordinating Comm.* (No. 24,871). The court's
resolution of the merits of the AEC's argument is discussed later in this chapter. For a
discussion of the program that preceded the 1972 Clean Water Act, see William L. Andreen,
*The Evolution of Water Pollution Control in the United States—State, Local, and Federal
Efforts, 1789–1972: Part II*, 22 Stan. Envtl. L. J. 215 (2003).

77. The problem was that the Conference Committee deleted Senator Jackson's
language in Section 101(c) which created a right "to a healthful environment" and gave no
attention to the question of judicial review of impact statements. Richard A. Liroff, *A
National Policy for the Environment: NEPA and Its Aftermath* 26–32 (1976). The best
discussion of the legislative history and the case for judicial review of NEPA decisions is
Eva H. Hanks & John L. Hanks, *An Environmental Bill of Rights: The Citizen Suit and the
National Environmental Policy Act of 1969*, 24 RUTGERS L. REV. 230 (1970), cited in *Calvert
Cliffs' Coordinating Comm.*, 449 F.2d at 1115–16 n.13.

implemented.[78]

Judge Wright concluded that the legislative history of Section 102(2), some of which was written by Myron Cherry, envisioned full compliance unless clearly prohibited by existing law.[79] Thus, if an agency decision was "reached procedurally without individualized consideration and balancing of environmental factors—conducted fully and in good faith—it is the responsibility of courts to reverse."[80] His rejection of the Commission's argument that they lacked the authority to consider thermal pollution followed from the court's "to the fullest extent possible" doctrine. The court construed Sections 102 and 103 of NEPA to create a presumption of authority to comply unless compliance was clearly inconsistent with the agency's existing statutory mandate. This conclusion is consistent with the intent of Senator Jackson, although NEPA's wording supports only a more limited reading. If an agency could comply with NEPA under their existing authority, they must.[81]

---

78. 42 U.S.C. § 4332 (2000).

79. National Environmental Policy Act of 1969, Conf. Rep. on S. 1075, 115 Cong. Rec. (Part 29) 39701, 39702–03 (1969). The full compliance analysis also swept away Commission objections that it had to limit the application of NEPA to post–1971 license applications even though no full operating license had been issued in order to ensure an "orderly transition" to full compliance. The final part of the opinion dealt with an issue that is no longer significant. In brief, the AEC rules allowed the Commission to accept a state water pollution agency certification that the plant met applicable water quality standards as the basis to conclude that there were no environmental impacts associated with the thermal discharge. To support this argument, the Commission invoked the Jackson–Muskie compromise reflected in Section 104. 42 U.S.C. § 4334 (2000). Section 104 provides that nothing in NEPA shall affect the obligations of federal agencies to comply with environmental quality standards. This section was added at the insistence of Senator Muskie who was concerned that NEPA could be used to weaken the existing and future strong air and water technology-forcing standards which would eventually become the Clean Air and Water Acts. Judge Wright found the legislative history too weak to support the AEC's position and held that the AEC could impose additional discharge limitations. However, Congress reversed holding this in 1972, 33 U.S.C. § 1371(c)(2), and in general, the thermal pollution problem has substantially been mitigated. Most of the plants built in the 1970s use cooling towers rather than once through cooling.

80. *Calvert Cliffs' Coordinating Comm.*, 449 F.2d at 1115.

81. The existing language replaced language that read, "[t]he Congress authorizes and directs that the policies, regulations and public laws of the United States, to the fullest extent possible, be interpreted and administered . . . " The enacted version was inserted in conference by the leading opponent of NEPA, Congressman Wayne Aspinall of Colorado. He clearly did not intend to create the strong presumption that Senator Jackson and Congressman Dingell of Michigan did. However, Senator Jackson and Congressman Dingell outmaneuvered Congressman Aspinall by inserting language in the conference report, on which Judge Wright relied, which contained the strong presumption interpretation. National Environmental Policy Act of 1969, Conf. Rep., Major Changes in S. 1075 as Passed by the Senate, 115 Cong. Rec. 40415, 40417–18 (1969); National Environmental Policy Act of 1969, Conf. Rep. on S. 1075, 115 Cong. Rec. 39701, 39702–03 (1969). The Report was

The substance-procedure dichotomy solved one barrier to invalidation of the AEC's rules by avoiding the hard question of whether NEPA contained sufficient substantive standards to evaluate an agency outcome. However, the focus on procedure did not fully justify the remand for two reasons. First, the AEC, unlike some other agencies, had not ignored NEPA; it was quite aware that it was one of the principal targets of the legislation. Second, it was not clear what procedure the statute mandated. There was no pre-existing model for an environment impact assessment.[82] An assessment is not a classic trial type-procedure because the inevitable scientific uncertainties about future impacts make it more than a search for "the truth." To construct a model of good NEPA procedure, Judge Wright fell back on another familiar legal principle then much in vogue and suggested by Petitioners:[83] the need to balance competing factors combined with the idea of an affirmative duty to consider environmental values. He found the AEC's environmental policy "a mockery of the Act" because it did not require an independent Commission balancing of environmental factors. The Commission's "responsibility is not simply to sit back, like an umpire, and resolve adversary contentions at the hearing stage. Rather, it must itself take the initiative of considering environmental values at every distinctive and comprehensive stage of the process beyond the staff's evaluation and recommendation."[84]

---

accepted without serious challenge by both houses of Congress. Richard A. Liroff, *A National Policy for the Environment: NEPA and Its Aftermath* 26–31 (1976).

82. An earlier version of the statute, drafted by William Van Ness and Daniel Dreyfus, contained a provision for "environmental findings" but this was changed to the requirement for a "detailed environmental statement" during the negotiations with Senator Edmund Muskie. There is no record of the reason for this, Frederick R. Anderson, *NEPA in the Courts: A Legal Analysis of the National Environmental Policy Act* 8 (1973), and one court observed that the findings requirement would have provided a firmer basis for judicial review. *See* City of New York v. United States, 344 F. Supp. 929, 936 n.16 (E.D.N.Y. 1972).

83. Petitioners first introduced the idea of balancing in the context of their argument that NEPA should apply to plants that were not fully licensed. They argued that the alternatives requirement required a balancing of the costs and benefits of each alternative. Brief of Petitioners' at 39, *Calvert Cliffs' Coordinating Comm.* (No. 24,871). However, the argument that NEPA required that agency to balance fully all of the statutory factors appeared in their reply brief. Petitioners' Reply Br. at 16, *Calvert Cliffs' Coordinating Comm.* (No. 24,871).

84. *Calvert Cliffs' Coordinating Comm.*, 449 F.2d at 1119. The quote is a paraphrase of language adopted by the Second Circuit in *Scenic Hudson Pres. Conference*, 354 F.2d at 620. A political scientist asserts that NEPA was intended to shift the federal government's role from an umpire to an environmental steward. Geoffrey Wandesforde–Smith, *National Policy for the Environment: Politics and the Concept of Stewardship, in Congress and the Environment* 205 (Richard A. Cooley & Geoffrey Wandesforde–Smith eds., 1970). Judge Wright subsequently developed a general theory of substantive review of agency rulemaking, premised on the agency's affirmative consideration of all relevant factors. J. Skelly

IV. The Immediate Impact of Calvert Cliffs'

Calvert Cliffs' had a dramatic immediate impact on the nuclear industry, although ultimately not on the Calvert Cliffs plant. Baltimore Gas and Electric decided to go ahead with the plant and prepared a full environmental impact statement; the first unit came on line in 1975. Today, the plant is a well-recognized landmark on Maryland's western shore. Two 850–megawatt generating units produce power for about one-third of the electricity customers in Maryland.[85] The initial licenses from the Nuclear Regulatory Commission (NRC) were valid through 2014 and 2016, but in 2000, Calvert Cliffs became the first nuclear plant to receive a license extension.[86] Somewhat ironically, the critical comments on the draft EIS prepared by the Union of Concerned Scientists noted the extensive discussion of fish and shellfish impacts but criticized the NRC staff for deeming the possible existence of a cancer cluster near the plant as "outside the scope of the environmental reviews."[87]

An historian of the anti-nuclear movement described *Calvert Cliffs'* as "the judicial opinion that had the most detrimental consequences on the development of nuclear power."[88] It stopped the licensing of all nuclear plants for eighteen months and fundamentally changed the nature of AEC licensing.[89] The case is therefore a validation of the power of lawsuits to delay actions and ultimately bring about administrative and political change. Nuclear power's allure dimmed in the 1970s. The AEC's promotional and regulatory functions were split in 1974. The Carter Administration's decision not to reprocess spent fuel for national security reasons created a back-end waste disposal problem that remains

Wright, *The Courts and the Rulemaking Process: The Limits of Judicial Review*, 59 Cornell L. Rev. 375, 388–93 (1974).

85. The plant is now owned by Constellation Nuclear, a unit of Constellation Energy Group. Information about the plant can be found at http://www.constellation.com/generation/ccnpp.asp.

86. Robin Roy & Andrew Moyad, *Nuclear Power Plants—Safety of Aging Power Plants*, in The Wiley Encyclopedia of Energy and the Environment 1137, 1138 (Attilio Bisio & Sharon Boots eds., 1997) cited the Calvert Cliffs' unit as an example of a reactor pressure vessel vulnerable to "embrittlement" from neutron bombardment.

87. Comments on Draft Environmental Impact Statement for Calvert Cliffs License Renewal Application, April 12, 1999 available at http://www.ucsusa.org/clean_energy/nuclear_safety/page.cfm?pageID=201. A history of what the AEC used to call "unscheduled incidents" relating to the plant can be found at http://www.ecology.at.nmi/site.php?site=Calvert+Cliffs.

88. Cook, *supra* note 35, at 44; *see also* Oliver Houck, *Unfinished Stories*, 73 Colo. L. Rev. 867, 887–88 (2002) for a discussion of the reason the AEC did not appeal to Supreme Court.

89. Joint Comm. on Atomic Energy, 92d Cong., 1st Sess., Selected Materials on the Calvert Cliffs' Decision, Its Origin and Aftermath 68–699 (Joint Comm. Print 1972) is collection of the relevant AEC reactions to *Calvert Cliffs'*.

unsolved to this day. The two oil price shocks in 1973 and 1979 helped to spur energy conservation and contrary to the Federal Power Commission's once endless upward slopping demand curve, the demand for energy fell. No new nuclear plants came on line after the crisis at Three Mile Island in 1979, and in the 1980s utilities, courts and public utility commissions struggled with the question of who should pay for cancelled or moth balled nuclear plants.

V. The Continuing Importance of Calvert Cliffs' Today

Calvert Cliffs' cemented the principle that the potential adverse environmental impacts and available alternatives of a wide range of government sponsored and licensed activities should be rigorously assessed in advance of the activities. It created a "common law" of impact assessment with substantial consequences for agency noncompliance. *Calvert Cliffs'* and its progeny democratized NEPA and environmental protection generally by (1) allowing citizens to challenge an agency's decision not to prepare an EIS as well as its adequacy, (2) creating inducements for agencies to open the scoping process to public involvement through comments, and (3) defining adequacy with sufficient detail that the agencies have opened up their processes to public involvement and outside sources of information to foreclose legal challenges to their final EISs.[90] However, the formulation of affirmative environmental policies—the original purpose for enacting the statute—has become increasingly divorced from the EIS process,[91] and NEPA has not developed in all the ways that Judge Wright envisioned. Both *Calvert Cliffs'* and subsequent Supreme Court decisions have contributed to the emphasis on process over substance or outcomes.

Judge Wright seems to have envisioned a more extensive EIS process than did Senator Jackson, and Judge Wright's view briefly prevailed. Judge Wright assumed that the agency would assemble the relevant environmental information and then use this information to make a reasoned choice, balancing between environmental and non-environmental values. However, this "rather finely tuned and 'systematic' balancing analysis" was immediately criticized by environmental lawyers and others as undermined by the substance-procedure dichotomy. Instead of forcing agencies to prefer more environmentally sustainable options, the dichotomy ensures that an agency need only seriously consider environmental values by displaying adverse impacts and agonizing a bit over the consequences of the proposed decision.[92] There is no

---

90. Lynton K. Caldwell, *Science and the National Environmental Policy Act* 72 (1982).

91. Lynton Keith Caldwell, *The National Environmental Policy Act: An Agenda for the Future* 50–55 (1998).

92. Courts have adopted the "hard look" standard. *E.g.,* Kern v. U.S. Bureau of Land Mgmt., 284 F.3d 1062, 1066 (9th Cir. 2002).

pressure to prefer consistently environmental to non-environmental out-comes.[93] Nonetheless, initially inspired by *Calvert Cliffs'*, a few district and courts of appeals used NEPA to probe deeply into agency decision-making.[94] The D.C. Circuit continued to read NEPA broadly and did not draw a hard and fast distinction between substantive and procedural review. It reversed major agency constructions of the Act in the spirit of *Calvert Cliffs'*. *Natural Resources Defense Council, Inc. v. Morton* held that, within reason, an agency had a duty to consider alternatives that it did not have the power to adopt or which required legislative authoriza-tion.[95] In 1973, the court, per Judge Wright, adopted a broad balancing test to determine when an EIS should be prepared for an ongoing nuclear research program.[96]

The uneasy balance between substance and procedure did not hold. The "detailed" EIS process that characterizes NEPA compliance has become a much more formal process limited to information disclosure rather than the balancing envisioned by Judge Wright. In the end, the analogy between an impact statement and Securities and Exchange Commission filing prevailed over Judge Wright's balancing theory. In 1971, a federal district judge tossed off the sentence that "[a]t the very least, NEPA is an environmental full disclosure law."[97] This character-ization of NEPA has been repeated consistently and has come to stand for the truthful teenager rule:[98] as long as the agency discloses the

---

93. Frederick R. Anderson, *NEPA in the Courts: A Legal Analysis of the National Environmental Policy Act* 256–58 (1973); A. Dan Tarlock, *Balancing Environmental Con-siderations and Energy Demands: A Comment on Calvert Cliffs' Coordinating Committee, Inc. v. AEC*, 47 IND. L.J. 645 (1972); Edmund S. Muskie & Eliot R. Cutler, *A National Environmental Policy: Now You See It, Now You Don't*, 25 Me. L. REV. 163 (1973); Joseph L. Sax, *The (Unhappy) Truth About NEPA*, 26 Okla. L. Rev. 239 (1973).

94. *E.g.*, Envtl. Def. Fund, Inc. v. Corps of Eng'rs of the U.S. Army, 325 F. Supp. 749 (E.D. Ark. 1971), *aff'd*, 470 F.2d 289 (8th Cir. 1972); Sierra Club v. Froehlke, 359 F. Supp. 1289 (S.D. Tex. 1973).

95. 458 F.2d 827 (D.C. Cir. 1972) (reversing Department of Interior refusal to discuss elimination of then-existing oil import quotas which benefitted independent southwest producers at the expense of New England). It is doubtful that this holding has much force today. Dep't of Transp. v. Pub. Citizen, 541 U.S. 752 (2004) held that the Department of Transportation did not have to issue an EIS for a North American Free Trade Agreement rule that allowed Mexican trucks into the United States. The Court conceded that the trucks would increase air pollution but concluded that the Department had no authority or ability to consider their environmental impacts. Only the President has the authority to prevent cross border truck traffic.

96. Scientists' Inst. for Pub. Info., Inc. v. AEC, 481 F.2d 1079 (D.C. Cir. 1973) (considering the impact of a liquid metal fast breeder reactor research program).

97. *Envtl. Def. Fund, Inc.*, 325 F. Supp. at 759.

98. Most parents of teenagers try to teach them to tell the truth about the misjudg-ments that they make and ultimately reward them for their candor.

required range of alternatives and adverse impacts, it has fulfilled its NEPA duties regardless of the environmental impact of its decision.

Judge Wright's view of NEPA was ultimately quashed by a series of Supreme Court decisions which vary between indifference and hostility toward NEPA.[99] The Court has instructed lower courts to defer to agency determinations of the scope of relevant alternatives[100] and on whether the agency was in fact engaged in regional planning or other similar action.[101] The Court also held that NEPA is limited to the physical environment,[102] and it turned the intent of the drafters on its head by holding that the Act does apply to appropriations requests.[103] Finally, in 1980 the Court held that NEPA does not permit a court to question the substantive decision taken by the agency, regardless of the environmental consequences of the decision.[104] As the Court subsequently put it, "NEPA itself does not mandate particular results, but simply prescribes the necessary process."[105] More generally, the Court has often spoken glowingly about the importance of NEPA but it has never reversed an agency's application of the statute.[106]

---

99. One of the many paradoxes of environmental law is that it has survived and thrived in the face of indifference or hostility from the Supreme Court. *See* Richard J. Lazarus, *Restoring What's Environmental About Environmental Law in the Supreme Court*, 47 U.C.L.A. L. Rev. 703 (2000); Daniel A. Farber, *Is the Supreme Court Irrelevant?: Reflections on the Judicial Role in Environmental Law*, 81 Minn. L. Rev. 547 (1997).

100. Vermont Yankee Nuclear Power Corp. v. Natural Res. Def. Council, Inc., 435 U.S. 519 (1978).

101. Kleppe v. Sierra Club, 427 U.S. 390 (1976).

102. Metro. Edison Co. v. People Against Nuclear Power, 460 U.S. 766 (1983) (holding that the psychological risks of restarting Three Mile Island need not be included in the EIS).

103. Andrus v. Sierra Club, 442 U.S. 347 (1979). *Andrus* resolved a dispute which went to the heart of the original theory of NEPA compliance but was not resolved in the legislation: the application of NEPA to the most powerful and least accountable agency, the OMB, or the Bureau of the Budget as it was known then. OMB's potential to force agencies to be more environmentally responsive was raised but not resolved in the legislative process. Frederick R. Anderson, *NEPA in the Courts: A Legal Analysis of the National Environmental Policy Act* 11–12 (1973). Section 102(c) finessed the issue by speaking only of legislative proposals and recommendations. During the Carter Administration, the Council on Environmental Quality adopted regulations which excluded appropriations, although the Nixon Administration Council had included them in the definition of "legislation." *See Environmental Quality—1979: The Tenth Annual Report of the Council on Environmental Quality* 577–84 (1979). *Andrus* resolved the issue by deferring to CEQ's regulations, although they are not binding on agencies. The exemption of OMB from the NEPA process has allowed it to increase the burden on agencies to justify environmental regulations rather than force agencies to consider the environmental consequences of budgetary decisions and alternative allocations.

104. Strycker's Bay Neighborhood Council v. Karlen, 444 U.S. 223 (1980).

105. Robertson v. Methow Valley Citizens Council, 490 U.S. 332, 350 (1989).

106. Weinberger v. Catholic Action of Hawaii/Peace Educ. Project, 454 U.S. 139 (1981). The Court held that NEPA applies to the military but that matters of national security contained in an EIS need not be disclosed to the public.

In spite of the Supreme Court's contraction of the Act, NEPA litigation has been a constant feature of environmental law. Litigation is fueled by the fact that since 1970, over 25,000 EISs have been filed. Complete statistics on the number of NEPA cases do not exist. The leading treatise, *NEPA: Law and Litigation*, lists over 3,000 Supreme Court, courts of appeals and district court cases decided since *Calvert Cliffs'*. Not surprisingly, since agencies have become more adept at compliance, it is harder to win NEPA cases alleging an inadequate EIS, but plaintiffs continue to win them.[107] The easiest case to win is when an EIS carries its own "death wound." For example, courts have reversed and remanded EISs where the agency's conclusion that there were no significant environmental impacts was inconsistent with the agency's own experts.[108] Courts are also much more willing to remand an EIS for an inadequate discussion of "secondary alternatives," alternatives that do not modify the project but are much less environmentally destructive.[109] The Supreme Court, however, has indicted little willingness to require supplemental EISs when new scientific information comes to light.[110]

In the end the importance of *Calvert Cliffs'* lies in what it set in motion within the agencies and throughout the world rather than in specific decisions holding that an EIS was inadequate. One of the editors of this series argues that "NEPA's greatest contribution—and it is both magnificent in its simplicity and deceptive in its power—is the environmental impact statement."[111] Judicial enforcement quickly led to an agency and industry culture of compliance or at least begrudging acceptance. One of the most important, but difficult to measure, indices of NEPA is the dog that it would not let hunt.[112] For example, in the very beginning, the Council on Environmental Quality reported on projects dropped or changes made in them because problems exposed in the EIS process.[113]

---

107. Professor Daniel R. Mandelker, author of *NEPA Law and Litigation*, disagrees and thinks that the government's success remains relatively constant. Interview by A. Dan Tarlock of Daniel R. Mandelker. However, Professor Mandelker counts both cases which review agency decisions not to file a full EIS and those—like *Calvert Cliffs'*—that review a completed EIS.

108. *E.g.,* Sierra Club v. U.S. Army Corp of Eng'rs, 701 F.2d 1011 (2d Cir. 1983).

109. Dubois v. U.S. Dep't of Agric., 102 F.3d 1273 (1st Cir. 1996).

110. Marsh v. Oregon Natural Res. Council, 490 U.S. 360 (1989).

111. Oliver A. Houck, *Is That All? A Review of the National Environmental Policy Act, An Agenda For the Future, By Lynton Keith Caldwell*, 11 Duke Envtl. L. & Pol'y F. 173, 190 (2000).

112. *See* Serge Taylor, *Making Bureaucracies Think: The Environmental Impact Statement Strategy of Administrative Reform* (1984).

113. *Environmental Quality: The Fourth Annual Report of the Council on Environmental Quality* 246–47 (1973); *Environmental Quality: The Sixth Annual Report of the Council on Environmental Quality* 628–32 (1975).

Despite NEPA's widespread acceptance in the United States and throughout the world it is difficult to evaluate NEPA's long term impacts because no cross-disciplinary consensus exists on the relative criteria to assess the success of the Act.[114] What is clear is that the EIS process continues to be contested and criticized. Opponents of NEPA argue that the process is too costly both in terms of EIS preparation and the delays that it causes to important activities.[115] Supporters of NEPA have criticized the gap between the collection of information and the actual decision.[116] They have sought ways to return NEPA to its original purpose: the reorientation of federal agencies.[117] The NEPA debate is long standing; it has taken a new turn as the Administration of George W. Bush has engaged in a concerned effort to weaken the statute.[118]

Conclusion

Calvert Cliffs' played a major role in establishing the EIS process as a fundamental principle of environmental law. *Calvert Cliffs'* helped to initiate a worldwide transition in the way in which decisions that threaten to impair the physical environment are made. Unfortunately, the case also helped to divorce the process of EIS from the underlying objectives of NEPA. Ultimately, the United States practice has fallen short of the transformation that the drafters of NEPA and Judge Wright envisioned. Perhaps, no more than the launch of a powerful legal ideal can be expected from even a self-consciously transformative decision. As Dean Kathleen Sullivan has said of the recent criticisms that *Brown v.*

---

114. Matthew J. Lindstrom & Zachary A. Smith, *The National Environmental Policy Act: Judicial Misconstruction, Legislative Indifference, & Executive Neglect* 127 (2001).

115. This criticism, couched in benign language, is the focus of *The NEPA Task Force Report to the Council on Environmental Quality: Modernizing NEPA Implementation* (Sept. 2003), *available at* http://ceq.eh.doe.gov/ntf/report/htmltoc.html. A study of EISs prepared between 1978–81 found that only ten percent of the statements were the subject of litigation. Taylor, *supra* note 112, at 359.

116. During the Clinton Administration, the Council on Environmental Quality conducted a major review of NEPA and not surprisingly pronounced it a success in need of reform. Council on Environmental Quality, *The National Environmental Policy Act—A Study of Its Effectiveness After Twenty-five Years* (Jan. 1997), *available at* http://cep.eh.doe.gov/nepa/nepa25fn.pdf.

117. *E.g.*, Environmental Law Institute Research Report, *Rediscovering the National Environmental Policy Act: Back to the Future* (1995); Bradley C. Karkkainen, *Toward A Smarter NEPA: Monitoring and Managing Government's Environmental Performance*, 102 Colum. L Rev. 903 (2002).

118. *E.g.*, John M. Carter, Mike Leahy & William J. Snape III, *Cutting Science, Ecology, and Transparency Out of National Forest Management: How the Bush Administration Uses the Judicial System to Weaken Environmental Laws*, 33 Envtl. L. Rep. 10959 (Envtl. L. Inst. 2003). The Healthy Forests Restoration Act of 2003, Pub. L. 108–148, 117 Stat. 1887, expedites NEPA reviews and limits the range of alternatives which need to be considered.

Board of Education failed to achieve real racial integration, "[i]t is too much to ask of a legal decision that it generate on its own the vast and complicated set of social policies to fulfill it."[119] *

---

119. Kathleen Sullivan, *What Happened to "Brown"?*, N.Y Rev. of Books, Sept. 23, 2004, at 47, 52.

* I would like to thank Patrick Haggarty, Chicago-Kent College of Law, Class of 2006, for his extremely thorough and helpful research, and my assistant, Vincent Rivera, for his preparation of the final manuscript, and Ms. Lucy Moss, Senior Reference Librarian, Chicago-Kent College of Law Library, for tracking down the briefs.

*

4

Holly Doremus

The Story of *TVA v. Hill*: A Narrow Escape for a Broad New Law

The story of *Tennessee Valley Authority v. Hill* is that of a remarkable new law, the Endangered Species Act (ESA), narrowly escaping its first major test against a powerful and intransigent federal agency. The law prevailed in the Supreme Court, despite doubts about its wisdom that the justices made no effort to hide. At the end of a long journey, both dam and fish also survived.

I. Social and Legal Background

The conflict that produced *TVA v. Hill* was rooted in the late 1960s and early 1970s, a period in which enactment of the first wave of ambitious federal environmental laws overlapped with the final stages of the post-war infrastructure development boom. TVA was struggling to extend its history of successful water project development; the Department of Interior was learning how to implement the Endangered Species Act, the most remarkable of the new environmental statutes; and citizens were experimenting with the new roles environmental statutes provided for them, both in agency proceedings and in litigation. By the time the case reached the Supreme Court in the late 1970s the energy crisis had added yet another wrinkle, causing politicians and the public to pull back from their earlier headlong rush toward strong environmental regulation.

A. The Agency

The Tennessee Valley Authority was the paradigmatic product of the New Deal—an experiment in aggressive government intervention in the private market. It was created in 1933, over the objections of private utilities, as an independent corporation owned by the United States, run by a three-member Presidentially-appointed board of directors.[1] TVA's enabling legislation authorized pursuit of a number of purposes, including flood control, navigation, electric power, improved agriculture and reforestation, and promoting "the economic and social well-being of the people" of the basin.[2]

TVA grew out of the technocratic conservation movement. Franklin Roosevelt envisioned the TVA as the first of a series of regional planning and development authorities.[3] The Tennessee River basin was a logical starting point in large part because it was one of the poorest corners of the Depression-locked country. Per capita income was less than half the national average.[4] Unemployment was high, agricultural and forest lands badly eroded, and government services virtually nonexistent.[5] TVA was expected to change all of that through well-planned use and development of the region's natural resources.

The new agency was given remarkable autonomy. It did not share its turf either with other federal agencies or with the private sector. It could build dams without involving the Corps of Engineers or Bureau of Reclamation. It could undertake agricultural programs without asking the Department of Agriculture. It could generate and sell electricity, manufacture and market fertilizer, and litigate on its own behalf. The early TVA was a dynamic agency brimming with self-confidence. It enjoyed the admiration of the public and a strong *esprit de corps*.

By the end of World War II, TVA had completed construction of a series of hydroelectric dams on or near the mainstem of the Tennessee River, as well as a number of coal-fired electric plants. The dams made the Tennessee navigable, protected communities like Chattanooga from floods, and primarily, driven by war-time demands, supplied energy. By 1945, TVA claimed to be the largest single producer of electricity in the nation.[6] During the War, it was a critical strategic power source, feeding power-hungry aluminum plants and the Manhattan Project work at Oak

---

1. Tennessee Valley Authority Act, Pub. L. No. 73–17, 2, 48 Stat. 58, 59 (1933) (codified as amended at 16 U.S.C. § 831 (2000)).

2. *Id.* at § 23, 48 Stat. 69.

3. Erwin C. Hargrove, *Introduction, in TVA: Fifty Years of Grass–Roots Bureaucracy* ix, xiv (Erwin C. Hargrove & Paul K. Conklin eds., 1983); Paul K. Conkin, *Intellectual and Political Roots, in TVA: Fifty Years of Grass–Roots Bureaucracy* 3,23 (Erwin C. Hargrove & Paul K. Conklin eds., 1983).

4. North Callahan, *TVA: Bridge Over Troubled Waters* 27 (1980).

5. Richard Lowitt, *The TVA, 1933–45, in TVA: Fifty Years of Grass–Roots Bureaucracy* 35, 37 (Erwin C. Hargrove & Paul K. Conklin eds., 1983)

6. William H. Droze, *The TVA, 1945–80: The Power Company, in TVA: Fifty Years of Grass–Roots Bureaucracy* 66, 68 (Erwin C. Hargrove & Paul K. Conklin eds., 1983).

Ridge National Laboratory, which for a time consumed as much electricity as New York City.[7]

After the war, TVA found itself at a loss. Its mission of spurring regional economic development came under direct attack by President Eisenhower, who denounced TVA as an example of the menace of "creeping socialism."[8] Long-time TVA employees including Aubrey "Red" Wagner, who became general manager in 1954 and chairman of the board in 1962, chafed at the idea that TVA might be relegated to the role of a mere power supplier. To revitalize the vision of regional economic development, with cheap power the means to that larger end,[9] Wagner pushed TVA toward development of the Tennessee River's tributaries. The Tellico Project, approved by TVA's Board of Directors in 1962 as the first large tributary project, was "the showcase" of this new mission.[10] The Project's symbolic importance to TVA leaders helps explain the tenacity with which the agency clung to its plans, even as costs and opposition mounted dramatically.

As it was promoting the Tellico Project, TVA was also battling steady erosion of once-solid public support. In the new environmental era, TVA's obsession with producing power as inexpensively as possible caused image problems. By 1965, the New York Times was reporting that TVA, "[l]ong a highly regarded institution and virtually immune from popular criticism," found itself "under increasing attack from conservationists" for its voracious appetite for strip-mined coal.[11] TVA, which by then generated most of its power at coal-burning plants, was the nation's largest coal consumer.[12] It claimed to be requiring coal suppliers to restore mined lands, but resisted all attempts to bring the terms of its coal contracts into the open.[13] TVA was also a major polluter, responsible for more than half of the sulfur dioxide pollution in the

    7.   Richard A. Couto, *New Seeds at the Grass Roots: The Politics of the TVA Power Program Since World War II, in TVA: Fifty Years of Grass–Roots Bureaucracy* 230, 231 (Erwin C. Hargrove & Paul K. Conklin eds., 1983).

    8.   William Bruce Wheeler & Michael J. McDonald, *TVA and the Tellico Dam 1936–1979: A Bureaucratic Crisis in Post–Industrial America* 12 (1986).

    9.   Erwin C. Hargrove, *The Task of Leadership: The Board Chairmen, in TVA: Fifty Years of Grass–Roots Bureaucracy* 89, 109 (Erwin C. Hargrove & Paul K. Conklin eds., 1983).

    10.   Wheeler & McDonald, *supra* note 8, at 22.

    11.   Ben A. Franklin, *TVA Is Attacked for Strip Mining*, N.Y. Times, July 4, 1965, at L27.

    12.   Dean Hill Rivkin, *TVA, the Courts, and the Public Interest, in TVA: Fifty Years of Grass–Roots Bureaucracy* 194, 202 (Erwin C. Hargrove & Paul K. Conklin eds., 1983).

    13.   *See* Natural Resources Defense Council v. Tennessee Valley Authority, 502 F.2d 852 (6th Cir. 1974).

Southeast.[14] TVA fought states over whether it had to apply for air pollution permits,[15] and EPA over whether it had to install "scrubbers" to control sulfur dioxide emissions. Even ratepayers were unhappy. TVA had once prospered by stimulating regional demand for electricity, using the resulting economies of scale to progressively lower rates. Now it found itself caught in the opposite spiral—every new plant was more expensive than the last, so that as more power came on line costs soared.[16]

The era of unbridled water development was coming to an end just as this project worked its way through the system. Both the economic and the environmental costs of water projects were increasingly apparent. Jimmy Carter, elected with strong environmentalist support, issued a "hit list" of pork-barrel water projects soon after his inauguration in 1977. In the short run, Carter's list accomplished little other than to alienate Congress and hurt his re-election prospects. The next appropriations bill funded almost all of the targeted projects.[17] But the incident foretold the future, "signaling the end of the era of federal dam-building."[18]

B. The Statute

As this dispute developed, federal protection of endangered species was still in its infancy. The Endangered Species Preservation Act of 1966[19] directed the major federal land management agencies to protect domestic endangered species and, to the extent consistent with their primary missions, to preserve the habitat of those species.[20] Three years later the Endangered Species Conservation Act[21] expanded protection to a broader range of species, but still relied on land acquisition and management.

---

14. Rivkin, *supra* note 12, at 211–16.

15. With the support of EPA, TVA successfully resisted. Hancock v. Train, 426 U.S. 167 (1976). But TVA's intransigence figured prominently in persuading legislators of the necessity for change, and in 1977 Congress amended the Clean Air Act to make federal facilities subject to state permit requirements. Clean Air Act Amendments of 1977, Pub. L. No. 95–95, 116(a), 91 Stat. 685, 711 (codified as amended at 42 U.S.C. § 7418 (2000)).

16. Richard M. Freeman, *Creation, Re–Creation, and Turmoil*, 49 Tenn. L. Rev. 687, 692–95 (1982).

17. Christine A. Klein, *On Dams and Democracy*, 78 Or. L. Rev. 641, 701 (1999); Marc Reisner, *Cadillac Desert: The American West and Its Disappearing Water* 317–43 (1986).

18. David H. Getches, *The Metamorphosis of Western Water Policy: Have Federal Laws and Local Decisions Eclipsed the States' Role?*, 20 Stan. Envtl. L.J. 3, 17 (2001).

19. Pub. L. No. 89–669, 80 Stat. 926 (1966).

20. *Id.*, 1(b).

21. Pub. L. No. 91–135, 83 Stat. 275 (1969).

Passage of the Endangered Species Act[22] (ESA) in 1973 radically changed that strategy, imposing strict regulatory limits on actions affecting listed species. Section 7 of the new Act required federal agencies to "insure that actions authorized, funded, or carried out by them do not jeopardize the continued existence" of any listed species "or result in the destruction or modification of habitat of such species which is determined ... to be critical."[23] Section 9 prohibited take of endangered fish or wildlife within the United States by any person.[24] "Take" was defined to include not only hunting but harassing, harming, capturing, or attempting to do so.[25] Like other environmental laws of the era, the ESA authorized private enforcement.[26]

The ESA "was one of the last pieces of environmental bandwagon legislation,"[27] enacted virtually without opposition.[28] In many ways, it was the most remarkable of the laws of that era. It lacked the utilitarian tone or public health implications of the Clean Air and Clean Water Acts. It could not be interpreted as strictly procedural, like the National Environmental Policy Act. It was not limited to a few selected places, like the Wilderness Act. Instead, it purported to protect all species against any activities, whoever the actor and whatever the location, that could cause extinction.

Although the statute's words seem clear, it is widely agreed that most legislators were not aware of the full scope of the ESA when they voted for it. Discussion had centered on appealing species such as grizzly bears, bald eagles, blue whales and the like.[29] Early drafts left considerable wiggle room in federal obligations, requiring consultation with the Fish and Wildlife Service (FWS) but mandating that agencies take only "practicable" steps to conserve listed species. That mandate was noncontroversial, and not much of a departure from the status quo. But a handful of White House and Congressional staffers reworked the bill, introducing a firm prohibition on federal actions that would jeopardize listed species. According to Curtis Bohlen, Undersecretary of Interior at

22. Pub. L. No. 93–205, 87 Stat. 884 (1973), codified as amended at 16 U.S.C. §§ 1531–1544 (2000).

23. Pub. L. No. 93–205, 7.

24. 16 U.S.C. § 1538(a)(1)(B) (2000).

25. 16 U.S.C. § 1532(19) (2000).

26. 16 U.S.C. § 1540(g) (2000).

27. Steven L. Yaffee, *Prohibitive Policy: Implementing the Federal Endangered Species Act* 48 (1982).

28. *See* Shannon Petersen, *Congress and Charismatic Megafauna: A Legislative History of the Endangered Species Act*, 29 Envtl. L. 463, 475 (1999).

29. *Id.* at 475–76.

the time, "[T]here were probably not more than four of us who understood its ramifications."[30]

When the Tellico conflict reached the Supreme Court, the ESA had scarcely been implemented, let alone tested. The courts had little administrative guidance because the first formal interpretations of its key provisions came as the case was being litigated. The FWS proposed regulations implementing section 7 just days before the Sixth Circuit issued its decision.[31] The proposed rules would have left substantial discretion to federal agencies to decide whether to initiate consultation[32] and whether a project had gone too far to stop, even if it would cause jeopardy.[33] The consultation regulations were issued in final form on January 4, 1978, after the Supreme Court had taken the Tellico case but before oral argument.[34] They made consultation mandatory if a federal action might affect a listed species or its critical habitat. The final rules also strengthened application of section 7 to ongoing actions, dropping the suggestion that action agencies could decide to continue with ongoing projects notwithstanding the potential for jeopardy.

When *TVA v. Hill* reached the Court, only two other appellate decisions had interpreted the ESA, and only one had even temporarily halted a project. The Eighth Circuit had refused to stop construction of a dam, finding that plaintiffs had failed to prove it would jeopardize the continued existence of the Indiana bat.[35] The Fifth Circuit, on the other hand, had enjoined work on an interstate highway until FWS agreed that it would not jeopardize the Mississippi sandhill crane or destroy its critical habitat.[36] The limited amount of litigation to this point did not comfort the public works community. A series of high-profile controversies were brewing. TVA's Columbia Dam, another tributary project, threatened two listed mussels. The Furbish lousewort stood in the way of the Dickey–Lincoln Dam in Maine. The Tennessee–Tombigbee Waterway, a navigation canal planned to connect the Tennessee River to the Gulf of Mexico, faced conflict with multiple species. The Grayrocks Dam in Wyoming had a problem with whooping cranes.

---

30. Charles C. Mann & Mark L. Plummer, *Noah's Choice: The Future of Endangered Species* 160 (1995).

31. Fish & Wildlife Service, Proposed Provisions for Interagency Corporation [sic], 42 Fed. Reg. 4868 (Jan. 26, 1977).

32. They stated that agencies "should" request consultation on activities which might affect listed species. *Id.* at 4871.

33. *Id.* at 4869.

34. National Oceanic & Atmospheric Administration and Fish & Wildlife Service, Endangered Species Act of 1973, Interagency Cooperation Regulations, 43 Fed. Reg. 870 (Jan. 4, 1978).

35. Sierra Club v. Froehlke, 534 F.2d 1289 (8th Cir. 1976).

36. National Wildlife Federation v. Coleman, 529 F.2d 359 (5th Cir. 1976).

The list of protected species was growing slowly, but there were indications that it might soon expand exponentially. A total of 126 domestic species had been listed under the early endangered species laws. Ten were added under the ESA in 1975, and roughly 60 more by the beginning of 1978. The prospect of many more listings was in the air. Environmentalists were beginning to try to force listings through the petition process.[37] The Smithsonian Institution had reported that some 3000 domestic plant species warranted listing,[38] prompting FWS to propose listing nearly 2000.[39] Most of those never actually reached the protected list, but the proposal fueled the perception that virtually any public works project might be stopped by the ESA.

II. Factual Background

The valley of the Little Tennessee River became the scene of the most important early confrontation between development and endangered species protection. The Little Tennessee rises in the mountains of North Carolina and flows northwest into Tennessee, joining the Tennessee River about 25 miles from Knoxville. Flanked by rolling hills, the Little Tennessee valley boasted some of the most fertile farm land in the region. It was dotted with historic, archeological, and cultural resources, including Cherokee villages and sacred sites,[40] a British fort from the French and Indian wars, and a U.S. Army blockhouse from the end of the eighteenth century.[41]

A. The Dam

TVA completed Fort Loudoun Dam on the mainstem of the Tennessee just above the confluence with the Little Tennessee in 1943. While

---

37. At least four petitions seeking listing were submitted in 1974. *See* U.S. Fish and Wildlife Service, Sea Turtles: Review of Status, 39 Fed. Reg. 29605 (Aug. 16, 1974); U.S. Fish and Wildlife Service, Freshwater Sponges: Review of Status, 40 Fed. Reg. 17764 (Apr. 22, 1975); U.S. Fish and Wildlife Service, Fresh Water Crustaceans: Review of Status, 40 Fed. Reg. 18476 (Apr. 28, 1975); U.S. Fish and Wildlife Service, Amendment Listing the Grizzly Bear of the 48 Conterminous States as a Threatened Species, 40 Fed. Reg. 31734 (July 28, 1975). Conservation opponents had also discovered the petition process. *See* U.S. Fish and Wildlife Service, American Alligator: Review of Endangered Species Status, 39 Fed. Reg. 26050 (July 16, 1974); U.S. Fish and Wildlife Service, Eastern Timber Wolf in Minnesota: Review of Status, 39 Fed. Reg. 40877 (Nov. 21, 1974).

38. Smithsonian Institution, Report on Endangered and Threatened Plant Species of the United States (1975).

39. Proposed Endangered Status for Some 1700 U.S. Vascular Plant Taxa, 41 Fed. Reg. 24524 (June 16, 1976).

40. Wheeler & McDonald, *supra* note 8, at 148; Zygmunt J.B. Plater, *Reflected in a River: Agency Accountability and the TVA Tellico Dam Case*, 49 Tenn. L. Rev. 747, 756 (1982).

41. William Bruce Wheeler & Michael J. McDonald, *TVA and the Tellico Dam 1936—1979: A Bureaucratic Crisis in Post–Industrial America* 49 (1986).

planning that project, TVA had contemplated eventually adding a second
dam just above the mouth of the Little Tennessee. The two reservoirs
would be connected by a canal so that water from the Little Tennessee
could turn the turbines in Fort Loudoun. Congress appropriated money
for this proposed Fort Loudoun Extension during World War II,[42] but the
War Production Board nixed it in favor of higher priority projects.[43]

TVA staff revived the Fort Loudoun Extension idea as the Tellico
Project, the centerpiece of the new tributary development program, in
1959. The primary purpose of the project was regional economic development, but alternative means to that end were never considered. Dams
were what the agency thought it did best. Therefore the project would be
reservoir-centered, whether or not that made sense from an economic
development standpoint.

TVA quickly ran into a roadblock. Both the executive branch and
Congress had begun demanding that the economic benefits of publicly
financed water projects outweigh their economic costs. Damming the
Little Tennessee would provide more flood protection for Chattanooga,
increase the hydropower yield of Fort Loudoun Dam, and make the
lower Little Tennessee navigable. The economic benefits, however, would
be modest. Power capacity would increase only 22 megawatts in a system
with total capacity exceeding 22,000 megawatts,[44] Chattanooga already
enjoyed good flood protection from the mainstem dams, and there was no
demand for barge traffic in the agricultural Little Tennessee Valley.
Consequently, the Tellico Project could not pass TVA's traditional cost-
benefit test. Even ignoring the considerable non-economic costs of flooding one of the last free-flowing rivers in the region and inundating
historic and cultural sites, TVA calculated in 1963 that the costs of the
Tellico Project would exceed its benefits.[45]

TVA's leaders, though, were too wedded to the Project to abandon it.
Instead, they revised their calculations until they could claim that the
Tellico Project was economically justified.[46] They downplayed costs and
inflated benefits in just about every way imaginable. Navigation benefits,
for example, were increased by assuming that thousands of acres along

42. U.S. Fish & Wildlife Service, Snail Darter Recovery Plan 1 (May 5, 1983).

43. *Id.* at 30.

44. *See* U.S. General Accounting Office, The Tennessee Valley Authority's Tellico
Dam Project–Costs, Alternatives, and Benefits, EMO–77–58 (1977) [hereinafter *GAO Report*].

45. Wheeler & McDonald, *supra* note 8, at 89.

46. Wheeler & McDonald provide a detailed overview of TVA's creative accounting.
Id. at 87–110. TVA's figures were strongly criticized by the General Accounting Office in a
1977 report to the Congress. *GAO Report, supra* note 44.

the reservoir would be developed for industries dependent upon water transportation.

TVA introduced new benefit categories to its calculations specifically to justify the Tellico Project. The largest claimed benefits were attributed to flatwater recreation. The calculations were highly questionable. Despite the presence of nearly two dozen other reservoirs within a fifty-mile radius, TVA assumed that Tellico reservoir would generate as many visits per mile of shoreline as other TVA reservoirs, and would not displace any of those visits. Furthermore, TVA ignored recreation costs, such as the loss of trout fishing in the lower Little Tennessee.[47]

TVA also claimed as benefits the expected increase in land values near the reservoir, reasoning that the Project should get credit for the economic boom it was meant to spark. The uncertainties surrounding future economic development left plenty of room for rosy projections. TVA assumed that no economic progress would occur without Tellico Dam. Competition with other areas for industrial development and costs attributable to the loss of existing economic activity were simply ignored. TVA did not worry about whether shorelands development benefits duplicated those already claimed as recreation or navigation benefits. Nor did it adjust its expectations in light of the disappointing rate of industrialization at a recently-completed dam nearby on the Clinch River.

Reliance on increasing land values to justify the project led to expansion of its footprint. To maximize the benefit of land appreciation, TVA planned to acquire more than twice the area the reservoir would inundate.[48] About 350 homes were ultimately condemned. Entire farms were taken even if only a few acres would end up under water.[49]

By late 1964, TVA had managed to gerrymander a benefit-cost ratio sufficiently high to justify taking the Tellico Project to the Bureau of the Budget,[50] which included it in the President's 1965 funding request. Funding was delayed a year by a Congressman who managed to get the money transferred to a different TVA project in his district, but was finally approved in late 1966.

Construction began in March 1967. The concrete portion of the dam was quickly completed, but there was much more to do before the river could be impounded. Roads had to be moved, bridges rebuilt, the canal

---

47. Walter L. Creese, *TVA's Public Planning: The Vision, the Reality* 127 (1990).

48. The Sixth Circuit upheld the condemnation of land beyond the reservoir pool in U.S. ex rel. Tennessee Valley Authority v. Two Tracts of Land Containing a Total of 146.4 Acres, More or Less in Loudon County, Tennessee, 532 F.2d 1083 (6th Cir. 1976).

49. Charles Seabrook, *Tellico: A Feud Resurfaces*, Atlanta Journal–Constitution, Oct. 19, 2003, at A1.

50. Now called the Office of Management and Budget.

constructed, and an earthen part of the dam erected. Costs quickly exceeded TVA's estimates. TVA had told appropriators that the Project would cost $43 million. By the middle of 1968, the expected cost had swollen to $67 million and was still climbing.

TVA was used to unquestioning local support of its projects, but did not get that for Tellico. Local constituencies were divided. The Tennessee Wildlife Resources Commission opposed the project because of its impacts on river fishing. The Governor's office changed position as it changed occupants, while the congressional delegation consistently favored the project.[51] Some local residents, believing TVA's promises of economic prosperity, favored the dam. Others, who stood to lose their farms or worried about impacts on the community, opposed it.[52]

Even before passage of the ESA, the Tellico Project ran into legal trouble. The National Environmental Policy Act[53] (NEPA) took effect on January 1, 1970. In July of that year, the head of the Council on Environmental Quality asked TVA whether it intended to file an environmental impact statement (EIS) for the Tellico Project. TVA replied that no EIS was required because construction had begun before NEPA's enactment. Local project opponents teamed with the fledgling Environmental Defense Fund to challenge that claim. On Jan. 11, 1972, Judge Robert Taylor of the Eastern District of Tennessee enjoined the project until an acceptable EIS was produced.[54] The Sixth Circuit affirmed.[55] At the time the injunction issued, TVA had spent about $29 million on the project, most of that on roads and land acquisition.[56] Although the injunction halted construction, TVA continued to acquire land for the Project.[57]

TVA filed its final EIS on February 10, 1973. Despite the objections of environmentalists, the courts upheld that EIS as adequate.[58] Judge Taylor dissolved the injunction on October 25, 1973.

B. The Fish

Tennessee, a state marked by unusual geologic and geographic diversity, has a rich freshwater fauna. Nearly 300 species of fish are

---

51. Department of the Interior, Endangered Species Committee, Transcript of Meeting 24 (Jan. 23, 1979).

52. Wheeler & McDonald, *supra* note 8, at 66–68.

53. 42 U.S.C. §§ 4321–4370f (2000).

54. Environmental Defense Fund v. TVA, 339 F. Supp. 806 (E.D. Tenn. 1972).

55. Environmental Defense Fund v. TVA, 468 F.2d 1164 (6th Cir. 1972).

56. *Id.* at 1170.

57. Wheeler & McDonald, *supra* note 8, at 145.

58. Environmental Defense Fund v. TVA, 371 F. Supp. 1004 (E.D. Tenn. 1973), *aff'd* 492 F.2d 466 (6th Cir. 1974).

native to the state, close to one-third of the species found in North America.[59] Of those, some 200 occur in the Tennessee River drainage.[60]

A new one turned up in the Tellico Project area just before the NEPA injunction was dissolved. In August 1973, David Etnier, a University of Tennessee ichthyologist, was snorkeling in the lower reaches of the Little Tennessee when he captured a small fish he had never seen before.[61] Etnier reportedly crowed to a bystander that he had found "the fish that will stop the Tellico Dam."[62] The fish turned out to be a new species, which Etnier dubbed the snail darter (*Percina tanasi*).[63] It was not a legal obstacle to the dam at the time of its discovery, but that changed a few months later with enactment of the ESA.

The snail darter is a small fish, growing to no more than about 3.5 inches.[64] It is intricately patterned in browns, greens, yellow and white to provide camouflage against the gravel substrates it prefers.

Despite their small size, darters are "fish with pizzazz,"[65] a diverse group of brightly colored fish that dart around the bottoms of streams, catching prey and avoiding predators. North America has 173 recognized species of darters,[66] forty in the genus *Percina* along with the snail darter.[67] Twenty of those occur in Tennessee.[68] The snail darter is distinguished from its relatives primarily by its food preference, which is responsible for its common name. Most darters feed on aquatic insects,[69]

---

59. John Fleischman, *Counting Darters*, Audubon, July–Aug. 1996, at 84, 86.

60. David A. Etnier & Wayne C. Starnes, *The Fishes of Tennessee* 18 (1993).

61. Zygmunt J.B. Plater, *The Snail Darter, the Tellico Dam, and Sustainable Democracy—Lessons for the Next President from a Classic Environmental Law Controversy* (2000), *at* http://www.law.mercer.edu/elaw/zygplater.html (last visited June 29, 2004); William Bruce Wheeler & Michael J. McDonald, *TVA and the Tellico Dam 1936–1979: A Bureaucratic Crisis in Post–Industrial America* 156–57 (1986); U.S. Fish & Wildlife Service, *Snail Darter Recovery Plan* 6 (1983).

62. William Bruce Wheeler & McDonald, *TVA and the Tellico Dam 1936–1979: A Bureaucratic Crisis in Post–Industrial America* 157 (1986).

63. David A. Etnier, *Percina (Imostoma) tanasi, a New Percid Fish from the Little Tennessee River, Tennessee*, 88 Proceedings of the Biological Society of Washington 469 (1976).

64. U.S. Fish and Wildlife Service, Endangered and Threatened Wildlife and Plants: Final Rule Reclassifying the Snail Darter (*Percina tanasi*) from an Endangered Species to a Threatened Species and Rescinding Critical Habitat Designation, 49 Fed. Reg. 27510 (1984).

65. John Fleischman, *Counting Darters*, Audubon, July–Aug. 1996, at 84.

66. Lawrence M. Page, *Etheostomatinae, in Percid Fishes: Systematics, Ecology and Exploitation* 225 (John F. Craig, ed., 2000).

67. *Id.* at 226.

68. Etnier & Starnes, *supra* note 60, at 565–94.

69. Page, *supra* note 66, at 228.

but the snail darter is partial to small river snails and limpets.[70] Its unusually large mouth accommodates this dietary specialization.[71] The snail darter is also distinctive in its behavior; unlike many darters it congregates in groups and is not territorial.[72]

The snail darter requires both relatively shallow gravel shoals with moderate or swift currents and deeper slackwater pools. The adults feed and spawn in the gravel shoals, which harbor the snails they eat.[73] The larvae drift downstream to deeper pools, where they develop into juveniles, which then return upstream to the shoals.[74] Snail darters live no longer than four years,[75] so interruption of spawning can quickly eliminate a population. The snail darter was probably once widely distributed in the upper Tennessee River and its tributaries,[76] but would have been eliminated from much of the system by construction of the mainstem dams.

TVA was on notice well before the litigation began that the project area might harbor endangered fish species. The NEPA litigation had produced the uncontested finding that "The free-flowing river is the likely habitat of one or more of seven rare or endangered fish species."[77] Etnier made no secret of his discovery of the snail darter, and by December 1973 TVA had agreed to fund a snail darter transplant study by one of his students.[78]

In the fall of 1974, Hiram (Hank) Hill a second-year law student at the University of Tennessee, brought the snail darter to the attention of Zygmunt Plater, a young law professor. During a suspension from law school, Hill had hung out with David Etnier's graduate students, who told him about the discovery of a fish that apparently existed nowhere other than in the middle of the planned Tellico Reservoir. Hill asked Plater if the potential effect of the fish on completion of the dam under the new Endangered Species Act would make a suitable topic for an

70. Etnier & Starnes, *supra* note 60, at 588.

71. *Id.*

72. U.S. Fish & Wildlife Service, Snail Darter Recovery Plan 14 (1983).

73. U.S. Fish and Wildlife Service, Proposed Endangered Status for the Snail Darter, 40 Fed. Reg. 25,597 (June 17, 1975).

74. Virginia Tech., Fish and Wildlife Information Exchange, Snail Darter Species Account (1996), *at* http://fwie.fw.vt.edu/WWW/esis/lists/e254004.htm (last visited July 14, 2004).

75. U.S. Fish and Wildlife Service, Division of Endangered Species, Species Accounts: Snail Darter (Percina (Imostoma) tanasi), *at* http://endangered.fws.gov/i/e/sae15.html (last modified Nov. 1992).

76. U.S. Fish & Wildlife Service, Snail Darter Recovery Plan 8 (1983).

77. Environmental Defense Fund v. TVA, 339 F. Supp. 806, 808 (E.D. Tenn. 1972).

78. Hill v. TVA, 419 F. Supp. 753, 758 (E.D. Tenn. 1976).

environmental law paper.[79] As Hill dug into the new Act and its legislative history, he convinced both himself and Plater that the ESA would not permit closure of the dam.

What should they do with that conclusion? They realized that TVA would have advantages not only in litigation but in the political arena as well. The law seemed straightforward enough, but their resources were severely limited. They would have to raise money by selling T-shirts and wildlife prints,[80] and learn to do their own public relations work. By contrast, TVA had abundant resources for both litigation and public relations.[81] The tiny fish would invite ridicule. They knew they would be accused of misusing the ESA to block a dam they opposed for other reasons. Litigation over the snail darter might even threaten the political future of the ESA.

But no other legal weapons were available.[82] NEPA had provided delay, but could offer no more. Tellico Reservoir would inundate historic sites, but the National Historic Preservation Act[83] lacked substantive bite. There was no legal forum in which to argue that Tellico Dam was simply a bad idea, a TVA fantasy whose real-world benefits would not come close to justifying its economic, social, and environmental costs. Theoretically opponents of the dam could make that case to Congress, but in reality the legislative process was a nearly impenetrable pork-barrel "iron triangle"[84] not likely to respond.

So, led by Plater and Hill, dam opponents gritted their teeth and decided to push the ESA angle for all it was worth. The first step was to get the snail darter on the protected list. David Etnier sent a packet of information to the Fish and Wildlife Service, which had the responsibility to list any species that was endangered or threatened. Just as it is today, FWS was reluctant to jump into a heated controversy. But the ESA provided a mechanism for interested parties to prod FWS into action: section 4 required that FWS undertake a status review if it was presented with a petition providing substantial evidence that listing might be warranted.[85] With the help of Etnier and his students, Plater

---

79. Zygmunt J.B. Plater, *Law and the Fourth Estate: Endangered Nature, the Press, and the Dicey Game of Democratic Governance*, 32 Envtl. L. 1, 11–12 (2002).

80. Plater, *supra* note 40, at 756–57 n. 29.

81. Professor Plater reports that TVA's legal division had a budget of $2.5 million in 1976, and that the agency's Information Offices had a staff of 64 and a budget of about $1.75 million. *Id.* at 769, n. 78, 79.

82. *Id.* at 769–70.

83. 16 U.S.C. § 470–470x–6 (2000).

84. *See* Daniel McCool, Command of the Waters: Iron Triangles, Federal Water Development and Indian Water 5 (1994).

85. Pub. L. 93–205, 4(c)(2), presently codified as amended at 16 U.S.C. § 1533(b)(3).

drafted a petition explaining that the snail darter was known only from this one location and would be destroyed by completion of the Tellico Project.

FWS received the petition on January 20, 1975.[86] On March 7, it commenced a status review.[87] It proposed to list the fish as an endangered species on June 17,[88] and finalized the listing on October 9.[89] The lower Little Tennessee River was designated as critical habitat on April 1, 1976.[90] The sequence was unusually rapid, especially in light of the controversy over the dam. Even so, listing took time. While the petition was pending, TVA sped up construction, to the point that work went on 24 hours a day.[91] TVA biologists were sent to transplant snail darters from the Little Tennessee to the Hiwassee River and to scour nearby waters for the little fish.

TVA did not back off when the listing was finalized. It continued building at a frenetic pace, arguing first that the listing was not legally effective until thirty days after Federal Register publication[92] and later that in any case it need not comply with the ESA until ordered to do so by a court.[93] When FWS demanded that TVA consult about the impacts of the Tellico Project on the fish, TVA agreed to meet but refused to discuss any alternatives other than dam completion.

As a practical matter, FWS could not use the courts to enforce the ESA against TVA. Like most federal agencies, FWS must convince the Department of Justice to litigate its claims.[94] The Department is understandably reluctant to sue one federal agency on behalf of another. It has done so a number of times, but there are political and sometimes even constitutional hurdles to overcome.[95] The circumstances under which a

---

86. U.S. Fish and Wildlife Service, Amendment Listing the Snail Darter as an Endangered Species, 40 Fed. Reg. 47505 (Oct. 9, 1975).

87. U.S. Fish and Wildlife Service, Joseph P. Congleton, et al. Endangered Species Petition, 40 Fed. Reg. 11618 (March 12, 1975).

88. U.S. Fish and Wildlife Service, Proposed Endangered Status for the Snail Darter, 40 Fed. Reg. 25597 (June 17, 1975).

89. U.S. Fish and Wildlife Service, Amendment Listing the Snail Darter as an Endangered Species, 40 Fed. Reg. 47505 (Oct. 9, 1975).

90. U.S. Fish and Wildlife Service, Snail Darter, 41 Fed. Reg. 13926 (April 1, 1976).

91. Charles Mohr, *Some Little Fish and a Mighty Law at Risk*, N.Y. Times, April 23, 1978, at sec. 4, p. 20; Plater, *supra* note 40, at 768.

92. Plater, *supra* note 40, at 768.

93. *Id.* at 769.

94. 28 U.S.C. §§ 515, 516 (2000).

95. *See* Michael Herz, *United States v. United States: When Can the Federal Government Sue Itself?* 32 Wm. & Mary L. Rev. 893 (1991).

regulatory agency can sue TVA remain in doubt today.[96] Tellico was not an attractive test case. FWS had not yet tried to enforce the controversial provisions of the ESA requiring consultation and prohibiting take. It was not likely to do so for the first time against another federal agency on behalf of an inconspicuous fish. But the ESA allowed Plater and his band of dam opponents to step into the void and they did so, filing a citizen's suit against TVA on February 18, 1976.[97]

Throughout the listing proceedings and the ensuing litigation, events also moved forward on the political track. TVA successfully sought additional appropriations for the Tellico Project after the snail darter problem became apparent. Appropriations for TVA are not directly earmarked for specific projects. They appear as lump sums in the final bills. But those bills are preceded by hearings before an appropriations subcommittee at which specific projects are discussed. Those projects are listed in the legislative reports that accompany the final bills. Beginning in 1975, the TVA appropriations hearings included testimony about the snail darter and its status. TVA testified that it would do its best to protect the darter, but that in any case the Project should be completed.[98] Both House and Senate Appropriations Committees repeatedly agreed.[99] The substantive committees with jurisdiction over the ESA played no role in these appropriations decisions.

III. Prior Proceedings

The plaintiffs accused TVA of violating ESA section 7, because the project would jeopardize the continued existence of the species, and section 9, because it would take snail darters. They concentrated on the section 7 claim, which they felt would be easier to prove.

The district court's findings of fact could hardly have been more favorable to the plaintiffs on the status of the fish. The reservoir behind

---

96. See Tennessee Valley Authority v. U.S. Environmental Protection Agency, 278 F.3d 1184, 1191–98 (11th Cir. 2002), opinion withdrawn in part by Tennessee Valley Authority v. Whitman, 336 F.3d 1236 (11th Cir. 2003).

97. Hill v. Tennessee Valley Authority, 419 F. Supp. 753, 756 (E.D. Tenn. 1976).

98. Public Works for Water and Power Development and Energy Research Appropriation Bill: Hearing Before the Subcomm. of the House Committee on Appropriations, 94th Cong., 467 (1975); Public Works for Water and Power Development and Energy Research Appropriation Bill, Hearing Before the Subcomm. of the House Committee on Appropriations, 94th Cong., 260–62 (1976).

99. In 1975, the House Committee directed in its report "that the project . . . should be completed as promptly as possible." H.R. Rep. 94–319 at 76 (1975). The Senate Committee wrote in 1976: "The Committee does not view the Endangered Species Act as prohibiting the completion of the Tellico project at its advanced stage and directs that this project be completed as promptly as possible in the public interest." S. Rep. 94–960 at 96 (1976). In 1977, the House Committee "strongly recommend[ed] that [the Tellico Project] not be stopped because of a misuse of the [ESA]." H.R. Rep. 95–379 at 103 (1977).

Tellico Dam would inundate the snail darter's designated critical habitat, making it unsuitable for adult fish, spawning, and egg development. Although TVA claimed to have found 50 or 60 snail darters below the dam, that hardly compared to the 10,000 or more above it. TVA had searched the upper reaches of the Little Tennessee, as well as some 60 or 70 other waterways in the region, without finding snail darters. It had transplanted several hundred fish to the Hiwassee River, but Dr. Etnier testified that there was little chance they would reproduce there. The district court concluded that "it is highly probable that closure of the Tellico Dam and the consequent impoundment of the river behind it will jeopardize the continued existence of the snail darter."[100]

Notwithstanding its factual findings, the district court refused to enjoin completion of the Tellico Project. Judge Taylor noted that the project had first been authorized in 1966, well before passage of the ESA. It was about 80% complete. More than $78 million had been committed, and Taylor agreed with TVA that over $50 million would be irretrievably lost if the project was halted.[101] Congress had appropriated money for the Project after the snail darter was discovered, and the President had signed the most recent appropriation bill after the darter was listed as endangered.[102]

Under the circumstances, Judge Taylor concluded that Congress could not have intended that the ESA halt the Tellico Project. "At some point in time," he wrote, "a federal project becomes so near completion and so incapable of modification that a court of equity should not apply a statute enacted long after inception of the project to produce an unreasonable result."[103] He was not troubled by the fact that TVA had worked feverishly, with full knowledge of the potential and then impending listing of the snail darter, to bring the Project to its current stage of completion.[104]

Judge Taylor conceded that striking the balance between endangered species and federal projects was "a legislative and not a judicial function."[105] He was convinced, however, that by continuing to fund the project Congress had struck that balance in favor of TVA. If he was wrong, he noted, "it is not too late for Congress to refuse to appropriate the funds to complete the project."[106]

---

100. Hill v. Tennessee Valley Authority, 419 F. Supp. 753, 757 (E.D. Tenn. 1976).

101. *Id.* at 759.

102. *Id.* at 758.

103. *Id.* at 760.

104. Zygmunt J.B. Plater, *Environmental Law in the Political Ecosystem—Coping with the Reality of Politics*, 19 Pace Envtl. L. Rev. 423, 444 (2002).

105. Hill v. TVA, 419 F. Supp. 753, 763 (E.D. Tenn. 1976).

106. *Id.* at 763 n.12

Plaintiffs appealed. The Sixth Circuit accepted the district court's findings of fact but took a sharply different view of the legal effect of the ESA. It concluded unequivocally that "TVA's Tellico project operations violate" section 7,[107] because the only known substantial population of snail darters would be drastically reduced, if not extirpated, by dam closure. Writing for the panel, Judge Celebrezze refused to read into the Act an exemption for projects already underway because to do so would undermine the ESA's ability to achieve its goals:

> Current project status cannot be translated into a workable standard of judicial review. Whether a dam is 50% or 90% completed is irrelevant in calculating the social and scientific costs attributable to the disappearance of a unique form of life. Courts are ill-equipped to calculate how many dollars must be invested before the value of a dam exceeds that of the endangered species.... Conscientious enforcement of the Act requires that it be taken to its logical extreme.[108]

The Sixth Circuit also rejected TVA's contention that Congressional appropriations implicitly exempted the Tellico Project from the ESA. The ESA was clear, and TVA's actions were plainly inconsistent with its terms. Allowing the Tellico Project to continue based on statements made by appropriations subcommittees would give those subcommittees unwarranted legislative authority.[109]

Having found that completion of the Tellico Project would violate the ESA and that Congress had not exempted the Project, the Sixth Circuit concluded that the district court had no discretion to deny an injunction. Congress could exempt the project from the ESA, but it would have to do so explicitly. The Sixth Circuit decision put the burden of galvanizing legislative action on TVA rather than on dam opponents.[110]

TVA still refused to give up, continuing construction work until the district court formally issued an injunction, and then seeking review by the Supreme Court. Although TVA has independent litigating authority, it obtained the support of the Office of the Solicitor General for its petition for certiorari.[111] The Solicitor General's views tend to command

---

107. Hill v. Tennessee Valley Authority, 549 F.2d 1064, 1069 (6th Cir. 1977).

108. *Id.* at 1071.

109. *Id.* at 1073.

110. *Id.* at 1075. Judge Wade McCree concurred separately but endorsed the key points of the majority opinion. *Id.* at 1074.

111. The agency's independent litigation authority was clarified in Cooper v. TVA, 723 F.2d 1560, 1565 (Fed. Cir. 1983). Whether TVA had the authority to seek Supreme Court review in its own right is unclear. Neal Devins, *Unitariness and Independence: Solicitor General Control Over Independent Agency Litigation*, 82 Cal. L. Rev. 255, 275 and

special respect from the Court, in large part because of the office's reputation for careful legal analysis separated from political considerations. Although in this case there was no circuit split and the legal issues did not appear difficult, the Solicitor General often supports independent agency certiorari requests, thereby forestalling demands by those agencies for expanded litigating authority.[112]

The Tellico dispute caused a rift within the Carter administration. Attorney General Griffin Bell argued for completion of the dam. Secretary of the Interior Cecil Andrus took the opposite view. The President himself tried unsuccessfully to change Bell's position, and then to broker a compromise between TVA and Interior.[113] In his memoirs, Bell justified his strong stance as necessary to preserve the treasured political independence of the Solicitor General's office.[114] Bell did agree, however, that the Department of Interior could present its views in the brief to the Supreme Court.

IV. The Supreme Court Decision

The Supreme Court's view of the Tellico case was largely in place before it granted certiorari.[115] The case was first discussed in the initial conference of the Justices at the outset of the term. Usually the Court decides whether to take up a case during that first discussion, but decision on this one was put off pending further consideration.

The delay was not caused by uncertainty about whether to grant certiorari. There were more than the four votes required for that. The issue was whether the Court would invite briefs and hear oral argument.

---

n. 104 (1994). In this case, it sought and received the solicitor General's support, see Transcript, Rex E. Lee, Conference on the Office of Solicitor General of the United States, 2003 B.Y.U. L.R. 1, 27 (remarks of Judge Daniel Friedman) (". . . I found myself the acting solicitor general in that case because Judge McCree had been a member of the panel of the Sixth Circuit that had decided the case. Then he came in as solicitor general and obviously could not participate in the case . . . And the TVA had authority to represent itself in the Supreme Court, but it preferred to have the solicitor general represent it. So, the case began with the petition stage, and we filed a petition for certiorari on behalf of the TVA").

   112. *Id.* at 288.

   113. Wheeler & Michael J. McDonald, *TVA and the Tellico Dam 1936–1979: A Bureaucratic Crisis in Post–Industrial America* 205 (1986).

   114. Griffin B. Bell & Ronald J. Ostrow, *Taking Care of the Law* 43 (1982). Bell recounts being "in a slow burn" because President Carter sought a change of position in the absence of any intervening change in the law or the facts, which could "undermine the respect traditionally accorded the Department [of Justice] and the Office of the Solicitor General by the justices on the Court."

   115. This discussion of events in the Supreme Court prior to the grant of certiorari is based on the Blackmun papers on file at the Library of Congress. All the draft opinions and memoranda mentioned can be found in Justice Blackmun's papers, as can all of the direct quotations.

There appeared to be five votes for summary reversal,[116] but by convention the Court would not take that drastic step without a sixth vote.[117] So the justices postponed the decision, and launched a flurry of drafts, counter-drafts, and memoranda.

The majority favoring reversal could not agree on a legal theory. Then–Justice William Rehnquist circulated a proposed opinion stating that, even assuming section 7 applied to the Tellico Project, the trial court had discretion to deny an injunction. Justice Lewis Powell agreed with the result, but not the reasoning. He circulated a draft arguing that section 7 simply did not apply. Chief Justice Warren Burger was strongly in the pro-reversal camp, but offered a third rationale. He suggested in a memorandum that "the Snail Darter Act" (as he called the ESA) had been amended by subsequent appropriations acts to exempt the Tellico Project. In a handwritten note to Justice Blackmun, headed "Re Snail Darters v. Elec. Power," Burger attributed this argument to Justice Byron White.

Justice Potter Stewart responded with a draft dissent describing section 7's requirements as mandatory, and noting that the parties did not dispute that closure of the dam would cause extinction of the fish. Under the circumstances, he wrote, both TVA and the courts lacked the power to balance the value of the dam against that of the snail darter. "That balance has already been struck by Congress." Justice Thurgood Marshall signed on to Stewart's dissent.

Justice John Paul Stevens also jumped into the fray, circulating a strongly worded dissent. He noted that the government did not seek summary action, and had not raised the argument relied on by Justice Rehnquist. His draft minced no words:

> Perhaps it is somewhat odd for Congress to place such a high value on the preservation of the snail darter. But it is even more odd for this Court to place a higher value on the investment in the Tellico Dam and Reservoir Project than on the proper allocation of decisional responsibility in the structure of our Government. For this Court to place its stamp of approval on proposed executive actions that will admittedly violate a federal statute is . . . lawless.

Justice Brennan did not sign on to any of the drafts, but he promised to write separately criticizing the decision if the case was not set for full briefing and oral argument.[118]

---

116. A note sent later from Justice Powell to Justice Blackmun indicates that Powell, Blackmun, White, Rehnquist and Chief Justice Burger voted for summary reversal.

117. H. W. Perry, Jr., *Deciding to Decide: Agenda Setting in the United States Supreme Court* 100 (1991).

118. Summary reversal by *per curiam* opinion, as five justices were prepared to do in this case, is "the most controversial form of summary disposition" within the Court itself.

The justices arguing for reversal could not swallow the apparent lack of common sense in stopping a water project more than 10 years and many millions of dollars after it was approved. A careful look at the Tellico Project would have revealed that in fact there was little common sense in continuing it,[119] but the justices don't appear to have looked beyond the documents submitted by the parties. Even the justices who opposed summary reversal did not question the value of the dam. They worried about the effect of the legal precedent the case would set, but not about extinction of the snail darter.

Ultimately, six votes could not be assembled for summary reversal. Still, a majority of the justices clearly favored reversal when, on November 14, 1977, the Court granted TVA's petition for a writ of certiorari.[120] The case was set for briefing and oral argument.

The brief for the United States, written by the Solicitor General's Office on behalf of TVA, argued first that the ESA did not apply to the Tellico Project. It asked the Court to interpret section 7 as applying only to the initial decision to authorize, fund or carry out an action, while there remained reasonable alternatives consistent with commitments already made. The U.S. did not limit that argument to projects predating passage of the ESA; it argued that any project begun before the listing of a species that later turned out to be in conflict with the project should be immune from ESA requirements. In case that argument did not fly, the U.S. had a fallback position: even if section 7 generally applied to projects that were already underway, continued appropriations for Tellico had implicitly exempted this specific project from the ESA. The brief did not argue that federal courts could deny injunctive relief if they found a violation of the ESA. Because of the compromise struck between Attorney General Bell and Interior Secretary Andrus, the brief closed with an unusual appendix. Entitled "Views of the Secretary of the Interior,"[121] it argued, directly contradicting the main brief, that section

Robert L. Stern, *Supreme Court Practice: for Practice in the Supreme Court of the United States* 5.12(c) (8th ed. 2002). Justice Marshall has explained that such opinions put the Court at "great risk of rendering erroneous or ill-advised decisions that may confuse the lower courts." Harris v. Rivera, 454 U.S. 339, 349 (1981) (Marshall, J., dissenting). The *TVA v. Hill* saga certainly supports Marshall's concern.

119. It would not have been difficult to look deeper. By this point, a draft of the GAO's devastating critique of TVA's inflated benefit-cost figures had been widely circulated and its conclusions reported in the press. The "cert. pool" memo drafted by a law clerk drew attention to the report, mentioning a Washington Post story discussing it. The final report was published October 14, before the Court granted certiorari. *GAO Report, supra* note 44.

120. TVA v. Hill, 434 U.S. 954 (1977).

121. Brief for Petitioner at 1a TVA v. Hill, 437 U.S. 153 (1978) (No. 76–1701). President Carter himself had authorized this appendix, and Attorney General Bell had

7 applied to the Tellico Project and that continued appropriations could not be interpreted as exempting the Project.

Attorney General Bell argued the case on behalf of TVA. Solicitor General Wade McCree had been on the Sixth Circuit panel before stepping down from the bench to accept his current position, and therefore could not appear as an advocate. Bell was an experienced attorney and former federal appellate judge. Understanding that striking facts can carry more weight than legal analysis even at the highest reaches of judicial decisionmaking, he focused on the common sense angle. After mentioning that there were nearly 90 kinds of darter in Tennessee, and more than 10 in the Little Tennessee River, Bell held up a small jar containing a dead snail darter.[122] He declined to argue openly that some species were entitled under the ESA to more protection than others, but no one could have missed the point that this particular species shouldn't stand in the way of an expensive (and presumably important) dam.

Under questioning, the shaky legal underpinnings of TVA's argument became apparent. Bell conceded that, although much work had been done, the dam was not finished. Completing it, he agreed, would be "an action,"[123] would modify designated critical habitat,[124] and according to the Secretary of Interior would cause the extinction of the snail darter.[125] Even the common sense argument suffered a bit. Bell admitted that, even as the oral argument was heard, Congress was considering an exemption for the Tellico project. Judicial intervention might not be necessary.

Professor Plater, arguing for the plaintiffs, also faced tough questions. The justices wanted to know whether a completed dam would have to be removed if snail darters were found behind it. Plater danced around that hypothetical, asserting that such a situation could not occur because any species truly threatened by the dam would necessarily disappear once the dam was complete.[126] He did insist, though, that the courts would have to enjoin completion of a project even if it was at the point where nothing remained but to close the gates when the conflict with a listed species was discovered.[127] When asked whether the snail

---

reluctantly acquiesced. Brian C. Kalt, *Wade H. McCree, Jr., and the Office of Solicitor General, 1977–1981*, 1998 Detroit C. L. Mich. St. L. Rev. 703, 723.

122. Transcript of Oral Argument at 6, TVA v. Hill, 437 U.S. 153 (1978) (No. 76–1701).

123. *Id.*at 21.

124. *Id.* at 22.

125. *Id.* at 25.

126. *Id.* at 38.

127. *Id.* at 53.

darter was good for anything, Plater did not point out the legal irrelevance of the question, but tried to turn the Court's attention to the more
obvious (albeit also legally irrelevant) values of the wild river the darter
needed to survive.[128]

In conference following oral argument, most of the justices stuck to
their earlier views. Brennan, Stewart, Marshall, and Stevens voted to
affirm, but none of them endorsed the ESA. Marshall commented that
"Congress can be a jackass." He and Stevens opined that Congress
would surely amend the ESA following the Court's decision. Rehnquist,
Powell and Blackmun voted to reverse. Burger did not announce his
vote, but it was clear that he favored reversal. Justice Byron White,
reportedly an early proponent of summary reversal, said he needed more
time. That left the Court apparently evenly divided. A few days later,
White sent a cryptic note to his colleagues reading simply: "My vote is to
affirm in this case." Chief Justice Burger then reversed his field and also
voted to affirm, making the vote 6 to 3 for affirmance. Burger assigned
himself the opinion.

The decision was issued on June 15, 1978. Despite his initial desire
to reverse, Burger wrote an opinion famous for its strong interpretation
of the ESA. Closing the gates of Tellico Dam would be a federal action,
and the Secretary of Interior had determined that closure would eradi-
cate the species. The Court was not empowered to balance the value of
the snail darter against the loss of millions of dollars through abandon-
ment of the partially complete project because the "plain intent of
Congress in enacting this statute was to halt and reverse the trend
toward species extinction, whatever the cost."[129]

Burger emphatically rejected the argument he had once endorsed,
that appropriations for the Tellico Project amounted to an implied
exemption from the terms of the ESA. Not only had Congress never
explicitly exempted the Project, none of the appropriations bills so much
as mentioned the Tellico Project in their text. Legislators voting on these
measures were

> entitled to operate under the assumption that the funds will be
> devoted to purposes which are lawful and not for any purpose
> forbidden. Without such an assurance, every appropriations measure
> would be pregnant with prospects of altering substantive legislation,
> repealing by implication any prior statute which might prohibit the
> expenditure.[130]

---

128. *Id.* at 43–45.

129. *Id.* at 184.

130. *Id.* at 190.

Finally, having found a violation of section 7 that would cause the extinction of a listed species, Burger held that the Court had no discretion to deny injunctive relief.

> Congress has spoken in the plainest of words, making it abundantly clear that the balance has been struck in favor of affording endangered species the highest of priorities.... Our individual appraisal of the wisdom or unwisdom of a particular course consciously selected by the Congress is to be put aside in the process of interpreting a statute. Once the meaning of an enactment is discerned and its constitutionality determined, the judicial process comes to an end. We do not sit as a committee of review, nor are we vested with the power of veto.[131]

Burger may have been trying to goad Congress into action. His memo assigning himself the case had noted that he planned to "serve notice on Congress that it should take care of its own 'chestnuts.' " He went out of his way to point out in a footnote exactly how trivial this species was, noting how many darter species occurred in the Tennessee system, how often new ones were discovered, and how hard it was to tell the species apart.[132]

Justice Powell, joined by Justice Blackmun, dissented, reiterating his view that the ESA must be interpreted in a way "that accords with some modicum of common sense and the public weal."[133] Powell pointed out that the prospects for future conflict were "breathtaking," because hundreds of thousands of species worldwide might qualify for protection.[134] He expressed confidence that Congress would amend the Act to save other federal projects from the fate of the Tellico Dam.[135] Rehnquist dissented separately. He continued to insist that even if closure of the dam would violate section 7, the district court had discretion to deny an injunction.[136]

V. The Immediate Fallout: First Round Goes to the Dam

Reaction to the Court's decision was immediate and sharply negative. Surprisingly TVA, which had fought so hard for so long for the Project, did not object. It had a new chairman, S. David Freeman, who was more interested in repairing the agency's environmental image than in pushing through the Tellico Project. Under Freeman's direction, TVA

---

131. *Id.* at 194–95.

132. *Id.* at 159, n.7.

133. *Id.* at 195.

134. *Id.* at 204, n.13.

135. *Id.* at 210.

136. *Id.* at 213.

cooperated with Interior on a study of alternatives to dam completion, including river-based development.[137] Public reaction was another matter. Major newspapers condemned the ESA's rigidity. The Wall Street Journal, for example, editorialized: "[T]he Endangered Species Act is pretty silly. . . . [it tries] to outlaw evolution itself."[138] Apparently the Journal believed that any species unable to adapt overnight to a change from river to reservoir had no business surviving.

Congress was poised to act quickly. The House and Senate committees with jurisdiction over the ESA had already been galvanized into oversight hearings by the Sixth Circuit decision.[139] A variety of proposals were floated, ranging from a specific exemption for Tellico to general authorization for action agencies to decide if their projects were too important to be stopped by endangered species. Minority leader Howard Baker (R–Tenn.), a co-sponsor of the 1973 ESA, favored the Tellico Project but initially opposed a specific exemption from the ESA. Baker and John Culver (D–Iowa), chair of the Senate subcommittee on Resource Protection, crafted a bill creating a new administrative exemption process. With the support of environmentalists who saw it as a compromise that would minimize damage to the Act, this bill became law on November 10, 1978.[140]

The new exemption process was highly constrained, a pressure-relief valve to be activated only when an explosion was imminent. It empowered an Endangered Species Committee consisting of the Secretaries of Agriculture, the Army, and Interior; the Administrators of the EPA and the National Oceanic and Atmospheric Administration; the Chairman of the Council of Economic Advisors; and a representative of each affected state (dividing one vote among them), to consider exemption applications.[141] Before an exemption application could even reach the Committee, a review board would have to find that the applicant had consulted in good faith, made a reasonable effort to identify and consider alternatives, and refrained from making any irreversible commitment of resources.[142] If so, the review board would hold a formal adjudicatory hearing, and make a recommendation to the Committee. In order to

---

137. Tennessee Valley Authority & U.S. Department of Interior, Alternatives for Completing the Tellico Project (Draft) (Aug. 10, 1978).

138. *Scopes Prosecution Vindicated*, Wall St. J., June 16, 1978, at 16.

139. Constance Holden, *Endangered Species: Review of Law Triggered by Tellico Impasse*, 196 Science 1426 (1977).

140. Endangered Species Act Amendments of 1978, Pub. L. No. 95–632, 92 Stat. 3751 (codified as amended at 16 U.S.C. §§ 1531–1544 (2000)).

141. *Id.* at 3 (codified as amended at 16 U.S.C. § 1536(e) (2000)).

142. Endangered Species Act Amendments of 1978, Pub. L. No. 95–632, 3, 92 Stat. 3751. The initial review is now conducted by the Secretary of the Interior. 16 U.S.C. § 1536(g)(3) (2000).

grant an exemption, at least five members of the Committee would have to agree that: 1) there was no reasonable and prudent alternative to the project; 2) the benefits of the project clearly outweighed the benefits of any alternative consistent with conservation of the species[143] and the project was in the public interest; and 3) the project was of regional or national significance. The Committee's membership was chosen to represent a diversity of viewpoints, expertise, and experience;[144] some members would be expected to be sympathetic to development, while others would tend to favor the listed species.

The 1978 amendments required that the Committee immediately consider exemptions for the Tellico Project and the Grayrocks Dam in Wyoming,[145] which had been enjoined because it would jeopardize whooping cranes downstream in the Platte River. The Committee, informally dubbed "the God Squad" because of its power of life and death over listed species, convened for the first time on January 23, 1979. The staff report exposed TVA's original cost-benefit calculations as a sham.[146] Charles Schulze, Chairman of the President's Council of Economic Advisors, summed up the Committee's conclusion: "The interesting phenomenon is that here is a project that is 95 percent complete, and if one takes just the cost of finishing it against the benefits and does it properly, it doesn't pay, which says something about the original design."[147] The committee voted unanimously against exemption. Interior Secretary Andrus reportedly said, "Frankly, I hate to see the snail darter get the credit for stopping a project that was ill-conceived and uneconomic in the first place."[148]

But the story was still not over. Although TVA was no longer actively pushing the Tellico Project, Senator Baker refused to give up. He tried but failed to dissolve the God Squad, and to openly exempt the Tellico Project from the ESA.[149] Eventually, in what may have been the original anti-environmental appropriations rider, Baker orchestrated attachment of a clause directing TVA to complete the Tellico Dam "notwithstanding the provisions of [the ESA] or any other law" to the

---

143. The Committee was specifically directed *not* to weigh the benefits of the project against the value of the species. H.R. Conf. Rep. No. 95–1804, at 20 (1978), *reprinted in* 1978 U.S.C.C.A.N. 9484, 9488.

144. H.R. Rep. No. 95–632, at 15 (1978), *reprinted in* 1978 U.S.C.C.A.N. 9453, 9465.

145. Endangered Species Act Amendments of 1978, Pub. L. No. 95–632, 5, 92 Stat. 3751, 3761.

146. *Id.* at 4.

147. Dept. of the Interior, Endangered Species Comm., Transcript of Meeting at 26 (Jan. 23, 1979).

148. *The Senator, the Darter and the Dam*, N.Y. Times, May 8, 1979, at A22.

149. Jared des Rosiers, *The Exemption Process Under the Endangered Species Act: How the "God Squad" Works and Why*, 66 Notre Dame L. Rev. 825, 848 (1991).

Energy and Water Development Appropriation Act for fiscal year 1980.[150] There was no debate on the rider in the House; almost no one even knew what it said.[151] The bill, with the Tellico rider attached, squeaked through the Senate. The majority leader endorsed it as a way to protect traditional legislative logrolling.[152]

President Carter, against the urging of his Interior Secretary and the Chair of the Council on Environmental Quality, signed the appropriation bill "with regret."[153] National environmental groups criticized Carter for caving in on Tellico,[154] but his decision should not have come as a surprise. Carter was concerned that a veto could undermine his other legislative priorities, including the treaty he was negotiating to transfer control of the Panama Canal to Panama.[155] The President was also told that a veto might precipitate amendments gutting the ESA.[156] That threat was real; funding had already been temporarily cut off, leaving Interior without resources to enforce the law.[157]

Once Congress had mandated completion of the dam, TVA wasted no time. Twelve hours after the appropriation bill became law, the bulldozers resumed work. The Cherokee tribe brought a First Amendment challenge, which was rejected.[158] That fall the last residents of the reservoir area were forcibly removed. The gates of the dam were closed on November 29, 1979.[159]

To everyone's surprise, the snail darter did not go extinct. As anticipated, it was extirpated from the Little Tennessee River. Contrary to Dr. Etnier's expectations, though, TVA's transplant program produced a reproducing population in the Hiwassee River. Furthermore,

---

150. Energy and Water Development Appropriation Act, Pub. L. No. 96–69, Title IV, 93 Stat. 437, 449 (1979). For examples of subsequent appropriations riders, see Sandra Beth Zellmer, *Sacrificing Legislative Integrity at the Altar of Appropriations Riders: A Constitutional Crisis*, 21 Harv. Envtl. L. Rev. 457 (1997); Sidney A. Shapiro, *The Information Quality Act and Environmental Protection: The Perils of Reform by Appropriations Rider*, 28 Wm. & Mary Envtl. L. & Pol'y Rev. 339 (2004).

151. Ward Sinclair, *Lawmakers Cutting Legal Corners to Save Tellico Dam*, Wash. Post, July 17, 1979, at A2.

152. Zygmunt J.B. Plater, *supra* note 104, at 466.

153. *Tellico Dam Gets Go–Ahead*, Endangered Species Tech. Bull., Oct. 1979, at 1, 3.

154. Luther J. Carter, *Carter's Tellico Decision Offends Environmentalists*, 206 Science 202 (1979).

155. Wheeler & McDonald, *supra* note 8, at 213; Reisner, *supra* note 17, at 340–41.

156. Luther J. Carter, *Carter's Tellico Decision Offends Environmentalists*, 206 Science 202 (1979).

157. *Stalking the Law*, Time, Oct. 16, 1978, at 84.

158. Sequoyah v. Tennessee Valley Authority, 480 F. Supp. 608 (E.D. Tenn. 1979), *aff'd* 620 F.2d 1159 (6th Cir. 1980).

159. Wheeler & McDonald, *supra* note 8, at ix.

although TVA's earlier search for snail darters elsewhere in the region had come up empty,[160] additional populations were later found in the lower reaches of several tributaries of the Tennessee.[161] These populations were small relative to that destroyed by the Tellico Dam.[162] Nonetheless, in 1984 the snail darter was downlisted to threatened.[163] Interest in the fish waned quickly once the controversy was over. At the time of downlisting, FWS acknowledged that it had no plans for ongoing monitoring.[164] It seems to have given no thought to the snail darter in the twenty years since then.

In 1982, TVA sold more than 11,000 acres at a handsome profit to the Tellico Reservoir Development Agency for industrial, commercial, and residential development.[165] TRDA, which like TVA found itself unable to attract much industry, later sold nearly 5,000 of those acres to a developer for construction of a resort community.[166] Today there is some industry at Tellico, employing over 3,000 people,[167] but making no use of water transportation.[168] There are also several up-scale residential developments, featuring golf courses, marinas, and luxury homes. The reservoir is not a recreational gem. It is in poor to fair ecological condition,[169] and Tellico anglers are advised not to eat catfish because of

---

160.   U.S. Fish & Wildlife Service, Snail Darter Recovery Plan 12 (1983).

161.   Etnier & Starnes, *supra* note 60, at 589; U.S. Fish & Wildlife Service, Final Rule Reclassifying the Snail Darter (*Percina tanasi*) From an Endangered Species to a Threatened Species and Rescinding Critical Habitat Designation, 49 Fed. Reg. 27510 (July 5, 1984).

162.   U.S. Fish & Wildlife Service, Division of Endangered Species, Species Accounts, Snail Darter (Percina (Imostoma) tanasi), *at* http://endangered.fws.gov/i/e/sae15.html (last modified Nov. 1992).

163.   U.S. Fish & Wildlife Service, Final Rule Reclassifying the Snail Darter (Percina tanasi) From an Endangered Species to a Threatened Species and Rescinding Critical Habitat Designation, 49 Fed. Reg. 27510 (July 5, 1984).

164.   Id. at 27511.

165.   TVA, *Tellico Reservoir Land Management Plan* 8 (2000); *TVA Gives Up Tellico Land Scheme*, Engineering News, Dec. 2, 1985, at 5.

166.   Worth   Wilkerson,   *Tellico   Village: Its   Origins*   (2002),   *at* http://www.tvpoa.org/AboutPOA/tellico_villageörigins.htm (last visited July 1, 2004); Joe W. McCaleb, *Stewardship of Public Lands and Cultural Resources in the Tennessee Valley—A Critique of the Tennessee Valley Authority's "New Deal,"* 1 Res Communes 2, 9 (1998–99).

167.   Tellico Reservoir Development Agency, *Tellico West Industrial Properties, Available Industrial Sites* (2002), *at* http://www.tellico.com/sites/Tellico_Prospect.pdf (last visited July 8, 2004).

168.   There is no barge traffic on Tellico Reservoir. Email communication from M. Ted Nelson, Manager of River Operations–Navigation, TVA, July 1, 2004 (on file with author).

169.   TVA, *Tellico Reservoir, Ecological Health Rating, at* http://www.tva.gov/environment/ecohealth/tellico.htm (last visited July 12, 2004).

possible PCB contamination.[170]

VI. The Lasting Effect of TVA v. Hill: The Statute Wins (or Rather Doesn't Lose) the War

The Supreme Court came close to gutting the ESA, and potentially other environmental laws as well, in *TVA v. Hill*. The Court's decision amounted to a ringing endorsement of the Act's power which continues to reverberate, but subsequent events in the legislature and executive branch agencies have held that power in check.

Allowing implied amendment through appropriations bills, as Burger and reportedly White had initially wanted to do, would have been the worst possible outcome for environmental protection. It is difficult enough for legislators to notice explicit exemptions or amendments of substantive law in appropriations bills, which often run to hundreds of dense pages, or to oppose them when the only choice presented is an up or down vote on the overall spending bill. But in this case, the only mention of either the Tellico Project or the ESA was found in appropriation committee reports and hearing transcripts. Even these discussions, for those who happened to find them, were cryptic. They did not directly say the project should be exempted, but instead combined the hope that transplants would succeed with the suggestion that the ESA should not stop the project. If that kind of statement were enough to amend the law, no statute would ever be safe from sly amendment by crafty appropriators. *TVA v. Hill* forces Congress to speak clearly, and in the legislation itself, if it wishes to exempt a particular project from a general law.

The second aspect of *TVA v. Hill* with continuing general importance is its establishment of an outer boundary on the discretion of federal courts to deny injunctive relief for statutory violations. In general, the Supreme Court has been reluctant to find that statutes implicitly restrict the traditional discretion of the courts to decide whether an injunction is appropriate. A few years after *TVA v. Hill*, the Court affirmed the lower courts' balancing of the equities to deny an injunction in *Weinberger v. Romero–Barcelo*,[171] where the Navy had failed to obtain a permit required by the Clean Water Act for weapons training exercises that resulted in the discharge of munitions to waters. *Romero-Barcelo* distinguished, and thus left intact, the holding in *TVA v. Hill* that federal courts have no choice but to enjoin substantive violations that threaten to undermine the legislative purpose of the statute. That is an important boundary for environmental protection, since, as *TVA v. Hill* shows, judges often do not understand or sympathize with the goals of

---

170. *Id.*

171. 456 U.S. 305 (1982).

environmental legislation. In the Supreme Court, none of the current justices is a reliable voice for environmental concerns, and several are notably hostile to environmental protection.[172] The justices in the majority in *TVA v. Hill* were motivated by their view of the relative roles of Congress and the courts, not by environmental sensitivity. But the decision ensures that Congress can, when it chooses to do so, protect the environment in ways that judges might think unwise.

Interpreting ESA section 7 as not applying to projects at a certain stage of completion (as Powell wanted to do), could have crippled the ESA even if it did not damage other environmental laws. If FWS and the courts always had to consider how far along a project was before an ESA conflict was discovered, or what alternatives might remain, when deciding whether it must be halted, it would never be clear whether the substantive provisions of the ESA applied. If completion of a dam was not subject to the ESA, agencies would have argued that *a fortiori* operation of existing projects could not be. The sunk costs argument would be even stronger in the case of completed projects, and would be bolstered by the expectations of people who had come to rely on the project. And the Supreme Court would already have established the precedent that not all federal activities were subject to the ESA. Both agencies and courts would have found themselves under heavy pressure to exempt projects of all sorts, and with a substantial rhetorical basis for doing so. Furthermore, action agencies would have had obvious incentives to ignore potential conflicts, or to speed up their work once the risk of a conflict was discovered, in hopes of pushing the project beyond the stage where ESA compliance would not be ordered. Finally, the regulatory agencies would have found it even more politically difficult than it currently is to list controversial species in a timely manner, as every day of delay would increase the probability that a project could escape the substantive bite of section 7. Unquestionably, species that are neither cute nor awe-inspiring would have been in grave trouble under Powell's interpretation.

Instead, *TVA v. Hill* established a broad interpretation of the term "action" in section 7 which persists today. Any discretionary federal involvement, no matter how long ago the project was authorized or how recently the species was listed, requires ESA compliance. That is especially important for water projects because, although the *TVA v. Hill* plaintiffs firmly denied it in oral argument, in fact it turns out that water projects can be in place for a long time before their impacts on the biota become fully apparent. *TVA v. Hill* ensures that action agencies must continue to consult on the operation of dams and irrigation

---

172. *See* Richard J. Lazarus, *Thirty Years of Environmental Protection Law in the Supreme Court*, 19 Pace Envtl. L. Rev. 619 (2002).

projects, and to address the impacts of project operations on listed species.[173] The obligation to consult often reveals that federal activities, including the operation of water projects, can be modified in ways that reduce their impact on listed species.

Perhaps the most lasting aspect of the decision is its rhetoric, rather than its holding. Courts and commentators continue to cite Chief Justice Burger's statements that the ESA "admits of no exception," that Congress has given endangered species "the highest of priorities," and that Congress intended to halt the trend toward extinction "whatever the cost" even though the statute and its implementation are considerably more nuanced than that language suggests. The decision's rhetoric is used by both proponents and opponents of endangered species protection; the former use it to argue for strong judicial adherence to the law's goals, while the latter use it to argue that legislative softening is needed.

Despite the positive outcome of the Supreme Court decision, the saga of *TVA v. Hill* and its aftermath vividly illustrates how difficult it is to implement and enforce laws protecting non-economic environmental resources from exploitation. Notwithstanding the ESA's clear and uncompromising language, the highest court in the land came within one vote of allowing a federal project everyone believed would cause the extinction of a listed species to proceed, and indeed almost reached that result without even hearing argument. Following the decision, Congress introduced an administrative exemption process, and when that process failed to give a green light to the Tellico Project, Congress stepped in to do so.

Since then, Congress has used its unquestioned power to exempt projects from the ESA only a few times, and never as emphatically as it did for Tellico Dam. In 1988, Congress declared that the requirements of section 7 would be deemed satisfied for the first phase of construction of the Mt. Graham observatory in Arizona, provided that construction complied with a specified alternative FWS had offered in a biological opinion.[174] In 2001, it enjoined implementation of reasonable and prudent alternatives called for in a biological opinion on Alaska groundfish fisheries, which affect the listed Steller sea lion.[175] In 2003, it prohibited

---

173. *See, e.g.,* Klamath Water Users Protective Ass'n v. Patterson, 204 F.3d 1206 (9th Cir. 1999); Rio Grande Silvery Minnow v. Keys, 333 F.3d 1109 (10th Cir. 2003), *vacated as moot,* 355 F.3d 1215 (10th Cir. 2004).

174. Arizona–Idaho Conservation Act of 1988, Pub. L. No. 100–696, 602, 102 Stat. 4571, 4597 (1988). There was some evidence that the biological opinion was not valid. *See* Victor M. Sher & Carol Sue Hunting, *Eroding the Landscape, Eroding the Laws: Congressional Exemptions from Judicial Review of Environmental Laws,* 15 Harv. Envtl. L. Rev. 435, 450–51 (1991).

175. Consolidated Appropriations—Fiscal Year 2001, Pub. L. No. 106–554, § 1(a)(4), 114 Stat. 2763 (2001).

the Bureau of Reclamation from reallocating water away from irrigation contractors to protect the endangered Rio Grande silvery minnow,[176] a step litigation had suggested might be required by the ESA.[177]

Exemptions have been even harder to get through the God Squad. At is first meeting, the Committee technically granted an exemption for Grayrocks Dam but imposed conditions that would prevent jeopardy. Since then, the Committee has been convened only once. In 1992, it voted to exempt thirteen of forty-four BLM timber sales in spotted owl habitat. That decision was remanded by the Ninth Circuit because it may have been affected by impermissible ex parte communications between the White House and members of the Committee.[178] A change of administration intervened, and President Clinton withdrew the exemption application.

The small number of congressional and God Squad exemptions does not mean that listed species are always uncompromisingly protected. At every stage of ESA implementation the implementing agencies drag their feet and introduce discretion where the law appears to allow none.[179] Legislators, while not willing to face the political costs of openly weakening the ESA, have tacitly endorsed such behavior.[180] This "slippage"[181] may be inevitable, given the strength of the economic interests at stake and the diffuse benefits of biodiversity protection. It makes the *TVA v. Hill* opinion even more important: only the availability of citizen suits bolstered by the Court's strong interpretation of the ESA has given the law any teeth when conservation conflicts with development.[182] While it remains imperfect and incompletely implemented, the ESA has developed into the strongest substantive legal tool available in the United States for the protection of nature, thanks in large part to the *TVA v. Hill* decision.

---

176. Energy and Water Development and Appropriations Act 2004, Pub. L. No. 108–137, § 208, 117 Stat. 1827, 1849–50 (2003).

177. Rio Grande Silvery Minnow v. Keys, 333 F.3d 1109 (10th Cir. 2003), *vacated as moot*, 355 F.3d 1215 (10th Cir. 2004).

178. Portland Audubon Society v. Endangered Species Committee, 984 F.2d 1534 (9th Cir. 1993).

179. *See, e.g.*, Oliver A. Houck, *The Endangered Species Act and Its Implementation by the U.S. Departments of Interior and Commerce*, 64 U. Colo. L. Rev. 277 (1993).

180. *See, e.g.*, Holly Doremus, *Adaptive Management, The Endangered Species Act, and the Institutional Challenges of "New Age" Environmental Protection*, 41 Washburn L.J. 50, 58 (2001).

181. *See* Daniel A. Farber, *Taking Slippage Seriously: Noncompliance and Creative Compliance in Environmental Law*, 23 Harv. Envtl. L. Rev. 297 (1999).

182. Doremus, *supra* note 180, at 58.

Conclusion

When the gates of Tellico Dam closed, dam opponents from the local and national communities had suffered a stinging defeat in the long-running dispute over the Project. The free-flowing river, family farms, and Cherokee spiritual sites disappeared under a reservoir. Those losses are unlikely to be remedied any time soon. But for the ESA and environmental law generally, the victory in the Supreme Court has proven more important. Had the decision come out the other way, the ESA would have become a mere paper law. Instead, it has substantial, albeit not unlimited, substantive bite. Fortified by the Court's decision in *TVA v. Hill*, the ESA has proven more effective than any other law in forcing society to take account of the impacts of new and continuing actions on the biota. The little fish, while it ultimately did not stop the pointless dam, did reinforce an important statute.

Today, the Tellico Reservoir stands as a monument to agency stubbornness and pork-barrel politics. It has not become the center of an economic revival, or even an important recreational destination. But the opinion in *TVA v. Hill* stands as a different kind of monument, to the power of the rule of law. A majority of the justices, in the end, rose above their individual doubts about the relative importance of the dam and the fish to enforce the law as Congress had written it.*

---

* I gratefully acknowledge the generosity of Professor Zygmunt Plater for sources, insights and drafts of his book on the *Tellico* case; Professors David Etnier and Albert Lin for their comments; and research assistants Emily Fisher and Jason Mov.

5

Thomas O. McGarity

The Story of the *Benzene* Case: Judicially Imposed Regulatory Reform through Risk Assessment

Introduction

During the unforgettable summer of 1968, as the country witnessed the assassination of Robert F. Kennedy in Los Angeles, and a police riot in Chicago, the author of this chapter was gainfully employed as a day laborer at a large petrochemical plant in Groves, Texas, in the middle of what was at that time the largest petrochemical complex in the world. Since it was not at all uncommon for a day laborer to wind up with greasy hands and arms in the course of performing his (there were no female day laborers) duties, laborers were instructed to clean up at a spigot attached to one of the thousands of pipes carrying liquids throughout the plant. This particular pipe was referred to as the "benzene line." Benzene was the solvent of choice for day-to-day cleanup at the plant because it circulated at room temperature, because it was very good at removing grease, and because it was believed to be as safe as water for workers so long as they did not drink any of it. Once it had accomplished its task, the benzene from the spigot flowed through the plant's concrete stormwater drainage system into the adjacent Neches River at a point less than a mile upstream from one of the largest marine estuaries in the country.

Benzene is a colorless liquid that rapidly evaporates under ordinary atmospheric conditions, but remains heavier than air and therefore does not quickly dissipate.[1] It is produced naturally by volcanoes and forest

---

1. Benzene Chemical Backgrounder, *at* http://www.nsc.org/library/chemical/benzene.htm (edit made Oct. 3, 2002); Indus. Union Dep't, AFL–CIO v. American Petroleum Inst., 448 U.S. 607, 615 (1980).

fires, and is present in the blood and other tissues of many plants and animals.[2] Benzene was and is an exceedingly important chemical for the U.S. economy. In addition to cleaning the dirty hands of day laborers, benzene is used to enhance octane levels in gasoline, to make synthetic rubber, detergents and pesticides, and as the basic chemical building block for the exceedingly important class of "aromatic" chemical compounds.[3]

Its use in gasoline means that benzene is a ubiquitous air pollutant in urban areas, but it is also emitted in large quantities by petroleum refineries, coke ovens, and other industrial facilities. In 1998 more than 8.5 million pounds of benzene were released into the environment, the vast majority of which consisted of air emissions.[4] Human exposure to the chemical is greatest among workers who come into contact with and breathe it on a regular basis. Workers at petrochemical plants, service station attendants, workers at coking plants in the steel industry, and workers in the rubber manufacturing industry receive regular exposures to benzene.[5] The Occupational Safety and Health Administration (OSHA) estimated that in the late 1970s, more than 629,000 employees were regularly exposed to benzene in the workplace.[6] Populations near refineries and other industrial facilities that emit benzene are also exposed to high levels of benzene in the ambient air, and virtually all urbanites are exposed to much lower levels of benzene in the air they breathe.

By the mid–1970s, a number of epidemiological studies had appeared in the literature indicating that workplace exposures to benzene caused leukemia in heavily exposed workers at plants like the Groves, Texas refinery.[7] Although toxicologists had known for decades that benzene exposure could cause various blood diseases, the fact that it caused cancer was a matter of particular concern, because most scientists were (and are) of the opinion that there is no level of exposure to a carcinogenic substance that poses zero risk of contracting cancer. Although not every person exposed to small amounts of benzene would contract leukemia, a relatively rare and usually fatal disease, the general scientific consensus was that benzene could cause leukemia in some people even at very low exposure levels. Workers in Texas refineries were blissfully ignorant of this characteristic of benzene in the 1960s, but once

---

2. Benzene Chemical Backgrounder, *at* http://www.nsc.org/library/chemical/benzene.htm (edit made Oct. 3, 2002).

3. *Id.*

4. *Id.*

5. *Indus. Union Dep't, AFL–CIO,* 448 U.S. at 615–16.

6. *Id.* at 615 n.6.

7. *Id.* at 618–20.

their unions became aware of it, they demanded that the government do something to protect their members from benzene's carcinogenic risks.

This chapter will explore how a relatively young agency created by Congress to protect workers from the health risks that chemicals like benzene struggled to implement its protective mandate over the determined resistance of the economically and politically powerful petrochemical industry. It will examine how the Occupational Safety and Health Administration attempted to use a standard-setting proceeding devoted to benzene to advance a broader and, to the affected regulated industries, much more threatening "generic carcinogen policy" over the objection that the law required that agency to balance the costs to employers of health standards for the workplace against the benefits that they would provide to their employees. Finally, it will probe the role of the Supreme Court in a highly contentious policy dispute that had serious implications not just for occupational health, but for all of environmental law.

I. The Historical Setting

Although *Industrial Union Department, AFL–CIO v. American Petroleum Institute*,[8] known universally as the *Benzene* case, involved only occupational exposures to benzene, it came at a critical inflection point in the historical flow of U.S. environmental law, and it had a profound impact on that body of law. The "environmental decade" of the 1970s was coming to an end, and the "energy crisis" of the late 1970s had taken a large toll on the American economy. EPA had become a well-established regulatory agency, and it was struggling to implement an increasing number of ambitious pollution control programs. It had promulgated National Ambient Air Quality Standards for the conventional air pollutants, and the states were (not entirely successfully) struggling to write and enforce state implementation plans to attain the standards by recently extended deadlines. It had also promulgated the first round of technology-based effluent standards for conventional pollutants under the Clean Water Act, and the states were busily incorporating those standards into federally required permits. Genuine improvement was already visible in many airsheds and streams.

None of this came without a price, and the regulated industries were beginning to complain bitterly about the cost of complying with environmental standards. Industry trade associations, like the American Petroleum Institute, argued that unless agencies could demonstrate that the regulations they were promulgating would yield demonstrable benefits that clearly outweighed the costs they were imposing directly on regulat-

---

8. 448 U.S. 607 (1980).

ed industries and indirectly on consumers, they should not be allowed to intrude into otherwise well-functioning markets.[9]

The regulated industries soon recognized that the suggestion that agencies should tolerate some degree of death and environmental devastation so as to avoid imposing economic costs on regulated companies might be deemed self-serving by an increasingly cynical post-Watergate citizenry. They therefore invested substantial resources in creating "think tanks" and supporting academic research aimed at demonstrating "objectively" that society as a whole was better off if the costs imposed by regulatory agencies on industry were not allowed to exceed the benefits of those regulations.[10] Economists in academia and think tanks produced studies purporting to demonstrate that regulation was costing consumers hundreds of billions of dollars a year.[11] Worse, government-imposed costs without compensating benefits were contributing to the spiraling inflation that was engulfing the economy in the late 1970s.[12]

When it came to regulating toxic substances, however, it could not credibly be maintained that regulation was having a substantial impact on the economy. EPA could point to a some modest successes in removing a few notorious pesticides, like DDT, aldrin/dieldrin and heptachlor/chlordane, from the market, but it had failed miserably in implementing the toxics provisions of the Clean Air Act and the Clean Water Act. An initial effort to regulate discharges of nine toxic water pollutants, most of which caused cancer in laboratory animals, became bogged down in interminable hearings that the agency ultimately abandoned, only to be forced by an environmental group lawsuit to resume again.[13] Similar efforts under the Clean Air Act to regulate hazardous air pollutants similarly bogged down to such an extent that EPA was extremely reluctant to add a pollutant to the list of hazardous pollutants. By 1980, standards existed for only four hazardous air pollutants.[14] The

9. Nat'l Econ. Research Assocs., Inc., *The Business Roundtable Air Quality Project: Cost–Effectiveness and Cost–Benefit Analysis of Air Quality Regulation* (1980).

10. James Allen Smith, *The Idea Brokers: Think Tanks and the Rise of the New Policy Elite* 22 (The Free Press 1991); Oliver A. Houck, *With Charity for All*, 93 Yale L.J. 1415 (1984).

11. Murray L. Weidenbaum, *The Future of Business Regulation* 23 tbl.3 (1979); Michael Andrew Scully, *The Alarming Price of Regulation*, Fortune, Dec. 31, 1979, at 78.

12. Allen V. Kneese & Charles L. Schultze, *Pollution, Prices, and Public Policy* 71 (1975); Stephen Breyer, *Analyzing Regulatory Failure: Mismatches, Less Restrictive Alternatives, and Reform*, 92 Harv. L. Rev. 549 (1979).

13. Ridgeway M. Hall, Jr., *The Evolution and Implementation of EPA's Regulatory Program to Control the Discharge of Toxic Pollutants to the Nation's Waters*, 10 Nat. Resources Law. 507 (1977).

14. John E. Bonine & Thomas O. McGarity, *The Law of Environmental Protection* 695 (2d ed. 1992).

regulated industries, however, recognized the potential for future regulations to have a huge economic impact if the regulatory agencies were able to surmount the procedural hurdles that had thus far stymied their efforts to regulate toxics in the environment.

At the time that the Supreme Court took up the *Benzene* case, industrial groups, environmental groups, and regulatory agencies were engaged in two fierce battles over the future of health, safety and environmental regulation. The first was a battle over the roles that scientific information and policy considerations should play in regulating chemicals that were relatively benign at high exposures, but could cause adverse chronic diseases, like cancer, at low exposure levels. It was largely this battle that continued to bog down EPA's efforts to cancel pesticides and to promulgate health-based standards for toxic air and water pollutants. The second battle was over the paradigm that should drive regulatory programs for toxic substances. Observing the potential for battles over the science to delay environmental improvement, environmental groups increasingly preferred technology-based standards as a first line of defense. The regulated industries and their allies in think tanks and academia argued that any regulatory controls had to be justified by a showing that their health and environmental benefits exceeded the costs that they imposed on industry.

II. The Science–Policy Battle

At the dawn of the environmental movement in the early 1970s, it was clear that human activities had soiled the planet. Air pollution had become so bad in some urban areas that driving was impaired and people afflicted with emphysema were forced to leave. Heavily polluted streams caused massive fish kills and rendered many of those fish that survived inedible. Rachael Carson's *Silent Spring* documented the adverse effects of agricultural pesticides on birds and aquatic organisms.[15] Well-known occupational diseases, like black lung disease and asbestosis, were killing and maiming workers in the mining and shipbuilding industries. Although it was often difficult to prove in individual cases that exposure to a particular pollutant caused a particular fish kill or a particular asthma attack, in the aggregate it was clear that ubiquitous conventional pollutants, like sulfur dioxide in the air and biochemical oxygen demand in the water, were causing a great deal of damage to human health and the environment. It could therefore safely be assumed that reducing the quantities of conventional pollutants emitted into the air and water would bring about appreciable improvement.

For toxic chemicals in the environment, matters were much more complicated. Since very little was known about the adverse effects of

---

15. Rachel Carson, *Silent Spring* (1962).

chronic exposures to small levels of chemicals, it was difficult for the
government to justify protective action by demonstrating a cause-effect
relationship between exposure to toxic chemicals in the environment and
the incidence of disease. Given the huge gaps in scientific knowledge, the
best that a government agency could do was to show that the chemical at
issue caused cancer in some highly exposed humans or in laboratory
animals and that human beings in large numbers were exposed to the
chemical in small concentrations. Any case for regulatory intervention
built on such a slim factual foundation had to rely heavily upon protective assumptions reflecting precautionary statutory policies. In other
words, when faced with large scientific uncertainties, the agency had to
"err on the side of safety," rather than rely exclusively on established
scientific facts, if it was to regulate at all.

The battle over the science began in earnest in the early 1970s as
OSHA attempted to address the carcinogenic risks that workplace con-
taminants like asbestos and vinyl chloride posed to workers and EPA
attempted to address carcinogenic risks to consumers posed by pesticides
like aldrin/dieldrin and heptachlor/chlordane. Reviewing courts were
initially quite sympathetic to aggressive agency attempts to fill gaps in
the factual evidence resulting from large scientific uncertainties with
protective policies. In upholding OSHA's asbestos standard in 1974, the
Court of Appeals for the District of Columbia Circuit, observed that
"some of the questions involved in the promulgation of these standards
are on the frontiers of scientific knowledge, and consequently as to them
insufficient data is presently available to make a fully informed factual
determination. Decisionmaking must in that circumstance depend to a
greater extent upon policy judgments and less upon purely factual
analysis."[16] In upholding EPA's early decision to cancel the pesticide
DDT, the same court concluded that within the "great mass of often
inconsistent evidence which was developed at the hearing," there was
sufficient evidence to support the rather drastic action, "although it
possibly might support contrary conclusions as well."[17]

Having persuaded at least one court that regulatory agencies should
have a good deal of leeway to employ protective policies in resolving
science-policy disputes at the "frontiers of scientific knowledge," both
EPA and OSHA decided to press the matter in a more formalized way by
reducing the interplay between science and policy to a generic set of
"cancer principles."[18] Although scientific bodies had for years attempted

16. Industrial Union Dep't, AFL–CIO v. Hodgson, 499 F.2d 467, 474 (D.C. Cir. 1974).

17. Environmental Def. Fund, Inc. v. EPA, 489 F.2d 1247, 1252 (D.C. Cir. 1973).

18. The following history of the "cancer principles" and the subsequent development
of generic carcinogen policies in the late 1970s is drawn from Thomas O. McGarity,

to articulate such principles, both EPA and OSHA seized upon a 1970 Report to the Surgeon General by a panel of scientists from government and academia assembled by Dr. Umberto Saffiotti, a scientist at the National Cancer Institute. The report was widely circulated among the federal agencies, and it accompanied Dr. Saffiotti's testimony in two 1971 Senate hearings.

Although framed as a set of scientific principles for "Evaluation of Environmental Carcinogens," the report was equally a statement of prudent regulatory policy. One of the principles stated that "[a]ny substance which is shown conclusively to cause tumors in animals should be considered carcinogenic and therefore a potential cancer hazard to man." Another stated that "[n]o level of exposure to a chemical carcinogen should be considered toxicologically insignificant for man. For carcinogenic agents a 'safe level for man' cannot be established by application of our present knowledge." In what was clearly a departure from science into the realm of policy, still another "principle" stated that "[t]he principle of a zero tolerance for carcinogenic exposures should be retained in all areas of legislation presently covered by it and should be extended to cover other exposures as well."[19]

OSHA relied heavily upon the Saffiotti report in a hearing addressing fourteen chemical carcinogens routinely found in the workplace, and the Third Circuit quoted from the report in upholding all but one minor aspect of the regulations that resulted.[20] EPA attorneys persuaded Dr. Saffiotti to testify in the DDT cancellation hearings, and attorneys in EPA's Office of General Counsel drew on his testimony and the report in hearings on the pesticides aldrin and dieldrin to craft a set of nine cancer principles in their brief to the Administrator. Soon thereafter, the nine cancer principles emerged in the agency's notice of intent to suspend the pesticides heptachlor and chlordane. After EPA suspended those pesticides, the D.C. Circuit rejected the manufacture's contention that the Administrator's reliance on the principles improperly biased him against the industry's position that the principles did not represent a scientific consensus.[21]

The attorneys' attempt to craft nine "cancer principles" attracted a great deal of criticism from the regulated community and from some scientists in EPA's Office of Pesticide Programs. One EPA scientist

OSHA's Generic Carcinogen Policy: Rule Making under Scientific and Legal Uncertainty, in Law and Science in Collaboration 55–104 (J.D. Nyhart & Milton M. Carrow eds., 1983).

19. Chemicals and the Future of Man: Hearings Before the Subcomm. on Executive Reorganization and Government Research of the Senate Comm. on Government Operations, 92d Cong., 1st Sess., 173, 180–81 (1971).

20. Synthetic Organic Chem. Mfrs. Ass'n. v. Brennan, 503 F.2d 1155 (3d Cir. 1974).

21. Environmental Def. Fund, Inc., 548 F.2d at 1006.

requested a National Cancer Institute review of the principles, and a Subcommittee of the National Cancer Advisory Board took up the matter in late 1975. Although the Subcommittee's report did not differ substantially from the Saffiotti principles on questions of science, it was much more restrained on questions of regulatory policy. Concluding that an adjudicatory hearing was probably not the best venue for crafting the agency's approach to regulating carcinogens, EPA's Administrator, Russell Train, created a new internal entity called the Carcinogen Assessment Group (CAG) in the Office of Research and Development, and he assigned representatives from all relevant programs to work with the group to come up with agency-wide guidelines for carcinogenic chemicals.

The product of the CAG's deliberations was a document called "Interim Procedures and Guidelines for Health Risk and Economic Impact Assessments of Suspected Carcinogens."[22] Strongly influenced by EPA's experience in regulating pesticides under a statute mandating risk-benefit balancing and in many ways limited to pesticides, the document prescribed a case-by-case "weight of the evidence" approach to addressing the carcinogenic risks posed by chemical substances. In addition to prescribing a flexible mechanism for classifying chemicals according to the likelihood that they were carcinogenic in humans, the document retained the "principle" that there was no threshold level of exposure to a carcinogen below which the cancer risk disappeared. At the same time, the document stated EPA's intention in the future to use quantitative risk assessment models in balancing the risks of carcinogenic pesticides against their benefits. The guidelines did not speak directly to how EPA should go about setting media quality-based standards in statutory contexts that required standards to protect the public, health, sometimes with a margin of safety, without regard to cost.

While EPA was struggling internally with how to go about addressing carcinogenic chemicals, one of its most aggressive advocates of a more generic approach left the agency. Anson Keller, who had been EPA's Associate General Counsel for Pesticides during the DDT and aldrin/dieldrin hearings, transferred to OSHA in 1975 to become a special assistant to the head of that agency. OSHA read its statute to preclude cost-benefit balancing in setting occupational health standards, and its interpretation had been upheld in three courts of appeal.[23] In

---

22. Interim Procedures and Guidelines for Health Risk and Economic Impact Assessments of Suspected Carcinogens, 41 Fed. Reg. 21402 (EPA May 25, 1976). The current version of the Proposed Guidelines for Carcinogen Risk Assessment, first published at 61 Fed. Reg. 17960–01 (EPA Apr. 23, 1996), is available at http://www.epa.gov/ord/Web-Pubs/carcinogen/alternate.html.

23. Society of Plastics Indus., Inc. v. OSHA, 509 F.2d 1301 (2d Cir.), *cert. denied sub nom.* Firestone Plastics Co. v. U.S. Dep't of Labor, 421 U.S. 992 (1975); Synthetic Organic Chem. Mfrs. Ass'n, 503 F.2d at 1155; *Indus. Union Dep't, AFL–CIO*, 499 F.2d at 474.

addition, OSHA was under a great deal of pressure from labor unions and their allies in Congress to speed up what had become a very cumbersome process for promulgating occupational health standards. Keller decided that the best way to approach carcinogen regulation was through a massive rulemaking exercise in which OSHA would promulgate a "Generic Carcinogen Policy" that, unlike the case-by-case "weight-of-the-evidence" approach that EPA was adopting for pesticides, would rely on protective regulatory policies to prescribe in advance the regulatory consequences of various findings concerning the carcinogenicity of workplace chemicals.

By the fall of 1976, Keller had prepared a draft Generic Carcinogen Policy, and OSHA published it in the *Federal Register* for public comment.[24] The preamble to the proposed regulation adopted in one form or another all of the Saffiotti principles. The regulation itself would have established a presumption that regulatory action would be taken with respect to any workplace chemical that increased the incidence of benign or malignant tumors in humans, two mammalian test species, a single mammalian test species in more than one experiment, or a single mammalian species if supported by additional short-term tests. An employer could, however, rebut the presumption of regulatory action by making one of five specified showings. If the presumption was not rebutted, OSHA would automatically issue an emergency temporary standard (in accordance with a model standard prescribed in the regulation) and issue a notice of proposed rulemaking for a permanent standard within the next sixty days (again in accordance with a model template). The model permanent standard required employers to reduce employee exposure to the lowest feasible level, unless they could feasibly substitute less hazardous substances. In the hearing that followed, the issues would be strictly limited to five topics specified in the generic regulation. One issue that would not be relevant in individual hearings was whether worker exposure to the substance at issue was below a threshold exposure for carcinogenic risk.

According to Keller, the immediate aim of the Generic Carcinogen Policy was to refocus attention in individual hearings from the recurring scientific questions to the important non-generic question of feasibility. An additional goal, however, was to precipitate a full-scale public shootout in which all interested parties could participate in the science-policy battle. Keller was disappointed with Administrator Train's decision to assign responsibility for resolving the science-policy debate to a small group of unaccountable agency employees deliberating behind closed doors. He preferred a wide-open public debate on how the government

---

24. Identification, Classification and Regulation of Toxic Substances Posing a Potential Occupational Carcinogenic Risk, 42 Fed. Reg. 54147 (OSHA Oct. 4, 1977).

should regulate carcinogens, and he hoped that the policy that he had crafted would serve as a model for other federal agencies, including EPA.

The OSHA Generic Carcinogen Policy differed dramatically from EPA's Interim Guidelines for pesticides. The former adopted a generic "one-size-fits-all" approach in the interest of speeding up what had become an extremely cumbersome regulatory process. The latter adopted a "case-by-case" approach that allowed the agency to consider all of the unique aspects of a particular chemical but could conceivably bog the agency down in endless arguments over whether the scientific information was sufficiently robust to support each "scientific" finding necessary to support regulatory action. The former approach did not require the agency to engage in a risk assessment modeling exercise in which policy judgments could become hidden in the assumptions underlying the model; the latter approach required exactly that.

The regulated industry greatly favored the EPA pesticides approach. Unlike OSHA's Generic Carcinogen Policy, EPA's approach did not foreclose industry's ability to wage the science-policy battle every time the agency acted. It provided a much better opportunity to challenge the factual basis for EPA conclusions both in discussions with agency staff prior to any decision and in the hearings and judicial proceedings that followed. Rather than being forced to rebut presumptions, the industry could insist that the agency come up with sufficient information to justify taking action against each particular chemical. In addition to allowing the industry to press the agency to adopt risk assessment models that generally yielded results to the industry's liking, regulation based upon quantitative risk assessment permitted the industry to argue that some quantitative risks were so tiny as to be de minimis. The Generic Carcinogen Policy, by contrast, did not admit the possibility of de minimis exposures; once a substance fell into the category of regulated chemicals, the only relevant issue was the feasibility of attaining the level that OSHA prescribed.

Environmental groups and labor unions much preferred OSHA's generic approach. Past experience with notoriously lengthy and expensive pesticide and health standards hearings suggested that free ranging science-policy debate in individual hearings was a prescription for regulatory paralysis. Dealing with toxic chemicals on a case-by-case basis had achieved three significant pesticide cancellations and suspensions, four major OSHA standards, four hazardous air pollutant standards and no standards for toxic water pollutants in seven years. Given the fact that hundreds of potentially hazardous pesticides and air and water pollutants remained to be addressed, this was not a record that inspired a great deal of confidence in the case-by-case approach. Furthermore, the environmental groups and unions did not trust quantitative risk assessment, pointing out that the uncertainties in the exercise were so huge that honest assessments could yield results that varied over several orders of magnitude for a single set of data about a single chemical. They worried about the likelihood that critical policy choices would be buried out of public view in the assumptions risk assessment "experts" employed in crafting the models.

Worried that the quantitative risk assessment tool would migrate from pesticides to other EPA programs, the Environmental Defense Fund petitioned EPA to establish a policy governing the classification and regulation of carcinogenic air pollutants under the Clean Air Act that was modeled on the OSHA Generic Carcinogen Policy. Industry groups were equally worried about the threat that Keller's generic carcinogen policy posed to its interests across several regulatory programs. One industry spokesperson opined that "[i]t's the domino theory. . . . If OSHA goes, so go EPA, CPSC and others."[25]

In the meantime, the voters in 1976 elected one the most consumer-oriented presidents in decades. In early 1977, President Carter appointed David Hawkins, one of the founders of the Natural Resources Defense Council, to be the head of air programs at EPA, and Hawkins quickly agreed to consider the EDF petition. Eula Bingham, an industrial hygienist with strong ties to labor unions, became the head of OSHA, and she soon let it be known that she was a strong supporter of Keller's efforts. It began to look very much like the proponents of the generic carcinogen approach would carry the day when the Consumer Product Safety Commission (CPSC) announced that it was immediately implementing an "Interim Policy and Procedure for Classifying, Evaluating and Regulating Carcinogens in Consumer Products" that was modeled on OSHA's generic approach.

The regulated industries viewed these developments with a great deal of alarm. Several affected industries launched a cooperative effort to kill the OSHA Generic Carcinogen Policy, and they created the American Industrial Health Council to provide a scientific veneer for its all-out attack on OSHA's approach. Potential regulatees spent millions of dollars preparing and presenting testimony at OSHA's lengthy hearings. Ultimately, as we shall see, the industry prevailed, but not in the public shootout that Keller had initiated. It defeated OSHA's Generic Carcinogen Policy in the quiet corridors of the United States Supreme Court.

On January 22, 1980, more than two years after it was proposed, OSHA published its final Generic Carcinogen Policy. The encyclopedic preamble to the regulation analyzed the massive hearing record in great detail and quoted at length from the testimony of the dozens of witnesses who had testified. On the important scientific and policy issues,

---

25. Ann Pelham, *Government Tackles Tricky Question of How to Regulate Carcinogens*, 36 Cong. Q. Wkly. Rep. 957, 961 (1978).

the final regulation did not depart from the proposal. It did, however, eliminate the automatic trigger that would have forced OSHA to act within sixty days. Instead, the agency created a priority-setting mechanism that allowed the agency to select from among ten chemicals at any given time. The presumption-rebuttal process and the model regulations, however, remained intact. The only relevant issue for a substance determined to be a carcinogen was the determination of the lowest feasible exposure level.[26]

III. *The Battle Over the Paradigm*

Because it was clear at the outset of the environmental movement that pollution was causing a great deal of damage, it was also clear that much environmental improvement could be accomplished if the sources of that pollution were simply required to reduce pollutants in their emissions and effluent. Since technologies were often easily available to control pollution, the problem was the lack of any incentive on the part of the polluters to install those technologies. Thus, the first round of pollution regulation in the early 1970s consisted primarily of state and federal attempts to identify polluters and force them to install readily available pollution control technologies for conventional pollutants. This was the explicitly articulated goal of the Clean Water Act Amendments of 1972.[27] Although the articulated goal of the Clean Air Act Amendments of 1970 was to achieve a level of ambient air quality sufficient to protect public health and the environment, in practice the early state implementation plans attempted to attain the air quality standards primarily by imposing technology-based controls on identifiable sources of conventional air pollutants.

Before long, however, the companies subject to these requirements began to complain about "technology for technology's sake." It made no sense, they maintained, to force companies to install expensive pollution control technologies unless it could be shown that the benefits to society of the reduced pollution exceeded the cost to industry of the controls. Any money expended complying with regulations beyond the value of the benefits derived therefrom was an waste of resources. In the inflationary times of the late 1970s, some economists argued that any unnecessary costs imposed on industry would only drive up prices, and this in turn would contribute to the inflationary spiral. Critics blamed federal regulation for a host of maladies ranging from productivity losses to increased unemployment. The solution was to force regulatory agencies like EPA

---

26. Identification, Classification and Regulation of Potential Occupational Carcinogens, 45 Fed. Reg. 5002 (OSHA Jan. 22, 1980) (codified at 29 C.F.R. pt. 1990).

27. Federal Water Pollution Control Act Amendments of 1972, Pub. L. No. 92–500, § 301(b), 86 Stat. 844 (1972) (codified as amended at 33 U.S.C. § 1311(b) (2000)).

and OSHA to subject their regulations to a cost-benefit decision criterion.[28]

Environmental groups and unions believed that forcing agencies to engage in detailed and expensive cost-benefit analyses could only further slow down the process of promulgating much needed protections. They were, in any event, highly skeptical of claims that accurate techniques existed for determining the benefits of health and safety regulations. Echoing their criticisms of risk assessment, they argued that the uncertainties surrounding attempts to regulate chemical carcinogens were so huge that the number of cancers prevented by any particular regulatory intervention could not be determined with any degree of confidence. More importantly, comparing the deaths prevented to the cost of the regulation would require the agency to calculate the dollar value of a cancer prevented, and this was tantamount to putting a dollar value on human life, an exercise that at the time was generally regarded as morally reprehensible.[29]

The debate over whether agencies should adopt the technology-forcing or cost-benefit paradigm was raging in Congress and within the Carter Administration as OSHA was promulgating its Generic Carcinogen Policy and its occupational health standard for benzene. President Carter in early 1978 created a new intergovernmental entity called the Regulatory Analysis Review Group, composed mostly of administration economists, and charged it with reviewing agency regulations with an eye toward reducing the overall cost of federal regulation.[30] The Senate Committee on Governmental Affairs, at the time controlled by the Democratic party, released a lengthy report at the end of a two-year study of federal regulation recommending that Congress enact legislation requiring agencies to calculate the costs and benefits of their major regulations.[31] A comprehensive report prepared for a special Commission of the American Bar Association by Professor Stephen Breyer made similar recommendations.[32] In 1979 alone, more than 150 "regulatory reform" bills were introduced in Congress.[33]

Despite these pressures from within and without the Administration, OSHA steadfastly adhered to its position that it could not adopt the

28. Tom Alexander, *It's Roundup Time for the Runaway Regulators*, Fortune, Dec. 3, 1979, at 126.

29. Timothy B. Clark, *Carter's Assault on The Costs of Regulation*, 10 Nat'l J. 1281 (1978).

30. Timothy B. Clark, *The Year of Regulation*, 11 Nat'l J. 108 (1979).

31. Study on Federal Regulation, S. Doc. No. 95–26 (1977).

32. Comm'n on Law & the Econ., Am. Bar Ass'n, *Federal Regulation: Roads To Reform* (1979).

33. Alexander, *supra* note 28, at 126.

cost-benefit paradigm because Congress had directed it to employ a feasibility-based technology-forcing approach. OSHA only half-heartedly complied with an Executive Order that required agencies to prepare regulatory impact assessment detailing the costs and benefits of major rules, contracting out the job to consulting companies.[34] Eula Bingham, then the chief of OSHA, explained that cost-benefit analysis was "currently not what is required in the Occupational Safety and Health Act. I have the law to uphold. That is my mandate."[35]

EPA also resisted demands that it adopt the cost-benefit paradigm in areas other than pesticides, following what it believed to be the dictates of its statutes. In relaxing the national primary ambient air quality standard for ozone, EPA was extremely careful to base the decision exclusively upon the scientific evidence on the health effects of ozone, and it went to great lengths to exclude cost considerations from its decisionmaking process.[36] The agency expanded its program of promulgating technology-based effluent standards under the Clean Water Act to include toxic pollutants. These exercises were not cost-oblivious, but they made no attempt whatsoever to quantify and monetize environmental benefits. Only with respect to pesticides regulation, where the statute rather clearly called for balancing the risks against the benefits of various pesticide uses, did the agency explicitly adopt the cost-benefit paradigm.

IV. *The Benzene Regulation*

The two escalating struggles over the future of health and environmental regulation merged in the industry's challenge to OSHA's occupational health standard for benzene. Industrial hygienists had known for many years that exposure to benzene at high levels could cause a number of acute and nonmalignant chronic diseases. It was, for example, well known that persistent exposure to benzene at concentrations exceeding 25–40 parts per million (ppm) could interfere with blood synthesis and cause aplastic anemia, a fatal disease.[37] Implementing a specific requirement of the 1970 Occupational Safety and Health Act (OSHAct), OSHA in 1971 had established a "consensus" standard for benzene of 10 ppm. This standard was uncontroversial because it was easily achieved in virtually all workplaces.[38]

---

34. Timothy B. Clark, *It's Still No Bureaucratic Revolution, But Regulatory Reform Has a Foothold*, 11 Nat'l J. 1596 (1979).

35. Donald P. Burke, *OSHA's Bingham Defies Both Policy and Logic*, Chemical Wk., Nov. 8, 1978, at 5.

36. American Petroleum Inst. v. Costle, 665 F.2d 1176 (D.C. Cir. 1981).

37. *Indus. Union Dep't, AFL–CIO*, 448 U.S. at 617.

38. Occupational Safety and Health Standards: Occupational Exposure to Benzene, 43 Fed. Reg. 5918 (Feb. 10, 1978).

Soon after epidemiological studies began to demonstrate that benzene was in fact a carcinogen in human beings, OSHA issued an "emergency temporary" standard for benzene reducing the allowable exposure from 10 ppm to 1 ppm.[39] The petroleum industry immediately appealed to the Fifth Circuit, and that court, without entertaining written or oral arguments, stayed the standard until a hearing could be scheduled.[40] By statute, emergency temporary standards expire six months after issuance.[41] Since the case did not come up on the court's docket during that time, the temporary emergency standard never went into effect, and workers continued to be exposed to higher levels of benzene.

OSHA then issued a notice of proposed rulemaking proposing to adopt a permanent standard of 1 ppm for benzene.[42] In that notice, OSHA requested evidence and argument on whether benzene caused leukemia in workers, but it did not invite comment on whether there was a "threshold" exposure below which worker exposures to benzene would be "safe." Instead, OSHA requested information on what the lowest feasible exposure level would be given existing technology and other economic considerations.[43] OSHA conducted an adjudicatory-type hearing from July 19 through August 10, 1977, at which ninety-five witnesses testified.[44] Grover Wrenn, who had worked closely with Anson Keller in drafting the Generic Carcinogen Policy, testified at the hearings that the agency's approach toward benzene was in fact consistent with the broader carcinogen policy that the agency was simultaneously promulgating in the generic proceeding.[45] After completing the hearings, OSHA promulgated a permanent 1 ppm standard.[46]

OSHA estimated that the cost of complying with the benzene regulation would include $266 million in capital investments, first year operating costs of $187–205 million and recurring annual costs of approximately $34 million.[47] Consistent with its carcinogen policy, OSHA did not attempt to quantify the benefits of the regulation. Justice

---

39. Occupational Exposure to Benzene: Emergency Temporary Standards; Hearing, 42 Fed. Reg. 22515 (May 3, 1977).

40. *Indus. Union Dep't, AFL–CIO*, 448 U.S. at 623.

41. 29 U.S.C. § 655(c)(1) (2000).

42. Occupational Exposure to Benzene: Emergency Temporary Standards; Hearing, 42 Fed. Reg. at 22515.

43. *Indus. Union Dep't, AFL–CIO*, 448 U.S. at 623.

44. American Petroleum Inst. v. OSHA, 581 F.2d 493, 499 (5th Cir. 1978).

45. *Indus. Union Dep't, AFL–CIO*, 448 U.S. at 623–25.

46. 29 C.F.R. § 1910.1028 (1979). The standard also required employers to provide medical examinations for workers exposed to benzene levels above 0.5 ppm.

47. *Indus. Union Dep't, AFL–CIO*, 448 U.S. at 628–29.

Stevens later opined that the rule was "an expensive way of providing
some additional protection for a relatively small number of employees."[48]
The companies that were the target of the rulemaking effort no doubt
agreed with this assessment, but the day laborers at the Groves, Texas
petrochemical complex, whose lives were at stake, might well have
phrased it differently.

V. The Race to the Courthouse

There was, of course, no doubt that OSHA's benzene rule would be
challenged in court. The petroleum and rubber industries were unhappy
with how the agency had resolved both the science-policy and the
paradigm debates. The broad industry coalition that had assembled to
challenge OSHA's Generic Carcinogen Policy also backed the benzene
appeal in the hope that a holding for the petroleum industry would
undermine OSHA's broader generic carcinogen effort. The Industrial
Union of the AFL–CIO was generally happy with the way that OSHA
had resolved the debates in the benzene proceeding, but it believed that
OSHA had not pressed the industry hard enough because even greater
protection was feasible.

It was not at all clear, however, which court of appeals would hear
the challenge. OSHA's refusal to engage in quantitative risk assessment
and employ a cost-benefit decision criterion had previously been upheld
in the Second, Third and D.C. circuits.[49] The Fifth Circuit had never
decided an OSHA case, but it had recently held that the Consumer
Product Safety Act required CPSC to balance costs against benefits, and
the language that the court relied on in that case was almost identical to
the OSHAct's definition of "occupational safety and health standard."[50]

The OSHAct provided that a person adversely affected by a standard
promulgated by OSHA could within sixty days challenge the standard in
the United States court of appeals for the circuit in which the person
resided or had its principal place of business.[51] The petroleum industry
challenged the benzene standard in the Fifth Circuit, and the Industrial
Union Department of the AFL–CIO filed its petition in the D.C. Circuit.[52]
At the time, a federal procedural statute applicable to all agencies

---

48. *Id.* at 628.

49. *See Society of Plastics Indus., Inc.*, 509 F.2d at 1301; *Synthetic Organic Chem.
Mfrs. Ass'n*, 503 F.2d at 1155; *Indus. Union Dep't, AFL–CIO*, 499 F.2d at 474.

50. Aqua Slide 'N' Dive Corp. v. Consumer Product Safety Comm'n, 569 F.2d 831
(5th Cir. 1978).

51. Occupational Safety and Health Act, Pub. L. No. 91–596, § 6, 84 Stat. 1593
(1970) (codified as amended at 29 U.S.C. § 655(f) (2000)).

52. The description below is drawn from Judge Leventhal's opinion in Industrial
Union Dep't, AFL–CIO v. Bingham, 570 F.2d 965 (D.C. Cir. 1977).

provided that in cases in which multiple appeals were properly filed in more than a single court, the court of appeals in which an appeal was "first instituted" would decide the case, unless "[f]or the convenience of the parties in the interest of justice" that court decided to transfer the proceedings "to any other court of appeals."[53] This provision had inspired a number of spectacular "races-to-the-courthouse" over the years as litigants went to great lengths to ensure that their challenges were heard in the forum of their choice.[54]

The curious race-to-the-courthouse in the *Benzene* case began on April 29, 1977, when Assistant Secretary Bingham hosted a meeting with representatives of twelve organizations that had participated in the rulemaking. During the meeting, Bingham ceremoniously signed an emergency temporary standard for benzene and described it to the participants. The meeting ended at about 10:00 am, and the union lodged its appeal in the D.C. Circuit eight minutes later. At 10:30 am, Assistant Secretary Bingham and Labor Secretary Ray Marshall held a press conference at which they announced to the rest of the world that OSHA had just issued the standard. The document itself was filed with the Office of the Federal Register at 10:55 am on the same day, and it was published in the *Federal Register* on May 3, 1977. A week after publication, the American Petroleum Institute filed its petition for review in the Fifth Circuit. After granting an interim stay of the emergency temporary standard, the Fifth Circuit transferred the case to the D.C. Circuit because the first petition had been filed in that court. The petroleum industry then petitioned the D.C. Circuit to transfer the case back to the Fifth Circuit.

The petroleum industry argued in the D.C. Circuit that the Union had jumped the gun in the race because it filed for review before the press conference at which the action was announced to the general public. That being the case, the first valid challenge was the industry's petition in the Fifth Circuit, and the D.C. Circuit was obliged to send the case back to that court.

D.C. Circuit judge Harold Leventhal concluded that Bingham's signing the standard was in fact the starting gun because it was done in the presence of representatives from most of the participants in the rulemaking. The D.C. Circuit therefore had jurisdiction over the petition. Judge Leventhal then proceeded to the question whether the court should "for the convenience of the parties in the interest of justice" transfer the case to the Fifth Circuit. Although the D.C. Circuit was

53. Pub. L. No. 85–791, § 2, 72 Stat. 941 (1958) (codified as amended at 28 U.S.C. § 2112(a) (2000)).

54. *See* Thomas O. McGarity, Multi–Party Forum Shopping for Appellate Review of Administrative Action, 129 U. Pa. L. Rev. 302 (1980).

clearly the most convenient court for all of the parties, Judge Leventhal thought that the "appearance of justice" was not served by keeping the case in the D.C. Circuit. He believed that "[w]hen a court of first filing of a petition for review materializes before even the substance of the agency decision is disclosed to the public at large, the appearance of justice is brought into serious question."[55]

Judge Fahy agreed with Judge Leventhal that the D.C. Circuit was the court of first filing and therefore had jurisdiction to decide whether to keep or transfer the case. He disagreed, however, that the interest of justice required transferring the case to the Fifth Circuit. Given that all of the parties challenging the regulation were present at the meeting at which the Assistant Secretary signed the order being appealed, he thought that it was reasonable for the AFL–CIO to conclude that the signing represented the final agency action. He saw nothing inequitable in deciding the merits in the D.C. Circuit.

Judge Wilkey, the third judge on the panel, disagreed with both Judges Leventhal and Fahy on the jurisdictional question. He believed that the AFL–CIO had in fact jumped the gun when it filed its petition before the general public was made aware of the action. That being the case, the Fifth Circuit had exclusive jurisdiction to decide whether to keep the case or transfer it back to the D.C. Circuit. This conclusion, however, left matters in a very unsatisfactory state of affairs with the two judges who believed that the court had the power to decide whether to transfer disagreeing on that question and one judge sitting on the sidelines because he believed the court lacked the power to decide. To break this odd impasse, Judge Wilkey acceded to the majority holding that the court had jurisdiction and then joined Judge Leventhal in voting to transfer the case to the Fifth Circuit.

It seems highly unlikely, in retrospect, that the Supreme Court would have taken up the *Benzene* case at all if Judge Leventhal had divined "the interest of justice" differently. The D.C. Circuit had already ruled in favor of OSHA and the unions on the critical cost-benefit paradigm question,[56] and it in fact followed that precedent in another case less than a year after transferring the *Benzene* case to the Fifth Circuit.[57] Absent the Fifth Circuit opinion, there would have been no split in the circuits and no particular reason for the Supreme to grant certiorari. Congress later amended the general procedural statute to replace the unseemly race-to-the-courthouse with a random selection process in cases of multiple appeals.[58] But the die had been cast in the

---

55. *Indus. Union Dep't, AFL–CIO*, 570 F.2d at 972.

56. Industrial Union Dep't, AFL–CIO v. Hodgson, 499 F.2d 467 (D.C. Cir. 1974).

57. AFL–CIO v. Marshall, 617 F.2d 636 (D.C. Cir. 1979).

58. Pub. L. No. 100–236, § 1, 101 Stat. 1731 (1988) (codified at 28 U.S.C. § 2112(a) (2000)).

Benzene case, demonstrating once again that weighty matters often turn on how judges resolve apparently trivial procedural issues.

The Fifth Circuit did not disappoint the industry petitioners.[59] The court agreed with their argument that the definition of "occupational safety and health standard" in § 3(8) of the OSHAct to mean standards that are "reasonably necessary" to provide safe or healthful places of employment required OSHA "to (1) attempt to determine the extent to which its standards will benefit workers, and (2) decide whether the projected benefits justify the costs of compliance with the standard."[60] The court rejected OSHA's view that Congress meant for § 3(8) to be read in light of the explicit requirement in § 6(b)(5) that OSHA set the standard as close to "safe" as was "feasible." Relying heavily upon its recent opinion interpreting the Consumer Product Safety Act, the court held that the use of the word "reasonably" in § 3(8) meant that OSHA was required to balance costs against benefits in setting occupational health standards. Since OSHA had admittedly not done that, the court set aside the standard.

VI. The Supreme Court Decision

The Supreme Court granted the Solicitor General's petition for certiorari, and it affirmed the Fifth Circuit holding without reaching the question whether the OSHAct required OSHA to adhere to the cost-benefit balancing paradigm. The Court's internal deliberations did not yield agreement or even a single majority opinion. Chief Justice Burger assigned the case to Justice Stevens after the initial conference after two of the Justices who originally voted to reverse the Fifth Circuit decision indicated that they might vote to affirm under Justice Stevens' theory of the case.[61] After Justice Stevens circulated a lengthy memorandum elaborating upon his theory, Justice Marshall circulated a five-page memorandum rejecting that theory and urging his colleagues to vote to reverse.[62]

Justice Marshall's overture was apparently persuasive, because only Justices Burger and Stewart joined Justice Stevens in his plurality opinion. Justice Burger also wrote his own concurring opinion. Justice Powell joined in most of the Stevens opinion, but he wrote a separate opinion to address the topic of cost-benefit analysis, an issue that the Stevens opinion did not reach. Justice Rehnquist joined the previous four

---

59. *American Petroleum Inst.*, 581 F.2d at 493.

60. *Id.* at 501.

61. Memorandum from Penda Hair, to Mr. Justice Blackmun (Jan. 17, 1980) (on file with author).

62. Memorandum from Thurgood Marshall, to the Conference (May 6, 1980) (on file with author).

justices in voting to set aside the agency action, but he did so on the
wholly separate ground that the OSHAct was an unconstitutional violation of the nondelegation doctrine. The four remaining justices joined in
Justice Marshall's dissenting opinion in which he concluded that OSHA's
analysis conformed to the statute. Although Justice Stevens' opinion
represented the views of only three of the Justices at the time that it was
written, the dissenting justices apparently accepted Justice Stevens'
resolution of the *Benzene* case when Justice Stevens joined them a year
later in holding that the OSHAct did not impose a cost-benefit decision
criterion in OSHA standard-setting.[63]

Justice Stevens was impressed with the "voluminous evidence of the
adverse effects of exposure to benzene at levels of concentration well
above 10 ppm,"[64] but was unconvinced of its relevance to exposures at or
below the current OSHA standard of 10 ppm. Since OSHA had not
seriously attempted to justify its 1 ppm standard by reference to benzene's noncarcinogenic effects on workers, Justice Stevens focused primarily on OSHA's application of its general carcinogen policy to the
leukemogenic effects of benzene, an exercise that clearly troubled him.
He noted that the agency's policy stance made it "irrelevant whether
there was any evidence at all of a leukemia risk at 10 ppm" so long as
"there was no evidence that there was *not* some risk, however small, at
that level."[65] He noted that OSHA had "rejected industry contentions
that certain epidemiological studies indicating no excess risk of leukemia
among workers exposed at levels below 10 ppm" were proof that there
was threshold level of exposure to benzene that would leave them free of
any risk of contracting leukemia.[66] It had also rejected an industry-
prepared quantitative risk assessment indicating that reducing benzene
exposures from 10 ppm to 1 ppm would prevent at most one leukemia
and one other cancer death every six years.[67]

OSHA thought it had good reasons for rejecting the threshold
hypothesis and the industry's attempt to quantify the workplace risks
posed by benzene. The government's brief noted that "a number of
scientists and public health specialists" had concluded that "a suscepti-
ble person may contract cancer from the absorption of even one molecule
of a carcinogen like benzene."[68] Justice Stevens, however, found this to
be largely irrelevant because, in his view, a workplace could be "safe"
and still pose a cancer risk to workers.

---

63.   American Textile Mfrs. Inst., Inc. v. Donovan, 452 U.S. 490 (1981).

64.   *Indus. Union Dep't, AFL–CIO*, 448 U.S. at 631.

65.   *Id.* at 625.

66.   *Id.* at 634.

67.   *Id.* at 635.

68.   *Id.* at 636.

The key to the Stevens plurality's legal analysis was § 3(8) of the OSHAct, which defined an occupational health standard as one that was "reasonably necessary and appropriate to provide safe or healthful employment," and the key to that definition was the word "safe." In Justice Stevens' view, " 'safe' is not the equivalent of 'risk-free.' "[69] He cited no authority for that conclusion other than what he believed to be common parlance:

> There are many activities that we engage in every day—such as driving a car or even breathing city air—that entail some risk of accident or material health impairment; nevertheless, few people would consider these activities "unsafe."[70]

Given this common understanding of the meaning of "safe," Justice Stevens concluded that "a workplace can hardly be considered 'unsafe' unless it threatens the workers with a significant risk of harm."[71] Consequently, prior to promulgating an occupational health standard, OSHA was "required to make a threshold finding that a place of employment is unsafe—in the sense that significant risks are present and can be eliminated or lessened by a change in practices."[72] Since OSHA had not even attempted to make this threshold showing, the standard had to be set aside.[73]

The plurality opinion did not feel compelled to defer to the agency's own interpretation of the word "safe" in § 3(8) because the agency had not attempted to interpret that word. OSHA had taken the position that § 6(b)(5)'s command that occupational health standards be set at the level "which most adequately assures ... that no employee will suffer material impairment of health or functional capacity" trumped the more general reference to "safe or healthful employment" in § 3(8). Justice Stevens disagreed. He noted that § 6(b)(5) "repeatedly uses the term 'standard' without suggesting any exception from, or qualification of, the general definition."[74] Even though § 3(8) was tucked away in the "definitions" section of the Act, "that fact does not drain each definition of substantive content," and Justice Stevens apparently understood the content of the word "safe."[75]

Having read the statute to require a threshold showing of "significant risk," the Court allowed that it was "the Agency's responsibility to

---

69. *Id.* at 642.

70. *Id.*

71. *Id.*

72. *Id.*

73. *Id.* at 653.

74. *Id.* at 642.

75. *Id.* at 640 n.45.

determine, in the first instance, what it considers to be a 'significant' risk."[76] Nevertheless, Justice Stevens offered some unsolicited guidance, no doubt based upon his understanding of risk and significance:

> Some risks are plainly acceptable and others are plainly unacceptable. If, for example, the odds are one in a billion that a person will die from cancer by taking a drink of chlorinated water, the risk clearly could not be considered significant. On the other hand, if the odds are one in a thousand that regular inhalation of gasoline vapors that are 2% benzene will be fatal, a reasonable person might well consider the risk significant and take appropriate steps to decrease or eliminate it.[77]

The plurality opinion noted that OSHA did not have "to calculate the exact probability of harm," nor did it have to support its significant risk finding with "anything approaching scientific certainty."[78] OSHA could even use "conservative assumptions" in assessing workplace health risks "so long as they [were] supported by a body of reputable scientific thought."[79] It did, however, have to support its significant risk conclusion with substantial evidence in the administrative record.

Given the agency's erroneous reading of § 3(8) with respect to the "significant risk" question, the Stevens plurality concluded that it was unnecessary for the plurality to decide whether the Fifth Circuit had correctly interpreted that section to require cost-benefit balancing in setting occupational health standards.[80] Justice Powell, however, disagreed with this assessment, and he wrote a concurring opinion in which he concluded that § 3(8) required "the agency to determine that the economic effects of its standard bear a reasonable relationship to the expected benefits."[81] Chief Justice Burger concurred in the Stevens plurality opinion, but added a brief concurring opinion to caution against judicial usurpation of congressionally delegated agency power and to suggest that OSHA was empowered to ignore *de minimis* risks.[82] Justice Rehnquist wrote separately to express his view that Congress had unconstitutionally delegated to OSHA the power to decide "whether the statistical possibility of future deaths should ever be disregarded in light of the economic costs of preventing those deaths."[83]

---

76. *Id.* at 655.

77. *Id.*

78. *Id.* at 655–56.

79. *Id.* at 656.

80. *Id.* at 640.

81. *Id.* at 667.

82. *Id.* at 662–63.

83. *Id.* at 672.

Justice Marshall filed a dissenting opinion, joined by Justices Brennan, White and Blackmun, in which he argued that the plurality opinion "flagrantly disregard[ed]" the principle that "a court is not permitted to distort a statute's meaning in order to make it conform with the Justices' own views of sound social policy."[84] The plurality's conclusion that § 3(8) required OSHA to make a threshold "significant risk" showing prior to regulating bore "no connection with the acts or intentions of Congress" and was, in the dissent's view, "based only on the plurality's solicitude for the welfare of regulated industries."[85] In addition, the plurality did not demonstrate sufficient appreciation for the difficulty of assessing and managing risks to workers in the context of huge scientific uncertainties. By placing the burden of demonstrating that status quo exposure levels posed a "significant risk" to workers, the plurality had "place[d] the burden of medical uncertainty squarely on the shoulders of the American worker, the intended beneficiary" of the OSHAct.[86]

The dissenters were especially worried that the plurality opinion would be interpreted to require OSHA to base its future "significant risk" findings upon quantitative risk assessment. Justice Marshall noted that "[t]o require a quantitative showing of a 'significant' risk ... would either paralyze the Secretary into inaction or force him to deceive the public by acting on the basis of assumptions that must be considered too speculative to support any realistic assessment of the relevant risk."[87] Ultimately, the dissenters feared that "the Federal Government's efforts to protect American workers from cancer and other crippling diseases may be substantially impaired."[88]

VII. Analysis of the Plurality Opinion

Justice Stevens' plurality opinion went to great lengths to avoid resolving the cost-benefit paradigm debate, but in the process it effectively resolved science-policy debate. The opinion made it very clear that OSHA was not permitted to substitute policy for science to the extent that it had in the Generic Carcinogen Policy. It could not simply jump from the scientific finding that the relevant contaminant caused cancer to the preordained policy conclusion that the best way to address the carcinogenic risk was to substitute another chemical or reduce exposures to the lowest feasible level. Justice Stevens believed that science was capable of more than that. It was capable of providing the basis for an

---

84. *Id.* at 688.
85. *Id.* at 690.
86. *Id.*
87. *Id.* at 716.
88. *Id.* at 688.

assessment of the risks with sufficient rigor to allow a decisionmaker to determine whether status quo exposures caused a "significant risk" of harm to workers. Although the opinion did not explicitly require OSHA to employ existing quantitative risk assessment techniques of the sort that EPA had recently adopted, it strongly implied that quantitative risk assessment offered the agency a safe harbor against future challenges. Policy could perhaps play a role in constructing risk assessment models and in choosing from among the available models, but objective scientific considerations should drive those decisions.

On the other hand, Justice Stevens clearly recognized that policy considerations would play a prominent role in determining which risks were "significant" risks, and it was the agency's "responsibility to determine, in the first instance, what it consider[ed] to be a 'significant' risk."[89] Perhaps because the statute itself did not use the work "significant," however, Justice Stevens felt obliged to provide some guidance on how this policy question should be answered. He suggested that a one-in-a-billion probability of contracting cancer from a drink of chlorinated water is insignificant while a one-in-a-thousand risk of dying from breathing gasoline vapors is significant. Far from providing useful guidance, however, this example demonstrated how poorly Justice Stevens understood the concept of risk.

At the outset, it should be observed that the example spoke only in terms of probabilities and neglected to mention the extent of exposure to the risk-producing activity, one of the most elementary concepts of risk assessment. If we assume that an average person takes only four drinks of chlorinated water per day, then 250 million Americans drink one billion glasses of water per day. On the average, then, one American will contract cancer each day under Justice Steven's "insignificant" risk hypothetical.

Justice Stevens did not specify how long a person would have to be exposed to gasoline vapors to suffer the one-in-a-thousand risk. Obviously, the risk is higher if exposure for one hour yields a one-in-a-thousand risk of cancer than if it takes a lifetime's exposure to yield that risk. Assuming that one would have to be exposed for a year to experience this risk, it would still be necessary to know how many persons are exposed to gasoline vapors to calculate the real risk. Justice Stevens apparently drew his hypothetical from the record of the case, which mentioned benzene risks to gasoline station attendants. At the time there were approximately 200,000 gas stations in the United States. Assuming two attendants per station, perhaps 400,000 workers would be exposed to a one-in-a-thousand risk of cancer under Justice Stevens' hypothetical. This risk would yield approximately 400 cases of cancer per

---

89. *Id.* at 655.

year, a number that is virtually identical to the 365 cases of cancer per year that the one-in-a-billion probability of getting cancer from drinking chlorinated water would yield. Yet Justice Stevens assures us that the former risk is significant, while the latter is insignificant.

The *Benzene* plurality opinion can be viewed as a politic attempt by well-meaning judges to steer an obstreperous agency gently into what they believed to be the mainstream of regulatory thought. The bipartisan "regulatory reform" movement that was enveloping Washington, D.C. in the late 1970s could hardly have escaped the attention of the Justices. History has demonstrated that some regulatory reformers who were eagerly awaiting the election of Ronald Reagan four months after *Benzene* was decided had much more drastic reforms in mind. Sending a not-too-subtle message to OSHA that it would be well advised to follow EPA's lead and adopt more objective quantitative approaches to addressing potential carcinogens was not an especially drastic judicial intervention. Justice Stevens may have thought the Court was saving the agency from itself.

A less intrusive and more protective option was available. A more deferential reading of the statute would have emphasized § 6(b)(5), which directs the Secretary in promulgating a health and safety standard for toxic materials to "set the standard which most adequately assures, to the extent feasible, on the basis of the best available evidence, that no employee will suffer material impairment of health or functional capacity.... " This phrase clearly requires OSHA to establish occupational health standards at a level that ensures that *no* employee will suffer material health impairment. Even the industry's quantitative risk assessment concluded that one employee would suffer leukemia (certainly a material health impairment) every six years if the benzene standard were not lowered to 1 ppm. This being the case, § 6(b)(5) required OSHA to set the standard at the lowest feasible level.

This less intrusive reading would have avoided the embarrassment of a judicially created and incoherently defined concept of "significant risk." OSHA would still have to engage in risk assessment to support a finding that at least one employee would suffer material health impairment at status quo exposures, but it would not be required to engage in highly uncertain and potentially deceptive quantitative risk assessment exercises.

VIII. *The Impact of the Benzene Decision*

A. The Impact on OSHA

The *Benzene* decision effectively resolved the science-policy battle in favor of the proponents of quantitative risk assessment. Although the decision did nothing to improve the quality or quantity of information available on the carcinogenic effects of low-level exposure to chemicals in the environment, it did send a strong signal to OSHA that it would be well-advised to adopt quantitative risk assessment if it expected its standards to be upheld in the future. Although the agency initially attempted to save face by proposing modifications to its Generic Carcinogen Policy at the end of the Carter Administration, the policy was quickly abandoned altogether in the next Administration. Under President Reagan, who had made OSHA a poster child for excessive regulation during the 1980 campaign, OSHA shifted its focus away from large-scale occupational health standards and toward co-operative efforts to help employers reduce workplace injuries due to accidents.[90]

The decision also had a perverse long-term impact on individual rulemakings as industry groups and even OSHA insisted that the agency was powerless to regulate substances that appeared to pose a smaller than one-in-one-thousand cancer risk. For example, when a risk assessment for formaldehyde projected a 1.5 in 10,000 risk of contracting cancer "for the great majority of workers" who were exposed to that substance at levels below the current 3 ppm standard, OSHA declined to act because the risk did not approach the 1 in 1000 risk threshold suggested by the *Benzene* plurality opinion.[91] Even the "minority" of workers exposed to levels near the existing three parts per million exposure limit faced "only a four in 1,000 risk—a level not elevated dramatically above the Supreme Court's benchmark for permanent rulemaking."[92] Quite apart from the agency's questionable portrayal of the risks as point estimates, its refusal to address what in most environmental programs would be viewed as very high risks suggests that the *Benzene* can be used by industry as a brake to slow down an aggressive agency and by a reluctant agency as an excuse to justify regulatory failures.

B. The Impact on EPA

At EPA, the Benzene decision was viewed as a strong endorsement of its position on quantitative risk assessment. As a result, quantitative risk assessment has flourished in all of the programs that that agency administers.[93] The agency has relied especially heavily on risk assessment models in establishing threshold levels for hazardous substance cleanups under the Comprehensive Environmental Response, Compensa-

---

90. *See* Thomas O. McGarity & Sidney A. Shapiro, *Workers at Risk* 61–182 (1993).

91. *Evidence of "Grave Risk" Lacking For Emergency Formaldehyde Rule, DOL Says*, 13 BNA Occupational Safety & Health Rep. 663 (1983).

92. *Id.*

93. *See* Office of the Science Advisor, Environmental Protection Agency, *An Examination of EPA Risk Assessment Principles and Practices* (Staff paper Mar. 2004), *available at* http://www.epa.gov/osa/ratf.htm.

tion and Liability Act (CERCLA). One of the nine specific criteria that must be considered in selecting the final remedy for a site is the "magnitude of residual risk remaining from untreated waste or treatment residuals remaining at the conclusion of the remedial activities," a factor that begs for the application of a quantitative risk assessment model.[94] EPA has not, however, felt constrained by the *Benzene* decision to employ a one-in-one-thousand risk threshold in determining what is "safe" under its statutes. For example, the Tenth Circuit upheld a CERCLA remedy that was based upon a risk assessment predicting that the risk to a child at a hypothetical day care center erected on a remediated waste disposal site would not exceed one-in-one-hundred-thousand.[95]

EPA struggled for a decade after the *Benzene* decision to list and promulgate standards for hazardous air pollutants based upon quantitative risk assessment before becoming utterly stymied by an almost incomprehensible D.C. Circuit opinion that applied the *Benzene* plurality's significant risk concept to the carcinogen vinyl chloride in the context of a statute that required EPA to establish standards sufficient to protect the public health with an ample margin of safety.[96] Congress mercifully intervened in 1990 and amended the statute to require EPA to take a technology-based approach.[97] Once that approach was in place, EPA began to move forward much more expeditiously to promulgate standards reflecting the maximum achievable control technology for hazardous air pollutants, including benzene. The agency now faces the challenge of addressing areas where ambient levels of hazardous air pollutants remain high, despite the implementation of the technology-based standards. Here, the amended statute instructs EPA to use a one-in-one-million risk threshold for carcinogens, a task that cannot easily be accomplished without an exercise in quantitative risk assessment.[98] The 1996 Food Quality Protection Act similarly allows EPA to establish pesticide tolerances for carcinogens at a level that will yield a one-in-one-million risk to the maximally exposed individual, but only if "the lifetime risk of experiencing the nonthreshold effect is appropriately assessed by quantitative risk assessment."[99]

94.   40 C.F.R. § 300.430(e)(9)(iii)(C)(1) (2004).

95.   United States v. Burlington N. R. Co., 200 F.3d 679 (10th Cir. 1999).

96.   Natural Res. Def. Council, Inc. v. EPA, 824 F.2d 1146 (D.C. Cir. 1987).

97.   Clean Air Act Amendments of 1990, Pub. L. No. 101–549, § 112, 104 Stat. 2399 (codified at 42 U.S.C. § 7412(d)(2) (2000)).

98.   *Id.* § 112(f)(2).

99.   Pub. L. No. 104–170, § 408, 110 Stat. 1514 (1996) (codified at 21 U.S.C. § 346a(b)(2)(B) (2000)).

Quantitative risk assessment has also come to play a prominent role in EPA's implementation of the Clean Water Act. With the apparent blessing of environmental groups, EPA for a decade abandoned its statutory obligation to manage the Clean Water Act's media quality-based program for toxic water pollutants. Instead the agency focused almost exclusively on promulgating technology-based standards for toxics under the 1977 Amendments to the Clean Water Act, a project that extended well into the 1990s. Although this effort brought about a great deal of improvement, it did not result in clean rivers and lakes. A renewed effort to write water quality standards for toxics and to establish maximum daily loads for segments that do not attain those standards is underway and may not be completed until after 2010. A large part of the problem remains the difficulty of writing water quality standards, a process that has, in light of the *Benzene* decision, become so dominated by quantitative risk assessment that litigation over water quality standards frequently focuses intensely on the details of these modeling exercises.[100]

There is some reason for skepticism, however, about EPA's wholesale embrace of quantitative risk assessment.[101] Despite some genuine advances, scientific understanding of the way that chemicals cause cancer in human beings remains incomplete. Different risk assessment models still result in vastly different predictions. Even a single risk assessment model can yield wildly uncertain estimates in the typical situation in which long-term human exposures are very difficult to determine. Yet EPA and other risk assessment proponents invariably portray the results of these modeling exercises as point estimates with little or no effort to communicate the sometimes huge uncertainties that accompany these predictions. While point estimates are no doubt comforting, they frequently convey a false sense of confidence that may suggest too strongly that the agency actually knows the magnitude of the risks that it is addressing.

Conclusion

If the *Benzene* case has had a profound impact on the science-policy battle, its impact on the battle over the cost-benefit paradigm has been minimal. Although Justice Powell would have required OSHA to employ a cost-benefit decision criterion, he did not participate in the Court's deliberations when it took up that issue a year later in the *Cotton Dust* case.[102] In that case, the Court held that OSHA was not required to

---

100. *See* Natural Res. Def. Council, Inc. v. EPA, 16 F.3d 1395 (4th Cir. 1993) (considering a challenge to Maryland and Virginia water quality standards for dioxin).

101. *See* Thomas O. McGarity, Sidney Shapiro & David Bollier, *Sophisticated Sabotage: The Intellectual Games Used to Subvert Responsible Regulation* 67–97 (2004).

102. *American Textile Mfrs. Inst., Inc.*, 452 U.S. at 490.

balance costs against benefits in setting occupational health standards. The majority opinion, in which Justice Stevens joined, reasoned that cost-benefit analysis was not required because Congress used the word "feasible" in § 6(b)(5), and that word could not be construed to imply a balancing approach. In the words of the Court, "cost-benefit analysis by OSHA is not required by the statute because feasibility analysis is."[103] In the intervening years, successful technology-based programs for reducing human exposure to toxic chemicals have justified statutes that have resolved the paradigm debate in favor of the technology-based approach.[104]

The *Cotton Dust* case did not, of course, end the matter. In 1995, proponents of a cost-benefit decision criterion came within two votes in the Senate of mandating a cost-benefit decision criterion for all health and environmental standard-setting.[105] Indeed, the battle continued to rage when President George W. Bush appointed John D. Graham, a strong proponent of cost-benefit analysis from the Harvard Center for Risk Analysis, to head the Office of Information and Regulatory Affairs (OIRA) in the Office of Management and Budget. This nomination was strongly supported by regulated industries and equally strongly opposed by public interest groups. From that position, to which he was confirmed in late 2001, Graham has overseen the centralized review process for health and safety regulations. To the chagrin of public interest groups and the joy of industry-funded think tanks, OIRA greatly stemmed the flow of health, safety and environmental regulation during the Bush Administration. Although EPA promulgated several important regulations, most of which were required by statute, OSHA did not promulgate a single significant health standard during the entire four years.

Although the battle over the paradigm rages on,[106] it is fair to say that quantitative risk assessment will continue to dominate the process of setting media quality standards in the foreseeable future. Despite its considerable practical limitations, the patina of objectivity that quantitative risk assessment lends to the standard-setting exercise will no doubt prove irresistible to EPA and other health and environmental agencies. Although policy considerations will necessarily play a very large role, the extent to which individual media quality standards depend upon policy, rather than science, will continue to remain obscure.

---

103. *Id.* at 509.

104. *See* Center for Progressive Regulation, *A New Progressive Agenda for Public Health and the Environment* ch. 5 (Christopher H. Schroeder & Rena Steinzor eds., 2004).

105. 141 Cong. Rec. 10,399 (1995) (cloture vote on "Dole Bill").

106. *See* Frank Ackerman & Lisa Heinzerling, *Priceless* (2004).

*

6

Jody Freeman

The Story of *Chevron*: Environmental Law and Administrative Discretion

Chevron v. NRDC is, without question, one of the most important cases in the history of American administrative law.[1] Consider this: at the time of writing, Westlaw counts 119 law review articles with *Chevron* in the title,[2] including many by the leading scholars and jurists in the field.[3] *Chevron* is also well on its way to being the most widely cited administrative law case of all time, with a conservative count yielding nearly 6800 citations in the federal courts.[4] Give an administrative law professor three seconds to name the most important case in the field, or a recent administrative law student which case (if any) stands out from class, and they are most likely to say, *Chevron*. What's more, the case

---

1. Chevron, U.S.A. Inc. v. Natural Res. Def. Council, Inc., 467 U.S. 837 (1984).

2. This is a conservative count arrived at by searching Westlaw's "Journals and Law Reviews" database.

3. The following is just a sample of the rich literature analyzing *Chevron*'s impact: Cynthia R. Farina, *Statutory Interpretation and the Balance of Power in the Administrative State*, 89 Colum. L. Rev. 452 (1989); John F. Manning, *Constitutional Structure and Judicial Deference to Agency Interpretations of Agency Rules*, 96 Colum. L. Rev. 612 (1996); Thomas W. Merrill, *Judicial Deference to Executive Precedent*, 101 Yale L.J. 969 (1992); Richard J. Pierce, Jr, *Chevron and Its Aftermath: Judicial Review of Agency Interpretations of Statutory Provisions*, 41 Vand. L. Rev. 301 (1988); Antonin Scalia, *Judicial Deference to Administrative Interpretations of Law*, 1989 Duke L.J. 511 (1989); Peter H. Schuck & E. Donald Elliott, *To the Chevron Station: An Empirical Study of Federal Administrative Law*, 1990 Duke L.J. 984 (1990); Kenneth W. Starr, *Judicial Review in the Post–Chevron Era*, 3 Yale J. on Reg. 283 (1986); Cass R. Sunstein, *Law and Administration After Chevron*, 90 Colum. L. Rev. 2071 (1990).

4. A conservative count from both the Westlaw and Lexis databases turns up between 6700 and 6800 citations to *Chevron* in the federal courts. *See also* Sunstein, *Law and Administration After Chevron*, 90 Colum. L. Rev. 2071, 2074–75 (1990), counting 1000 citations in the first six years after *Chevron* was decided.

has legs. Its progeny[5] have produced their own cottage industry of commentary,[6] and there appears to be no end in sight. Very few cases have such a long and active life, especially when they do not involve a constitutional challenge.

Yet what of *Chevron's* place in environmental law? Perhaps because of the sensation it caused in administrative law, it is easy to forget that *Chevron* is an enormously important Clean Air Act (CAA) case as well.[7] After all, at issue in *Chevron* were some of the most complicated and stringent provisions of the (at the time) relatively new 1977 amendments to the CAA.[8] This was the first case involving the controversial use of "bubbles" in air regulation to reach the Supreme Court, an auspicious moment that marked the debut of market approaches like netting and offsetting in environmental regulation.

It is hard to discern any of this complexity and importance from the decision itself, however. Justice Stevens' unanimous opinion offers only the most superficial analysis of the relevant statutory provisions,[9] and instead frames the case more generally, in administrative law terms. *Chevron* is known, as a result, as the case in which the Supreme Court announced a sweeping rule of deference to agency interpretations of law.[10] What people remember is not the details of the EPA's controversial bubble policy, which was at issue in the case, but the Court's two-part test for when to accept agency interpretations: Has Congress addressed the precise question in issue? If not, is the agency interpretation "reasonable"? If the answer to the first question is no, and the answer to the second yes, the court defers.[11] In a field as statutory as

---

5. Christensen v. Harris County, 529 U.S. 576 (2000); United States v. Mead, 533 U.S. 218 (2001).

6. Michael P. Healy, *Spurious Interpretation Redux: Mead and the Shrinking Domain of Statutory Ambiguity*, 54 Admin. L. Rev. 673 (2002); Ronald M. Levin, *Mead and the Prospective Exercise of Discretion*, 54 Admin. L. Rev. 771 (2002); Thomas W. Merrill, *The Mead Doctrine: Rules and Standards, Meta–Rules and Meta–Standards*, 54 Admin. L. Rev. 807 (2002).

7. 42 U.S.C. § 7402 (2000).

8. *See* 42 U.S.C. §§ 7502, 7503 (2000).

9. That *Chevron* involves the complicated "New Source Review" (NSR) provisions of the CAA Amendments of 1977 seemed almost incidental. This is especially apparent when one sees the extent to which the Court adopted the administrative law framing of the Petitioner's brief and declined to grapple with the statutory complexity provided by the Respondent's brief.

10. In adopting this new rule of deference, the Supreme Court dismissed, with almost no serious discussion, a complex body of law aimed at calibrating judicial deference on matters of law to a number of relevant considerations (including agency expertise, the timing of the legal interpretation, and the relative consistency of the agency's position over time).

11. Even environmental law casebooks tend to present *Chevron* in a section devoted to administrative law standards of review rather than in a chapter devoted to air quality.

environmental law, and as subject to conflicting policies and goals, deference determines important outcomes, as *Chevron* itself demonstrates.

But there is more to the story. *Chevron* is in the environmental law pantheon for additional good reasons. It was the first (and only) Supreme Court case to memorialize the turn toward market mechanisms in environmental regulation. The bubble concept was among the earliest emissions trading ideas to take root in EPA regulations.[12] The rationale for trading policies such as bubbles, netting[13] and offsetting[14] in these early days was to reduce the cost of compliance with environmental standards by affording firms the flexibility to achieve them in the least-cost manner. Yet at the time, and to this day, critics saw the bubble as a regulatory shell game.

In the ensuing years, emissions trading has become both more widespread and more sophisticated, evolving from controversial techniques like bubbles, to cap-and-trade programs like the acid rain provisions of the CAA that attract extensive praise. And the trading concept has leapt the fence of air regulation to make inroads into water regulation, habitat conservation and even wetlands preservation.[15] While contemporary trading programs are meaningfully different from, and serve distinct purposes than, the bubble concept, the bubble is still fairly viewed as an early ancestor of today's market mechanisms.[16]

See e.g., Roger W. Findley, Daniel A. Farber & Jody Freeman, *Environmental Law* 138 (6th ed. 2003).

12. The earliest example appears to be the EPA's offset rule, adopted in the late seventies to avoid a construction moratorium in states that had not yet met attainment deadlines, and which ultimately found its way into the NSR provisions in the 1977 amendments to the Act.

13. Netting is an approach through which a company modifying one point in a source can avoid CAA abatement requirements by reducing emissions from other points within the source. The source's net emissions thus stay at the same level. *See* Richard A. Liroff, *Reforming Air Pollution Regulations: The Toil and Trouble of EPA's Bubble 6 (1986)*.

14. Through offsetting, companies can construct or modify pollution sources as long as they reduce emissions from existing sources to a greater extent. *Id.* at 7.

15. *See* James Salzman & J.B. Ruhl, *Currencies and the Commodification of Environmental Law,* 53 Stan. L. Rev. 607 (2000); *see also* Environmental Protection Agency, "A Summary of U.S. Effluent Trading and Offset Projects," available at http://www.epa.gov/owow/watershed/trading/traenvrn.pdf.

16. On the difference between the early bubble strategy and more recent cap and trade programs, NRDC's David Doniger says, "Cap and trade is distinctly more sound. The cap determines the total permitted pollution. The allowances and continuous emissions monitoring provide a near-foolproof way to assure that the cap is met. If a pollutant is broadly fungible and the cap and timetable is calculated to meet the public health and environmental goals, then a cap and trade program can be idea. But neither netting nor bubbles had an environmental motivation or justification. They were purely for evasion of

In a related vein, the case began a pattern that continues to this day, of industry efforts to minimize the CAA's reach by circumscribing the ambit of the New Source Review (NSR) program, along with countervailing efforts by environmental groups to expand the reach of that program as broadly as possible.[17] First introduced in rudimentary form in 1970, but significantly strengthened by Congress in the 1977 Amendments, the NSR program is intended to regulate strictly the introduction of additional air pollution when plants either install new equipment or update existing equipment. The process applies with greatest rigor to all new or modified sources in "non-attainment zones"—the dirtiest parts of the country, where states have not yet attained air quality standards.[18]

Among other steps, NSR requires owners to install state-of-the-art pollution control technology that will achieve the "lowest achievable emission rate" (LAER) possible for that type of source. In addition, each new or modified source must secure offsetting reductions of pollution from other sources in the area. Not surprisingly, to avoid these burdens, firms generally wish to avoid NSR.

The issue in *Chevron* was whether the EPA could authorize states to use a plantwide definition of stationary source in the NSR program in addition to the unit-by-unit definition. The effect of this new approach would be to treat all the polluting units or "points" (such as boilers or blast furnaces) at a plant as if they constituted a *single* source under an imaginary "bubble." The concept would allow a firm to trade emission increases at one unit for emission reductions at another; NSR would not be triggered because emissions under the entire bubble would not increase.

This abstract policy idea had real world implications: the widespread use of bubbles threatened to slow or reverse efforts to improve air quality in non-attainment zones, where health risks, and damage to crops and habitat, due to air pollution were most serious. Just when Congress had singled out these areas for stringent regulation, the EPA was proposing to adopt a regulatory reform concept that seemed to

---

rules the industry advocates lacked the votes to change legislatively." Email from David Doniger, March 15, 2005 (on file with author).

17. The dispute over NSR that began in *Chevron* has far reaching effects, and is still relevant today. See the discussion of NSR reform, *infra* note 121 and accompanying text. NSR reform is a key element of the Bush administration's proposed Clear Skies legislation, which, if it passes, will be the first significant amendment of the CAA in fifteen years. The bill has recently faced significant setbacks, failing to reach the full Senate due to a 9–9 vote by the Environment and Public Works Committee. *See* Michael Janofsky, *Bush-Backed Emissions Bill Fails to Reach Senate Floor*, N.Y. Times, A24:5 March 10, 2005.

18. As discussed below, NSR also applies to a program known as "Prevention of Significant Deterioration" (PSD), where the goal is to avoid the degradation of air quality. However, the NSR provisions at issue in *Chevron* concerned non-attainment zones.

march in the opposite direction. In support of the idea, industry claimed that going through the NSR permit process, meeting the LAER standard, and securing offsets was excessively costly and time consuming for little real air quality gain. Further, they argued, NSR created a potential disincentive to modernizing plants: firms would avoid updating equipment to avoid triggering the program's requirements.[19] On the other hand, environmentalists argued that the bubble was a sleight of hand—a gimmick that would allow industry to avoid making air quality improvements as they made capital investments, and enabling them to grandfather old pollution rates indefinitely.

This was the context in which *Chevron* arose, and why the stakes were so high for environmental policy.

I. The Clean Air Act and the Birth of the Bubble Approach

Traditionally, air pollution, like most environmental issues, had been a matter handled locally by the states. Yet the states had done precious little to control it, even in the face of growing public concern. As early as 1948, a four-day air inversion in Donora, Pennsylvania, had made the news when it led to numerous excess deaths.[20] Similar incidents occurred in the 1950s and 1960s and were blamed for yet more fatalities.[21] By the 60s, the consequences of state inaction were apparent to the naked eye, as smog engulfed major cities and soot damaged buildings and crops. Studies emerged showing that polluted air would take a toll on human health, raising the risk of death from heart disease and cancer.[22]

Such scientific findings became more alarming in the wake of several high-profile incidents that alerted the country to the air pollution problem. Los Angeles's infamous smog was perhaps the most persistently glaring problem; in 1965, the city's carbon monoxide concentrations violated what would later become the federal air quality standard 78 to 99 percent of the time.[23] The problem pervaded the northeast as well.[24] On Thanksgiving Day in 1966, an inversion episode in New York City

---

19. The requirements in PSD areas are slightly different because the goal of the PSD program is to maintain air quality in areas where the federal ambient air standards are already met.

20. Indur Goklany, *Clearing the Air* 24–25 (1999).

21. *Id.* at 26.

22. *See* Oliver A. Houck, *More Unfinished Stories: Lucas, Atlanta Coalition and Palila/Sweet Home*, 75 U. Colo. L. Rev. 331, 386 & n. 357 (2004) (citing Council on Environmental Quality, *Environmental Quality: Fifth Annual Report of the Council on Environmental Quality* 12–14 (1974), reporting death rates from heart disease rising from 137 per 100,000 to 362 in 1970 and death rates from cancer rising from 64 per 100,000 to 163.8).

23. *Id.* at 27 and studies cited therein.

24. *Id.*

was blamed for approximately 170 deaths.[25] Eventually, the public outcry reached Washington, D.C.

After trying unsuccessfully to induce the states to act,[26] Congress passed the CAA amendments of 1970, launching the nation's first real experiment with a strong federal pollution control law. The legislation instructed the EPA to set, for a class of pervasive "criteria pollutants," health-based national ambient air quality standards (NAAQS),[27] which all states would be required to meet.[28]

Chevron arose because the initial deadlines Congress set for state compliance with the NAAQS were, whether intentionally or not, wildly optimistic. The statute required the states to develop state implementation plans (SIPs) for achieving attainment with the federal standards by 1975 (with some exceptions).[29] Yet for a variety of reasons, there was widespread non-compliance. Unquestionably, the initial deadlines were simply unrealistic in terms of the time needed to develop and install controls on the regulated sources. There were other contributing factors as well, however: EPA was under-resourced and over-tasked; many states dragged their feet while others, if willing, lacked the technical and administrative capacity to generate accurate SIPs; industry opposed the

---

25. *See id.* at 26 and studies cited therein.

26. Congress had passed the Air Pollution Control Act, the first federal legislation aimed at curbing air pollution, in 1955 but this early legislation sought primarily to induce more state regulation by providing research support along with technical and financial aid to the states.

27. To meet NAAQS for these pollutants, states would be required to produce state implementation plans (SIPs)—essentially a collection of emission limits, standards, and other constraints that the states would impose on the various sources of pollution (both stationary and non-stationary) within their respective jurisdictions. This approach allows states to take the lead in meting out the pain of complying with federal standards, but it reserves to the federal government the power to approve or disapprove those plans. In theory, when the EPA approves a SIP, it is saying that the measures adopted in it will, collectively, ensure attainment of NAAQS by the statutory deadlines.

28. The EPA is authorized to set standards for a small set of pervasive and harmful air pollutants (the so-called "criteria pollutants," including sulfur dioxide, carbon monoxide, particulate matter, nitrogen oxides, lead and ozone), at a level that is "requisite to protect human health with an adequate margin of safety." *See* CAA §§ 108—109, 42 U.S.C. §§ 7408–7409 (2000).

29. Although the harm-based approach to setting national ambient standards, which are then implemented through regulations devised in state plans, remains the core of the Act, this approach has been supplemented by a variety of technology-based emissions standards that are directly imposed on individual sources of pollution, depending on where they are located, what they emit, when they are built and whether they are considered "major" or not under the Act. These emission limits apply in addition to whatever measures states adopt in their SIPs to guarantee compliance with federal ambient standards. A single stationary source of pollution may be subject to a host of requirements. For a summary of these requirements, see Mark S. Squillace & David R. Wooley, *Air Pollution* 61–67 (1999).

regulations at every turn; environmental groups litigated to push the EPA further than it wanted to go; and new unanticipated problems arose.[30] Thus, because of a combination of legislative misjudgment or optimism (or both), technical difficulty, complexity, opacity, and outright resistance, compliance with the law was, to put it mildly, incomplete.[31]

Still, the NAAQS gave citizens and policymakers, for the first time, a way of gauging whether the air they were breathing was "healthy." And the news was not good. As of 1975, 153 of 247 air quality control regions—over 60%—were expected to fall short of the ambient air quality standards. Fueling public concern, scientific studies and media reports increasingly linked this air pollution to serious illness and even death. In one study, the excess annual number of angina attacks due to carbon monoxide (CO) exposure in Los Angeles was expected to be between 530,000 and 690,000.[32]

Awareness of carcinogens was also rising. Noting that between 60 and 90 percent of cancer was caused by environmental factors, the Council on Environmental Quality (CEQ) drew a connection between air pollution and higher-than-normal cancer death rates.[33] It was increasingly clear, as well, that air pollution was costly for the nation. In 1972, the EPA suggested that $25 billion was a "conservative" estimate of the annual cost of air pollution.[34] Given the public's already heightened concern about the detrimental effects of air pollution, compliance that was spotty at best was seen as a potent public threat. Widespread non-attainment was a source of fear and outrage—and a driving force for reform.

To address the problem of non-compliance Congress amended the Act only seven years later. The 1977 CAA amendments extended the deadlines for achieving NAAQS for non-attainment areas to 1982 (and in some cases 1987),[35] and strengthened the rudimentary NSR program.

---

30. John P. Dwyer, *The Pathology of Symbolic Legislation*, 17 Ecology L.Q. 233 (1990).

31. On incomplete compliance generally, see Daniel A. Farber, *Taking Slippage Seriously: Noncompliance and Creative Compliance in Environmental Law*, 23 Harv. Envtl. L. Rev. 297 (1999).

32. Council on Environmental Quality Ann. Rep. 168 (1977).

33. Council on Environmental Quality Ann. Rep.17, 19 (1975).

34. Environmental Protection Agency, The Economics of Clean Air, S. Doc. No. 92–67, at 1–10 (1972).

35. However, as the 1987 deadline approached, it was clear that many areas of the country still had not achieved compliance with NAAQS. As a result, much of the population continued to breathe unhealthy air. Congress moved to extend the deadlines again in 1990, and most observers expect they will need to be extended yet again, particularly in light of the EPA's 1997 rulemaking which set still tighter standards for ozone and particulate matter. Clearly, the non-attainment problem is serious, and ongoing.

Going forward, NSR would require all new or modified sources in non-attainment zones to obtain state issued permits; to equip their new or modified sources with state-of-the-art pollution control technology (or to make other process changes) capable of achieving the LAER; and to secure offsets of pollution from other sources in the region so that the net result, after the offsets, will guarantee that the state is making "reasonable progress" toward compliance with the national air standards. Finally, under NSR, plant owners were required to certify to the state that all of the facilities under their control were in compliance with the requirements of the state's implementation plan.[36]

As the EPA began to implement the 1977 Amendments, however, it struggled with how to balance the statutory requirement of forcing states to meet air quality standards with the political imperative of allowing them to continue to pursue a reasonable amount of economic growth. The stage was set for the bubble.

II. The Debate Over the Bubble Approach

The bubble rule at issue in *Chevron* did not appear overnight. As the EPA began implementing the CAA in the early seventies, the agency began to consider the merits of using the bubble in a variety of CAA programs.[37] This was part of a larger move toward adopting emissions trading, a policy tool that was quickly swept up in the politics of environmental regulation.[38]

In theory, the bubble concept seems completely unobjectionable. It simply treats all the polluting units in a firm as if there were a tent over them, with a single hole for emissions, and allows firms to distribute emissions reductions among the individual units in whichever manner they choose. The bubble concept is a way of affording firms flexibility to make operational decisions about how to reach a given regulatory target in the cheapest way possible, providing they meet the target. Why does this benefit firms? Given the cost of technology, it can be much more expensive to squeeze the last increment of pollution control out of a new piece of equipment than to take other steps—such as shutting down an

---

36. 42 U.S.C. §§ 7502–7503.

37. On the history and rationale of the bubble policy generally, see Michael H. Levin, *Building a Better Bubble at EPA*, 9 Regulation 33 (1985). For the history of emissions trading, see Tom Tietenberg, *Emissions Trading: An Exercise in Reforming Pollution Policy,* Resources for the Future, 1985.

38. *See generally* Liroff, *supra* note 13; *see also* Michael H. Levin, *Getting There: Implementing the "Bubble Policy" in Social Regulation: Strategies for Reform* 68–69 (Bardach & R. Kagan eds., 1982) (hereinafter Levin, *Bubble Policy*) (claiming that the bubble was originally proposed in the Nixon administration by major smelters, "a heavily polluting and recalcitrant industry," and was "fiercely opposed by EPA's Air Programs and Enforcement Offices on enforcement and equity grounds").

older and less efficient unit, switching fuels, or finding other practices to change at the facility that will yield improvements in air quality. The bubble allows firms to choose their poison.[39]

To see the potential benefits of such an approach, consider what Mike Levin,[40] the head of EPA's Office of Planning and Management (OPM) at the time,[41] often did in cafeterias around the country to illustrate it.

> Take a salt shaker and a pepper shaker. Assume that command and control regulation typically requires uniform reductions from each emission point within an industrial category.[42] If the shakers each are stacks at (say) a refinery, and each currently is allowed to (and does) emit 250 tons per year (TPY) of volatile organic compounds, a new rule would require each to reduce by 100 TPY. But let's say it will cost 5 times as much to reduce 100 tons at Salt as at Pepper because, for example, there's not enough room to install control equipment there, or because Salt's location is much hotter, so it will have to install condensers & refrigeration to make control equipment work reliably.

> Why not allow Pepper (or Pepper plus another unregulated refinery source emitting the same pollutants) to reduce by 200 tons instead? Costs might not only be reduced fivefold in this case, but industry resistance to issuance of the rule in the first place could be reduced. So would foot-dragging on compliance, or applications for "variances" on grounds of cost-effectiveness (which if granted, would require little or no reduction at Salt). More important, the rule suddenly seems reasonable, because it allows adjustment for site-specific variations that regulators knew nothing about. Still more important, it encourages regulated sources to come forward with superior and more efficient reduction options than they had previously had reason to seek or disclose. Regulators can use this information to secure further reductions with less friction on a

---

39. For an explanation and defense of the rationale behind the bubble, see generally Levin, *Bubble Policy, supra* note 38.

40. Levin had gotten into the "reform game" as the Deputy Director of an Occupational Health and Safety Reform Act task force in the Carter administration, and was hired at EPA by Doug Costle at the end of the Carter Administration.

41. For a history of the role of OPM in developing the bubble during the late seventies, see Levin, *Bubble Policy, supra* note 38, at 69–87. *See also* Liroff, *supra* note 13, at 37.

42. Command and control regulation, generally, is described as a centralized, uniform and highly prescriptive approach. A classic example is traditional, technology-based standard-setting, in which all firms are required to meet a given regulatory standard, which they usually do by adopting the same technology the agency used in the setting the standard.

system-wide basis, as long as they do so without directly penalizing the sources that came forward this way.[43]Over time, regulators' jobs get easier, and more real reductions are secured.[44]

Understood in these terms, bubbles seem eminently sensible.[45] Indeed, as an abstract policy idea, the bubble concept garnered praise from everyone: EPA officials, representatives of industry, and even environmentalists.[46] Yet the disagreement lay in details of the *application* of the bubble concept by EPA in nonattainment zones. There is a vast difference between using a bubble to help existing sources achieve compliance under approved state plans, and using it to allow offsets between units in non-attainment zones, as the EPA's bubble rule did.[47]

To appreciate the "dark side" of the bubble[48] consider these objections: as implemented by EPA in nonattainment zones, the bubble allowed firms to retire or modify old units and apply the resulting emission credits to new or modified units. And this would occur without requiring the firm to install pollution control technology that would force an even greater reduction in emission levels over time. Allowing this kind of offsetting essentially enables firms to perpetuate existing emission levels indefinitely. They "bank" the excess pollution from old units, converting existing pollution levels into an entitlement going forward. The public never sees the air quality benefit of retired units with this approach. Over time, the bubble could also result in firms capturing future credits for what are called "anyway" tons—tons of

---

43. "Agencies easily can strike that balance by, for example, committing to impose new requirements which are based on this information, only to all sources in a category across-the-board—not just to the sources that showed they could reduce further. In this way, the incentives to come forward can become self-reinforcing because sources receive tangible balance sheet rewards. At the same time, the regulatory system gets a feedback loop for continuous improvement." Email from Mike Levin, March 15, 2005 (on file with author).

44. *Id.*

45. Levin Email, *supra* note 43. Levin's point then, and now, is that bubbles represented a superior alternative to the NSR program as it operated in reality, though not, perhaps, as it might have operated in an ideal world of perfect implementation. Sources were already getting variances from SIP rules for existing sources in nonattainment zones without producing any emissions reductions, so NSR was being "evaded" already. In his view, there were so many escape hatches from NSR that the notion of the bubble costing the nation "foregone" NSR reductions was fanciful.

46. David Doniger, *The Dark Side of the Bubble*, 4 The Environmental Forum 32 (1985) (hereinafter Doniger, *Dark Side*). After skewering the EPA's for its application of the bubble concept in non-attainment zones, Doniger writes: "Notwithstanding these criticisms of the application of the bubble, NRDC *likes* the concept itself; it has the real potential to do good in the fight for clean air." *Id.* at 35.

47. For this reason, it is more appropriate to describe *Chevron* as a case about "netting" rather than the bubbles.

48. Doniger, *Dark Side*, *supra* note 46; Doniger Email, *supra* note 16.

pollution that would have been retired anyway, as firms, in the regular course of business, replace old equipment with new units.[49]

Moreover, when examined closely, the EPA's application of the bubble in fact allowed firms to calculate a net *increase* in pollution as if it were equivalent to no net increase. This was the result of the agency's definition of what constituted a "significant increase" for purposes of triggering NSR. Under the agency's definition, for example, a forty ton increase in emissions would not be considered significant.[50] So using bubbles in nonattainment zones would actually allow air quality to degrade in areas of the country where health risks were perceived to be greatest.

Perhaps the most fundamental objection to the bubble, was that companies were evading controls "obviously intended to apply when new capital commitments were made, by opportunistically seizing the inevitable 'headroom' between the actual operation of existing sources and the regulatory requirements applicable to them."[51] The command and control limits "had always left considerable headroom in that the regulator's strategy was to impose a requirement tough enough to make a company install controls, but not so tough as to give the company a legitimate issue as to whether the controls would meet the limit. What the regulatory reforms sought to do was to capture this headroom and give it back to the companies, not to the public."[52] The result for nonattainment zones then, was the exact opposite effect of what Congress

---

49. Many examples of beneficial trades are vulnerable to criticism on grounds that, when closely examined, those trades are of dubious value. *See e.g.*, the example, cited by Liroff, of Armco's trade of fugitive emissions from blast and oxygen furnaces for reductions in road dust. Fugitive particulate emissions escape through windows and vents without going through stacks, so controlling them can be costly. In the Armco example, removing 587 tons of emissions (about 92% of emissions) would have been $7.5 million using conventional controls. But reducing particulate emissions from the company's open dust sources (through road paving, road sweeping, chemical treatment of unpaved roads and a variety of other controls) would be much cheaper (a reduction of 3,965 tons per year, nearly seven times greater than the 587 tons expected from conventional controls on fugitive emissions). In theory, this example demonstrates how the cost per ton of emissions controlled would be substantially less for the firm using the alternative strategy. *See* Liroff, *supra* note 13, at 76–77. Yet furnace emissions are likely to be smaller and impregnated with toxics whereas road dust is likely to be on the high end of the size scale and relatively free of toxics. Unless such trades are for very large ratios, there is little rationale for them.

50. *See* Respondent's Brief, NRDC v. Gorsuch, 685 F.2d 718 (D.C. Cir. 1982), D.C. Cir. No. 81–2208, at 44–45. *See also* Transcript of Official Proceedings of the Supreme Court of the United States, Chevron, Inc. v. NRDC, Inc., at 8 where David Doniger points this out to the Court. Indeed, each instance of using the bubble could produce a relatively small increase in pollutants when looked at alone (i.e., a net increase of forty tons which would not be considered "significant" under the EPA's regulation), but lead to a substantial increase in the aggregate (when these forty ton increases were added together).

51. Doniger Email, *supra* note 48.

52. *Id.*

seemed to require.[53] Finally, industry's argument that NSR would retard modernization was dubious: pollution control costs, it was argued, are only one factor in a firm's investment decisions.[54]

Leading the opposition to the bubble on these grounds was the Natural Resources Defense Council (NRDC),[55] which had emerged by the mid-seventies as a forceful advocate for the environment (and which, of course, ultimately ended up as the plaintiff in *Chevron*).[56] In the NRDC's view, widespread adoption of the bubble would at worst reduce, and at best delay, the air quality gains that would otherwise have been made under NSR.

Perhaps surprisingly, many states opposed the bubble idea as well. They worried that this new policy idea would provide industry with new

---

53. A less obvious point is that if bubbles apply to modified or new units at existing plant in non-attainment zones, the effect could be to stifle economic growth by precluding the construction of entirely new plants in those areas. After all, under the CAA, states must ensure that they are making "reasonable further progress" toward the federal air standards. By foregoing gains that might otherwise be made due to installing technology at existing plants, states would have no choice but to more closely control the construction of new ones. Indeed, deploying the bubble in this way seems to favor existing firms that wish to expand or update their facilities over newer firms that might locate in the non-attainment zone. By allowing existing firms to expand without applying the most stringent pollution control technology, the bubble rule potentially shifts the burden of emissions reductions to other sources in the same region. The bubble appears to ease the burden on some firms at the expense of others. This point is not an argument against the bubble. In fact bubble advocates would likely agree that simply shifting the burdens around is perfectly consistent with achieving compliance with NAAQS. The real goal, they would say, is to ensure that SIPs guarantee compliance, however the burdens of doing so might be allocated. In this view, the SIP is the insurance policy against any tinkering that might be done with NSR. By contrast, opponents of the bubble believed that NSR was a minimum set of requirements for all new sources in non-attainment zones, the floor over which the SIP process would be laid.

54. That is, even if the marginal cost of controlling pollution from new units is greater than the cost of controlling older ones, this fact alone will not necessarily deter modernization. A firm might still choose to invest in new sources even if it means adopting expensive technological controls, either because the new sources will be more efficient, or because other factors suggest that doing so would be in the firm's interest. *See* Liroff, *supra* note 13, at 108–09.

55. In the late seventies the NRDC was arguably the major non-governmental player in air and water pollution policy and enforcement. Created in the late sixties by entrepreneurial Yale Law School graduates, and funded by the Ford Foundation, the organization was, by the late seventies, litigating hundreds of suits under both the CAA and the Clean Water Act. Its efforts were nothing short of Herculean in these early and relatively lean years, especially considering the resources and political influence wielded by the chemical and petroleum industries (among others) and their trade associations in Washington, D.C. *See* Robert Gottlieb, *Forcing the Spring—The Transformation of the American Environmental Movement*, 140–43 (1993); Marshall Robinson, *The Ford Foundation—Sowing the Seeds of Revolution*, Environment 11 (April 1993).

56. For a history of the inter-agency conflict over the 1979 proposal, and a description of its contents, see Liroff, *supra* note 13, at 42–48.

opportunities to litigate, potentially interfering with the states' attempts to revise their SIPs, and generally undermining ongoing enforcement efforts.[57] Moreover, a number of states believed they already had the authority to use bubbles, and some were already doing so; they thought they possessed the flexibility that the EPA wanted to bestow upon them.[58]

The divide over bubbles also pervaded the agency itself. Scratch the surface of *Chevron* and one finds not a united EPA seeking policy flexibility and judicial deference, but a struggle within the agency based on two very different views of the law. On one side were regulatory reformers like Mike Levin, who believed that the promise of market mechanisms—in terms of cost savings, ease of administration, and incentives to modernization—outweighed the inflated predictions about what command and control strategies would otherwise achieve.[59] They argued that chasing every small emissions increase was a misallocation of resources that would cost firms dearly for little air quality gain. Command and control regulation was reaching its limits in terms of effectiveness. Bubbles would simply afford states flexibility as they wrote SIPs, and the SIPS could be relied upon to guarantee compliance with NAAQS.

On the other side were many career employees in the agency, both in the Office of Air Quality Planning and Standards (OAQPS) and the enforcement office, who believed that most of the progress on air pollution had been, and would continue to be, the result of forcing firms to apply technology to their sources (as in the New Source Performance Standards Program).

Their perspective was perhaps best embodied by engineers like Walt Barber (who directed OAQPS in the late seventies), and by lawyers like David Hawkins, the EPA's Assistant Administrator for Air quality programs (who had formerly been one of the NRDC's primary air lawyer),[60] who were sympathetic to the view that installing "hardware" on sources was the best way to achieve air quality gains. As one former EPA staff attorney put it, "The engineers didn't care about law and regulations. They wanted to see hardware on productions units. They trusted hardware, not regulations. That's where they thought they'd get the reductions."[61] To them the bubble was an abstraction they could not

---

57. *Id.* 38–39.

58. *Id.* at 44–45.

59. This characterization is based in part on a Telephone Interview of Michael Levin, January 13, 2005 (transcript on file with author).

60. Hawkins subsequently returned to NRDC.

61. Telephone Interview with Peter Wyckoff, November 16, 2004 (transcript on file with author).

verify, an example of how the regulatory "reformers" in OPM were simply gaming the system to facilitate industry evasion of air pollution control.

It was in the heat of this internal debate that the EPA moved forward toward adopting the bubble approach.

III. Prior Bubble Litigation

The EPA first adopted the bubble in 1975, for purposes of implementing the New Source Performance Standards (NSPS) of the CAA. The NSPS program requires that all new or modified sources of pollution meet emissions standards set according to the best demonstrated technology,[62] on an industry-by-industry basis. The program's purpose is to ensure that all new sources of pollution adopt at least a minimal level of pollution control technology. In the NSPS provisions, Congress defined "stationary source" as "any building, structure, facility or installation" emitting an air pollutant. It defined "modification" as any change in a stationary source that increases emissions of any air pollutant.

In 1975, under pressure from both the smelting industry and the Department of Commerce, the EPA proposed using a bubble concept for modified sources in the NSPS program. The agency would not deem there to be a "modification" triggering NSPS if plants could offset increases in emissions from one unit with decreases in emissions from another unit at the same plant. As discussed above, this offered significant potential savings to plant owners.

In *ASARCO, Inc. v. EPA,* the first bubble case to reach the federal courts, the D.C. Circuit invalidated the agency's rule.[63] The Court reasoned that Congress intended the NSPS provisions to improve air quality. The plantwide definition of stationary source was incompatible with congressional intent because "netting out" emissions (subtracting reductions against increases to achieve no net increase) would simply maintain air quality at the same level. "Treating whole plants as single sources," said the Court, "would grant the operators of existing plants permanent easements against federal new source standards—and the worst polluters would get the largest easements. The 'best' pollution control technology would never have to be installed, and existing plants would use up much of the available clean air, inhibiting construction of new plants...."[64] In their first at-bat, the regulatory reformers had struck out.

---

62. Of course, this effectively results in firms adopting the technology that was used to set the standard.

63. 578 F.2d 319 (D.C. Cir. 1978).

64. *Id.* at 329–30 n.40.

Yet this proved a weak deterrent. The agency next deployed the bubble when implementing the PSD program, designed to prevent air quality in cleaner areas of the country from degrading below federal standards. The PSD program was adopted by the EPA in 1974 in response to a lawsuit by the Sierra Club, and ultimately added to the Act, with minor modifications, by Congress in 1977.[65] The PSD provisions limit the annual increment by which air pollution can increase— essentially capping and controlling the rate of air quality degradation. The program requires all proposed new or modified sources to go through a pre-construction review and permitting process to ensure that their emissions will not lead to an exceedance of the allowable increments. In addition, these sources must comply with a Best Available Control Technology standard (BACT), which must be at least as stringent as the NSPS standards. There would, however, be no need for preconstruction review or compliance with BACT if, using the bubble concept, the increases from one point of pollution could be offset by decreases from another point at the same plant.

This time, in *Alabama Power Co. v. Costle,* a different panel of the D.C. Circuit upheld the regulations.[66] Not only was the plantwide definition permissible in the PSD program, held the Court, it was mandatory. This was because the purpose of the PSD program, was not to *improve* air quality, as was the case with the NSPS provisions in *ASARCO*, but merely to *maintain* it. Bubbles were consistent with this goal. Indeed, the Court found that Congress had "clearly envisioned" that entire plants could be sources because the relevant section lists fourteen different types of "plants" as examples of stationary sources.[67] The opinion emphasized that the agency had discretion to define the meaning of "stationary source" in light of the different programs of the Act. The Court reasoned that in adopting the PSD provisions, Congress was concerned with controlling emissions of new sources "only where industrial changes might increase pollution in an area, not where an existing plant changed its operations in ways that produced no pollution increase."[68] Modifications that result in no net increase in pollution, then, "are not 'modifications' at all."[69]

Thus, *Chevron* was the first case involving the bubble rule to reach the Supreme Court, but the third to have been heard by the D.C. Circuit. These two prior cases set the stage for *Chevron*, which seemed, on first

---

65. *See Sierra Club v. Ruckelshaus*, 344 F. Supp. 253 (D.D.C. 1972). For the EPA regulations, see 39 Fed. Reg. 42510, December 5, 1974.

66. 636 F.2d 323 (D.C. Cir. 1979).

67. *Id.* at 397.

68. *Id.* at 401.

69. *Id.*

glance, more akin to *ASARCO* than *Alabama Power*. After all, the EPA was again proposing to use the plantwide definition in a program designed to improve air quality. Why would the Court allow it this time?

IV. Setting the Stage for Chevron: *The EPA's Adoption of the Bubble in Non–Attainment Zones*

Chevron addressed the most controversial use of the bubble: the possibility of applying it to new and modified sources in non-attainment zones. The EPA had already taken a step in this direction in its 1976 "offset" policy, which allowed the addition or modification of sources as long as the new emissions could be offset with reductions from other sources in the area. Congress largely adopted this policy in the 1977 Amendments to the Clean Air Act, when it added the other NSR provisions, though it went further in prescribing additional requirements. Thus, while Congress did not forbid all new construction in these areas, it did establish a detailed set of preconditions under which economic development could proceed.

The EPA originally proposed using bubbles for existing sources only in non-attainment zones in 1977.[70] By all accounts, the idea was put forward by Armco Steel, which, like much of the steel industry, was at the time struggling to comply with air pollution regulations. Still, as noted earlier, the EPA remained internally divided over the wisdom of using the bubble in this context. And environmental groups were dead-set against it.

During the final years of the Carter Administration the agency tiptoed up to promulgating the plantwide definition of source. First, it modified its offset policy to allow netting in non-attainment areas (though only where states had revised their SIPs). Then, in 1980, the agency went so far as to issue a Notice of Proposed Rulemaking formally adopting the plantwide definition.

Yet at the last minute, EPA dropped the idea.[71] The Carter Administration's definition of "stationary source" for the NSR program remained as it had been: each individual unit of equipment, such as a boiler or blast furnace, could be a stationary source, as could an entire plant—the so-called "dual definition" of source. Specifically, the regulation defined "stationary source" to mean "any building, structure, facility, or installation which emits or may emit any air pollutant subject to regulation under the Act."[72] For obvious reasons, this approach expands the reach of the NSR Program. Every time a firm modifies a single unit, it triggers the application of the NSR requirements.

---

70.   Liroff, *supra* note 13, at 4.

71.   For an excellent chronology of these events, see Liroff, *supra* note 13, at 26.

72.   *See* 40 C.F.R. 51.18 (j) (1)(k)-(iii) and 52.24(f)(1)-(3).

When the Reagan Administration swept into office on a deregulatory platform looking for ways to ease what they viewed as excessive burdens on industry, the regulatory reformers at the EPA had a sympathetic ear. President Reagan appointed Ann Gorsuch, an anti-regulatory crusader, to head the EPA. The administration quickly embraced the bubble concept and moved it high on the agenda.[73] In short order, the EPA adopted the bubble rule in nonattainment zones, stating clearly in the rulemaking record that the new definition was the result of "a Government-wide reexamination of regulatory burdens and complexities."[74] The agency had simply changed its mind. It now felt that the dual definition was a disincentive to modernization and would "retard progress in air pollution control by discouraging the replacement of older, dirtier processes and equipment."[75]

Given the depth of disagreement over the bubble approach, the agency's new interpretation of "stationary source" was, to say the least, controversial. Congress had not defined the term in the NSR program, or anywhere else in the new non-attainment provisions. (Indeed, there is no evidence that Congress even considered the matter.) The agency itself had long rejected the "plantwide" definition of source in non-attainment zones; environmentalists had been resisting efforts to adopt it in other programs under the CAA since at least 1975; and industry had been pushing the idea for years behind the scenes. This was bound to wind up as a lawsuit.

V. *The* Chevron *Litigation*

The NRDC challenged the EPA's NSR bubble rule in 1982 in *NRDC v. Gorsuch*.[76] Various industry groups intervened in support of the regulation, including the Chemical Manufacturer's Association, the American Petroleum Institute and Chevron Inc. The panel was comprised of Judges Mikva, Ginsburg (Ruth Bader) and Jameson.[77] The NRDC's strategy was, in the words of David Doniger, who argued the case, to "ride the distinction the Court had drawn in *Alabama Power*."[78]

---

73. The bubble concept falls well short of later proposals to adopt more full-blown market mechanisms (such as the sulfur dioxide trading scheme adopted in the 1990 Amendments to the Act) it was among the earliest ideas sanctioned by economists and championed by industry as an alternative to traditional command and control regulation.

74. *See* Petitioner's Brief, NRDC v. Gorsuch, 685 F.2d 718 (D.C. Cir. 1982), D.C. Cir. No. 81–2208, at 12; 46 Fed. Reg. 16281 (1981).

75. *See* Petitioner's Brief, NRDC v. Gorsuch, 685 F.2d 718 (D.C. Cir. 1982), D.C. Cir. No. 81–2208 at 13.

76. 685 F.2d 718 (D.C. Cir. 1982).

77. None of the members of the panel had heard either of the prior two bubble cases. Judge Jameson was a Senior District Judge from Montana.

78. Telephone Interview with David Doniger, July 28, 2004 (transcript on file with author).

Indeed, this appears to have worked. The Court ruled unanimously that the agency's new interpretation of "stationary source" was unlawful.

The Court claimed to be controlled by its prior decisions in *ASARCO* and *Alabama Power*, which together established a "bright line test" for determining when the bubble concept is permissible.[79] Then judge (and now Justice) Ruth Bader Ginsburg's unanimous opinion claimed that the bubble was "mandatory for [CAA] programs designed merely to maintain existing air quality; it is inappropriate...in programs enacted to improve [air quality]."[80] Because improving air quality was the "raison d'etre"[81] of the non-attainment provisions, the Court was "impelled by the force of [its] precedent"[82] to hold that the EPA's new definition of stationary source for in the non-attainment program was unlawful. In so holding, the D.C. Circuit rejected the government's argument that there were a variety of plausible interpretations of "source;" that it was used inconsistently throughout the statute; and that the agency should be free to exercise its discretion unless its interpretation was contradicted by the statute.[83]

Yet the NRDC's strategy would come back to haunt Doniger when the case reached the Supreme Court. In reflecting on the litigation strategy, Doniger (now returned to the NRDC after serving at the EPA during the Clinton administration) said that he did not appreciate, until the Reply stage before the D.C. Circuit, that the best argument against the bubble rule was based on the statute's plain meaning. The term stationary source simply *had to* mean each individual unit or the other specific NSR requirements would not make sense. Though he would go on to advance this argument in his Supreme Court brief (relying heavily on the legislative history of the 1977 amendments), he had argued it only in Reply to the D.C. Circuit. As a result, the Court's rationale was heavily dependent on the dubious distinction between *ASARCO* and *Alabama Power*. The Court appeared to be inventing its bright line test. In the words of Jose Allen, the head of the Environmental Defense Section at the Department of Justice, who argued the case for the government, the decision seemed to impose a "straitjacket" on the agency that wasn't there.

A. Seeking *Certiorari*

According to Allen, it was not obvious at the outset that the government would seek *certiorari* in *Chevron*. On the one hand, the

---

79.   685 F.2d at 726.

80.   *Id.*

81.   *Id.*

82.   *Id.* at 720.

83.   Telephone Interview with Jose Allen, August 2, 2004 (transcript on file with author). Allen wrote the brief and argued the case for the government in the D.C. Circuit.

bubble policy had become an important part of the Reagan administration's de-regulatory agenda, so when the D.C. Circuit ruled against the EPA, the decision had political consequences for the administration. There was considerable pressure from officials at the Office of Management and Budget, and in the White House, to seek *certiorari* in the case. And it was clear that Chevron, Inc. was going to seek *certiorari*, so the Solicitor General might do better to proceed as petitioner to get control.[84]

On the other hand, however, there were those in both the EPA and the Solicitor General's office who took the view that the case presented a close question as to the appropriate definition of "stationary source" and perhaps did not merit a *certiorari* petition.

Similarly, many career staff at the EPA were sympathetic to the D.C. Circuit's holding, and did not favor the administration's position on the bubble policy. There was considerable concern among line personnel at the agency that if the Supreme Court reversed, and gave the agency the policy flexibility the regulatory reformers sought, it would ultimately hinder the advance of air pollution regulation.[85] Moreover, as Allen points out, even if the Court of Appeals' bright line test was dubious, to seek *certiorari* the government would need to argue that the D.C. Circuit had been mistaken in its judgment, regardless of its reasoning.[86]

The discussion within the administration went back and forth until finally it resolved in favor of filing the petition, presumably for political reasons. Indeed, Doniger recalls "pitching" the Deputy Solicitor General, in a couple of conversations, that the government should not seek *certiorari*. Though critical of the D.C. Circuit's approach, the Deputy seemed convinced by Doniger's argument that the bubble was not consistent with the statutory text. He told Doniger that he would recommend against the petition. Yet Doniger later learned that the Deputy had been overruled, on the orders of the White House.[87]

Just as the government's decision to seek *certiorari* was not a foregone conclusion, it was far from clear that the Supreme Court would take the case. As Bill Pedersen (who drafted the merits brief at the EPA) points out, there was no split in the Circuits, the case raised no

84. This was Mark Levy's understanding of the rationale for seeking certiorari, though he did not participate in contemporaneous discussions in the Solicitor General's office at the time. *See* Telephone Interview with Mark Levy, August 3, 2004 (transcript on file with author).

85. *Id.* Allen reports that it was difficult to get a consistent position out of the EPA regarding how sweeping the argument should be and how strongly to argue what the agency's past positions were. The memo to the Solicitor General requesting certiorari went back and forth to EPA numerous times. It was hard to get consensus from the agency because of the internal division.

86. *Id.*

87. Doniger Email, *supra* note 48.

constitutional issue and the interpretive issue was a small part of a single regulatory statute. Yet when the Court did take it, Pedersen says, Paul Bator, the Deputy Solicitor General, and others on the government side, thought they had a winner.[88] Why would the Court take it to affirm?[89]

B. The Briefs

Consistent with Doniger's new strategy of emphasizing the "plain meaning" of the statute, the respondent's brief is a detailed, sustained argument that Congress clearly intended to preclude a plantwide definition of stationary source in the non-attainment zone provisions. The NRDC argued that the agency was due no deference because there was simply no statutory ambiguity.

Doniger's brief, pared down, argued as follows: The non-attainment zone provisions require permits for any new or modified major stationary source. Section 302(j) defines "Major stationary source" as any "stationary facility or source" which emits at least 100 tons per year of pollution. This restates but does not solve the interpretive problem concerning the term "source." However, Section 111 (the NSPS provisions) defines stationary source as any "building, structure, facility, or installation." Thus, a major stationary source is simply a large source as defined in Section 111. And the plainest meaning of each of the terms in Section 111 leads to the conclusion that at least two of them are incapable of a plantwide definition. While "facility" and "installation" could conceivably encompass a plant, neither "building" nor "structure" can.[90]

Further, the brief argued, any other reading would effectively rewrite the non-attainment provisions. The Act imposes five separate conditions on new or modified sources in non-attainment zones: a complete SIP; offsets with other area sources to ensure net reduction in pollution; the application of LAER; and certification of company-wide compliance with all CAA requirements (plus, in areas with extended deadlines, a cost-benefit analysis).[91] The government's construction of the Act would allow a project to be built when only *one* of these conditions is met. That is, Doniger's brief argued, if the plant complied with the offset condition alone it would not be a major stationary source. In the NRDC's estimation at the time, adopting a plant-wide definition of stationary source would exempt 90% of the sources otherwise subject

---

88. Telephone Interview with Bill Pedersen, June 1, 2004 (transcript on file with author).

89. Pedersen attributes this thought to Paul Bator, who voiced it in an internal meeting. *Id.*

90. *See* Respondent's Brief, Chevron v. NRDC, S. Ct. Nos. 82–1005, at 29.

91. *Id.* at 32.

to NSR.[92] By not requiring the installation of state-of-the-art technology on all new or modified sources, the EPA would achieve a lesser level of control. This, the NRDC's brief argued, would directly contradict congressional intent.

The Petitioner's brief, by contrast, placed administrative law principles of deference at the center of its argument. It accused the court of appeals of inventing a "bright line test of its own ... a test creating a set of rigid statutory pigeon-holes whose function is to strip the Administrator of any discretion whatever in working out the details of the non-attainment program."[93] The D.C. Circuit's decision "constitutes an unwarranted usurpation" of the authority reserved to the agency.[94] This is remarkable, argued the government, when the lower court admits that that text and legislative history do not provide a definition of the term in question.

The brief emphasized that giving states the option of using the bubble best balances the competing purposes of the Act: improving air quality and encouraging industrial growth.[95] The government raised the specter of severe economic consequences: "The resulting expense and delay" that would result from rejecting the plantwide definition, would "create a substantial disincentive to expand capacity or replace outmoded and inefficient equipment, hampering growth and retarding modernization."[96]

The government did, however, have some problems. For example, the EPA had been inconsistent in its definition of "stationary source" over time and this flip-flopping might undermine the argument for deference. On the claim that the bubble was necessary to spur modernization, the evidence offered was a single hypothetical, and a citation to the EPA's rulemaking record, which itself relied on two anecdotal industry letters—hardly a compelling case for the bubble.[97]

---

92. This figure was produced as a result of a single study by Communities for a Better Environment which was cited in the Respondent's brief. The assertion was not challenged in the litigation. Even if this figure is overstated, it is conceivable that widespread state adoption of the bubble concept would lead to substantial losses—in the form of foregone gains—in air quality. This conclusion seems inescapable unless one assumes that requiring firms to meet the most stringent technology standard inhibits modernization to such an extent that it effectively cancels out the beneficial effects of requiring compliance with the standard in the first place. I thank Craig Oren for making this point. Telephone conversation, October 24, 2004 (on file with author).

93. Petitioner's Brief, Chevron v. NRDC, S. Ct. Nos. 82–1005 at 16.

94. *Id.* at 19.

95. *Id.* at 17.

96. *Id.* at 29.

97. *See* Respondent's Brief, Chevron v. NRDC, S. Ct. Nos. 82–1005, at 44–45. The brief is also somewhat misleading in suggesting that a plantwide definition "would not

Even without much empirical evidence, however, framing the case in terms of "environment versus economy," may have been an especially wise move. Bill Pedersen credits Paul Bator with this framing, and speculates that it made the case seem more consequential to the Court. Perhaps, he speculates, it reinforced the Supreme Court's decision to grant *certiorari* in the first place.[98]

The brief did two other things that may have been especially effective. First, whereas the *certiorari* petition had ended with the administrative law argument, the merits brief began with it. The petitioners took the view that it was in the overall interest of the government for agencies not to have their hands tied; that giving the expert regulators discretion was sensible in cases of such ambiguity and complexity; and that as long as the agency had a reasoned explanation, it could change its mind as administrations came and went.[99]

Second, the brief stressed that the D.C. Circuit was simply making things up. Its bright line *ASARCO/Alabama Power* rule seemed too contrived.[100] How could the bubble be required in some instances and prohibited in others if it was not even mentioned in the statute? Paul Bator and Mark Levy (an Assistant to the Solicitor General at the time, who wrote the brief with significant input from the EPA), were not environmental lawyers and saw the case through an administrative law lens. Levy's approach played into the frustration the Supreme Court had recently expressed about the tendency of some judges on the D.C. Circuit to roll up their sleeves and wade into searching review of agency decisions. In *Vermont Yankee Nuclear Power Corp. v. Natural Resources Defense Council, Inc.,*[101] the Supreme Court had already tried to rein in this kind of thing. Yet the D.C. Circuit was at it again.

C. Oral Argument

By all accounts, oral argument was a dismal affair.[102] Neither side thought it went well. The Court was skeptical of the administration but gave the NRDC an equally difficult time. Some of the Justices appeared, at least at times, not to fully grasp the complexities of the case. Justice

materially affect *net* air quality, especially if one considers the aggregate and long term effects of the policy." As mentioned earlier, the EPA's calculation of "significant increase" allows for a net increase in emissions without triggering NSR. *Id.* at 29–30. *See* Respondent's Brief at page 45 for the counter-argument.

98.   Pedersen Interview, *supra* note 88.

99.   *Id.*

100.   Levy Interview, *supra* note 84.

101.   *See* Vermont Yankee Nuclear Power Corp. v. Natural Res. Def. Council, Inc., 435 U.S. 519 (1978).

102.   This characterization of oral argument is based on interviews with a number of people who were present, and from my own reading of the transcript.

Rehnquist walked out at the start of oral argument and never returned.[103] There was both puzzlement and displeasure coming from the Bench. For example, at different points, Justice O'Connor seemed annoyed at Deputy Solicitor General Paul Bator, who at times appeared blustery, and who, on occasion, revealed a less than complete mastery of the intricacies of the statute.[104]

After the argument, both sides were nervous. The only thing Jose Allen thought the government had going for it was that the Supreme Court "didn't rule with environmental interests."[105] At the EPA, there was some anxiety that the Deputy Solicitor General had not fared well in oral argument and that the Justices did not seem to understand the case. For his part, the NRDC's Doniger, in his first Supreme Court argument, got bogged down in the minutiae of the definition of "source," trying painstakingly to illuminate how the plain meaning argument worked. Later, when pressed by Justice Stewart about the effect of the bubble (the Justice assumed that pollution levels before and after netting were the same), he tried to impress on the Justice that in fact netting in this instance would result in emissions *increases*. The Justice did not look pleased.

Doniger also misinterpreted the intent behind a crucial question from the Bench. When Justice Stevens asked him, during an exchange, "So you think *Alabama Power* was wrongly decided?" Doniger answered yes, thinking that the Justice was persuaded by his newly minted plain meaning argument, and saw that the D.C. Circuit had simply used the wrong rationale for the right decision. But this was not at all what Justice Stevens meant. He thought the D.C. Circuit's bright line test was dubious. Doniger had no choice, however. He was boxed in by his plain meaning argument. He *had* to say that *Alabama Power* was wrongly decided.

This was a setback to Doniger, who had gone into oral argument feeling optimistic. His spirits had been lifted earlier that day when, after attending the morning session, he went to grab a bite in the cafeteria. There he overheard a conversation between two clerks discussing the afternoon cases, in which one clerk complained to the other about *Chevron*. The complaining clerk had initially thought it would "an interesting case about economics," but it turned out to be "just an

---

103. Doniger Interview, *supra* note 78.

104. For example, Bator did not seem to know the answer to a question from the Bench about the justification for the rule deeming increases in emissions up to 100 tons to be not "significant," when the statute on its face required new source review for "any increase." *See* 1984 U.S. Trans Lexis 68 at 5. The effect of this aspect of the rule is to allow emissions to *increase* under the bubble, rather than require that they net out. In the aggregate, this would lead to poorer air quality, a point Doniger tried to make.

105. Allen Interview, *supra* note 83.

ordinary administrative law case."[106] Doniger thought this was a good sign—that the clerks would be focused on the statutory interpretation issues. Little did he know.

D. The Supreme Court Decision

The result in Chevron shocked everyone. Doniger was stunned to lose 6–0. The government, including Jose Allen and Mark Levy, had not anticipated the one-sidedness of their victory, or the sweeping nature of the decision. Indeed, no one involved in the litigation, or who was close to it, appears to have foreseen that *Chevron* would be a major administrative law case. True, the building blocks of Justice Stevens' opinion were laid out for the Court in the government's argument for deference, but as Levy observes, the opinion "is more path-breaking than the brief was."[107] It appears that the Solicitor General's office, along with everyone else, thought the administrative law questions would be resolved by applying established principles and precedents. No one thought it was a "big" case.

Everyone immediately recognized, however, what it meant when it was handed down. The Court had made new law, and in rather dramatic fashion. Justice Department and EPA officials knew that the case would be very helpful in ongoing battles over EPA regulatory programs, which were being litigated in federal courts all over the country. Academic commentators began to express concern about the latitude that would now be enjoyed by executive branch officials, and the incentives *Chevron* created for them to find and exploit statutory ambiguities. Would the government simply have to assert ambiguity in order to get *Chevron* deference, or would courts engage in scrupulous statutory interpretation? Those EPA officials who had always been uncomfortable with bubbles, and those who, more generally, did not want the kind of interpretive discretion being accorded to them, worried about what it would mean when "the other guys" got into power and got their hands on the doctrine.[108]

The Court itself did not seem to anticipate this reaction. From his review of the Marshall papers, Professor Percival concludes that the Justices did not realize the full implications of *Chevron*.[109] He notes that

---

106. Doniger Interview, *supra* note 78.

107. Levy Interview, *supra* note 84.

108. Doniger recalls running into Joe Cannon, then head of the air program, shortly after the decision came down. Cannon told him, "I shudder to think what you'll do with deference when *you* get into power." Doniger replied that by then, the doctrine would be cut back. "And sure enough by the time of the Clinton administration, it was." Doniger Interview, *supra* note 78.

109. *See* Robert V. Percival, *Environmental Law in the Supreme Court: Highlights from the Marshall Papers*, 13 Environmental Law Reporter 10606, 10613 (Oct. 1993).

there was no comment in the written exchanges among the Justices that "reflect any appreciation of the major change in administrative law the decision effected." Percival notes that Justice Stevens' draft opinion was circulated on June 11, 1984 and that, within a week, four justices had already indicated, with little or no comment, that they would join it.[110]

If the Court failed to anticipate the impact of its holding on administrative law, surely the Justices were even less aware of *Chevron's* implications for air pollution regulation. The transcript of oral argument leaves some doubt as to the Justices' appreciation of the technical statutory issues, let alone the larger policy debate over the use of bubbles. And Justice Blackmun's handwritten notes from Conference reinforce that impression.[111] For example, he quotes Justice Stevens as saying that he is "not at rest," and that "when I am so confused, I go with the Agency." And he indicates that Justice O'Connor was leaning toward deferring to the agency because "the bubble makes sense as a concept" and "industry is suffering."[112]

The Court's failure to engage meaningfully with the environmental implications of the case should not be surprising. Environmental statutes were fairly new at the time, and the CAA stood out as the apotheosis of technical complexity. Four years earlier, dissenting from a denial of *certiorari*, Justice Rehnquist had commented that "the requirements of the Clean Air Act Amendments virtually swim before one's eyes..."[113] and it is easy to imagine that he was not alone in this view.

Even the clerks at the time seemed to have no appetite for environmental statutes. As Percival notes, Justice Marshall's papers contain a clerk's note about a 1977 Clean Water Act case that says, "This certainly qualifies as the most boring this Term. I'm sure it's not Justice Stevens'

---

110. *Id.*

111. *Id.*

112. *Id.*

113. *See* United States Steel Corp. v. EPA, 444 U.S. 1035, 1038 (1980) (Rehnquist J., dissenting from denial of certiorari: "The fact that the requirements of the Clean Act Air Amendments virtually swim before one's eyes is not a rational basis, under these circumstances, for refusing to exercise our discretionary jurisdiction"). *See also* The Official Papers of Justice Harry Blackmun, Box 591, CMA v. NRDC & USEPA v. NRDC, Case Nos. 83–1013 & 83–1373, Box No. 416, Note Taken During Oral Argument by Justice Blackmun (November 6, 1984) ("What a dull case") (it is not clear whether this note was written by the Justice or by another Justice who was sitting next to Blackmun during oral argument and who jotted it on Blackmun's paper, which appears to have happened sometimes). There are repeated references in the Justices' oral arguments notes in environmental cases to how the cases were not necessarily the most interesting. *See, e.g.*, The Official Papers of Justice Harry Blackmun, Gwaltney v. Chesapeake Bay Foundation, Case No. 86–473, Box 490, Notes Taken During Oral Argument (October 5, 1987) ("I am getting sleepy" and the advocate "drones").

fault." A memo from one of Justice Blackmun's clerks during this period confirms the sentiment: "I don't know what to advise you about these petitions. The clerks all call them 'those horrible EPA cases.' "[114]

Especially interesting in light of how monumental the case would become, the Court in *Chevron* was at less than full strength: Justice Marshall did not participate in the case at all (he was apparently too ill to attend oral argument); then Justice Rehnquist was absent for the Conference because he had not participated at argument—he eventually recused himself; and Justice O'Connor, while attending both argument and Conference, eventually recused herself as well, due to a conflict of interest.[115] Justice O'Connor explained in a memo to the Court that the estate of her father, who had died after oral argument, owned stock in Chevron.[116]

Yet the case was also closer than the final decision would lead one to believe. Justice Blackmun's notes indicate that the initial vote in Conference was 3–3. What ultimately swayed the Justices who were wavering? In the absence of any written exchanges among them, and without disclosures by clerks, it is hard to know. Some Justices may ultimately have seized on the administrative law principles raised by the case as a way out of the statutory morass. Perhaps some believed that in a case of such complexity, an interpretive "tie" ought to go to the runner—in this case the agency. Some Justices undoubtedly responded to the Solicitor General's skillful invitation to rebuke the D.C. Circuit—yet again—for its usurpation of executive prerogative through aggressive review.[117] (Doniger believes that this determined the outcome, and that the clerk's comment foretold it: the Court needed to put the D.C. Circuit in its place.) The government had given the Court an administrative law principle on which to hang its hat, and the Justices appeared to take the opportunity.

---

114.   The Official Papers of Justice Harry Blackmun, Box 591, Arkansas v. Oklahoma & EPA v. Oklahoma, Case Nos. 90–1262 & 90–1266, Preliminary Memorandum to Justice Blackmun from Law Clerk (March 29, 1991). *See* Percival, *supra*, note 109, at 10617.

115.   The Official Papers of Justice Harry Blackmun, Case Nos. 82–1005; 82–1247; 82–1591, Box 397.

116.   *See* Justice O'Connor, Memorandum to the Conference, June 14, 1984 in the Official Papers of Harry Blackmun, Box 397.

117.   It is entirely plausible that the Supreme Court viewed *Chevron*, six years after *Vermont Yankee*, as an opportunity to again rebuke those members of the D.C. Circuit who had a penchant for overly aggressive review of agency decision making, whether on matters of fact, policy, or in the case of *Chevron*, law. Here they had done it again: in rejecting the agency's interpretation of "stationary source," the D.C. Circuit panel had announced a bright line test regarding when bubbles could and could not be used under the Clean Air Act—a test that had no basis in the Act itself.

Conclusion

Scholars have now spent over twenty years debating *Chevron's* theoretical and practical implications for administrative law, including its potentially enormous impact on the separation of powers. The Supreme Court's test appears to shift to the executive branch interpretive authority traditionally lodged in the judiciary on the theory that Congress' failure to address "the precise question in issue" evidences an intent to delegate interpretive authority to the implementing agency—a controversial rationale, to say the least.

Yet while the deference issue and its separation of powers implications have come to dominate scholarly commentary on *Chevron*, the substantive battle in the case, it should not be forgotten, centered on the legal and policy implications of using bubbles in the NSR program.[118] The progeny of this dispute are alive today in the debate over how to reform NSR after twenty-five years of experience, at a time when, according to the most recent EPA figures, approximately 126 million people still live in areas designated as nonattainment for at least one of the criteria pollutants; when people young and old across the country continue to breathe unhealthy air on many days of the year.[119]

In 2002, the EPA promulgated an NSR reform package that significantly altered NSR's applicability to existing sources.[120] In 2003, the EPA

---

118. Indeed, the bubble approach exists today in the form of Plantwide Applicability Limits (PALs) which allow firms to trade emissions among units under their control providing they achieve the established regulatory target. This is the more pure form of bubbles described earlier. PALS arguably supplant NSR. In return for limiting all of their emissions, PAL sources are allowed to use a much less demanding NSR regime than other sources (PAL sources may use an accounting mechanism for their emissions known as that is more favorable to the firm whereas other sources may not). PALS are intended help firms comply with their Title V permit limits by giving them operational flexibility. *See, e.g.,* Prevention of Significant Deterioration (PSD) and Nonattainment New Source Review (NSR), 61 Fed. Reg. 38,250, 38,264 (July 23, 1996) (*codified at* 40 C.F.R. §§ 51–52) (defining PAL for purposes of the proposed NSR Reform Rule). However, the 2002 NSR rule did not invent PALS; they have existed since 1994 by guidance document and case by case permit decisions.

119. *See* Environmental Protection Agency, *Air Pollution Trends* (2002) *at* http://www.epa.gov/airtrends/non.html.

120. Prevention of Significant Deterioration (PSD) and Nonattainment New Source Review (NSR): Baseline Emissions Determination, Actual- to Future-Actual Methodology, Plantwide Applicability Limitations, Clean Units, Pollution Control Projects, 67 Fed. Reg. 80,186 (Dec. 31, 2002) (*codified at* 40 C.F.R. pts. 51, 52). The Package proposed, among other things, to expand the time frame for establishing a firm's "pre-modification baseline emissions," allowing sources greater flexibility in establishing the baseline; alter the basis on which existing sources can calculate emissions in a manner that is more favorable to them by providing an alternative to the "past actual versus future potential" calculus previously applicable; and establish a bubble-like "plantwide applicability limit" program for facilities that wish to make changes under an imaginary cap without triggering NSR. It adopted a rule clarifying the longstanding exemption to NSR permitting requirements for "routine maintenance, repair and replacement activities." This rule sought to more clearly define which process changes would amount to "routine maintenance" of equipment that would not trigger NSR versus which changes would amount to a "modification" that would trigger NSR.[121] The rule was subsequently stayed by the D.C. Circuit and is currently being reconsidered by the agency. NSR reform is also a key aspect of the Bush Administration's Clear Skies legislation.[122]

Clearly, the question of whether, and for how long, to "grandfather" existing sources by allowing them to make capital improvements or to "modernize" without triggering strict pollution control requirements, remains as pressing as ever. The seeds of this dispute were sown in *Chevron.*

Beyond the matter of whether the bubble policy was a lawful interpretation of the statutory term "stationary source"—the key legal issue in *Chevron*—there remains the question of whether the bubble concept is good policy. At the time, there was little empirical evidence one way or the other; the likely effect of the bubble's widespread adoption was a matter of pure speculation.[123] So the policy debate turned mostly on a normative argument about whether using such a strategy would be, in theory, superior to the alternative of the unit-by-unit approach required by command and control. One's view of this depends heavily on one's beginning assumptions about the appropriate baseline from which to make comparisons. In the debate over whether the EPA's

---

was reconsidered by the agency, see 68 Fed. Reg. 63,021 (Nov. 7, 2003) (*codified at* 40 C.F.R. pts. 51, 52).

121. The new rule provided that the replacement of identical or functionally equivalent component parts would not be deemed a "modification" but instead would be deemed "Routine Maintenance" if (1) the replacement does not change the basic design parameters of the unit; (2) the replacement does not cause the unit to exceed applicable emissions or operation limits; and (3) the cost of the replacement activity does not exceed twenty percent of the replacement value of the process unit. *See* 68 Fed. Reg. at 61,252 (*codified at* 40 C.F.R. pts. 51, 52).

122. Clear Skies Act of 2005, S. 131, 109th Cong. (2005).

123. *See* Levin, *Bubble Policy, supra* note 38, at 70 on the absence of economic data for the bubble's asserted benefits in non-attainment areas. In a study conducted for the Conservation Foundation and published in 1986, Liroff concluded that many of the claims about the benefits of bubbles turned out to be overstated, or true only under certain circumstances. For case studies, see Liroff *supra* note 13, at 67–98. In some cases, the reductions in emissions only existed on paper, and amounted to administrative recognition of past emissions reductions. In other cases, administrative accounting techniques enabled firms to avoid reductions that would otherwise have been necessary or to make process changes that, one might argue, they ought to be required to make in any event. Still, Liroff's study did conclude that under certain circumstances, bubbles can reduce compliance costs, speed compliance and spur technological innovation. And Levin argues that EPA tried hard in the ensuing years to prohibit such trades.

bubble strategy would advance or retard progress toward the federal air quality standards, a key question was, and still is, "What, realistically, would NSR have *otherwise* required?"

This kind of conflict over baselines arises often in environmental regulation, especially in the context of air regulation. Should we assume that a command and control program will be perfectly implemented, and then compare the anticipated results to a market approach? Or is it more realistic to assume incomplete implementation, and to consider the cost and administrative expense associated with the command and control approach, when comparing it to the market alternative? And what are the transaction costs and compliance rates of the market alternative?

Whether trading of this sort, in any of its applications, is good policy, is not a "snapshot" issue. That is, any attempt at a real world answer must take account of how the policy has evolved over time, whether it has been reformed in light of criticism (in the case of the bubble, to eliminate the opportunity for "phony" paper trades).[124] And, most importantly, answering this question requires continually comparing the trading option to the (also evolving and also imperfect) alternatives. Would we have been better off without the bubble? Would cap-and-trade programs—now the preferred policy tool for addressing greenhouse gas regulation—have developed even if *Chevron* had come out the other way? The answer is unclear.

Industry and environmentalists still fight over such baseline issues and, as they did in *Chevron*, they continue to disagree over whether market instruments will work as well in practice as they sound in theory. At the root of these disagreements are very different views not only about appropriate baselines, but also about the narrowness and breadth of definitions and exemptions, and the accuracy of conflicting claims about what will induce modernization and technological innovation. The early stages of all of these disputes can be located in the history of the bubble policy, and in the briefs and arguments in *Chevron*. Despite its legacy as a high impact administrative law case then, *Chevron* remains a case very much at the heart of contemporary environmental law.*

---

124. In theory, the more questionable uses of the bubble are no longer permissible. *See* Final Emissions Trading Policy Statement 51 FR 43,814 (Dec. 4, 1986).

* I would like to acknowledge the contributions of Jose Allen, David Doniger, Michael Levin, Mark Levy, David Menotti, Bill Pedersen and Peter Wyckoff, all of whom played a role in the Chevron litigation; Professor Craig Oren for his comments; and Chris Baker, Paul Blanco, Miriam Seifter and the reference librarians at the UCLA School of Law for their research assistance.

*

7

William W. Buzbee

The Story of *Laidlaw*: Standing and Citizen Enforcement

Friends of the Earth, Inc. v. Laidlaw Environmental Services (TOC), Inc.,[1] hardly exudes significance. The Supreme Court permitted three environmental groups, Friends of the Earth, Inc., the Sierra Club, and CLEAN, to proceed with their lawsuit against a polluter, as expressly provided by statutory law. That polluter, Laidlaw, had been a chronic violator of its Clean Water Act permit. Hundreds of similar cases had been brought to successful conclusion since Congress in the early 1970s had added "citizen suit" provisions to most environmental laws. The Court's ruling thus at first blush appears ordinary, almost preordained. And yet virtually all environmental lawyers and judges would nevertheless agree that *Laidlaw* is among the most significant environmental law decisions of the last twenty years.

Laidlaw arrived before the Supreme Court during a period of tremendous flux in the law pertaining to citizen litigation and, in particular, citizen standing doctrine, which determines whether particular litigants will be allowed to go to court and pursue their claims. Between 1993 and 2000, when the *Laidlaw* decision was released, environmentalists had suffered a series of significant setbacks in seeking access to the courts. When the Fourth Circuit dismissed the plaintiffs' case in *Laidlaw*, the very viability of citizen enforcement of environmental law stood in the balance. That ruling left the *Laidlaw* plaintiffs remediless, without fees, and Laidlaw escaping without paying any penalties despite a record of hundreds of illegal discharges, hundreds of reporting violations, and substantial economic benefits from those violations. That decision, and several other similar appellate court setbacks,

---

1. 528 U.S. 167 (2000).

threatened to turn already challenging Supreme Court precedents into a minefield through which few environmental plaintiffs could pass.

The Fourth Circuit ruling, however, also presented a good vehicle for environmentalists to regain lost ground. The district court judge had found that the plaintiffs did have standing, and had found that the state's enforcement action against Laidlaw was not a "diligent prosecution." The illegal discharges involved mercury, a pollutant no one could trivialize. Furthermore, to determine the appropriate penalty, the trial judge had taken extensive evidence on Laidlaw's many violations and resulting economic advantage of over a million dollars due to its permit violations. The district court had reduced the ultimate penalty, in part due to a troublesome finding of no proof of environmental harms traceable to the permit violations, but his findings and the laborious work of lawyers at the trial level created a powerful factual case. The Fourth Circuit's devastating ruling dismissing the case on mootness grounds highlighted the problematic reach of these cases. Through a combination of fortuity and strategy, *Laidlaw* became the vehicle through which environmentalists sought to rescue citizen suits from the brink.

I. Citizen Suits and Standing

To understand the strategic choices of the *Laidlaw* lawyers and the significance of the case result, one must first have a basic understanding of how citizen suits and linked standing doctrine work. A logical question for someone new to environmental law is why the viability of citizen-initiated environmental litigation matters. After all, the executive branch can enforce the law, as can states when they assume enforcement roles under delegated program federalism schemes offered by most modern environmental laws. In reality, government actors frequently fail to enforce the law, sometimes (as in *Laidlaw*) entering into lax settlements that arguably undercut the law. In addition, government officials are frequently themselves the problem, missing deadlines and violating statutory and regulatory edicts. Citizens play a critical role in redressing these environmental law implementation failures, much as they have under the Administrative Procedure Act (APA) for decades, but with special additional functions under citizen suit provisions.

Under statutory citizen suit provisions, "any person" may sue a broad category of persons, including government officials, who violate legal obligations set forth in statutes, regulations, or pollution control permits.[2] They may also sue state and federal officials where they fail to carry out "nondiscretionary" duties such as issuing regulations by a

---

2. *See, e.g.,* Clean Water Act, 33 U.S.C. § 1365; Clean Air Act, 42 U.S.C. § 7604; Endangered Species Act, 16 U.S.C. § 1540(g).

statutory deadline.[3] Citizens must, however, in most circumstances first provide advance 60 day notice letters both to the target of their likely lawsuit as well as federal and state regulators. If prior to or during that time federal or state officials "diligently" prosecute the polluter or other violator of the law, then citizen action can be preempted, although citizen intervention rights provide an additional procedural option. Polluters' noncompliance is usually beyond debate. Under the Clean Air and Clean Water Act, they must self-report their compliance status, with substantial civil and criminal penalties discouraging false reporting. As occurred in *Laidlaw,* a polluter's Discharge Monitoring Reports (DMRs) establish the polluter's compliance status. If there are violations, the polluter is strictly liable, regardless of the polluter's good faith, negligence, or the reasonableness of its permit. A polluter's good faith efforts can, of course, influence relief provided by the courts, but good faith and diligence cannot eliminate the underlying liability.

If the citizen suit is allowed to proceed, citizen enforcers can seek injunctive relief and imposition of civil penalties. Plaintiffs who prevail typically may recover their attorney's fees and costs, although penalties imposed by a court go to the federal treasury. This kind of legislatively authorized direct citizen enforcement against polluters in citizen suit provisions was a major statutory innovation. It went well beyond citizen roles under the APA and other earlier regulatory regimes.

Although citizen suits were once characterized in a Supreme Court standing opinion as just reflecting the "government-policy preferences of political activists," such a view fails to note how such suits must be consistent with preceding enacted law.[4] Citizen litigants cannot even begin a case, let alone win it, unless their preferences comport with several layers of political judgments that are part of duly enacted statutory law and subsequent politically and judicially accountable steps of regulatory implementation. First, citizen litigants must step through the citizen suit procedural hurdles. Second, they must be able to point to a clear violation of legal obligations set forth in a statute, regulation, or permit. In the permit violation setting, a citizen plaintiff is actually enforcing multiple layers of politically accountable (and often litigated) judgments. Categories of polluter and pollution must, by statutory edict, be regulated by EPA. Those regulatory judgments themselves go through a notice and comment process, typically followed by litigation. If those regulatory judgments are upheld, they in turn must be rolled into permitting decisions at individual polluting facilities. These permitting

---

3. Eleventh Amendment immunities, however, may limit the relief available against states. *See* Hope Babcock, *The Effect of the Supreme Court's Eleventh Amendment Jurisprudence on Environmental Citizen Suits: Gotcha,* 10 Widener L. Rev. 205 (2003).

4. Steel Co. v. Citizens for a Better Env't, 523 U.S. 83, 104 (1998) (Scalia, J., writing for the Court majority).

judgments can be negotiated with federal regulators, but typically are handled by state regulators and themselves subject to participatory public process and potential challenges in administrative or judicial venues. When citizens sue to rectify pollution permit violations, they thus are acting in accord with many preceding democratically and judicially accountable judgments. Only if citizen political preferences are in sync with these enacted, promulgated and permitted political judgments do they have a chance of success.

Citizens are, however, likely more motivated than many government officials to act against environmental violators. First and foremost, environmentalists are often ardent advocates of a cleaner environment. They are eager to enforce the law and discourage polluters or government officials from violating environmental laws. Furthermore, not-for-profits dedicated to environmental goals need to show their members and funders evidence of their activism and achievements.[5] In addition, the added incentive of attorney's fee recoveries create strong monetary incentives to sue polluters, provided the probabilities of success and recovery are sufficiently high. It was just this likelihood of real enforcement that legislators identified when adding citizen suit provisions to environmental laws starting the 1970s.[6] The Environmental Protection Agency has similarly embraced the value of citizen suits, at least suits directed at pollution violators. Even during the Reagan administration, when many administration policies were viewed as anti-environmental, Administrator Ruckelshaus explicitly lauded such suits' benefits in "complement[ing] the EPA program"; subsequent policy memoranda did so in even greater detail.[7] This combination of democratically expressed goals, environmental aspirations of environmentalists, and attorney monetary incentives were critical to the *Laidlaw* plaintiffs' decision to commence their citizen suit.

Mere compliance with statutory prerequisites, however, does not ensure success. A citizen plaintiff must also surmount constitutional and prudential standing hurdles. It was litigation over the content of these constitutional hurdles that took *Laidlaw* to the Supreme Court. Constitutional standing doctrine is attributed primarily to Article III of the

---

5. *See* Daniel A. Farber, *Politics and Procedure in Environmental Law,* 8 J. L. Econ. & Org. 59 (1992).

6. *See* James R. May, *Now More Than Ever: Trends in Environmental Citizen Suits at 30,* 10 Widener L. Rev. 1, 1, 5–10 (2003) (quoting 1970s legislative and judicial statements about the purposes of citizen suits, and discussing "why citizen suits matter").

7. Telephone interview with Carolyn Smith Pravlik (August 27, 2004); Memoranda regarding "EPA Response to Citizen Suits" from William D. Ruckelshaus, EPA Administrator, to Regional Counsels and Administrators (July 30, 1984); Memoranda regarding "Clean Water Act Citizen Suits: Support of Federal Government" from Glenn Unterberger, Assoc. Enforcement Counsel for Water to Regional Counsels (Oct. 3, 1986).

Constitution's limitation of federal courts' jurisdiction to "Cases" and "Controversies," although Article II also adds something to the mix. From that slender textual base, the Supreme Court has built a substantial body of law regarding a plaintiff's suitability to bring a case.

Since the Court first applied standing doctrine to environmental litigation in the 1970s, most significantly in *Sierra Club v. Morton*,[8] it vacillated in its willingness to countenance significant citizen litigation under environmental laws. The Court in *Sierra Club* rejected a public interest group's ability merely to seek to enforce the law without showing some tangible links to the underlying threatened natural resource. The Court also, however, stated with clarity that recreational and aesthetic interests in an environmental amenity were indeed interests that were to be recognized by the courts, provided the plaintiff could show a link to those threatened or injured interests. For the next decade, courts devoted little attention to environmental litigants' standing, with most litigants able to show the requisite link to the environmental amenity at interest.

The composition of the lower courts and the Supreme Court was changing, however, as was the rise of increasingly active environmental groups willing to sue polluters and the government. By the late 1980s, many citizen suit actions were being brought against polluters and government agencies alleged to have violated legal obligations set forth in environmental laws, regulations and pollution permits. In an array of areas of public law litigation, many courts by the late 1980s embraced statutory, constitutional and prudential doctrines that reduced access to the courts afforded to regulatory beneficiaries such as environmental citizen suit plaintiffs.

As discussed in greater detail below, starting with the two *Lujan* cases that recast constitutional standing doctrine to deny judicial access even to citizens suing under expressly granted statutory citizen suit causes of action, the Supreme Court during the 1990s sent particularly mixed and confusing signals to courts and environmental litigants.[9] These mixed signals were rendered even more opaque due to the divided Supreme Court they reflected. The *Lujan* standing decisions and several other 1990s standing cases that followed, both in the environmental and non-environmental area, were often in five to four decisions that included multiple opinions. They seesawed in their conclusions and in their receptivity to citizen standing. One could fairly ask whether these cases set forth a body of law at all, or merely revealed the justices' divided

---

8. 405 U.S. 727 (1972).

9. Lujan v. Defenders of Wildlife, 504 U.S. 555 (1992) (*Lujan*); Lujan v. National Wildlife Federation, 497 U.S. 871 (1990) (*Lujan/NWF*).

political preferences.[10] A raft of critical law review scholarship and a well publicized white paper led to front page coverage by the New York Times in an article questioning the Supreme Court's apparent hostility to citizen environmental litigation.[11] After all, the environmental standing cases added up to an increasingly problematic set of barriers for citizen litigants. These sometimes irreconcilable Supreme Court opinions spawned an even more confused body of lower court law. From that morass, *Laidlaw* emerged.

II. Laidlaw's *Litigation History: The Lawyers and Facts*

Bruce Terris's law firm is a rarity, a small for-profit law firm that spends most of its time bringing environmental citizen suit actions. He and his partner, Carolyn Pravlik, acted as attorneys for Friends of Earth (FOE), Sierra Club, and Citizens Local Environmental Action Network (CLEAN) during the many years of the *Laidlaw* litigation. In *Laidlaw* and numerous other cases, they drew on their expertise and an established relationship with FOE and the other plaintiff environmental groups to identify and sue chronic pollution permit violators.

Bruce Terris was among the nation's earliest environmental litigators, having acted as an attorney for an environmentalist friend of court *amicus* filing in the first major environmental standing case, the Mineral King *Sierra Club v. Morton* case that recognized environmental standing. His Harvard Law School degree and eight years divided between the Department of Justice and Solicitor General's office prepared him well for sophisticated public law litigation. During his government years, he argued twelve cases before the Supreme Court, with four more (including *Laidlaw*) after he went into private practice. When he set up his own firm, its work was seventy to eighty percent environmental. Initially, even not-for-profit firms would hire him and pay his fees by the hour. This continued during the 1970s and early 1980s. During the 1980s, however, the volume of profitable plaintiff-side environmental work with clients who paid his fees on a time-billed basis dried up.

Pravlik worked with Terris during this period of transition, having joined the firm after graduation from Catholic University Law School and a short stint with the honors program of the United States Department of the Interior Solicitor General's office. When the controversial James Watt was appointed to head the Department of the Interior by President Reagan, he eliminated the honors program and the class of attorneys selected for the honors program by the outgoing administra-

---

    10. Richard J. Pierce, Jr., *Is Standing Law or Politics?*, 77 N.C. L. Rev. 1741 (1999).

    11. *See* William Glaberson, *Novel Antipollution Tool Is Being Upset by Courts*, N.Y. Times, at A1, June 5, 1999 (quoting and discussing report of Georgetown Environmental Policy Project and views of its director, John Echeverria).

tion. The wholesale firing of Pravlik and her classmates "solidified" Pravlik's commitment to work to protect the environment.[12] She joined Terris's firm and in the subsequent decades became the firm's lead lawyer in vetting potential citizen suits and advising other lawyers about such cases.

Once environmental plaintiff groups took much of their legal work in house, Terris and his firm had to come up with a new means to combine the need to make a living with their desire to improve the environment. From that point forward, utilizing citizen suit provisions, he and his firm, in his words, "generated our own environmental cases."[13] As characterized by Pravlik, their firm has "marching orders" from various environmental organizations with which they have worked to "alert them" if the firm "finds cases worth bringing."[14] Friends of Earth President, Dr. Brent Blackwelder, similarly describes their relationship, stating that his organization has such a standing request because they "want to crack down, that is something our membership wants, [we] want to keep enforcing the law."[15] Attorneys from the Terris–Pravlik firm study DMR reports in state databases to identify chronic violators. Once they identify violators potentially worth suing due to the seriousness of their violations, the firm consults with environmental groups such as Friends of the Earth (FOE), the American Canoe Association, and others, to see if they agree with commencement of such a suit. If these not-for-profits' leaders agree, then the groups provide Terris's firm with names and numbers of members in the affected areas who might be interested in serving as representatives for the organization during the litigation. This process is a "laborious and expensive proposition."[16]

Terris and his clients prefer cases that will not present problems under citizen suit doctrine, generally meaning cases that lack problematic factual complexity. The overwhelming majority of cases he has brought for environmental plaintiffs have been successful, with many settling early and before significant attorney's time and fees build up. Others, however, can end up "horrendously complicated" and seemingly "last forever."[17] Terris's and Pravlik's firm survived this change in practice, but today, with only nine lawyers, Terris believes that his firm is the biggest profit driven plaintiff-side environmental law firm in the

---

12. Telephone interview of Carolyn Smith Pravlik (August 27, 2004).

13. Telephone interview with Bruce Terris (July 6, 2004).

14. Telephone interview with Carolyn Smith Pravlik (Aug. 27, 2004).

15. Telephone interview with Dr. Brent Blackwelder, President, Friends of Earth (Oct. 1, 2004).

16. Telephone interview with Bruce Terris (July 6, 2004).

17. *Id.*

country.[18] In recent years, a few notable victories have been accompanied by far more numerous cases that, like *Laidlaw*, remain mired in a slow, hearing and motion-laden litigation process that result in few truly final victories. According to Pravlik, the last significant citizen suit case resulting in a favorable conclusion, including actual payment of attorney's fees, was in 2001. Others may bear fruit, including a 2004 multimillion dollar fee award by a district court, but appeals and challenges on the merits and the fee will delay any potential actual payment. As of late 2004, a three year environmental citizen suit drought is underway for their firm.

The *Laidlaw* complaint was filed in 1992. *Laidlaw* appeared to be one of the easy cases, with an industrial discharger whose DMRs revealed hundreds of permit violations involving a seriously toxic pollutant, mercury, and hundreds of other monitoring and reporting violations. Later, when plaintiffs decided to seek Supreme Court review of their case, the serious and toxic nature of mercury pollution influenced the decision to choose *Laidlaw* as a vehicle to cut back on harmful standing decisions of the 1990s. Well before they got to the Supreme Court, however, *Laidlaw* had became for Terris, Pravlik and their clients a long and drawn out case.

The polluter, Laidlaw, operated a large hazardous waste incinerator in Roebuck, South Carolina. The water pollution discharges that created Laidlaw's legal troubles emanated from a wastewater treatment plant for water used in air pollution control devices for the incinerator. Laidlaw purchased the facility from ABCO Industries, Inc. in 1986.[19] Shortly after the acquisition, the State of South Carolina revisited the facility's water pollution permit and ratcheted down permissible mercury discharges from 20 parts per billion (ppb) to 1.3 ppb, with an interim 10 ppb limit during 1987. Laidlaw contracted with consultants to devise strategies to meet the much more stringent 1.3 ppb limit, but initial attempted technological fixes did not do the trick. A 1988 fish kill into the North Tyger River was attributed to Laidlaw's effluent, leading to a state enforcement action. The state, through the South Carolina Department of Health and Environmental Control (DHEC), ordered Laidlaw to investigate treatment technologies so it would comply with its permit, replace the killed fish, and pay a $20,000 fine. Despite retention of another consultant and installation of a new pollution control system, Laidlaw still struggled to comply with its permit, violating its mercury permit limitation hundreds of times in the next few years.

---

18. *Id.*

19. Subsequent corporate ownership changes actually modified the name of Laidlaw, but as in the Supreme Court's decision, this chapter refers to the defendant as Laidlaw.

These mercury violations, plus hundreds of other monitoring and reporting violations, were found by Terris's firm. Following conversations with FOE and CLEAN and identification of FOE members willing to testify to their concerns about Laidlaw and their linkages to the North Tyger River, Terris sent a notice letter to Laidlaw, South Carolina and federal officials, as required by the Clean Water Act's citizen suit provision.

At this point, Laidlaw's counsel came into the picture. By the time the case was before the Supreme Court, a small team worked on Laidlaw's behalf, but initially the case's defense was led by the Atlanta and South Carolina offices of Ogletree, Deakins, Nash, Smoak & Stewart, a primarily corporate and defense firm specializing in labor law. Ogletree is the third largest labor firm in the country, with 215 lawyers.[20] Their tenacious and effective defense of *Laidlaw* was led for most of the case by Donald Cockrill. Although Cockrill started work on this case with less environmental experience than Terris's firm and no Supreme Court background, he proved himself an effective advocate and opponent. He too had impressive credentials, with a University of Virginia Law degree and six years of work with the United States Department of Justice fraud division prior to joining the Ogletree firm. He had occasional involvement with environmental law prior to *Laidlaw,* but nothing like Terris's and Pravlik's near total immersion in environmental litigation.

As Laidlaw's lawyers devised their legal strategies, Laidlaw began to get its violation problems under control. Although it continued to violate its permit after plaintiffs' notice letter, after the state (kind of) sued Laidlaw (more about that in a few pages), and after plaintiffs filed their complaint, the number of violations dwindled. They finally came into consistent compliance as the litigation continued, especially after its permit was revised to allow higher permit discharges, but over a different time period.

Defendant's counsel in *Laidlaw* utilized virtually every potential defensive strategy, forcing plaintiffs, plaintiffs' counsel, and the district court judge to battle through multi-day hearings and extensive motion practice. Although the fact of Laidlaw's hundreds of permit violations remained uncontroverted, the accreted array of available defensive strategies gave defendant numerous means to test plaintiffs and their counsel. That the case has taken years and millions of dollars in attorney time is not a testament to a congressionally created gravy train. Instead, the citizen suit device, intended to make more real and certain effective environmental enforcement, now is more like a maze filled with fatal traps.

---

20. Telephone interview with Donald Cockrill (July 2, 2004).

The defendant's first challenge was rooted in express statutory language. As plaintiffs counted the sixty days after their notice letter before they could file their complaint, Laidlaw's attorneys were busy trying to knock out the suit before it could get started. As provided by citizen suit provisions, if federal or state authorities diligently prosecute a permit violator, those enforcement actions can preclude the citizen's action, or at least relegate citizens to intervention in a government-initiated suit. Laidlaw's attorneys did not want to get mired in litigation, however. They wanted to bring closure to their potential liability before it got out of control.

Their strategy? Convince the state to sue and settle with Laidlaw, with Laidlaw's attorneys doing all the work. Off they ran to the chief of water pollution control at DHEC, Russell Sherer, asking DHEC to file an action in court against Laidlaw. Sherer demurred, stating that DHEC's usual practice was to pursue an administrative action. Under a literal reading of the Clean Water Act, however, a mere administrative action might not protect Laidlaw against future suits, in particular the threatened suit on behalf of FOE and its co-plaintiffs. Laidlaw persisted in its entreaties, this time with success. As trial Judge Anderson stated, the state "DHEC filed a judicial action against the Defendant solely because counsel for the Defendant requested that DHEC file a judicial action instead of an administrative action," with the goal of "bar[ring] the Plaintiffs' proposed citizen suit in federal court." [21]Rather than proceeding in an adversarial relationship, the state agreed to Laidlaw's doing all of the state's work. Laidlaw drafted the complaint, filed it, paid associated fees, and wrote up a simultaneous consent order memorializing settlement of the case. A judge signed this consent order the day after the court papers were filed, on the last day before plaintiffs could file their own case. In DHEC officials' recollections, no other enforcement matter ever moved so quickly to settlement.[22] This rapid settlement was explicitly intended to preempt the threatened citizen suit, a goal inconsistent with the state's usual stated policy of not filing actions at defendants' request to prevent a citizen suit.[23] As part of this settlement, Laidlaw agreed to a fine of $100,000, $20,000 less than initially sought by the state.

As *Laidlaw's* attorney Cockrill conceded, there was "an odor to it," but he and his client saw it as essential "to avoid getting mired in litigation."[24] When the environmental plaintiffs filed their complaint,

---

21. Friends of the Earth, Inc. v. Laidlaw Envtl. Serv., 890 F. Supp. 470, 478–79 (D.S.C. 1995).

22. *Id.* at 479.

23. *Id.*

24. Telephone Interview with Donald Cockrill (July 2, 2004).

Laidlaw moved to dismiss based on a "diligent prosecution" theory, as explicitly provided under the citizen suit provision. Such early and quick settlements, often on lax terms, are found in many reported environmental citizen suit cases, but do not always survive "diligent prosecution" scrutiny. Nevertheless, Cockrill expected to win on this motion. After all, a suit had been filed in court, a consent order entered, and Laidlaw had agreed to pay what it viewed as a substantial fine.

Much to Laidlaw's surprise, the Judge did not view this matter as one that could be resolved based on motion papers. Instead, due to factual issues he saw as unclear, he ordered an evidentiary hearing and put the attorneys through a substantial round of briefing. The court heard seven days of testimony over a period of three months, sought and received two *amicus* briefs from the United States Department of Justice, which supported plaintiffs' challenge to the diligence of the prosecution, and received memoranda from the parties about the facts and law concerning a "diligent prosecution" defense. Judge Anderson further received a request to reconsider and certify the question of diligence after an initial ruling for plaintiffs. He also requested and received additional briefs on *res judicata* principles as applied to citizen suit actions commenced after a state-defendant settlement under the Clean Water Act. This was, on issues of law and fact, an exhaustive and exhausting inquiry, but only concerned the ability of plaintiffs to bring their case.

In a twenty nine page ruling, Judge Anderson ruled for plaintiffs. He took into account the litigation history, recounting in detail the state's and Laidlaw's cooperative dealings, which he characterized as "somewhat suspect," but not themselves dispositive to his conclusion that there was not a diligent prosecution.[25] He ultimately found most significant the state's failure even to try to calculate, let alone recoup, the economic advantage to Laidlaw attributable to its permit violations. Federal and state policies both required consideration of economic advantage in determining penalties for permit violations. The $100,000 penalty was nowhere near the $2,270,000 that the state could have sought under its laws. Despite the court's concession that DHEC retained enforcement discretion, Judge Anderson found the state's utter failure to recover or even consider the economic benefit to Laidlaw critical. The suit could proceed.

Laidlaw was not finished, however, in trying to knock the citizens' case out at an early stage. Defendant's counsel attacked the plaintiff FOE's standing in a summary judgment motion, going beyond the offered affidavits of representatives of the plaintiffs. They were each deposed and motion practice followed. Several of the plaintiffs' represen-

---

25. *Laidlaw*, 890 F.Supp. at 489.

tatives testified to linkages to the river and Laidlaw, but in depositions left a great deal of uncertainty and confusion about the nature and extent of those connections. Defense counsel was able to point out numerous contradictions between affidavits and actual testimony, but the plaintiffs' counsel was still able to find snippets of testimony supporting standing arguments. Collectively, the representatives' sworn statements confirmed proximity to the illegally polluted river, concern about the pollution, somewhat wavering assertions about avoidance of the river due to its polluted state, but few direct physical or tangible linkages between Laidlaw's illegal pollution and the representatives' lives or activities. Oddly, defendant challenged the standing of only one of the three plaintiff organizations, apparent due to the belief that the other two plaintiffs would be dismissed on other grounds.[26] After yet another lengthy hearing, the trial judge found this motion to present a close question, but ultimately concluded that plaintiffs satisfied standing prerequisites.

Even then, more motion practice awaited. In 1995, three years after the case was commenced, cross motions for summary judgment were filed, with plaintiffs focusing on the mere fact of the hundreds of violations. Laidlaw, however, raised a defense under the Supreme Court's important and complicated *Gwaltney* case.[27] *Gwaltney* had held that citizen suits under the Clean Water Act could proceed only if there were ongoing violations when the suit was commenced. "Wholly past" violations were held not cognizable under the Clean Water Act. Despite Laidlaw's many violations, the only violations that were ongoing at the time plaintiffs filed their case were the mercury effluent discharges. Following the Supreme Court's convoluted *Gwaltney* opinion, the district court therefore dismissed the plaintiffs' many other claims, limiting their case to the ongoing mercury discharge violations. By so doing, the court substantially limited the penalties faced by Laidlaw.

To decide on those penalties and other potential relief against Laidlaw, Judge Anderson found that a trial was necessary. After a three day trial and further briefing, Judge Anderson was finally ready to decide the case on the merits, which he did in a ruling issued in 1997, five years after the commencement of the litigation. He declined to provide injunctive relief, since Laidlaw by 1997 had cured its mercury violation problems. He found that Laidlaw had gained an economic advantage of $1,092,581 due to its violations, but imposed a penalty of $405,800, taking into account Laidlaw's efforts to comply, lack of proof

---

26.   Email correspondence with Donald Cockrill (Sept. 25, 2004) (explaining that that earlier portion of litigation was handled by others, and suggesting that because the other plaintiffs had not sent notice letters, defendant expected them to be dismissed).

27.   Gwaltney v. Chesapeake Bay Found. Inc., 484 U.S. 49 (1987).

of environmental harms, and the attorney's fees it anticipated would soon be paid by defendant.[28]

Laidlaw then appealed to the Fourth Circuit. On the eve of the argument, the Supreme Court issued its ruling in *Steel Co. v. Citizens for a Better Environment*,[29] dismissing environmentalists' claims because the defendant had belatedly filed toxic release reporting forms prior to plaintiffs' actually filing their compliant. Because the *Steel Co.* defendant was already in compliance with the law, and penalties for the illegally delayed forms would go the U.S. treasury, the Supreme Court concluded that plaintiffs had no redressable claim, a key prong in standing analysis.

During the appeal argument, the Fourth Circuit *Laidlaw* panel focused on the implications of *Steel Co.* When the Fourth Circuit's *Laidlaw* ruling was issued, it was devastating to the plaintiffs. Despite plaintiffs' string of victories in the trial court and proof of longstanding, repeated illegal discharges of mercury before and after they had filed their complaint, the Fourth Circuit read Supreme Court law to require dismissal of plaintiffs' case. The Fourth Circuit's 1998 short opinion rejecting the *Laidlaw* plaintiff's case on mootness grounds built mainly upon *Steel Co.* Because Laidlaw had ceased its violations and the district court had granted no injunctive relief, plaintiffs' only live claim was for penalties. Therefore, the Fourth Circuit reasoned, "[a]pplying the reasoning of *Steel Co.*, we conclude that this action is moot because the only remedy currently available to plaintiffs—civil penalties payable to the government—would not redress any injury Plaintiffs have suffered."[30] Furthermore, the Court concluded that plaintiffs also could not receive any attorney's fees and costs since they could no longer obtain relief on the merits. The Fourth Circuit did not revisit the district court's grant of standing to the *Laidlaw* plaintiffs.

This Fourth Circuit *Laidlaw* ruling had recast the Supreme Court's *Steel Co.* standing redressability discussion as implicating mootness doctrine, but was not a far-fetched construction of the implications of the Court's 1990s standing cases. If allowed to stand, however, virtually any sloppy polluter could potentially escape liability and payment of fees merely by belatedly improving compliance efforts. If a defendant's compliance with its permit could at any time render a plaintiff's case moot, then most citizen suits would face dismissal with no penalties, court orders or attorney's fee awards, even where a plaintiff prompted that delayed compliance. Basically, only citizen suits based on pollution

---

28.   Friends of the Earth, Inc. v. Laidlaw Envtl. Serv., 956 F. Supp. 588 (D.S.C. 1997).

29.   523 U.S. 83 (1998).

30.   Friends of the Earth, Inc. v. Laidlaw Envtl. Serv., 149 F.3d 303, 306–07 (4th Cir. 1998). This decision was reversed by the Supreme Court, as discussed throughout this chapter.

violations that a defendant simply could never control would be worth bringing. The most compelling cases, involving polluters able to do better, but which had failed to invest the requisite money and effort, would predictably be a waste of plaintiffs' time because, under the Fourth Circuit's logic, they could readily be mooted and dismissed. *Laidlaw,* like several other contemporaneous cases, revealed the potentially expansive implications of the Court's 1990s standing opinions.

In the meantime, Laidlaw confronted other business problems unrelated to its pollution control efforts. As the Clean Water Act case wound on, Laidlaw shut down its operations and eventually filed for bankruptcy. Laidlaw argued against surrender of its pollution permit rights, but as of 2004 it remains in Chapter 11 bankruptcy. The Roebuck facility is no longer operational.

III. The Standing and Mootness Challenges: From **Lujan** to **Steel Co.**

Prior to the Supreme Court's *Laidlaw* ruling, the Court's constitutionally based standing and mootness standards threatened to create an insuperable obstacle to citizen litigants. Much of *Laidlaw's* importance lies in its clear rejection of these obstacles. This section reviews the increasingly problematic and confused standing law terrain leading up to *Laidlaw.* Only by understanding the difficult strategic choices faced by the *Laidlaw* plaintiffs can the remarkable result in *Laidlaw* be fully appreciated.

During the 1990s, Supreme Court pluralities or majorities, with Justice Scalia writing for the Court, recast constitutional doctrine in ways that reduced the viability of citizen suit provisions for environmental plaintiffs. The 1990s undercutting of citizen litigation arguably has its intellectual roots in a law review article written over twenty years ago by Justice Scalia.[31] Then-Judge Scalia argued that the doctrine of standing served a crucial constitutional "separation of powers" function and should be reinvigorated. He noted the rise of the "full-time public interest law firm" and not-for-profit national organizations committed to civil rights goals.[32] He bemoaned that such groups could enforce or force upon the executive branch "adherence to legislative policies that the political process itself would not enforce."[33] He argued that empowering citizen litigants would undercut the "ability to lose or misdirect laws[,] . . . one of the prime engines of social change." To avoid excessive interference with the executive branch's enforcement discretion, Justice

---

31. Antonin Scalia, *The Doctrine of Standing as an Essential Element of Standing of Powers*, 17 Suffolk U. L. Rev. 881 (1983).

32. *Id.* at 891, 893.

33. *Id.* at 896.

Scalia argued that the courts should do much more to ensure that plaintiffs really have a stake in their case.

For Justice Scalia, as reflected in this chapter and his subsequent opinions for the Supreme Court, a plaintiff's standing is largely contingent on a court's independent determination that the plaintiff really has a concrete interest that is harmed or threatened. This determination, in turn, is determined through a search for common law-like injuries or threats. The opposing view is that all standing analysis should be influenced heavily by congressionally created statutory interests and procedures. This analytical divide explains much of the Court's vacillating standing jurisprudence during the 1990s. This analytical divide was largely resolved by *Laidlaw*, although over a vociferous dissent by Justice Scalia, joined by Justice Thomas.

A reinvigorated and more restrictive standing doctrine first began to take form as Supreme Court law in 1990, in a five to four decision in *Lujan v. National Wildlife Federation (Lujan/NWF)*, with Justice Scalia writing for the majority. Although *Lujan/NWF* did not involve a citizen suit provision, its standing language, particularly its underlying stated rationale, limited the likely future roles of citizen and public interest litigants. Plaintiffs in *Lujan/NWF* had alleged broad illegality by the Bureau of Land Management in connection with a "land withdrawal program," with millions of acres of land affected. The breadth of the alleged illegality was critical to the Court's conclusion that plaintiffs lacked standing. No plaintiff could show adequate linkages to allegedly threatened lands, in large part due to the huge area allegedly affected. Mere use and enjoyment of lands "in the vicinity" of lands allegedly mismanaged was inadequate for the majority. *Lujan/NWF* language explaining the stringent standing hurdles echoed Justice Scalia's earlier article: "[Plaintiffs] cannot seek *wholesale* improvement of this program by court decree, rather than in the office of the Department or the halls of Congress, where programmatic improvements are normally made." The broad allegations of illegality were thus transformed, in the Court's language, into calls for "programmatic improvements," and courts were to play a limited role in responding to such claims.

Lujan/NWF was not, however, a clear disaster or change in the law. Its requirement that a plaintiff have a connection to a threatened environmental amenity was largely consistent with *Sierra Club v. Morton*. Furthermore, as discussed in *Lujan/NWF* and further amplified upon in the much more recent *Norton v. Southern Utah Wilderness Alliance*,[34] litigation claims based on broad statutory or regulatory language or broad agency initiatives always present difficulties. They will often lack the "final agency action" needed to initiate an APA-based

---

34.   542 U.S. 55 (2004).

action; linking a plaintiff to particular harms is difficult as those harms become more amorphous or widespread. Where underlying statutory or regulatory language is broad, it is frequently difficult to show that an agency lacked discretion under such broad mandates. Furthermore, *Lujan/NWF* was different from the 1990s standing cases that followed in one critical respect. The plaintiffs had to bring their challenge based on the typical APA Section 702 provision allowing for challenges to illegal or unjustified government action by "adversely affected or aggrieved" persons.[35] The Court acknowledged that its analysis regarding broad claims of illegality would be different if the case had been brought under other statutes that "permit ... broad regulations to serve as the 'agency action,' and thus to be the object of judicial review directly."[36]

It was *Lujan v. Defenders of Wildlife (Lujan),* that much more directly raised the stringent litigation hurdle posed by standing doctrine. In denying the plaintiffs standing in a case brought under the Endangered Species Act ("ESA"), the Supreme Court's decision created potentially significant problems even for plaintiffs, like the *Lujan* plaintiffs, whose causes of action were rooted in explicit statutory citizen suit provisions.[37] The Court's majority opinion, authored by Justice Scalia, required, at a minimum, that Article III courts only recognize standing for litigants if the courts find that the litigants have suffered constitutionally sufficient "injury in fact" that is traceable to the defendant and redressable by the courts. This much was not terribly notable, in fact much like *Sierra Club v. Morton.* Going well beyond *Lujan/NWF* or *Sierra Club,* however, *Lujan* decisively rejected the idea that the presence of a legislatively conferred cause of action could end standing analysis. The Court held that Article III courts must, at a minimum, determine that a litigant has a sufficiently real stake in the litigation such that she satisfies an Article III court's judgment that there exists an "injury in fact." The Court majority rooted this conclusion in separation of powers conceptions, including brief discussion that standing doctrine has it roots in Article III's "case" or "controversy" requirement, as well as Article II's allocation of enforcement power and the obligation to "faithfully execute" the law to the President. How Article II factors into standing analysis remains uncertain. It has barely been mentioned in majority standing opinions since *Lujan.*[38]

To understand why *Lujan* was a significant change and how *Laidlaw* provided a critical clarification of standing doctrine and narrowing of

---

35. Lujan v. National Wildlife Federation, 497 U.S. at 882 (1990).

36. *Id.* at 891.

37. Lujan v. Defenders of Wildlife, 504 U.S. 555 (1992).

38. Justice Scalia's *Laidlaw* dissent relies heavily on Article II, but spoke only for two justices.

Lujan, one has to understand what was at stake in this and the standing cases that followed. In *Lujan,* the Court concluded that named plaintiffs had not established at the summary judgment stage a sufficient link to an injury.[39] The plaintiffs in *Lujan* were challenging a new regulation interpreting the ESA as inapplicable to foreign projects supported by U.S. dollars.[40] In accordance with this interpretation, no consultation concerning endangered species impacts occurred regarding several foreign projects. Seemingly satisfying *Lujan/NWF's* requirements, the plaintiffs' representatives had provided sworn affidavits attesting to their connections to and ongoing interest in the particular locations abroad where endangered species existed and where United States funding, if unconstrained by the ESA, might have contributed to harm to these species. In no sense did the plaintiffs' representatives lack linkages to the threatened sites. The Court majority, however, found their connections to threatened areas inadequate to uphold their standing.

Although never stating so explicitly, the Court's approach to standing in *Lujan* had the effect of invalidating on constitutional grounds application of dozens of statutes' citizen-suit provisions in accordance with their language.[41] The majority opinion made clear that, while Congress can create causes of action for injuries not previously cognizable in the courts,[42] the mere intent of Congress to confer such a cause of action does not end Article III analysis. All plaintiffs must be able to show that their threatened interest and alleged injury add up to a type of interest or injury that the courts determine to be "actual," "particularized," and "concrete." The Court rejected the proposition that "the public interest in proper administration of the laws (specifically, in agencies' observance of a particular, statutorily prescribed procedure) can be converted into an individual right by a statute that denominates it as such, and that permits all citizens (or, for that matter, a subclass of citizens who suffer no distinctive concrete harm) to sue."[43] The existence of an agency procedural misstep or an erroneous statutory interpretation, even with broad citizen-suit conferral of a cause of action, was insufficient by itself to create standing for the *Lujan* plaintiffs. This

---

39. *Lujan,* 504 U.S. at 560.

40. *Id.* at 558–59.

41. *See* Karl S. Coplan, *Refracting the Spectrum of Clean Water Act Standing in Light of Lujan v. Defenders of Wildlife,* 22 Colum. J. Envtl. L. 169 (1997); Cass R. Sunstein, *What's Standing After Lujan? Of Citizen Suits, "Injuries," and Article III,* 91 Mich. L. Rev. 163 (1992) (critiquing *Lujan* and also exploring linkage of Justice Scalia's earlier article and his later Supreme Court *Lujan/NWF* and *Lujan* opinions).

42. The Court stated that Congress can "elevat[e] to the status of legally cognizable injuries concrete, *de facto* injuries that were previously inadequate in law . . . . " *Lujan,* 504 U.S. at 578.

43. *Id.* at 576–77.

approach was contrary to analysis by then Professor William Fletcher in an article relied on by the Supreme Court in an earlier standing Supreme Court opinion issued shortly before *Lujan*.[44]

Critical to understanding what *Lujan* actually decided and what *Laidlaw* clarified is close parsing of language in the so-called concurrence by Justice Kennedy, joined by Justice Souter. Without their agreement on the result and rationale in *Lujan*, there was no majority joining Justice Scalia. Justice Scalia and the majority appeared to have placed courts in a crucial judgmental role in evaluating standing. In their concurrence, Justices Kennedy and Souter were unwilling to adopt the Scalia opinion's "nexus" discussion and, it appears, the Scalia opinion's emphasis on common law-like injury. Justices Kennedy and Souter also refused to join in the redressability portions of Justice Scalia's opinion. In a somewhat obscure phrase, they "join[ed] Part IV of the Court's opinion with the following observations."[45] In telling language arguably converting ostensibly majority portions of Justice Scalia's opinion into a minority position, but certainly creating doctrinal confusion, they stated that "Congress has the power to define injuries and articulate chains of causation that will give rise to a case or controversy where none existed before, and I do not read the Court's opinion to suggest a contrary view."[46] For Justices Kennedy and Souter (who with Justice Stevens' concurrence on other grounds and the dissenters constituted a majority), Congress retains authority to articulate "new rights of action that do not have clear analogs in our common-law tradition."[47]

This dense discussion of congressional power and standing spawned substantial lower court litigation and scholarly comment. It also created a critical ambiguity regarding standing analysis, especially for environmental litigants. To what extent do underlying statutes providing a cause of action influence what kinds of claims and injuries will be adequate to justify standing? Is judicial judgment about the presence of "injury," or legislative goals and means to achieving those goals, critical to standing analysis? Relatedly, is the analysis called for of injury or threatened injury to interests of the plaintiff, or need courts find harm to the underlying environment? These key interrelated questions were left uncertain by *Lujan*. A mere citizen suit cause of action clearly did not end standing analysis, but the exact mode of standing analysis erected by *Lujan* was rife with ambiguity.

---

44. *See* International Primate Protection League v. Administrators of Tulane Educ. Fund, 500 U.S. 72, 77 (1991) (citing William Fletcher, *The Structure of Standing*, 98 Yale L.J. 221 (1988) and stating that "standing is gauged by the specific common-law, statutory or constitutional claims that a party presents.").

45. *Lujan,* 504 U.S. at 580.

46. *Id.*

47. *Id.*

Litigants and courts predictably worked with the new questions and opportunities created by *Lujan*. A unanimous Court in *Bennett v. Spear*, in yet another opinion by Justice Scalia, upheld standing for plaintiffs whose economic interests in lake waters had allegedly been harmed by government action under the Endangered Species Act.[48] After rejecting a prudential "zone of interest" standing analysis that would have disqualified claimants seeking to limit the reach of the law, the Court, as in *Lujan*, had to deal with Article III standing criteria where a sequence of statutorily required actions rendered uncertain what would happen if a court intervened. Despite granting standing, the Court's approach was potentially problematic for environmentalist plaintiffs. Such plaintiffs frequently can identify illegal government action, but cannot with certainty predict results if a defendant government agency were forced to follow the law. Rather than merely stating that the Court's remand to the relevant agency to do its "biological opinion" work in conformity with the ESA would constitute redress, the *Bennett* Court appeared independently to look for a "coercive" or "virtually determinative effect."[49] The Court ultimately concluded that this document and the ESA process had a sufficient effect on the action agency to find the claims redressable. The broad judicial gatekeeping approach utilized in *Bennett*, however, has been little utilized since the decision. In addition, as discussed below, *Laidlaw* both showed a far more deferential attitude toward Congress and articulated standing criteria in a way easing environmentalist plaintiffs' burdens.

Justice Scalia again wrote for the Court in *Steel Co. v. Citizens for a Better Environment*,[50] the case relied on so heavily by the Fourth Circuit in *Laidlaw*. In *Steel Co.*, the Court denied standing to environmentally motivated plaintiffs who sought imposition of penalties and limited injunctive relief against a company that had failed to file forms required by a federal toxic substances information disclosure statute known as EPCRA. The case was problematic for plaintiffs from the start due to the case's posture. Defendant had promptly filed the required forms once it received notice of the plaintiffs' intent to sue,[51] and no violations occurred after the suit was commenced. The case thus stood in a posture much like the 1987 Clean Water Act *Gwaltney* case, where the alleged violations had occurred in the past.[52] But *Gwaltney* turned on close parsing of the Clean Water Act's "pervasive" use of the past tense to conclude as a statutory matter that "wholly past" violations could not be

48. 520 U.S. 154 (1997).

49. *Id.* at 169–70.

50. 523 U.S. 83 (1998).

51. *Id.* at 88.

52. Gwaltney v. Chesapeake Bay Found. Inc., 484 U.S. 49 (1987).

the subject of citizen suits; *Steel Co.* lacked such dispositive statutory language. As in *Lujan,* however, constitutional arguments carried the day for the *Steel Co.* defendant. The Court, in a series of somewhat disparate opinions, found that plaintiffs lacked standing due to a lack of redressability; penalties would not flow to plaintiffs, and injunctive relief requiring legal compliance was not necessary due to the company's belated, but pre-complaint, rectifying of their failure to file reports.[53]

The *Steel Co.* majority opinion regarding Article III standing focused primarily on redressability issues, but contained brief language further shedding light on the relative roles of courts and Congress in assessing "injury in fact." The Court briefly mentioned the lack of reporting as relevant to standing, but in a way that inconclusively raised the issue of whether courts evaluating standing should wrap statutory interests and "injury" together: "We have not had occasion to decide whether being deprived of information that is supposed to be disclosed under EPCRA— or at least being deprived of it when one has a particular plan for its use— is a concrete injury in fact that satisfies Article III."[54]

Steel Co. thus further limited citizen standing, eliminating citizen suit viability at least in settings where illegal actions ceased pre-complaint. The crucial question left by the case concerned standing and citizen suit relief. Its finding that there was no redressable claim threatened to mean that citizen suit plaintiffs would have standing only where there were post-complaint violations justifying injunctive relief. After all, citizen suit penalties always go to the government, and fees and costs awarded to prevailing plaintiffs could not be bootstrapped into a basis for finding redress.

IV. *Reducing Standing Hurdles:* Akins *and Legislative Power*

This string of four standing opinions authored by Justice Scalia, all of which had the effect of limiting environmentalist plaintiffs' access to the courts, and all of which empowered courts to the arguable expense of Congress, came to an abrupt halt in a non-environmental case, *Federal Election Commission v. Akins.*[55] Justice Breyer's *Akins* opinion for the Court, as well as the subsequent *Laidlaw* majority opinion by Justice Ginsburg, adopted an analytical approach that differed substantially from the earlier 1990s majority standing opinions. *Akins,* as well as the later *Laidlaw* case, revived the viability of citizen litigation. Critical to this turn of the tide was how the Court majorities gave paramount importance to the "statutory universe" of legislative judgments and

---

53. *Id.* at 105–09.

54. *Id.* at 105.

55. 524 U.S. 11 (1998).

goals.[56] The Court in these cases did not engage in or call for independent judicial assessment of the existence of a sufficient injury or redressability.[57]

In *Akins,* the Court found that the respondents satisfied both prudential and Article III standing requirements in their complaint alleging that the Federal Election Commission had failed to require a lobbying group to disclose legally required information under the Federal Election Campaign Act of 1971.[58] The Court retained the "injury in fact" analysis prong, characterizing it as a "requirement that helps assure that courts will not 'pass upon ... abstract, intellectual problems,' but adjudicate 'concrete, living contest[s] between adversaries.' "[59] *Akins* stood in stark contrast to the *Lujan* apparent majority's focus on some judicial conception of injury with common law roots. Instead, the Court in *Akins* looked at this Article III question by repeatedly linking analysis of the petitioners' interests with interests made legally actionable by the statute: the " 'injury in fact' that respondents have suffered consists of their inability to obtain information ... the statute requires that AIPAC make public." The Court further stated that a plaintiff suffers an "injury in fact" when "the plaintiff fails to obtain information which must be publicly disclosed pursuant to a statute."[60] Taxpayer standing cases requiring a "logical nexus" between the "status asserted and the claim sought to be adjudicated" were inapposite, in the Court's view, because in *Akins* "there is a statute which ... does seek to protect individuals such as respondents from the harm they say they have suffered.... "[61] Standing analysis in *Akins* thus wrapped the Article III constitutional question with judicial deference to the statutory universe of interests and incentives created by the legislature.

The *Akins* Court's redressability discussion, without citation to or overt criticism of the contrasting *Bennett* language, called for a redressability analysis that created far fewer problems for claimants seeking to require government actions that would lead to indeterminate results. Rather than looking for some near-certain tangible changed result that would flow from the FEC's appropriate exercise of its authority on remand, the Court stated that the agency on remand could reach an

---

56. William W. Buzbee, *Standing and the Statutory Universe,* 11 Duke Envt'l L. & Pol. Forum 247 (2001).

57. *See* Cass R. Sunstein, *Informational Regulation and Informational Standing: Akins and Beyond,* 147 U. Penn. L. Rev. 613 (1999).

58. 524 U.S. at 19–26.

59. *Id.* at 20 (citing Coleman v. Miller, 307 U.S. 433, 460 (1939) (Frankfurter, J., dissenting)).

60. *Id.* at 21(citing Public Citizen v. Department of Justice, 491 U.S. 440, 449 (1989)).

61. *Id.* at 22.

identical result, but that the respondent's claim was nevertheless redressable and traceable. "[T]he courts ... can 'redress' respondents'
'injury in fact'" and find "causation" even though the courts "cannot
know" that the FEC would exercise its discretion in the way desired by
respondents.[62] "Agencies often have discretion about whether or not to
take a particular action. Yet those adversely affected by a discretionary
agency action generally have standing to complain that the agency based
its decision upon an improper legal ground."[63] Hence, the *Akins* Court
made agency conformity with legally required substance and process the
touchstone for finding standing causation and redressability, not separate independent judicial assessment that the statutorily required criteria or process mattered.[64] This was radically different from the analytical
process in *Bennett,* and also offered an approach in substantial tension
with *Lujan.*

V. Appellate Court Expansions of Lujan's Barriers

Around the time that *Akins* perhaps began to turn the tide in
standing doctrine, two Court of Appeals decisions and the Fourth Circuit's *Laidlaw* ruling revealed just how constraining recast standing and
related mootness doctrine could be for citizen litigants, particularly in
the environmental arena. They melded and arguably expanded upon
language and logic in the *Lujan* cases and *Steel Co.* to deny standing to
environmental plaintiffs suing under citizen suit provisions. Notably,
both they and *Laidlaw,* all of which were litigated by the Terris–Pravlik
firm, involved more classic citizen suit pollution cases than did the
preceding Supreme Court 1990s standing cases. *Lujan* involved a challenge to a government regulation implicating U.S. funded actions abroad,
Lujan/NWF involved government land management, *Steel Co.* involved
belatedly filed forms, and *Bennett* involved allegedly inadequate environmental analyses. None involved the bread and butter of citizen litigation,
cases in which a polluter violates its permit and citizens seek to compel
compliance and force the defendant to pay statutory penalties.

The Third and Fourth Circuits' opinions on environmental standing
in *Public Interest Research Group of New Jersey v. Magnesium Elektron,
Inc.,*[65] and *Friends of the Earth v. Gaston Copper Recyling Corp.,*[66]
respectively, arose out of the classic citizen suit fact pattern, as did
Laidlaw. All three cases involved pollution discharges in excess of levels
allowed by the defendants' Clean Water Act ("CWA") permits. In both

---

62. *Id*. at 24–26.

63. *Id*. at 25.

64. *Id*. at 25–26.

65. 123 F.3d 111 (3d Cir. 1997).

66. 179 F.3d 107 (4th Cir. 1999), *rev'd en banc,* 204 F.3d 149 (4th Cir. 2000).

Magnesium Elektron and *Gaston*, defendants sought to defeat the environmentalist plaintiffs' standing by extending the Supreme Court's *Lujan* decision, arguing that there was no proven harm to the environment. The defendants argued that due to the inability of plaintiffs to trace defendants' permit violations to particular discernible degradations of the illegally polluted receiving waters, plaintiffs could not show injury in fact that was traceable or redressable. The defendants in these cases succeeded, prompting opinions utilizing a mode of standing analysis in which courts would independently determine that legal violations actually resulted in what the courts found to be tangible "touch and feel" harm.[67]

The *Magnesium Elektron* opinion acknowledged that the CWA explicitly states that its purpose is to "restore and maintain the chemical, physical, and biological integrity of the Nation's waters." The court nevertheless rejected the environmental plaintiffs' argument that this statutory goal allowed plaintiffs to sue to maintain a river's " 'pristine state.' "[68] The court saw itself as having to determine independently if there was "actual or threatened injury" to the environment, and, in turn, these plaintiffs.[69] The court acknowledged that in *Lujan* the plaintiffs "had no plausible connection to the situs of the injury," while plaintiffs before the *Magnesium Elektron* court "no doubt . . . use[d] the Delaware River."[70] Again and again, however, the Third Circuit panel stated that it had to find on its own the presence of "actual, tangible injury to the River or its surroundings," even where plaintiffs were users of the River receiving illegal amounts of pollution and Congress made such violations actionable by citizens.[71] The court looked for proof of "increases in the River's salinity, or a decrease in the number of fish, or any other negative change in the River's ecosystem."[72] The court even claimed that some violations "actually benefitted the Creek's ecosystem" by adding nutrients to an area that was not "nutrient rich."[73]

In short, for the *Magnesium Elektron* court, the statute's explicit goal of "chemical, physical and biological integrity" was insufficient to make actionable pollution resulting from permit violations that by definition interfered with that integrity, albeit in ways difficult to establish

---

67. *Gaston*, 179 F.3d at 120 (Wilkinson, J., dissenting).

68. *Magnesium Elektron*, 123 F.3d at 120.

69. *Id.* For a critique of concepts of causation and discussion of *Magnesium Elektron*, see Richard Pierce, *Causation in Government Regulation and Toxic Torts*, 76 Wash. U.L.Q. 1307, 1333–35 (1998).

70. *Magnesium Elektron,* 123 F.3d at 120.

71. *Id.* at 121.

72. *Id.*

73. *Id.* at 123.

as tangible harms. If added nutrients led to flourishing of other species, then by definition (according to the court), this was no harm at all. The court in effect took the judge-centered view of standing in *Lujan*, *Bennett* and *Steel Co.* and expanded it to call for independent judicial assessment of the existence of environmental harm.

The *Gaston* case was also litigated by Bruce Terris's firm and, as in *Laidlaw* and *Magnesium Elektron*, the firm encountered difficulties. The *Gaston* court faced a case with conceded CWA violations, but this time with plaintiffs who alleged not only environmental and aesthetic impairments, but economic impairments due to perceptions that real property and businesses using the excessively polluted receiving waters faced resultant economic losses. Furthermore, testing of the type and concentrations of excessive pollution at issue for toxicity concededly showed "observable effects" on test organisms. The court, however, looked for proof that particular permit violations could be traced to particular harms to the receiving waters. In the absence of such proof, the court found that plaintiffs could not actually have suffered any injury in fact that was traceable to defendant.[74] Judge Wilkinson, in dissent, characterized the majority as "encroach[ing] on congressional authority" by requiring "evidence that [the court majority] can touch and feel."[75]

The Fourth Circuit's *Laidlaw* opinion did not share this focus on proof of environmental harm in evaluating standing, but like these other cases, built upon the Supreme Court's standing cases to create a substantial hurdle for citizen suit plaintiffs. As discussed above, if a defendant could come into compliance with its permit at any time, then under the Fourth Circuit's mootness logic, which in turn built on *Steel Co.*, at any time plaintiffs could suddenly find themselves knocked out of court, with no injunctive relief, penalties or award of fees. In the trial court's decision on penalties, however, *Laidlaw* did contain the conclusion that "even with the permit exceedances ... [there was] no demonstrated adverse affect on the environment."[76]

All three cases thus created disincentives for citizen suit plaintiffs to sue polluters except in the rare instance where plaintiffs could determine with confidence that a defendant simply could not come into compliance and also could establish that the illegal pollution created tangible, egregious harm. This evidentiary challenge would be burdensome and perhaps impossible to prove in settings of large water bodies or air sheds, or rapidly moving waters.

---

74. *Id.*

75. *Id.* at 120.

76. 956 F. Supp. at 603.

VI. Laidlaw *Before the Supreme Court*

A. Choosing *Laidlaw*

These appellate cases were thus tremendously problematic for environmental claimants, but also were potential vehicles to shift standing and mootness doctrine, or at least limit the damage. Deciding whether to seek Supreme Court review always involves an array of factors, especially in significant public law areas such as civil rights and environmental law. Much as civil rights litigators strategically chose case vehicles to set the stage for the result of *Brown v. Board of Education,* environmentalists needed to consider more than just which appellate court results were bad.[77] The stakes were high.

Gaston and *Magnesium Elektron* were substantial and problematic expansions of standing barriers, and *Laidlaw* was a problematic expansion of the *Steel Co.* standing discussion to justify a dismissal on mootness grounds. By clearly going beyond the core holdings in *Lujan* and *Steel Co.*, these cases were vulnerable to reversal by the Supreme Court. After all, despite the sequence of adverse standing decisions, the Court's center was uncertain. Even *Lujan* included the key Kennedy concurrence (joined by Justice Souter) that refused to view injury and standing merely through a common law lens; Congress had the power to "define injuries and articulate chains of causation" that did not have roots in "our common law tradition." Furthermore, although Justice O'Connor had sided with the majority in *Steel Co.*, she had joined a blistering dissent by Justice Blackmun in *Lujan,* criticizing the majority for its hostility to environmental citizen litigation. In *Akins,* which had adopted a standing approach more respectful of congressional statutory goals and means, a majority including Chief Justice Rehnquist and Justice Kennedy upheld the complaining voters' standing. Thus, only Justices Scalia and Thomas were virtually certain to be lost causes for environmentalists seeking to turn the standing tide, with Chief Justice Rehnquist also a likely but not certain adverse vote. Justices Kennedy and O'Connor were potential swing votes, with Justices Ginsburg, Breyer and likely Souter perhaps ready to revise standing doctrine in ways more deferential to Congress and amenable to environmentalist citizen litigants.

The question was which case to pursue. *Magnesium Elektron's* language was horrendous and a huge expansion of *Lujan,* but even if in error, would a case with an explicit ruling that no environmental harms had resulted from illegal pollution grab those swing voters? If anything, removing from the federal courts harmless pollution violations might appeal to Justices Kennedy and O'Connor. Chief Justice Rehnquist

---

77. 347 U.S. 483 (1954).

would almost certainly find plaintiffs in such a case unworthy of standing. *Gaston* had some good facts establishing harms impinging on property owners' interests, but it too involved minimal to nonexistent proven environmental harms.

Laidlaw offered much more compelling facts, with district court findings of lack of diligent prosecution, affirmation of plaintiffs' standing despite motion practice and a court hearing, and proof of substantial economic advantage resulting from the illegal pollution discharges. It was far from perfect, however, due to its penalty conclusion that the permit violations had not been shown to harm the environment. Nevertheless, the Fourth Circuit's complete dismissal on mootness grounds seemed a misreading of mootness doctrine and also had the effect of nullifying in many cases the efficacy of citizen suits created by Congress. Most significantly, mercury was a pollutant no Supreme Court justice could trivialize. The Fourth Circuit's ruling focused on mootness, not standing, however, and hence if corrected by the Supreme Court might only incrementally begin to weaken the 1990s standing precedents. Considered as a package, however, *Laidlaw* appeared to be the most compelling vehicle for Supreme Court review. Friends of the Earth President Dr. Brent Blackwelder recalls that because *Laidlaw* involved such a "severe pollutant," it was viewed as a good "precedent-setting case."[78] Others familiar with deliberations over which case was best to place before the Supreme Court similarly recall the fact of mercury violations as central to the choice to petition for a writ of certiorari in *Laidlaw*. The other case results, bad as they were, could either stand or await potential rehearing if the Supreme Court heard and provided a positive result in *Laidlaw*.

B. *Laidlaw*'s Briefing and Argument

The Supreme Court was petitioned to hear *Laidlaw* and granted that petition with the Fourth Circuit's mootness decision as the focus. The plaintiffs-petitioners' initial brief focused on the mootness issue, spending much of their initial brief arguing that the Fourth Circuit's ruling was in conflict with language in the Supreme Court's 1987 *Gwaltney* decision. The plaintiff-petitioners placed the underlying facts before the Court, including some emphasis on the mercury discharges and, several pages into the brief, discussion of how the Fourth Circuit's approach would undercut all citizen suit litigation. Their initial emphasis, however, was on *Gwaltney* and how mootness and the grounds for denial of injunctive relief should not be conflated. The defendant-respondent, Laidlaw, supported the mootness ruling below, but provided plaintiffs and environmentalists a major opening when it devoted much of its

---

78. Blackwelder interview (October 1, 2004).

brief to questioning the plaintiffs' standing. Up until that time, neither the Fourth Circuit nor the Supreme Court had indicated that plaintiffs' standing was in dispute. The Supreme Court in *Laidlaw* unavoidably had to clarify the implications of *Steel Co.*, a standing case, but until the plaintiffs put standing in issue, it did not appear that standing would be a disputed issued in *Laidlaw*. Plaintiffs in their reply addressed these standing arguments.

The oral arguments shifted focus, sometimes focusing on the mootness question, but also substantially focusing on standing and the question of deterrence. Bruce Terris also engaged in a colloquy with a Justice about whether citizen suit litigation is private, as the Justice implied in his (or her) question, or public litigation since it is explicitly authorized by statute. Terris, however, resisted the Court focusing or ruling on the standing question, arguing that it was not before the Court. After the United States argued in support of the environmentalists' position, Donald Cockrill argued for Laidlaw. When a Justice's questions turned to the constitutionality of *qui tam* actions, Justice Scalia interjected with a largely impenetrable quip, "Qui tam squared, you might say." Cockrill provoked laughter with his response, "I'll agree with that, although I'm not sure I understand it." Reflecting later on the case and his argument, Cockrill explained he was thinking: "Anything this guy says, I'm agreeing with him." He knew he had Scalia and Thomas on his side.[79] The argument otherwise revealed little. The questions hinted that the Court might confine itself to the mootness question, but also raised broader questions related to the nature of citizen suit actions, standing, and the deterrent effect of penalties under the Clean Water Act.

C. The Decision

Much to Court-watchers' surprise, the *Laidlaw* Court issued an opinion focused as much on standing as on mootness. It appeared that the Court reached out to make law on the standing issue, perhaps seeing a need to quell the growing discord among courts and lawyers regarding standing doctrine. The Court decisively rejected lower court expansions of the Supreme Court's already challenging standing criteria. In fact, it resolved *Lujan* ambiguities in clear favor of environmental plaintiffs, and limited the reach of *Steel Co.* Picking up on a countertrend first started in *Akins,* it further continued giving statutory frameworks a prominent, if not paramount role, in standing analysis. The existence of numerous post-complaint permit violations gave the *Laidlaw* Court crucial room to distinguish *Steel Co.*

---

79.   Telephone interview with Donald Cockrill (July 2, 2004).

The *Laidlaw* Court emphatically rejected defendant's argument that, as embraced in *Gaston* and *Magnesium Elektron*, plaintiffs in environmental cases had to establish harm to the excessively polluted river that in turn injured the plaintiffs. Instead, the seven Justice majority stated that "[t]he relevant showing for purposes of Article III standing, however, is not injury to the environment but injury to the plaintiff."[80] The Court stated that it saw "nothing 'improbable' about the proposition that a company's continuous and pervasive illegal discharges of pollutants into a river would cause nearby residents to curtail recreational use of the waterway" or cause them "other economic and aesthetic harms." The *Laidlaw* Court tied this focus on the plaintiff's injury and reasons courts cannot require additional proof of environmental harm by once again emphasizing the statutory framework: "[t]o insist upon the former [injury to the environment] rather than the latter as part of the standing inquiry . . . is to raise the standing hurdle higher than the necessary showing for success on the merits alleging noncompliance with a [Clean Water Act] permit."[81] The plaintiffs' somewhat weakly stated links to the polluted river were sufficient for Article III "injury in fact": "environmental plaintiffs adequately allege injury in fact when they aver that they use the affected area and are persons 'for whom the aesthetic and recreational values of the areas will be lessened' by the challenged activity."[82] The Court's emphasis was on plaintiffs' stated actual interests in the environmental amenity protected by statute.

Laidlaw thus firmly rejected an inordinate focus on proof of harm to the environment, in so doing adopting a standing framework that deferred to legislative judgments. Standing litigation will continue, especially in claims regarding government regulatory actions allegedly affecting the environment, but in citizen versus polluter cases, *Laidlaw* will seldom give defendants grounds to knock out a plaintiff on standing grounds.

Laidlaw also bluntly rejected any expansion of *Steel Co.* that would allow post-complaint compliance to moot a case. The Court characterized as misleading and unfortunate its own earlier cases describing mootness as "the doctrine of standing set in a time frame."[83] Instead, as frequently

---

80.   Friends of the Earth, Inc. v. Laidlaw Envtl. Serv., 528 U.S. 167, 181 (2000).

81.   *Id.*

82.   *Id.* at 183 (quoting Sierra Club v. Morton, 405 U.S. 727, 735 (1972)), and further citing *Lujan's* statement that "the desire to use or observe an animal species, even for purely esthetic purposes, is undeniably a cognizable interest for purposes of standing." Lujan v. Defenders of Wildlife, 504 U.S. 555, 562–63 (1992).

83.   *Laidlaw*, 528 U.S. at 189.

stated in other cases, a case is only moot if it is "absolutely clear that the allegedly wrongful behavior could not reasonably be expected to recur."[84]

Although better for citizen litigants than the Fourth Circuit's approach, *Laidlaw* was by no means a crystal clear win in its mootness discussion. Prior to *Laidlaw*, the typical lower court approach to mootness in the setting of penalty claims had been quite absolute: penalty claims could not be mooted. The Court's opinion in *Laidlaw*, however, was far from ideal in its clarity. The Court rejected the Fourth Circuit's expansive recasting of *Steel Co.* to find the plaintiff's case moot. It did not, however, embrace the typical rule on mootness and penalty claims, as citizen litigants surely hoped. Its remand implied that the plaintiffs' case could be mooted if it was "absolutely clear" that violations could not again occur. But if the usual penalty-mootness approach survived the Supreme Court's opinion, the imposition of penalties meant the case could not be mooted. On the other hand, the Court also did not flag its mootness discussion as a significant change. Unsurprisingly, this critical ambiguity has led to disparate lower court treatments about what *Laidlaw* calls for in assessing defense claims of mootness.[85]

The Court's limitation of *Steel Co.* and affirmance that civil penalties can serve a deterrent role was a critical victory for citizen plaintiffs. Despite language in *Steel Co.* to the contrary in a case under a different statute and in a different posture, the *Laidlaw* Court found that penalties can provide a plaintiff redress, even if penalties go to the treasury. For this proposition, the Court had to recharacterize *Steel Co.*, as well as rely on its own earlier Clean Water Act precedents and Clean Water Act legislative history stating the rationale for citizen suit penalties. The seven justice majority distinguished *Steel Co.* by emphasizing the different case postures. *Steel Co.* lacked post-complaint permit violations, while *Laidlaw* indisputably experienced post-complaint violations before it came into sustained permit compliance. The Court's explanation for why these penalties sufficed to preserve the plaintiffs' standing was again largely based on the Court's deference to legislative judgment. "Whether the prescribed conduct is to be deterred [by a range of potential sanctions] is a matter within the legislature's range of choice."[86] The Court continued, "[t]his congressional determination [about the deterrent effect of penalties] warrants judicial attention and respect."[87] The Court therefore found, based substantially on the Court's deference to legislative judgments, that penalties would serve both to

---

84. *Id.* (citations omitted).

85. *See* John D. Echeverria, *Standing and Mootness Decisions in the Wake of* Laidlaw, 10 Widener L. Rev. 183, 191–99 (2003).

86. *Laidlaw*, 528 U.S. at 187 (quoting Tigner v. Texas, 310 U.S. 141, 148 (1940)).

87. *Id.* at 185.

abate current violations and prevent future ones. *Steel Co.* was hence largely limited to its particular statute and factual posture.

Due to the Laidlaw facility's shutdown, the Court could not in a final way resolve the mootness claim, and hence the case was remanded, where the case still languishes in 2004 due to Laidlaw's bankruptcy filing. The Court's language and the complete shutdown of the Laidlaw facility mean, however, that even if this particular case might end up being held moot, it would be a rare citizen suit case that would be dismissed for mootness grounds. Other citizen suit hurdles that can drag out a case, however, do increase the risk that some post-complaint events will give defense counsel colorable arguments that a claim has become moot. Seldom will they succeed, but litigation over mootness has not and will not disappear.

VII. Assessing **Laidlaw**

It is difficult to overstate how completely *Laidlaw* revived citizen suits for environmental plaintiffs. After the Court's ruling, will post-complaint compliance moot a case? Only rarely. Will environmental plaintiffs have to prove actual tangible harm to the environment? No, just harm to themselves and their interests. Might penalties going to the government provide deterrence and hence redress for environmental plaintiffs? Yes, the Court responded, greatly limiting the reach of *Steel Co.*, but still leaving to future courts harmonizing of the somewhat clashing *Steel Co.* and *Laidlaw* majority opinions and uncertainty about mootness and penalties. Do courts still have the broad latitude threatened in court of appeals rulings in *Laidlaw*, *Gaston* and *Magnesium Elektron* to decide on the presence of a sufficient injury based on their own judicial assessments, rather than with heavy deference to legislative frameworks? A decisive "no" was provided in *Laidlaw*, further confirmed in the earlier *Akins* decision, clarifying a critical *Lujan* ambiguity in a way that decisively reduced standing hurdles.

Justice Scalia, in a dissent joined by Justice Thomas, did not try to argue *Laidlaw* was somehow distinguishable. He directly admitted the extent of the loss, pointing out ways the majority opinion was inconsistent with language and implications of earlier standing cases. He correctly stated that after *Laidlaw*, "[i]f there are permit violations, and a member of a plaintiff environmental organization lives near the offending plant, it would be difficult not to satisfy today's lenient standard."[88] Regarding the majority's penalty deterrence-redress conclusion, Justice Scalia was similarly blunt, perhaps a bit hyperbolic: The Court "has promulgated a revolutionary new doctrine of standing that will permit the entire body of public civil penalties to be handed over to enforcement

---

88. *Id.* at 201 (Scalia, J., dissenting).

by private interests."[89] In reality, plaintiffs will still need to establish their link to the harm or threatened environment, and the Court's ruling was hardly "revolutionary," but a fair resolution of a body of unsettled law. Apart from those caveats, however, Justice Scalia did accurately characterize the breadth of the *Laidlaw* Court's ruling. The seven justice *Laidlaw* majority had pulled citizen suits back from the precipice.

A. The Citizen Suit Gauntlet and Incentives for Citizen Plaintiffs

The somewhat lost story of *Laidlaw,* however, is just how difficult the *Laidlaw* case has been in its twelve years (and counting) of litigation and waiting. *Laidlaw* does not appear atypical. Citizen suit litigation remains a potentially significant option for victims of pollution, environmental groups, and others concerned with violations of environmental laws and regulations. The gauntlet through which the *Laidlaw* plaintiffs have had to run, however, reveals an increasingly complex and unrewarding citizen suit jurisprudence that awaits all citizen suit plaintiffs.

During the approximately thirty years of citizen suit litigation, with most such litigation occurring the past twenty years, effective and often innovative litigation by defendants has gradually built up a complex body of law. That Bruce Terris's firm, with only nine lawyers, is possibly the largest plaintiff side environmental firm run on profits hints at the challenging nature of this body of law. Were plaintiff-side environmental work through citizen suits the cakewalk apparently assumed by critics of citizen litigation, one would expect a legion of lawyers doing such work. Instead, most such work is done by not-for-profits reliant on foundation or membership funding, with a far smaller practice by for-profit firms. Few if any firms rely exclusively on citizen suit litigation.

As occurred in *Laidlaw* and surely will still occur in the future, citizen suit plaintiffs will still confront diligent prosecution challenges, and often will be knocked out of court due to state enforcement actions brought, as occurred in *Laidlaw*, just to preclude a plaintiff's case. Standing challenges remain a likelihood, although *Laidlaw's* more forgiving treatment of injury and redress should mean most actions against polluters will survive. *Gwaltney* challenges remain a substantial likelihood when defendants appear able to rectify discharge violations.

The complexity and duration of citizen suit litigation increases opportunities for defendants to point to production changes and, as a result, raise linked colorable mootness arguments. Mootness litigation is further complicated now due to the Court's failure to clarify whether claims for civil penalties will ever be moot, even if injunctive relief is

---

89. *Id.* at 209.

completely unnecessary.[90] Citizen litigants, especially those involved in long, drawn-out cases like *Laidlaw*, can anticipate that mootness defenses will be regularly raised. As stated by Pravlik, after the Supreme Court's *Laidlaw* ruling, standing challenges have "died off," but mootness challenges have increased. The Court's opinion created "a door for a defendant's lawyer to say 'let me try this.' "[91]

This increasingly complex citizen suit litigation process creates a paradox. Many of these defenses were developed as a means to limit citizens' access to the courts. The cumulative impact, however, is to create incentives for drawn out litigation, especially if lengthy litigation battles create the possibility of a later mootness claim. Furthermore, plaintiffs' attorney's fees increase as each defense is asserted. These defenses have the potential to lead to a defense victory, but if they do not, then aiming for a long shot victory to avoid massive fees becomes a more and more tempting strategy. As fees increase, then litigation over fees itself will often require another trial.

The hard-nosed defenses litigated by Cockrill and his firm for Laidlaw resulted in plaintiffs spending vast hours working on the *Laidlaw* case. That litigation time and the threat of a large fee award drove Laidlaw to continue to litigate, in defense counsel's opinion. When asked why Laidlaw did not settle the case early on, or at least after Judge Anderson imposed the $405,800 penalty, Cockrill attributed Laidlaw's decision to continue litigating on the high attorney's fees and costs plaintiffs would be awarded. Terris similarly perceives that in citizen suit litigation, cases typically only settle if they settle early. After substantial plaintiff and defense attorney time, defendants hope for a victory.

In *Laidlaw,* attorney's fees climbed rapidly as the litigation wound on. Terris and Cockrill anticipated that plaintiffs would be awarded something slightly over a million dollars in fees, had the case concluded after Judge Anderson's penalty decision. Even excluding the substantial fees surely paid to defense counsel, attorney's fees were more than double the underlying penalty. By the time the appeals were finished and the Supreme Court had issued its ruling, fees for plaintiffs alone had climbed close to three million dollars.[92] When one factors in defense counsel's bills, it is a virtual certainty that total attorney time on this case could have cost Laidlaw well over five million dollars, over ten times the court-imposed penalty. Of course, Laidlaw's decision to file for bankruptcy brought plaintiffs' hopes for court-ordered compensation to a halt. Eventually, plaintiffs will perhaps recover a few cents on every

---

90. *See* Echeverria, *supra* note 85.

91. Telephone interview with Carolyn Smith Pravlik (Aug. 27, 2004).

92. Telephone interview with Donald Cockrill (July 2, 2004).

dollar, provided the trial judge on remand does not find that Laidlaw's cessation of business and discharges render the plaintiffs' claims moot.

Due to Laidlaw's bankruptcy, this case may never get to this last major litigation phase in many citizen's suits, litigation over the appropriateness and size of an attorney's fee award. According to Carolyn Pravlik, even after a victory on the merits, the fees litigation phase has in most citizen's suit litigation become yet another major hurdle. Despite the strict liability regime that underlies citizen suit litigation against polluters under most environmental laws, the battles over fees can be fierce, assuming an attorney ever gets to that phase. The Supreme Court's recent ruling in the *Buckhannon* case, which under numerous statutes eliminated attorney's fee awards based on a "catalyst" theory, has further created incentives for litigation to a judgment rather than early settlement.[93]

When asked in the summer of 2004 when the Terris and Pravlik firm last had won a citizen suit case, including an award and payment of attorney's fees and costs, Pravlik could only mutter "good gosh," searching for any case that had gotten to that phase. As she talked through the docket of recent citizen's suit cases, one after the other was lost somewhere in the middle of motion practice, awaiting rulings, or on interlocutory or final appeals. No case in recent memory had resulted in a substantial victory and award of fees. She subsequently recounted a settlement "victory" that included payment of fees and costs three years earlier, in 2001. Their firm instead has been surviving on an array of non-environmental cases, especially ongoing work monitoring compliance under a couple of large civil rights case consent decrees. In the fall of 2004, their firm received a large award of fees and costs in a district court ruling, but that too will likely be appealed and delayed.[94]

Justice Scalia has at times characterized citizen litigants seeking payment of fees as acting in a role tantamount to that of an "extortionist,"[95] and characterized citizen suit litigants as having "massive bargaining power."[96] From the viewpoint of environmental plaintiffs' counsel, however, their position is by no means easy or one of strength. Far from standing alone as an illusory victory, *Laidlaw* is one of numerous environmental citizen suit cases where a victory has brought few or no penalties, and modest or no award of fees or costs, but has required years of litigation. For example, a leading Georgia environmental public

---

93. Buckhannon Bd. & Care Home Inc. v. W. Va. Dep't of Health & Human Res., 532 U.S. 598 (2001).

94. *See* Interfaith Comm. Org. v. Honeywell Int'l, Inc., 336 F.Supp.2d 370 (D.N.J. 2004).

95. *Buckhannon,* 532 U.S. at 618.

96. Friends of the Earth, Inc. v. Laidlaw Envtl. Serv., 528 U.S. 167, 209 (2000) (Scalia, J., dissenting).

interest law firm has in recent years earned, at most, 27% of its income from citizen suit attorney's fee awards; in one year, no awards were made.[97] A leading national environmental group has similarly found citizen suit litigation to be a poor vehicle to finance the practice of law. As an attorney stated, occasional large fee awards are possible, but the income stream is far too "lumpy," with long periods generating no awards of fees.[98] Early efforts to fund an enforcement project with such fees failed to generate net income, instead generating large debts.[99] A western state law firm active with citizen suit litigation under federal and state law has in recent years earned a maximum of 16% of its revenue from fee awards for cases that had lasted several years; in another year they earned as little as 1% from such fees, but likely average about 5% in most years. Furthermore, many potential cases investigated at length by attorneys for citizen suit plaintiffs end up not even being filed. Nothing about citizen suits is easy these days.

As the smoke clears from the *Laidlaw* decision, standing and moot-ness hurdles have been lowered for citizen litigants,[100] but those and numerous other defenses create potentially lengthy, intensive litigation. Citizen litigation can still be dismissed after substantial investments of time, even in cases where the underlying violations are beyond dispute. Moreover, a broad category of post-*Laidlaw* cases still confront difficult standing hurdles. In a range of cases challenging impact statements, resource management and other non-regulatory and regulatory actions, settings closer to the *Lujan* posture than the *Laidlaw* citizen versus polluter case, courts may still look for highly-particularized linkages between harms to the citizen plaintiff and the questioned act.[101]

B. *Laidlaw* and the Future of Standing Law

The most significant question, however, is whether the Supreme Court is actually finished with its decade-long standing and citizen suit

---

97. Email interview with Justine Thompson, Director, Georgia Center for Law in the Public Interest (Sept. 13, 2004).

98. Telephone interview with Nancy Marks, Senior Attorney, The Natural Resources Defense Council (Sept. 20, 2004).

99. Kristi M. Smith, *Who's Suing Whom? A Comparison of Government and Citizen Suit Environmental Enforcement Actions Brought Under EPA-Administered Statutes, 1995–2000*, 29 Colum. J. of Envtl. L. 359, 393 (2004) (citing 1994 interview with NRDC attorney Marks recounting that the project ended up " '$1,000,000 in the red' ") (citations omitted).

100. *See, e.g.*, Am. Soc'y for Prevention of Cruelty to Animals v. Ringling Bros., 317 F.3d 334 (D.C. Cir. 2003).

101. *See, e.g.*, Echeverria, *supra* note 85; Sierra Club v. EPA, 292 F.3d 895 (D.C. Cir. 2002) (denying standing to environmental organization due to the court's inability to link alleged damages that would result from a rule regarding wastewater sludges to particular members adequate to find standing traceability and redress).

roller coaster. *Laidlaw* was a decisive victory for plaintiffs, but the result did little to simplify a citizen suit jurisprudence that will continue to engender intensive litigation. Plaintiffs should seldom lose, but additional litigation delays of months if not years will create another disincentive for citizen litigation. *Laidlaw* did "smooth away some of the more troublesome rough edges in previous opinions," as aptly observed by Professor Daniel Farber, but neither it nor any other single case can undo these confused and complex crosscurrents of citizen suit litigation law.[102] Citizens and their attorneys with the capacity to ride out the long litigation process stand a good chance of victory, but even more extended wars of attrition will discourage the plaintiffs' bar.

In sum, the decisive *Laidlaw* majority opinion's embrace of a legislation-centered view of injury bodes well for citizen plaintiffs. On the other hand, defense counsel have already begun exploiting opportunities left open by *Laidlaw* and defenses long available under citizen suit language, the *Gwaltney* case, and in the setting of attorney's fee litigation. Furthermore, uncertainties in Supreme Court standing and mootness doctrine certainly leave room for yet another recasting of Supreme Court jurisprudence. The Court could soon have to resolve the question about mootness in the setting of imposition of penalties. It also might need to revisit the continued application of *Lujan*-like approaches in suits against agencies for allegedly unjustified regulatory actions. Plaintiffs in such a setting face potential difficulty when they seek to establish a link to a particular harm; they typically will seek both to prove a negative regarding what would happen if the government acted differently, and also to establish actual current harms attributable to an allegedly illegal regulatory act. New rules of broad impact will always present challenges for citizen litigants, as established in *Lujan/NWF* and *Lujan,* as well as the more recent *Southern Utah* case. *Laidlaw* provided reassurance to citizen litigants, but it did not purport to overrule any of these cases. *Laidlaw* and *Akins* manifested deference to legislative judgments, but did not foreclose revival of more judge-centered, common law-like conceptions of harms to survive a standing challenge. How Article II fits into standing analysis remains uncertain.

Perhaps of even greater significance, there appears to be little surrender by any of the Justices of hard line adherence to their particular approach to citizen litigation and standing. *Laidlaw,* with its posture of a suit against a polluter, allowed three Justices (Chief Justice Rehnquist, and Justices O'Connor and Kennedy) to side with the plaintiffs without rewriting law in the setting most threatening to Justices concerned with preserving the executive's enforcement primacy. Justices

---

102. Daniel A. Farber, *Environmental Litigation After* Laidlaw, 30 Envtl. L. Rep. 10516 (2000).

Scalia and Thomas continue vehemently to advocate their far more
rigorous standing approach, an approach that places judges in a powerful
role of assessing the reality of underlying alleged injury. With ongoing
play in the law, vigorous disagreement on the Court, posture distinctions
allowing for ongoing adherence to earlier, tougher standing approaches,
little reason exists to expect a cessation of standing and mootness
disagreement on the Supreme Court or in the lower courts. It is highly
unlikely that any of the current Justices will, in the interest of fealty to
precedent or stability in the law, concur in standing results despite their
personal disagreements. With the increasingly aged members of the
Court, and a reelected President who touts Justice Scalia as his model
Justice, soon a new Justice or two will assume a role on the Supreme
Court. Plenty of room remains for new twists in the law.

Conclusion

The *Laidlaw* case's lower court rulings offered compelling facts and
illustrated the problematic implications of the Supreme Court's 1990s
standing doctrine revival. The Supreme Court's decisive *Laidlaw* majority resolved many of these open questions and problematic implications,
preserving the viability of citizen suit litigation. *Laidlaw* did not, however, render citizen environmental litigation simple. Numerous challenges
will continue to be raised against plaintiffs, deterring many attorneys
from even venturing into this area. Remaining play in the law and
disagreement on the Supreme Court virtually ensure that this chapter is
far from closed. *Laidlaw* was critical, however, to preserving citizens'
ability to sue polluters and government actors violating their legal
commitments. As long as the nation's environmental laws continue to
have strong citizen support and remain law, citizen enforcement guaran-
tees that those laws will still have an effect, even during periods of
executive or state enforcement laxity. Citizen litigants must be prepared
for contentious and extended litigation, but constitutional impediments
have been lessened, at least for now.*

---

* I would like to acknowledge with gratitude the research assistance of Jeremy
Corcoran, Julie Bowling and Amy Clark, as well as the personal insights of several
participants in the *Laidlaw* litigation cited in this work.

8

Carol M. Rose

The Story of *Lucas*: Environmental Land Use Regulation Between Developers and the Deep Blue Sea

"The fact that tangible property is also visible tends to give rigidity to our conception of our rights in it that we do not attach to others less concretely clothed. But the notion that the former are exempt from the legislative modification required from time to time in civilized life is contradicted not only by the doctrine of eminent domain, under which what is taken is paid for, but by that of the police power in its proper sense, under which property rights may be cut down, and to that extent taken, without pay."—Oliver Wendell Holmes[1]

I. Introduction

In *Lucas v. South Carolina Coastal Council (Lucas)*,[2] a private land developer successfully challenged South Carolina's beachfront protection statute as a "taking" of his property under the Fifth and Fourteenth Amendments to the United States Constitution.

This blank fact deserves a moment's pause. Most of the leading environmental cases described in this volume have nothing to say about "takings" of property. While there have been many challenges to the Clean Air Act (CAA), there have been no major takings cases, even though billions of dollars have been at stake for industrial interests regulated by the Act. The Clean Water Act's (CWA) pollution control requirements were contemplated to force a substantial number of busi-

---

1. Block v. Hirsch, 256 U.S. 135, 155 (1921).
2. 505 U.S. 1003 (1992).

nesses to fail,[3] yet these controls have generated no major takings cases. The legislation that established the Superfund (CERCLA) has generated reams of litigation about private responsibilities for cleaning up hazardous materials deposited on land, but these cases seldom raise the issue of governmental takings of property, and instead generally involve parties' efforts to pass the buck to other parties.

But those pollution control cases stand in contrast to the major conservation-oriented statutes that pit landowners against legislative attempts to preserve wetlands, endangered species, and, as in *Lucas*, coastal areas. Unlike the pollution control aspects of the CWA, the Act's wetlands protection provisions have produced some serious and occasionally successful takings claims.[4] Similarly, the Endangered Species Act, which also often revolves around marine life, reproduces the wetlands litigation pattern in a subdued form, that is, a number of complaints about takings of private property, albeit not very successful ones.[5] Coastal regulation, as we shall see, has been a hotbed of takings litigation.

But regulations change in many areas, including environmental ones; why does environmental *land use* legislation generate all of this heat over property rights when other kinds of environmental legislation do not? One clue is in the quotation from Holmes with which this chapter begins: land is the most visible and tangible of things you can own, and that quality captures your attention, and enhances your sense of entitlement. Perhaps because it is so tangible, so very much *there*, land is also the easiest of all resources to turn into property: it is fixed; it can be fenced; trespassers can easily be identified and repelled in the exercise of that quintessential symbol of property, the right to exclude. By contrast, typical "environmental" resources like water or air or wildlife are elusive, spread-out, hard to capture, easily subject to invasion, and in general "propertizable" only with considerable effort, if at all.

Attentiveness to property is not a bad thing. Indeed, the great claim for property is that property does engage our interest, and makes us weigh our decisions carefully, knowing that as owners we will take the

---

3. *See, e.g.*, Ass'n of Pacific Fisheries v. EPA, 615 F.2d 794, 808 (9th Cir. 1980) (observing that Congress expected adoption of pollution control measures would result in plant closings).

4. One notable successful claim was Florida Rock Indus., Inc. v. United States, 18 F.3d 1560, 1568–73 (Fed. Cir. 1994).

5. For a summary of ESA cases claiming property takings see Robert Meltz, *The Endangered Species Act and Claims of Property Rights "Takings": A Summary of the Court Decisions* (2003), *available at* http://resourcescommittee.house.gov/Press/reports/esa/esaproprights_crs.pdf (noting cases but also noting that most have been unsuccessful).

gain from good decisions and bear the cost of bad ones. But from an environmental perspective, the problem with land is that land gets all the attention, even though land uses interact so deeply with the very much less "propertizable" environmental resources. To take a prosaic example, cutting down a particular tree removes habitat for a bird population, at the same time that it increases runoff into a stream, and ever so slightly reduces the scrubbing of carbon dioxide from the atmosphere. Taken one by one, cutting each tree has only very small marginal effects, and those effects usually fail to claim the specific attention of anyone in particular. Hence the members of the public are slow to notice environmental problems and even slower to feel responsible for them. By the time they do, the older landowners have already invested in houses in the clearing, and newcomers claim that they should be able to clear their lots, too. When environmentalists call for some land use control to deal with some of the cumulative effect of these actions, they may expect a sharp and focused opposition from landowners.

In the American legal experience, this pattern—growing environmental concern facing sharp landowner opposition—has nowhere been more noticeable than at the beach. Many coastal areas faced serious degradation before American legislatures responded, but coastal regulation has stirred a witches' brew of takings cases, including three major Supreme Court cases on takings of property.[6] Through holdings at least partially favorable to private landowners, these cases have much roiled the waters of takings jurisprudence in the United States. Perhaps even more important, these cases have invigorated the notion that private property must necessarily be opposed to environmental protection, a mistaken idea that can badly damage the texture of legal and lay thought about both property and environmental protection, since so much of environmental law actually does aim at protecting property interests.

Of all of these takings cases, the most important to date has generally been thought to be *Lucas v. South Carolina Coastal Council*. The basic narrative of David Lucas' battle with the South Carolina Coastal Council has been recounted many times, sometimes favorably to Lucas, quite understandably in the case of his own book,[7] but often much more critically, as in the very able narrative and critique by the legal scholar Vicki Been, in the volume on *Property Stories* in this series of legal "stories."[8]

---

6. In addition to *Lucas*, the cases are *Nollan v. California Coastal Commission*, 483 U.S. 825 (1987), and *Palazzolo v. Rhode Island*, 533 U.S. 606 (2001).

7. David Lucas, *Lucas vs. The Green Machine* (1995) [hereinafter *Green Machine*]. Another sympathetic and very interesting account is by the economist William A. Fischel, *Regulatory Takings: Law, Economics, and Politics* 59–63 (1995).

8. Vicki Been, Lucas v. *The Green Machine: Using the Takings Clause to Promote More Efficient Regulation? in Property Stories* 221 (Gerald Korngold & Andrew P. Morriss

These and most other accounts of the case describe a set of parallel stories. One begins with David Lucas, his development activities on the Isle of Palms near Charleston in the later 1970s and his purchase (or possibly retention) of two nearby beachfront lots in the mid 1980s (lots that he held with somewhat ambiguous plans for future development). Meanwhile, the parallel story starts with South Carolina's long effort to manage its shifting coastline: the state's adoption of a coastal zone statute in 1977 in response to federal encouragement of coastal planning; then its 1988 amendment of the earlier act, creating the beachfront setback requirements that made Lucas' lots essentially unbuildable. Those setback amendments set the stage for the collision of the two stories: Lucas claimed that South Carolina's regulation had deprived his property of all economic value and hence constituted an uncompensated "taking" of his property. He won in the trial court, lost in the South Carolina Supreme Court, and wound up, finally, in the United States Supreme Court, which ruled that the state's beachfront regulation was a prima facie taking of his property, subject only to certain limited defenses based on the state's common law of property.

The great jurisprudential drama here is the doctrinal significance of Lucas' victory for "takings" doctrine in the United States. How distinguishable is *Lucas* from other cases, given the lower court's unrefuted finding that South Carolina's regulations caused his lots to lose all economically beneficial use? What defenses might still be available to regulating bodies after *Lucas*, even if regulation causes an owner a similarly drastic loss of value? Those questions are very significant for property law, and this chapter on *Lucas* will necessarily take up some of them.

But it is the parallel story—the background of coastal zone management efforts—that I plan to explore somewhat more extensively here. This story will wind the reader through a brief history of the modern pressures on the coast, and then take up the only partially-successful federal drive in the 1970s to encourage state land use regulation. Some lessons from other states' coastal management acts follow, along, of course, with South Carolina's own experiences—and all these regulatory efforts will be related to an evolving "takings" jurisprudence over the same time period. The reason for the focus on regulation is that modern environmentalism, for better or worse, is very frequently a story of legislative efforts to manage resources, given what appears to be the failure of private market activity to do so.[9] *Lucas* is the leading exemplar

---

eds., 2004). For another very interesting though briefer critical account, see Oliver A. Houck, *More Unfinished Stories: Lucas, Atlanta Coalition, and Palila/Sweet Home*, 75 U. Colo. L. Rev. 331 (2004)

9. Some clearly think legislation worse than the market, however. *See, e.g.*, Terry L. Anderson & Donald R. Leal, *Free Market Environmentalism* (Rev. ed. 2001).

of the property-based briar patch that this legislation can encounter in the land-use context, but one needs to put *Lucas* into a longer scenario to notice the larger patterns that the case represents.

To give a brief preview, one leitmotiv of this chapter is that certain consistent political factors—especially property-related and local governmental opposition—drove the various stages of coastal zone management towards narrow regulatory "solutions," even when the issues were considerably broader. But unfortunately, that same narrow scope eventually made coastal legislation vulnerable to the takings charges that culminated in *Lucas*. At the same time, the case and its aftermath also revealed the fragility of the major theories behind takings jurisprudence. Indeed the story suggests the need for a more pragmatic view of takings law, as a means to police and thus to ease regulatory transitions.

Why does this matter to environmentalists? It matters because transitional strategies are critical to the success of environmental land use regulation generally, not just for coastal management. In turn, land use controls are critical to some parts of environmental law, perhaps increasingly so as we face a new generation of environmental issues that go beyond gross controls on major pollution sources. Because land is so much easier to turn into property than typical environmental resources like water or air, and because land is so noticeable as property, new environmental controls of land uses are always likely to raise the decibel level. Nevertheless, environmentalism needs to explore ways to approach this problem constructively. Ultimately, that is why a chapter on *Lucas*, a case about property takings, belongs in a book of "Environmental Stories."

II. Who Cares About the Coast?

Drama comes easily in the places where large bodies of water meet the land. Waves billow and crash against rocky shores, or they lap sonorously against long sweeps of sands. Sunsets and sunrises redden distant horizons as sailors take warning or delight. Birds swoop or stalk in search of unwary fish. Weirdly shaped plants extend grasping roots into the deep, swampy muds of coastal wetlands, reeking of decay while teeming with life.

But all of the sea's appeals to the senses were met only by limited audiences until relatively recent times, at least among Europeans and European settlers; until the eighteenth century, most found the seashore unattractive, even malignant.[10] This is not to say that the seas and seacoasts were unimportant, however. Quite the contrary, in an age

---

   10. For a quite vivid account of pre-eighteenth century Europeans' dread of the sea and seashore, see Alain Corbin, *The Lure of the Sea: The Discovery of the Seaside in the Western World 1750–1840* 1–18 (Jocelyn Phelps trans., 1994).

when roads were few and rough, waterways were supremely important for travel and trade; and at a time when protein was not so easy to come by, fish comprised an important element in diet.[11] To serve the ends of travel, commerce and provisioning, European law going back to the Romans consistently stressed that waterways and lands washed by the tides would be open for navigation and fishing, except insofar as the sovereign created or permitted special private rights for these "public trust" purposes.[12] Tidal wetlands might have seemed inaccessible and spooky, but even these areas had their own populations who learned how to use the local wildlife, fish, and plant materials, as with the "fen people" of medieval England or the Acadian transplants of Louisiana's swamps.[13] And, of course, dunes, reefs, barrier islands and their vegetation have always served a more passive function, protecting ports and upland areas from the ravages of storms.

But it was only in the eighteenth century that Europeans and European settlers began to *enjoy* the beach, beginning with English travelers who increasingly saw the seaside water and air as healthful and pleasurable. In response, coastal recreation businesses emerged; one of the more unusual examples was the "bathing machine," a kind of horse-drawn cubicle that would halt in the water while the modest occupants undressed, swam, and dressed again.[14] The bathing machines are a backhanded reminder that then, as now, sex was an element in the beach's allure: the warm sun, the lazy days, the glimpse of flesh.[15] Who could resist? By the nineteenth century, other European countries, and the United States, too, had followed Britain's lead.[16]

Improved land-based transportation was a factor in the increasing recreational uses of the beach, a pattern that continues to this day. In

---

11. For fish in the European diet, see, e.g., Kathy L. Pearson, *Nutrition and the Early–Medieval Diet*, 72 Speculum 1, 9 (1997).

12. For an extensive account of Roman and subsequent law of the "public trust," see Patrick Deveney, *Title, Jus Publicum, and the Public Trust: An Historical Analysis*, 1 Sea Grant L.J. 13, 21 (1976).

13. Fred P. Bosselman, *Limitations Inherent in the Title to Wetlands at Common Law*, 15 Stan. Envtl. L.J. 247, 265–74 (1996) (medieval fen people); Herbert R. Padgett, *Physical and Cultural Associations on the Louisiana Coast*, 59 Annals Ass'n Am. Geographers 481, 481–84 (1969) (Acadians).

14. John Travis, *Continuity and Change in English Sea–Bathing, 1730–1900: A Case of Swimming With the Tide, in Recreation and the Sea* 8, 12–13 (Stephen Fisher ed., 1997). For pictures of bathing machines, see *id.* at 18, 28.

15. Lena Lencek & Gideon Bosker, *The Beach: The History of Paradise on Earth* 48–50, 56–58, 106, 284 (1998) (describing the continuing association of bathing and the beach with sexual adventure).

16. John K. Walton, *The Seaside Resorts of Western Europe, 1750–1939, in Recreation and the Sea, supra* note 14, at 36, 40–41.

the late nineteenth century, the relevant transport was the railroad.[17] Rail lines took the French Impressionist painters from Paris through the French countryside to the coastal tourist spots, where they chronicled beach activities.[18] Rail lines brought Philadelphians to the beaches of New Jersey and New Yorkers to Coney Island.[19] Automobiles and highways made the shore even more accessible. Long before the national interstate highway system brought coastlines within relatively easy reach to so many, Robert Moses, New York's master planner from the 1920s through the 1960s, built the parkways that took New Yorkers to nearby Long Island beaches.[20] Expanding recreational interest in beach areas spawned real estate development, including summer homes, hotels, and shoreline businesses that promoted recreational boating, swimming, fishing, and eating. Local governments were important players in this development from the start, providing lifeguards, boardwalks, and other elements of security, ambience and infrastructure, all to attract tourists and summer people and their money.[21]

With increasing temporary or permanent populations at the beach, however, came considerable alteration in the shore itself. In the 1890s, in a portent of things to come, the developer of Palm Beach, Florida completely rearranged the natural landscape, filling wetlands and inlets and constructing roads and a seawall.[22] On eroding beaches in New Jersey, shoreland owners built jetties to preserve their own sand beach or seawalls to protect their houses, thus preventing the waves and currents from re-nourishing the beach itself, and causing the beach to diminish all the more.[23]

In a sense, the recreational or amenity use of the waterfront is only one of a number of ways in which the shoreline has become open to commerce, or to what we might now call "globalization." Another obvious example is port facility improvement, especially with the emer-

---

17. *Id.* at 42.

18. Richard Brettell, *The Impressionist Landscape and the Image of France, in A Day in the Country: Impressionism and the French Landscape* 27, 40–49 (Andrea P. A. Belloli ed., 1985). It might be noted that at least some observers thought even then that the French coast was being ruined by what was seen as tawdry development. *Id.* at 43.

19. Lencek & Bosker, *supra* note 15, at 139–40 (Philadelphia—New Jersey), 165–66 (New York—Coney Island).

20. Robert A. Caro, *The Power Broker: Robert Moses and the Fall of New York*, 170–71, 233, 237 (1974).

21. Walton, *supra* note 16, at 50–51 (describing the importance of municipal government in English resort development); Lencek & Bosker, *supra* note 15, at 130, 140 (boardwalks and steps), 146 (lifeguards and security).

22. Lencek & Bosker, *supra* note 15, at 204–05 (Palm Beach), 279 (Atlantic coast).

23. Cornelia Dean, *Against the Tide: The Battle for America's Beaches* 53, 56–58 (1999).

gence of containerized shipping from around the globe. Now, more than ever, seaports require extensive dredging and alterations of the natural features of bays and inlets.[24] But other aspects of globalization have their impact, too. In the 1930s it became commercially feasible to produce oil and gas at rigs off the shores of the Gulf States; offshore drilling followed in California in the 1960s and Alaska in the 1970s.[25] Those operations put the coastline at risk of spills, or, as in the case of Louisiana's massive Gulf Coast Achafalaya wetlands, onshore channel construction that brings salt water intrusions and the disruption of native plants and animals.[26] More recently, aquaculture industries in coastal waters in the United States and abroad have produced marine food products for wider markets, but shrimp production can cut into soil-holding mangrove swamps, while fish farms throw off organic pollutants into the surrounding waters.[27]

Upstream development has also had a major impact on the coast, albeit less directly. A critical sanitation improvement in nineteenth century urban areas was the introduction of sewerage systems, but those same sewers shunted waste matter into rivers and poisoned downstream fisheries.[28] Along with the great expansion of coastal development, up-stream residential development—especially the growth of the suburbs—has ballooned in the years since the Second World War, and this growth affects downstream waters. While sewage discharge is now more likely to be treated, there is more of it, and there are also such factors as increased runoff, street waste and siltation.[29] We now know that even the gentle farming of Pennsylvania's Amish communities affects water quality in the Chesapeake Bay, and it should be no surprise that concentrated commercial feedlots can have massive effects on downstream aquatic systems.[30] Even automobile air pollution affects the beach, since nitrogen

---

24. Lawrence Juda & Richard Burroughs, *Dredging Navigational Channels in a Changing Scientific and Regulatory Environment*, 35 J. MAR. L. & COM. 171, 174–79 (2004).

25. William R. Freudenburg & Robert Gramling, *Oil in Troubled Waters: Perceptions, Politics, and the Battle Over Offshore Drilling* 17–23 (1994).

26. *Id.* at 42–45.

27. Shannon R. Wilson, *Sustainable Aquaculture: An Organizing Solution in International Law*, 26 T. Jefferson L. Rev. 491, 500 (2004); Rosamond L. Naylor et al., *Nature's Subsidies to Shrimp and Salmon Farming*, 282 Science 883, 883–84 (1998); U.S. Department of Commerce, National Oceanic & Atmospheric Admin., National Ocean Service, *Trends in U.S. Coastal Regions, 1970–1998*, at 11–12 (Aug. 1999) *available at* http://www.oceanservice.noaa.gov/websites/retiredsites/natdia_pdf/trends_addendum.pdf [hereinafter *Trends*].

28. *See, e.g.*, City of Hampton v. Watson, 89 S.E. 81 (Va. 1916) (permitting city to continue using stream as sewer outlet despite contamination of oyster beds).

29. *Trends, supra* note 27, at 4–5 (coastal population increase), 15–16 (wastewater and nonpoint pollution).

30. David A. Fahrenthold, *Pennsylvania Pollution Muddies Bay Cleanup; State Lags in Curbing Runoff from Farms*, Wash. Post, May 16, 2004, at A1 (Amish); *Trends, supra* note 27, at 11 (feedlot effects).

byproducts of auto exhaust add substantially to the eutrophication of downwind bays and lakes.[31] Even more important over the long run, all sorts of combustion, from lawn mowers to coal-fired power plants, add gases to the environment that raise global temperatures and bring the oceans ever higher up onto the beach and inlets.[32] The coastal area, in short, is a vulnerable one, filled with fragile environmental and visual features, and sensitive to vast numbers and kinds of assaults, from near and far.

Taken together, all of these assaults simply represent competing uses of the waterfront, but as is the case for many environmental goods, much of this competition is unmediated by overt markets. Such non-market effects, economists say, can be placed roughly into two categories: externalities, on the one hand (damage to the beach from outsider uses such as oil drilling or upstream pollution), and the commons problem, on the other (the mutual damage that shore users inflict upon one another, generally from development activities). Until the dawn of the modern environmental era in the 1970s, insofar as there was any mediation of these effects at all, it came simply from property owners and—sometimes—from local regulation. But by the 1960s there were many who thought that those two sources of authority had failed, not only for the beach but for land-related resource uses more generally.

III. Regulating the Beach

A. Federal Land Use? A Failure and a Success

The late 1960s and early 1970s were a period of massive legislative change on environmental issues.[33] As is discussed elsewhere in this volume, these years set out the basic environmental planning structure for federal projects (the National Environmental Policy Act or NEPA), for air pollution control (the Clean Air Act or CAA), for water pollution (the Federal Water Pollution Control Act, now known as the Clean Water Act or CWA), and for the protection of threatened wild plants and animals (the Endangered Species Act or ESA).

Land uses did not go unnoticed in this flurry of major legislation. Aside from NEPA's review of federally-sponsored activities, the Clean

---

31. Peter Whorisky, *Bay Pollution Progress Overstated; Government Program's Computer Model Proved Too Optimistic*, Wash. Post, July 18, 2004, at A1.

32. *See, e.g.*, Jeffrey W. Niemitz, *A Line in the Sand: Global Climate Change and the Future of Coastal Management Policy*, 8 Dick. J. Envtl. L. & Pol'y 1, 3–8 (1999).

33. *See, e.g.*, E. Donald Elliott, Bruce A. Ackerman, & John C. Millian, *Toward a Theory of Statutory Evolution: The Federalization of Environmental Law*, 1 J.L. Econ. & Org. 313 (1985) (elaborating a theory of political competition to explain the wave of environmental law after the late 1960s).

Water Act subjected wetlands alterations to federal approval;[34] the ESA included provisions to protect habitat;[35] and even the Clean Air Act, at least for a time, contemplated land use controls on "indirect" air pollution magnets like shopping centers.[36] But Congress also addressed land use control in a more global sense, debating several different bills for a national land use planning act between 1970 and 1974.[37] A notable promoter was Senator Henry Jackson of Washington, who introduced a national land use bill early in 1970 as a followup to the then just-signed NEPA. As Secretary of the Interior Rogers C. B. Morton was to assert later in the debates, "land use, in fact, is the key to all the rest of our environmental problems."[38]

Land use has traditionally been a highly localized regulatory area, in part because land issues genuinely vary greatly from place to place, and in part because local officials have so carefully guarded this major source of their authority and revenue. But by the 1970s local land use regulators had been under attack for well over a decade for what was seen as their parochialism and their systematic capitulation to developers; the power, cohesiveness and intensity of the developers, it was said, permitted them to overwhelm weak and scattered local opposition, and thus to "capture" local governments particularly easily.[39]

The local-level capture theory suggested that more centralized decisionmaking would be preferable, but the major federal land use bills took the theory only part way; they aimed not so much at establishing a national program, or even national standards, as at supporting state land

---

34. Clean Water Act § 404, 86 Stat. 884 (1972) (codified as amended at 33 U.S.C. § 1344 (2000)).

35. *See* Babbitt v. Sweet Home Chapter of Cmtys. for a Great Oregon, 515 U.S. 687 (1995) (upholding regulations treating habitat destruction as "harm" under ESA § 9); *see also* ESA § 10(a), 16 U.S.C. § 1539 (2000) (authorizing habitat conservation plans as condition of "incidental taking" of endangered species).

36. *See* Patrick Del Duca & Daniel Mansueto, *Indirect Source Controls: An Intersection of Air Quality Management and Land Use Regulation*, 24 Loy. L.A. L. Rev. 1131, 1152–54 (1991) (describing EPA's initial demand for indirect source control, then Congress' withdrawal of support in 1977 and 1990 amendments to the CAA).

37. Noreen Lyday, *The Law of the Land: Debating National Land Use Legislation 1970–75* (1976).

38. Rogers C.B. Morton, Letter to the Editor, Wash. Post, Jan. 4, 1972, *cited in* Daly, *infra* note 40, at 24.

39. Frank J. Popper, *The Politics of Land–Use Reform* 4, 10 (1981) (describing concern over developers' capture of local government); Carol M. Rose, *Planning and Dealing: Piecemeal Land Controls as a Problem of Local Legitimacy*, 71 Cal. L. Rev. 837, 841, 858–63 (1983) (describing early critiques). More recently, however, William Fischel has argued that the more important though generally benign "captors" of local government are homeowner-voters, who often oppose development. *See* William A. Fischel, *The Homevoter Hypothesis: How Home Values Influence Local Government Taxation, School Finance, and Land–Use Policies* (2001).

use regulation. To be sure, the major bills would have shifted control away from local governments especially with respect to environmentally sensitive areas, large-scale developments, and the siting of major regional facilities like energy plants and airports.[40] Presumably if decisionmaking were simply kicked upstairs as far as the state level, better decisions would result: less development-dominated, less insular, more attentive to regional impacts and needs, and presumably environmentally friendlier.[41] But even in those heady days of optimism about national environmental controls for air and water pollution, in the case of land use regulation, centralization at the state level would be centralization enough. Any further step toward nationalization undoubtedly seemed too insensitive to regional variations, too much a departure from past practice, and too hot a political potato.[42]

To further allay the two major expected sources of opposition, i.e., local governments and property rights proponents, the Council on Environmental Quality sponsored two books during the debates over national land use legislation. In the first, *The Quiet Revolution in Land Use Control*, Fred Bosselman and David Callies described what they said was a gathering trend to shift land use control from local to state authorities. The second, *The Taking Issue*, dealt with property law: here the same authors (joined by John Banta) argued that past takings jurisprudence granted governments liberal authority to regulate property without triggering the requirement to compensate affected owners. Both books became influential over the long run, but at the time, the *Taking* book particularly alarmed the opposition, and perhaps set off what was to become a long project by some business persons, lawyers, and conservative academics to protect private property against what was thought to be overreaching regulation.[43]

---

40. Jayne E. Daly, *A Glimpse of the Past—A Vision for the Future: Senator Henry M. Jackson and National Land Use Legislation*, 28 Urb. Law. 7, 9–12, 20, 25 (1996). Both Daly, at 20–21, 25–26, and Lyday, *supra* note 37, at 21–22, 30, note the influence of the American Law Institute's Model Land Development Code on the Nixon administration's bill, which affected later compromise bills.

41. Daly, *supra* note 40, at 20 (concerning the view that local governments were too small to take regional concerns into account); Lyday, *supra* note 37, at 20–21 (same); Popper, *supra* note 39, at 3–4 (describing the impact of Ralph Nader and capture theory on land use reform proposals), 46–55 (outlining this and other problems of local land use control, including fragmented jurisdictions, corruption, developer dominance, and insularity).

42. Lyday, *supra* note 37, at 26, 31, 36, 41 (noting local variations and traditions, a few failed efforts for specific national standards); Daly, *supra* note 40, at 14, 29 (same).

43. Fred Bosselman & David Callies, *The Quiet Revolution in Land Use Controls* (1971); Fred Bosselman, David Callies, & John Banta, *The Taking Issue: A Study of the Constitutional Limits of Governmental Authority to Regulate the Use of Privately–Owned Land Without Paying Compensation to the Owners* (1973). For the CEQ role and the effect of the books, see Lyday, *supra* note 37, at 20, 41–42, 46; for the origins of the property

Thus despite significant political support, the national land use bills faced growing opposition from conservative and business groups, who attacked on predictable grounds: that the bills extended federal authority into traditional local domains, and that they extended governmental authority too far over private property rights. In the end all of the bills failed. The final blow came in 1974, when the last of Jackson's bills passed the Senate but lost on a procedural motion in the House.[44]

Thus the Coastal Zone Management Act (CZMA), passed in 1972, became in a sense only a surviving remnant of a much more sweeping effort for national intervention into land use controls. For a time, the CZMA was under discussion simultaneously with the various national land use bills, and each of these legislative initiatives influenced the other.[45] Like the land use bills, the CZMA was motivated by the sense that local governments were not "up to the task" of coastal management.[46] Like those bills, the Act centered on federal financial support for voluntary state planning, with only quite general criteria for federal approval. Like those bills, the CZMA offered the states an additional payoff for coastal planning: once a state coastal plan was approved, the Federal government was required to make its own projects and licenses "consistent" with the state plan insofar as possible.[47] Also like the more general land use bills, the CZMA was careful to mention that state coastal planning should not stifle appropriate economic projects.[48]

But there were some differences, and the differences were part of the reason why the CZMA succeeded where the more general bills failed. Coastal bills enjoyed a major publicity advantage; they followed in the wake of the dramatic uproar over the Santa Barbara oil spill in 1969,[49]

rights movement, see Houck, *supra* note 8, at 343–44; *see also* Douglas T. Kendall & Charles P. Lord, *The Takings Project: A Critical Analysis and Assessment of the Progress So Far*, 25 B.C. Envt'l Aff. L. Rev. 509 (1998).

    44. Lyday, *supra* note 37, at 37–39, 41–48; Daly, *supra* note 40, at 135 (describing property and federalism concerns). Lyday, *supra* note 37, at 43, also argues that the absence of national standards weakened environmental support for the bills.

    45. Lyday, *supra* note 37, at 20–21; Zigurds L. Zile, *A Legislative–Political History of the Coastal Zone Management Act of 1972*, 1 Coastal Zone Mgmt. J. 235, 263, 269–72 (1974).

    46. Staff of the Senate Comm. On Commerce, 94th Cong., 2d Sess., Legislative History of the Coastal Zone Management Act of 1972, as Amended in 1974 and 1976 with a Section-by-Section Index 2 (Comm. Print 1976); Zile, *supra* note 45, at 236.

    47. Coastal Zone Management Act § 307(c), 86 Stat. 1285 (1972) (codified as amended at 16 U.S.C. § 1456(c) (2000)); Daly, *supra* note 40, at 19 (concerning National Land Use conformity provisions).

    48. Coastal Zone Management Act § 303(2)(D), (3), 86 Stat. 1281 (1972) (codified as amended at 16 U.S.C. § 1452(2)(D), (3) (2000)).

    49. At least one conservative rationale for coastal planning was to calm public reaction over such spills and leaks. *See* Keith C. Clarke & Jeffrey J. Hemphill, *The Santa*

and in the same year, the so-called Stratton Commission's major report on coastal issues, which itself urged federal assistance to state coastal planning.[50] Another obvious difference was the limited ambit of the CZMA; this Act dealt with only a small range of sensitive topographies. Though the CZMA bills gradually broadened to include estuaries as well as beaches,[51] the early symbolism of the visible and popular beach may have sharpened legislative and constituent attention in a way that eluded the more general land use bills. Moreover, the narrower focus of the Act also served to reduce—though certainly not eliminate—opposition from the usual sources, local governments, real estate interests and property rights proponents. Some had thought the CZMA would only be a stepping stone to a national land use act; as it turned out, that path went nowhere. The CZMA's relative success was to presage later events in state coastal legislation, where a narrow focus could be a source of political strength, limiting local and landowner opposition. But the state stories were also to reveal some of the costs of this strategy, both environmental and jurisprudential.

B. Models for South Carolina? A Near Neighbor and a Distant Hussy

Most of the thirty-five eligible states submitted plans within a few years of the CZMA's passage, reflecting different state histories and interests in their particular coasts: Atlantic, Gulf, Pacific, Bering Sea, and Great Lakes. From the beginning, two leading states were California and North Carolina; they offered somewhat different models of coastal planning that are both relevant to South Carolina's later efforts.

North Carolina's legislature had to consider a very complicated shore. On the east are the Outer Banks, a long rope of barrier islands that serve as beach and wildlife preserve areas. But behind the Banks are deep and substantial estuaries, some among the largest on the east coast.[52] Accordingly, the state's Coastal Area Management Act (CAMA) of 1974 included areas relatively deep into the uplands, since activities there clearly affect estuaries. The CAMA drew in the entire areas of all the twenty shoreline and estuarian counties, which were required to submit coastal plans according to state guidelines.

Barbara Oil Spill: A Retrospective, 64 Yearbook of the Ass'n of Pacific Coast Geographers 157, 157–62 (Darrick Danta ed., 2002), *available at* http://www.geog.ucsb.edu/?kclarke/Papers/SBOilSpill1969.pdf.

50. Comm'n on Marine Science, Eng'g and Res., *Our Nation and the Sea: A Plan for National Action* (Jan. 1969), *available at* http://www.lib.noaa.gov/edocs/stratton/title.html.

51. Zile, *supra* note 45, at 236.

52. Thomas J. Schoenbaum, *The Management of Land and Water Use in the Coastal Zone: A New Law is Enacted in North Carolina*, 53 N.C. L. Rev. 275, 275–76 (1974).

But development interests and local governments had opposed the CAMA sharply, and in order to pass the Act, the legislature took several steps to appease them. First, special state permits were only required within "areas of environmental concern;" even there, local officials decided on most projects aside from "major developments." An even more direct conciliation was the prominent inclusion of local governmental nominees and development interests on the state-level Coastal Resources Commission, a measure that one 1974 commentator feared would lead to serious conflicts of interest.[53] In general, then, while North Carolina's CAMA has evolved considerably over time, the basic state strategy has been to treat a broad area as the coastal zone, but to manage only selective matters within that broad zone, and to engage local officials throughout the process.

California's strategy was quite different, and considerably more audacious. Several factors converged to focus popular concern on the state's beaches in the late '60s and early '70s: the Santa Barbara oil spill, of course, but also new and looming beachfront development, accompanied by ever-greater impediments to public access and ocean views.[54] California's assertiveness also resulted from the process through which coastal protection became law. After several plans failed in the legislature—due in part to the opposition of then-Governor Ronald Reagan—an energetic state coalition of environmentalists succeeded in driving a coastal management act through the initiative process. This manner of adoption gave some particular twists to the legislation. First, rather like the CZMA itself, the Act's proponents limited resistance and gathered support by focusing specifically on what was most popular, particularly the beach and estuarian areas. And second, the initiative process meant that the Act came into being without the usual legislative concessions.[55] The result was a coastal act that focused on a narrow geographical area, but that was quite uncompromising within it.

The 1972 Act contemplated further legislative action, which issued in a second coastal act in 1976. This act was slightly more conciliatory to development interests, but all the same, California's coastal management

---

53. *Id.* at 282 (local opposition), 291–92 (permits), 300–01 (board makeup); Milton S. Heath, Jr., & David W. Owens, *Coastal Management Law in North Carolina: 1974–1994*, 72 N.C. L. Rev. 1413, 1413–18 (1994). Schoenbaum's concern over conflict of interest was addressed by the legislature in a 1989 amendment. *See* Heath & Owens, *supra*, at 1418.

54. Robert G. Healy & John S. Rosenberg, *Land Use and the States* 80–85 (2d ed. 1979).

55. Popper, *supra* note 39, at 101 (noting reformers concentration on the popular area); William J. Duddleson, *How the Citizens of California Secured Their Coastal Management Program, in Protecting the Golden Shore* 3, 3–15 (Robert G. Healy ed., 1978) (describing the campaign to pass the law); Healy & Rosenberg, *supra* note 54, at 85–89 (same).

soon became a kind of template for what was possible for state coastal management.[56] This was the case not only vis-a-vis the Federal government, where the California Commission challenged the offshore oil leasing plans of now-President Reagan's administration,[57] but also vis-a-vis California's own landowners and developers.

California's environmental coalition had initially mollified local governmental opposition by its definition of the landward coastal zone only as a relatively shallow area (one thousand yards landward from shore, in addition to the state's seaward limit of three miles). But within this limited stretch, the state commission and its six affiliated regional commissions were authorized to veto or place conditions on all development projects, even those approved by local governments. While some of the rural northern counties were less enthusiastic about controls, the state commission and the urban regional commissions were especially aggressive, unwilling to make exceptions and ever-ready to tell coastal landowners with great specificity what they could and could not do on their properties, to assure their compatibility with the coastal character.[58]

Because of the narrow geographical range of the coastal zone, only a relatively few property owners were affected, but these landowners and developers complained bitterly. Some fought back in the courts, soon to be assisted by the newly-formed conservative public interest group, the Pacific Legal Foundation. In the early years, however, these cases were more significant for their harassment value than for legal precedent.[59] On the other side, California's citizens appeared to have quite firm views that they themselves had rights to views of and access to the coast, and the state's coastal law gave them ample opportunity to appeal land

56. Popper, *supra* note 39, at 99–100 (describing California's original law and the 1976 modifications).

57. The California Commission lost this battle when the Supreme Court held that the leases were not subject to consistency requirements, hinting that federal activities located outside the state zone did not "directly" affect the zone. *See* Secretary of the Interior v. California, 464 U.S. 312 (1984). But over the long-run California did better; Congress amended the federal CZMA itself in 1990, to include activities "within or outside" the coastal zone. *See* Coastal Zone Management Act § 30(c), 104 Stat. 1388–307 (1990) (codified at 16 U.S.C. § 1456(c), (d) (2000)).

58. Healy & Rosenberg, *supra* note 54, at 86–90, 105–106 (stringency and specificity of coastal regulation and regional variations); Popper, *supra* note 39, at 100–01, 126–27, 135–37, 142–43 (same; also noting small numbers of landowners in narrow strip).

59. Popper, *supra* note 39, at 100–01, 131–32, 150–51 (few owners, landowner or developer objections and lawsuits); Duddleson, *supra* note 55, at 25–26 (legal challenges). The Pacific Legal Foundation was founded in 1973, by several figures associated with then-Governor Reagan. *See* Kendall & Lord, *supra* note 43, at 540–42; *see also* The Pacific Legal Foundation website, *at* http://www.pacificlegal.org/PLFProfile.asp.

development.[60]

Indeed, for a considerable time, the California commission seemed invincible, or so it appeared to one disgruntled California land use lawyer, Michael Berger, who complained that the Commission always won.[61] Invincible, that is, until 1987, when the Supreme Court decided the case of *Nollan v. California Coastal Commission*,[62] and agreed with a landowner that the Commission had "taken" property without compensation, in violation of the First and Fourteenth Amendments to the United States Constitution.

IV. Coastal Zone Management Goes to Court

A. Takings Doctrine Evolves

The idea behind Constitutional "takings" doctrine has always been, roughly, that individuals or small groups should not be singled out to bear the cost of measures that benefit the public as a whole. Various theories have been offered for this basic premise, but most fall into one of three more or less conventional types: first, equality or fairness (people's property should be treated equally); second, political structure (majorities or more powerful political groups should not be able to pick on weaker ones); and third, efficient decisionmaking (governments should have to take costs into account in order to make better decisions).[63] Certain aspects of the *Lucas* case challenge all three of these theories, and so I will come back to them later. In any event, perhaps because a variety of conceptions can be marshaled behind takings doctrine, Constitutional takings jurisprudence is a notably murky area of the law.

Nevertheless, as a doctrinal matter, the many actual takings cases over time have yielded a number of prima facie claims, along with some equally well-established defenses, and if one is content to leave theory more or less to one side, one might understand takings jurisprudence simply as a set of variations on these doctrinal claims and defenses. To give a lightening rundown, with a few leading cases: The earliest and strongest prima facie claim for compensation has always come (1) when a government takes formal title to land; it may do so by eminent domain, but it has to pay fair market value.[64] The second and third claims arise,

---

60. Healy & Rosenberg, *supra* note 54, at 84 (citizen sense of ownership); Duddleson, *supra* note 55, at 25–32 (citizen participation).

61. Michael M. Berger, *You Can't Win Them All—Or Can You?*, 54 J. St. B. Cal. 16 (1979) (complaining about Commission's string of court victories).

62. 483 U.S. 825 (1987).

63. For a brief account of these three major theories, see David A. Dana & Thomas W. Merrill, *Property: Takings* 32–52 (2002)

64. One notable argument to the contrary is Morton J. Horwitz, *The Transformation of American Law, 1780–1860* (1977) (arguing that early nineteenth century courts allowed roads and public improvements on private land without compensation).

respectively, with (2) physical invasion of a property, *and/or* (3) diminution in its value. The reason for the "and/or" is that the leading early case to expand "takings" beyond takings of title, *Pumpelly v. Green Bay Co.* (1872),[65] involved the flooding of some land because of a legislatively-authorized dam; this newly-designated taking thus involved *both* a physical invasion and a complete or almost complete loss of its value.

Of all of these claims, those involving solely "diminution in value," sometimes called "regulatory takings," have proved to be particularly nettlesome in the twentieth century. The case that seemed to establish diminution in value alone as a potential taking was *Mahon v. Pennsylvania Coal Co.* in 1922,[66] in which Oliver Wendell Holmes famously stated that a regulation might be treated as a taking if it "goes too far" in diminishing the value of a property. This maddeningly imprecise formulation has dogged takings jurisprudence ever since. What is "too far"? And compared to what? That is, what is the "denominator," the underlying property interest to which the loss is compared?

Turning from prima facie claims to defenses, by the time of *Mahon* there were also a number of well-established routes through regulatory bodies might rebut takings claims, and indeed Holmes' opinion as well as Brandeis' dissent referred to most of them. One defense that was to become particularly relevant in the *Lucas* case might be called the "no-right" defense: the regulation was not a taking if it simply prevented the property owner from doing something that exceeded her rights (e.g., perpetrating a nuisance, or building in such a way as to encroach on a public way, or in some cases, charging monopoly profits). Another standard defense was that the regulation itself brought some "reciprocal benefits" to the allegedly harmed property, thus implicitly compensating the claimant (e.g. building height limits enhanced general fire safety).[67] Still another defense was that the offending legislative act actually affected large numbers of people, so that it was not so much a singling out of the particular owner for ill-treatment, as it was an in-kind tax on

---

65. 80 U.S. 166 (1872).

66. 260 U.S. 393 (1922). At issue in the case was a Pennsylvania statute that prohibited a coal firm from mining so as to cause subsidence to a surface structure, even though the surface property had been purchased from the coal company in a deed that ostensibly relinquished subsurface support rights. *Mahon* was not an open-and-shut diminution in value case, however, since Pennsylvania recognized a separable property interest in a "support right," and thus its taking was akin to a taking of title. For this and some ambiguities about the deed interpretation, see Carol M. Rose, *Mahon Reconstructed: Why the Takings Issue is Still a Muddle*, 57 S. Cal. L. Rev. 561, 563–64, 578–79 (1984).

67. *Mahon*, 260 U.S. at 414 (referring to defense of "average reciprocity of advantage"), 416 (citing rent control cases, which were based on a temporary monopoly in emergency theory), 418 (Brandeis, J., dissenting) (citing reciprocal benefits and nuisance defenses); *see also* Mugler v. Kansas, 123 U.S. 623, 667–70 (1887) (discussing nuisance defense).

everybody (or at least a lot of people).[68] Obviously, both the prima facie claims and the defenses varied in strength under different circumstances, and in addition, it was not entirely clear if every defense could counterbalance every prima facie case. But at a minimum, these various claims and defenses gave and continue to give some doctrinal shape to an otherwise highly contentious area of the law.

At the time of the *Mahon* decision, municipalities were already intensifying their land use regulations, particularly using the new device of zoning. The Supreme Court upheld zoning in 1926 in *Village of Euclid v. Ambler Realty Co.*[69] Thereafter and for the next several decades, the Supreme Court for the most part took a hands-off approach to land use controls, hearing relatively few cases and generally upholding land regulations, thus giving local land regulators considerable latitude for experiment.[70]

The year 1978, however, signaled something of a change, when the Court accepted an important new takings case. In *Penn Central Transportation Co. v. City of New York,*[71] the city's historic preservation ordinance effectively prevented the owner of Grand Central Station from building a tower of a bulk equivalent to that of surrounding buildings, while extending a carrot by allowing a transfer of the unused "development rights" to some other location. The Court majority upheld the legislation, and in the course of doing so stated that these cases had to be considered through "essentially *ad hoc*, factual inquiries" involving several "factors;" the Court mentioned the economic effect of the regulation, and particularly the extent to which the accused regulation disrupted an owner's "investment-backed expectations," as well as the "character of the governmental action" (mentioning here physical invasion).

Penn Central's majority came out favorably to regulation, but in a sense it marked the end of an era, and a self-insertion of the Court into takings claims. Significantly, Justice Rehnquist issued a widely-discussed dissent in *Penn Central,* saying among other things that the City had effectively acquired an uncompensated easement in the property—i.e., something akin to a taking of title—and the only question was whether that taking had been sufficiently compensated. As Rehnquist became Chief Justice and the composition of the Court gradually became more

---

68. This defense was not mentioned in *Mahon,* but it was stated in *Richards v. Washington Terminal Co.,* 233 U.S. 546, 553–56 (1914) (holding that the legislature may authorize a public nuisance, though not a private one that amounts to a taking).

69. 272 U.S. 365 (1926).

70. One exception was *Nectow v. City of Cambridge,* 277 U.S. 183 (1928), requiring local zoning bodies to take special hardships into account when they did not disrupt the overall zoning plan.

71. 438 U.S. 104 (1978).

conservative, *Penn Central's* ad hoc and generally pro-regulatory approach seemed ever more embattled. After *Penn Central*, the Court accepted more takings cases to its docket; although Court majorities continued to uphold regulations in some of these cases and evaded direct substantive decisions in others,[72] some of the justices must have been looking for harder-edged rules.

In the 1982 case of *Loretto v. Teleprompter Manhattan CATV Corp.*, they found their opportunity, in the old rubric of physical invasion; *Loretto* held that a regulation causing a physical invasion was a categorical taking of property, even though the actual damage was minimal.[73] Soon after *Loretto's* adoption of a bright-line rule, Richard Epstein's 1985 book, *Takings*,[74] emerged as the first major legal academic challenge to the Council on Environmental Quality's 1973 pro-regulatory *Taking Issue*. Epstein's libertarian views galvanized conservative property rights proponents, and now ever more takings claims started to pop up in the courts. Clearly, more of these were going to reach the Supreme Court's docket.

It should be observed that these sea changes in takings jurisprudence emerged a good ten to fifteen years *after* the great flurry of environmental legislation of the early 1970s. Although property rights had been discussed in the earlier environmental legislation, that legislation had been debated and passed in a much more permissive jurisprudential climate. But by the mid–1980s, environmental legislation—and especially environmental legislation involving land use control, like coastal zone management—had came directly in the firing line.

B. The Court Goes to the Beach: The Come–Uppance in California

In 1987, the Court accepted and decided three major land use cases. One, *Keystone Bituminous Coal Ass'n v. DeBenedictis*,[75] continued the

---

72. *See, e.g.*, San Diego Gas & Elec. Co. v. City of San Diego, 450 U.S. 621 (1981) (avoiding decision on jurisdictional grounds); Agins v. City of Tiburon, 447 U.S. 255, 260–62 (1980) (rejecting takings claim). For a summary of the cases between *Penn Central* and *Lucas*, see Richard J. Lazarus, *Putting the Correct "Spin" on Lucas*, 45 Stan. L. Rev. 1411, 1415–16 (1993). Lazarus, *supra*, at 1417, notes that a "disproportionate" number of the cases in which the Court granted review came from California.

73. 458 U.S. 419 (1982). The Court prominently cited the old *Pumpelly* case for the proposition that a physical invasion counts as an automatic taking, but this considerably overstated *Pumpelly*, since the flooding in that case had combined a physical invasion with a total or at least very great loss of value. The new emphasis on "physical invasion" soon spawned a mini-jurisprudence of what was and what was not a physical invasion. *See, e.g.*, Yee v. City of Escondido, 503 U.S. 519 (1992) (holding that a rent control ordinance did not effect a physical invasion of a landlord's property).

74. Richard A. Epstein, *Takings: Private Property and the Power of Eminent Domain* (1985).

Penn Central line: a sharply-divided Court upheld a state mining regulation, with the majority using an ad hoc balancing analysis. A second
case, *First English Evangelical Lutheran Church of Glendale v. County
of Los Angeles,*[76] moved away from permissiveness as it got closer to the
beach; it involved a regulation imposing a building moratorium in a
particular floodplain. The again-divided Court sidestepped the question
whether the regulation itself effected a taking of property, but the
remedial portions of the opinion sent a shudder down the spines of state
and local planners: the Court held that successful takings claimants were
not restricted to injunctive relief, that is, merely invalidating an offending regulation, but that they could also claim damages during the period
of the taking.[77]

The third case of this trilogy was *Nollan v. California Coastal
Commission.*[78] Centered in the Court's sights was another land-water
interface, but now it really was the beach, and the target was the coastal
management of that especially active state board, California's. In *Nollan*,
a coastal landowner had sought permission to rebuild a house on his
property, but the California Commission had conditioned the permit on
his granting the public a right to cross his property, which happened to
be located between two state parks. Such conditions for public access had
become standard practice for the Commission's handling of development
permits—and it was a practice very aggravating to beachfront owners,
who like Nollan, could hear the *vox populi* passing only a few feet from
their front porches.[79] The Pacific Legal Foundation took Nollan's case
and persuaded another divided Supreme Court to side with the owners.
The new conservative Justice Antonin Scalia wrote the opinion, holding
that the condition was an unconstitutional taking of Nollan's property,
and stating that the Commission could only impose conditions that had
some "nexus" to the vindication of a legitimate public interest.[80]

---

75.   480 U.S. 470 (1987). The mining statute in *Keystone* was very like the one that
had been overturned in the old *Mahon* case.

76.   482 U.S. 304 (1987).

77.   In so holding, the Court rejected the argument made both in the dissent and in
an earlier decision of the California Supreme Court: that the prospect of damages could
have a serious chilling effect on cash-strapped governmental bodies, making them shy away
even from valid and needed regulations. Agins v. City of Tiburon, 598 P.2d 25, 30–31 (Cal.
1979), *aff'd on other grounds*, 447 U.S. 255 (1980).

78.   483 U.S. 825 (1987).

79.   Healy & Rosenberg, *supra* note 54, at 117. For a picture of Nollan's rather
narrow beach, see Jesse Dukeminier & James E. Krier, *Property* 1201 (5th ed. 2002).

80.   Scalia hypothesized that a public interest in viewing the beach might have been
enough, even one that was threatened by the "cumulative impact produced in conjunction
with other construction," but he said that such an interest was not related to this
particular condition. *Nollan*, 483 U.S. at 835–37.

Nollan was certainly enough to take the California Commission down a peg, though it was not clear quite how far.[81] The Commission at least had to reconsider its freewheeling ways and to find justifications for particular conditions, all a matter of particular delicacy in the light of *First English's* approval of money damages for winning landowners. And *Nollan* was certainly enough to make at least one long-term critic of the California Commission happy; as lawyer Michael Berger now crowed in print, "Happy Birthday, Constitution!"[82]

On the other hand, in a certain sense *Nollan* could be read in a much more limited fashion, indeed, as a minor variation on much older themes in takings jurisprudence. It was easy to characterize the Coastal Commission's regulation as a physical invasion, or even a taking of title, since the Commission had wanted Nollan to grant the public an easement to walk across the property.

What was left hanging was that especially troubling category of purely "regulatory takings," the claims that involved neither title nor physical invasion, but only some loss of value. Would governing boards be treated so roughly in pure value-loss cases? Left hanging too was the question of defenses: supposing that an owner could make out some prima facie case of a taking, what avenues were still open for governing boards to rebut the claim? And finally, there was the question of the environmental context: did environmental motivations strengthen governing bodies' defenses, or weaken them? No board could have been more interested than California's Coastal Commission.

These issues resurfaced five years later in *Lucas v. South Carolina Coastal Commission*. Now, of course, a different coastal board was facing an irate owner. But it may well be that South Carolina was something of a pawn for another intended target: not South Carolina, which had been relatively cautious about coastal zone management, but rather big, brassy, imperious California, the real state leader of what David Lucas would call "The Green Machine."[83]

---

81. *See, e.g.,* Robert A. Jones & Judy Pasternak, *Decision May Force Changes in Access Rules,* L.A. Times, June 27, 1987, at 1 (citing Coastal officials saying both that their job would become more difficult and that the decision would not much affect the Commission's work).

82. Michael M. Berger, *Happy Birthday Constitution: The Supreme Court Establishes New Ground Rules for Land–Use Planning,* 20 Urb. Law. 735 (1988) (praising *First English,* in which Berger represented the landowner, and *Nollan,* in which he wrote an amicus curiae brief in support of the landowner).

83. *Green Machine, supra* note 7. Some of the California Commission's major critics were involved in *Lucas* as well; e.g., the Pacific Legal Foundation filed an amicus brief, and Michael Berger filed a brief for the National Association of Home Builders. Richard Lazarus has called attention to Justice White's slip in oral argument, referring to the

V. *Showdown in South Carolina*

A. **South Carolina Regulates Its Coast**

Unlike show-time California on the far "left coast," and even unlike the tarheel environmentalists in the other Carolina just across the northern border, South Carolina had been relatively slow off the mark in establishing a coastal regulation. After all, this was a politically conservative state, dominated by Dixiecrats in the past and increasingly shifting to the Republican party as the national Democratic party became more liberal.[84] In 1972, the year that Congress passed the CZMA, all of the Atlantic seaboard states had already passed legislation at least protecting coastal wetlands—all except South Carolina.[85] That same year, South Carolina did establish a program to review all construction or dredging below the mean high water mark, but this was a rather modest step, given that lands below that mark were already widely viewed as belonging to the state as a part of the traditional "public trust."[86] That program was not enough to qualify South Carolina for CMZA approval or implementation grants, though the state did get planning grants as its legislature struggled to find an acceptable formula for coastal management.[87]

No one should conclude, though, that the coastal area was a matter of indifference to South Carolina. The coast of just under 200 miles makes up the entire southeastern leg of this triangular state, and it is a major tourist attraction as well as an historical and cultural resource. The northern half of the coastline, roughly, is the "Grand Strand" of superlative white-sand beaches. Among other things it was at these beaches that lowlanders created the Shag, now the state dance, a kind of low-key, sand-between-the-toes rhythm-and-blues routine.[88] At the

---

South Carolina Supreme Court as "the California court." Lazarus, *supra* note 72, at 1417–18.

84. Cole Blease Graham, Jr., & William V. Moore, *South Carolina Politics & Government* 66–69 (1994).

85. Bradford W. Wyche, *Note: The South Carolina Coastal Zone Management Act of 1977*, 29 S.C. L. Rev. 666 (1978).

86. *Id.* at 666 n.5 (construction review program), 667–68 (South Carolina precedent for state ownership of tidelands); *see also, e.g.*, State v. Pacific Guano Co., 22 S.C. 50 (1884) (same). For other states, see Deveney, *supra* note 12, at 52–54; *see also* Glenn J. MacGrady, *The Navigability Concept in the Civil and Common Law: Historical Development, Current Importance, and Some Doctrines That Don't Hold Water*, 3 Fla. St. U. L. Rev. 513, 547–50 (1975) (citing treatises of Kent and Angell on public ownership of foreshore, though author thinks them historically inaccurate).

87. Wyche, *supra* note 85, at 670.

88. *See, e.g.*, Phyllis Speidell, *Shaggin': Dancers Are Cool on Hot Summer Nights*, Virginian–Pilot (Norfolk, Va.), June 30, 2004, at E1 (boldly claiming that South Carolina has no monopoly on shag); *cf.* Roddie Burris, *Author Says State Dance Originated at Black*

Strand's north end is Myrtle Beach, a famous new-ish city known especially for its golf facilities; south of the Strand is Charleston, a much older port city, famous as well for its early city planning and historic buildings. In between is Georgetown, once the unofficial capital of South Carolina's rice-growing tidewater plantations. For many years, ex-slaves and their descendants lived on the islands stretching south of Charleston; until the middle of the twentieth century and beyond, some of these were places seemingly frozen in time, as their residents fished, farmed, wove reed baskets, and spoke an English–African creole "Gullah" dialect that would soon be made famous by Pat Conroy's book, *The Water is Wide*, and the movie based on it, *Conrack*.[89] Adding to the drama of the coast are storms, of which the very most dramatic are hurricanes: South Carolina's long coast is a prime landfall for the maelstroms that swirl across the Atlantic from Africa each summer. Much less dramatic, but of enormous long-term significance, is the effect of global warming: an insidious but relentless rise in ocean water levels, driving the beachfront ever back toward the shore.

But probably most important in the calls for coastal management, South Carolina by the 1970s had already attracted major real estate development. Particularly notable was the development on the sea island of Hilton Head just off the far south shore of the state, the very island where a century earlier Union troops had set up the Port Royal plantation for runaway slaves, and where their twentieth century descendants would soon find their lives changed forever. The first of the new resort "plantations" got underway on this history-drenched island in the 1960s, complete with golf courses and the first gates on the island; and more developments were on the way.[90]

Clearly the coast's economic and cultural importance—and its increasing development as well as its increasingly well-understood vulnerability—put coastal management into sharp public focus, and perhaps caused the legislative debates to drag on for so long. It took the legislature four years before the two houses finally agreed on a bill in 1976. But this bill that was vetoed, revived, and then vetoed again by the Governor, on grounds that followers of the CZMA might have anticipat-

---

Club, The State (Columbia, S.C.), Mar. 8, 2003, at 1 (claiming origin of shag at Charleston club). Both articles note that the shag is now the South Carolina state dance.

    89. Pat Conroy, *The Water is Wide* (1972); *Conrack* (Twentieth Century Fox 1974). *See also* Michael N. Danielson, *Profits and Politics in Paradise: The Development of Hilton Head Island* 9–12 (1995) (Hilton Head Island prior to development). For some remarkable photographs of the sea islanders around the turn of the last century, see Edith M. Dabbs, *Face of an Island: Leigh Richmond Miner's Photographs of Saint Helena Island* (1970).

    90. Town of Hilton Head Island Municipal Government, *A History Timeline of Hilton Head Island*, at http://www.hiltonheadislandsc.gov/Island/history.html (last visited Feb. 5, 2005). For a more extensive history, see Danielson, *supra* note 89, at 39–79.

ed: that the proposed legislation would violate property rights and undercut local authority. Only in the following year did both legislative houses and the Governor finally agree.[91]

South Carolina's Coastal Zone Management Act of 1977 appeared to borrow from neighboring North Carolina in defining the coastal zone: as in North Carolina, the Act defined all eight of its seacoast counties to be part of the coastal zone, a significant percentage of the entire state's land area.[92] But despite this appearance, in other ways the Act's strategy was much more akin to California's combination of a narrow geographic reach, but intense regulation within it. As in California, the state Coastal Council approval was required only within a very limited "critical area" of the coastal zone, an area indeed considerably narrower even than California's zone. But inside that narrow band, again as in California, all land alterations—not just major developments, as in North Carolina— would require the Coastal Council's approval.[93]

South Carolina's "critical area" included the sea out to the usual three-mile limit, but it extended landward only to include "tidelands" (i.e., areas washed by the tides and adjacent waters and estuaries), and beaches up to the front-row dunes. The Council initially interpreted its beach jurisdiction to exclude dunes more than 200 feet from the high water mark, and it also excluded beach areas upland of then-existing structures. (The latter exception appeared to create a set of vulnerable "backyard sand dunes" behind existing beach houses and other struc- tures.)[94] A 1978 analysis of the Act noted that since the coast is so deeply affected by upland activities, such a narrowly-defined "critical area" might not meet the CZMA requirements for effective control of land uses having a significant impact on the coast.[95]

Thus South Carolina, even more than California before it, adopted the strategy of intense regulatory scrutiny within a very tightly focused

---

91. Wyche, *supra* note 85, at 667. For the governor's vetoes, see Douglas Mauldin, *Tidelands Bill Vetoed by Edwards*, The State (Columbia, S.C.), June 19, 1976, at 1A; Douglas Mauldin, *Tidelands Charges Hurled*, The State (Columbia, S.C.), July 23, 1976 at 1A.

92. South Carolina Coastal Zone Management Act, 1977 S.C. Acts 123 (codified as amended at S.C. Code Ann. §§ 48–39–10 to –220 (West Supp. 2004)). The Act also gave each of the eight counties one representative on the eighteen-member Coastal Council. *See Id.* § 48–39–40.

93. *Id.* §§ 48–39–10,–130,–210.

94. Wyche, *supra* note 85, at 673–74.

95. *Id.* at 672–74. To counterbalance this problem, the Council came to agreements with other relevant state agencies—mining, highways, etc.—that they would make their own projects conform to the coastal plan. *See Tidelands Bill May Be Needed to Keep Funds*, The State (Columbia, S.C.) July 29, 1976, at 1B (federal official remarked that then-current bills were not approvable).

strip, and even that strip "grandfathered" out pre-existing structures. Echoing California and the CZMA itself, one great advantage of this strategy was political: it concentrated attention on a specific and popular part of the coastal area, the beach, while leaving only a very slim segment of property owners (and local governmental jurisdictions) to be affected, thus isolating potential opposition. But one obvious cost to the strategy was environmental, since constricted geographical limits left the coastal environment very much at risk from even very nearby upland change. This was a problem that, as we shall see shortly, the Coastal Commission proposed to remedy in the later1980s. But by that time, another cost of narrow regulation—one that had been much less obvious in the 1970s—was emerging from the federal jurisprudence of property rights, as the Supreme Court turned up the temperature of its takings cases.

The problem was this: the strategy of geographical narrowing that made the Act politically palatable also made it jurisprudentially suspect. The very geographical isolation of the most-affected owners made them appear subject to political "singling out"—the usual gravamen of takings claims—subject to special regulatory burdens not shared by their neighbors. As in so many instances of takings jurisprudence, the owner's question is, "why me?" That question was getting louder, and the *Nollan* case from California suggested that the coastal boards would need to have a good answer.

B. The Beachfront Management Act of 1988

"The Beaches Are Made of Continents." So stated the third chapter in Wallace Kaufman and Orrin Pilkey's 1979 book, *The Beaches Are Moving*.[96] Pilkey, a geology professor at Duke, emerged in the 1970s and 1980s as a leading scientific spokesman for the idea that beaches are by nature a migrating interface between water and land, and that beach armoring (and the upland structures whose owners insist on armor) only accelerate the loss of this valuable resource. South Carolinians by the mid–80's were paying attention to this North Carolina academic and to North Carolina's then-recent legal changes.[97]

In 1987, ten years after the passage of South Carolina's Coastal Zone Management Act and within a year after a severe winter storm caused new devastation on the beaches, a "Blue Ribbon Committee on

---

96. Wallace Kaufman & Orrin H. Pilkey, Jr., *The Beaches are Moving: The Drowning of America's Shoreline* 27 (2d ed. 1983). For Pilkey, see Dean, *supra* note 23, at 16, 53, 83–85, 99–102, 153, 194.

97. Pilkey's Duke group was later invoked at the *Lucas* trial by Christopher Jones, a coastal process specialist testifying for the Council. Transcript of Record to South Carolina Supreme Court at 69, Lucas v. South Carolina Coastal Council (S.C. Ct. C.P. 1989) (No. 89–CP–10–66) [hereinafter Record].

Beachfront Management" issued its report. The Report identified beach/
dune erosion as a critical problem for the tourism industry and leisure
activities, for storm protection, and for dune-based vegetation and wildlife. To deal with beach erosion, it adopted a Pilkey-inspired long-term
policy of "retreat."[98]

A major problem, according to the Report, was development too
close to the shore, and especially owners' use of seawalls, bulkheads,
revetments, and other armor to protect their beachfront structures.
Implicitly following Pilkey's increasingly influential theories, the Report
called for sharp curtailment and gradual phasing-out of beach armoring,
saying that these structures only added to overall erosion and loss of the
sand and dunes. Indeed these structures illustrated a kind of "commons
problem" among front owners: their efforts to preserve their own
beachfront removed sand from down-current properties at the same time
that the armoring devices chopped up the great visual expanse of the
beach itself. But the Coastal Council was not authorized to control these
structures; what was worse, sometimes a seawall itself limited the
Council's jurisdiction by defining the upward wash of the waves.[99]

In addition to beefing up the Council's anti-armoring authority, the
Report called for an increased landward reach for the Council's regulatory authority, a reach that could shift geographically to follow beach
erosion. Adopting a technique that the North Carolina legislature had
put in place several years earlier,[100] the Report recommended a somewhat complicated array of "baselines" and "setbacks" for development.
For stable beaches, baselines were recommended at the dune crest; for
the often-shifting shorelines around tidal inlets, the baseline was to be
the point of furthest erosion over the previous three decades. To these
baselines would be added further setbacks, calculated to account for
expected erosion over thirty years into the future.[101] Existing structures
would not be affected so long as they remained intact, but no new
construction or reconstruction was to be allowed seaward of the baseline,
and within the larger setback area, construction and reconstruction
would require Council approval, which was to be given in accordance

---

98. *Report of the South Carolina Blue Ribbon Committee on Beachfront Management.*
i-ii, iii-iv, 6 (Mar. 1987) [hereinafter *Blue Ribbon Report*].

99. *Id.* at 1–2; *see also* Gered Lennon, William J. Neal, David M. Bush, Orrin H.
Pilkey, Matthew Stutz & Jane Bullock, Living with the South Carolina Coast, 180–81
(Duke U. Press 1996).

100. For North Carolina's setback rules adopted during the early 1980's see Heath &
Owens, *supra* note 53, at 1430 n.148.

101. *Blue Ribbon Report, supra* note 98, at 4–10. In later defending the Beachfront
Management Act in the *Lucas* case, the Council's brief pointed out that North Carolina was
even more strict with its setback. Coastal Council's Trial Memorandum at 7, Lucas v.
South Carolina Coastal Council (S.C. Ct. C.P. 1989) (No. 89–CP–10–66).

with stated guidelines as to size and location of the structure. The baselines and accompanying setbacks were to be revised periodically, giving the Council an adjustable authority to accompany the shifting lines of the coast.

The Beachfront Management Act (BMA) came up in the legislature soon thereafter, and after considerable controversy and much backing and filling, the lawmakers passed the Act the following year, making some modifications from the Report proposal but in many parts copying it verbatim. One modification turned the thirty-year policies and setbacks into forty-year ones.[102] Debate had swirled around another modification that was to became particularly significant: in addition to restrictions on building within the "setback," the Act flatly prohibited construction or reconstruction in a minimum "no-build" or "dead zone" area, extending twenty feet landward of any baseline, whether the beach was eroding or not.[103] As in the Report, the main idea informing the final Act was that of a gradual retreat, to be effected by an enlarged substantive and geographical jurisdiction for the Council.

The BMA was amended significantly in 1990—of which more will be said shortly—but by then two major events had occurred, and both affected the Act. One came from nature: Hurricane Hugo had paid a devastating visit to the South Carolina coast. The second came from law, and to some degree, politics: David Lucas, a Republican activist and landowner on the Isle of Palms near Charleston, decided to challenge the Act as a taking of his property.

C. Lucas' Challenge

David Lucas was not just any landowner, and the Isle of Palms was not just any land. Following in the pattern of the highly publicized Hilton Head, developers had tagged the Isle of Palms as another potential resort area. Lucas knew some of the original developers from his own Republican party activities, and when they decided to sell their interests in 1984, Lucas formed the Wild Dunes Associates partnership to buy them out. Over the next two years, he and his partners built the very successful Wild Dunes, a project of 1500 acres and 2500 condominiums, with attendant golf courses and marinas. But Lucas had a falling out with his partners, and in 1986 he sold his interest to them. Nevertheless, in a somewhat odd transaction, he quickly bought back

---

102. 1988 S.C. Acts 634 (codified at S.C. Code Ann. §§ 48–39–250 to 360 (West Supp. 2004)); see also Cindi Ross, 'Dead Zone' Dominates Beach Work, Talks Center on Issue of Construction in Area, The State (Columbia, S.C.), May 26, 1988, at 1C; Lou Kinard, Major Provisions of the Beachfront Protection Legislation Bill is Approved as Tide Rises in Favor of Beach Protection, The State (Columbia, S.C.), June 2, 1988, at 1A.

103. 1988 S.C. Acts 634 § 3 (adding S.C. Code Ann. 48–39–290 and–300, current version at 48–39–290 (West Supp. 2004)).

two waterfront lots, with, he said, the intention to build a home for himself on one and an investment home on the other.[104]

Lucas' lots were in a part of the island that was classed as an "unstabilized inlet," and although the area was generally accreting, like many inlet areas it was subject to extreme erosional episodes in storms. Lucas' own lots had been completely underwater on several occasions in the forty years prior to the BMA.[105] Such deep past erosions meant that the statutory baseline (together with the minimum twenty-foot no-build zone) might be so far landward as to prevent construction on many properties even in accreting inlet areas, and even though they were now hundreds of feet from shore. Indeed, this was a concern that was supposed to be adjusted in the period between 1988 and the final 1990 BMA.[106] But Lucas got to the courthouse first.

At trial before Judge Larry Patterson, Lucas professed to disclaim any attack on the BMA's public goals of beach protection. Instead, he simply alleged that the baseline/setback rules covered so much of his property that it was undevelopable, causing its market value to drop to zero from an alleged prior value of over $2 million.[107] This was at least a minor overstatement, since the BMA would have permitted walkway structures and camping, which presumably had some value. It was more of an overstatement to say that Lucas was not attacking the BMA itself, at least insofar as it applied to properties like his. The trial transcript strongly suggests that he and his lawyers thought it silly to apply stringent development setbacks on a beach that had been growing wider. The Council witnesses, on the other hand, were clearly concerned that even a one-time storm over-wash would send owners scrambling for armor and other coast-damaging "protections."[108] As it turned out, the Council witnesses were right: within a few years, the beach receded once again, and as they predicted, Wild Dunes owners clamored for armored beach protection.[109]

---

104. Been, *supra* note 8, at 225–26. Been questions whether Lucas' transaction was a new purchase or a disguised retention of lots that Lucas had previously selected for himself, intimating that the transaction might have been set up either to avoid capital gains tax or to bolster a takings claim, or both.

105. Record, *supra* note 97, at 81–84 (testimony concerning beach moving across Lucas' lots in past).

106. Lennon, Neal, Bush, Pilkey, Stutz & Bullock *supra* note 99, at 183.

107. Complaint, Lucas v. South Carolina Coastal Council (S.C. Ct. C.P. 1989) (No. 89–CP–10–66).

108. Record, *supra* note 97, at 25–26 (testimony of Lucas of preference for accreting beach), 88–95 (testimony about accretion on cross-examination), 85–86, 101–06 (Council witness discussing past and potential future demand for hard protection, and sand scraping).

109. Lynne Langley, *Owners Wait for Decision on Erosion*, The Post and Courier (Charleston, S.C.), July 23, 1996, at B1.

At the time of the trial, however, Judge Patterson, may have been more influenced by the aerial photographs, stipulations, and occasional testimony that showed that the properties neighboring Lucas' had all been built up, unaffected by BMA because of its grandfathering provisions.[110] This information made it seem that Lucas alone, or almost alone, was the target of the BMA's setback requirements.[111] In the end, the judge agreed with Lucas that the BMA had removed any reasonable economic use from the lots and had rendered them valueless, a finding that—importantly—was never overturned through the remainder of the litigation. Since according to Patterson's opinion, a regulation causing the loss of all economically viable use was an unconstitutional taking, the policies behind the BMA were irrelevant; the only remaining issue was the value of the property and related costs, which Judge Patterson set at just over $1.2 million.[112]

The Council appealed, but just weeks after the trial, Hurricane Hugo struck the South Carolina coast with winds of one hundred thirty-five miles per hour, causing twenty-seven deaths and billions of dollars in damage and, among other things, inundating much of the Isle of Palms.[113] Perhaps impressed with the fury of the storm, the South Carolina Supreme Court reversed *Lucas* in early 1991, though not without dissent.[114] The state Court held that by not contesting the legislature's findings—that continued beachfront erosion was a serious public harm, that the harm was exacerbated by development, and that close-in development required regulatory control—Lucas had in effect conceded the "nuisance exception" in takings jurisprudence. That is to say, he was claiming compensation for something he had no right to do in the first place.

The U.S. Supreme Court accepted *Lucas* for review for the 1991–92 term, and by now the case was being closely watched by real estate developers and conservative public interest groups, as well as coastal states and environmental groups. Together, they filed a great sheaf of amicus briefs.[115] For the conservative groups, *Lucas* was a golden oppor-

110. Record, *supra* note 97, at 12 (stipulation of neighboring houses), 32 (testimony that area was built out), 44 (judge inquired about other buildings).

111. Lucas himself seemed to think this. *See Green Machine*, *supra* note 7, at 91.

112. Lucas v. South Carolina Coastal Council, No. 89–CP–10–66, slip. op. (S.C. Ct. C.P. Aug. 10, 1989).

113. Joseph H. Golden et al., *Hurricane Hugo: Puerto Rico, The U.S. Virgin Islands, and South Carolina, Sept. 17–22, 1989* at 166 (deaths), 172 (speed), 227–29 (Isle of Palms) (Nat'l Acad. Of Sciences 1994). The report noted that "proximity to open water" was correlated with greater damage. *Id.* at 229.

114. Lucas v. South Carolina Coastal Council, 404 S.E.2d 895 (S.C. 1991).

115. For the briefs and especially the jockeying within the federal government about a Justice Department brief, see Houck, *supra* note 8, at 348–52.

tunity to further the reining-in of land use regulation begun with the 1987 *Nollan* case; the conservative Pacific Legal Foundation, whose lawyers had defeated the California Coastal Commission in *Nollan*, called Lucas to ask if the PLF could help.[116] For the environmentalists and regulators, on the other hand, the case seemed to portend the crippling of their ability to stave off development-related environmental assaults.

Neither hope nor fear was entirely realized, but at the time, the case seemed a clear victory for property rights over environmental concerns. The majority opinion was written by Justice Scalia, who had also written the *Nollan* majority opinion in 1987.[117] Since there was no ostensible taking of title or physical invasion in *Lucas*, the only remaining claim rested on diminution in value—this in a case in which no one had been able to dislodge the trial court's finding that Lucas's property had lost all viable economic use. That finding became the key to the success of the property-rights argument over the short term, but something of an Achilles Heel over the longer term.

In dealing with this pure diminution-in-value case, Scalia skirted the notorious "denominator" question, that is, what was the underlying property interest to which the diminution in value was to be compared? As Stevens' dissenting opinion pointed out, developers could slice and dice any larger property down to a seemingly total loss of an affected part,[118] a point that might have been relevant to David Lucas' lots, in light of their somewhat ambiguous relationship to his earlier and much larger interest in the Wild Dunes development. Scalia put this issue to one side, however, and focused only on the lots in litigation, concluding that whatever might constitute "enough" of a diminution of value, the loss of all economically beneficial uses was enough to constitute a prima facie case of a taking.

There was a certain caution in this opinion, all the same. Scalia made much of the point that it was *land* at issue, intimating that takings questions would not be taken so seriously in a non-land context. In addition, his opinion made clear that regulators could still mount defenses even to a prima facie case of total taking. One of those was the traditional "no right" defense, that is, that the owner's activities went beyond his legal rights, as in the case of a harmful or noxious use.

But Scalia's opinion would have narrowed that traditional no-right defense: where an uncompensated governmental regulation deprived land of all beneficial economic use, he said, it was not enough that a

---

116. *Green Machine*, *supra* note 7, at 168–69.

117. *Lucas*, 505 U.S. at 1003.

118. *Id.* at 1065–66.

legislature simply announce that some property use was noxious or otherwise outside the owner's rights. Rather, such a serious constraint had to "inhere in the title itself," according to the "background principles of law" that would have been enforceable at common law by a court at the behest of a neighbor or a public body. Moreover, Scalia suggested that it would be difficult to find such an inherent common-law "background principle" if the activity had been widely practiced by others, presumably like all those other Wild Dunes neighbors in Lucas' vicinity, whose houses were grandfathered in by the Act. The narrow, common-law scope of the no-right defense was clearly the most controversial aspect of Scalia's opinion; even Justice Kennedy's concurrence took issue on this point, and like the dissenters, he would have allowed legislatures more room for adjustments of owners' rights over time.

In the end, the case was remanded to the South Carolina Supreme Court for a finding on the defenses, specifically, whether there were state law limitations inherent in Lucas' title that would have negated his claim to compensation for a total taking. The South Carolina court found no such limitation, sealing a victory for David Lucas.

What happened next? Several things happened, and all of them have interesting theoretical ramifications for environmental law.

VI.   After Lucas—Then What?

A.   What Happened to the Lucas Lots? A Story about the "Cost Internalization" Theory of Takings

The logical starting point for "what happened next" is the notorious Isle of Palms lots: After a modicum of further legal jostling and negotiation, South Carolina bought out David Lucas' lots for a bit less than $1.6 million. Within a short time, South Carolina resold the property for rebuilding, a fact that caused a considerable amount of crowing among more conservative commentators. When governments have to pay for their projects, they have argued, those in charge will come to better decisions about relative costs and benefits.[119]

In the chapter on Lucas in the Property Stories volume in this series, however, Vicki Been has illustrated the serious weaknesses in this "cost internalization" argument. Her first point is a practical one: as a matter of fact, cost internalization had little to do with the Council's sale of the property for development. Rather, as she notes, this outcome that was virtually foreordained in the wake of Hurricane Hugo's devastation. So many structures were damaged, and so many owners demanded the right

---

119. See, e.g., Henry N. Butler, Regulatory Takings After Lucas, Regulation: The Cato Review of Bus. & Gov't, 1993, at 76, available at http://www.cato.org/pubs/regulation/reg16n3g.html; Fischel, supra note 7, at 61, 364–65.

to rebuild, that first the Coastal Council and then the state legislature backed down.[120] It was a straw in the wind that after Hugo, Senator Jim Waddell, who had been a leader in pressing for the 1988 BMA, heeded his irate Hilton Head constituents and called for a softening of the Act.[121] The 1990 amendments to the BMA dropped the twenty-foot "dead zone" and even permitted construction seaward not only of the setbacks but even of the baselines, so long as the owners agreed to clear out if the ocean threatened to chew them up again.[122] Indeed, well before the U.S. Supreme Court's Lucas opinion, Lucas himself could have applied for a permit to build under the newly-amended BMA.[123] In 1993, the Council itself was reined in by a restructuring that placed it under the jurisdiction of the state's Department of Health and Environmental Control.[124] Thus in the wake of Hugo, South Carolina environmentalists' earlier hope for a gradual "retreat" from the beach had at best been postponed. Under the circumstances, it would have been pointless to deny construction on the former Lucas lots.

Been's second point confronts the whole takings theory that revolves around cost internalization, the idea that regulators will arrive at more efficient decisions if they have to internalize the costs of their decisions by buying out property owners. The generalized environmental *benefits* of regulation are diffused through the population, and they are much more difficult to weigh than the specific costs to specific property owners. For this reason, cost internalization theory in practice yields only half the balance. When governmental bodies weigh those costs, while shortchanging the benefits, they are led not to efficient regulation but rather to inefficient inaction.[125]

As a postscript to the whole episode, the ocean did indeed come back to chew up the intruders. The Wild Dunes development has suffered floods a number of times since the *Lucas* case, and the beach itself has migrated back and forth, causing beachfront owners—including the purchasers of Lucas' lots—to scramble for protection via beach bulldoz-

---

120. Been, *supra* note 8, at 235–36, 244–45; *see also* Charles Pope & Cindi Ross Scoppe, *Permits Will Speed Beachfront Repair*, The State (Columbia, S.C.), Sept. 29, 1989, at 1A (Council's rebuilding permits within dead zone).

121. Cindi Ross, *Whatever the Approach, Beach Bill Likely to Be Overhauled*, The State (Columbia, S.C.), Feb. 18, 1989, at 1C.

122. 1990 S.C. Acts 60, § 3 (amending S.C. Code Ann. § 48–39–290 (West Supp. 2004)) (providing that owners building seaward of the baseline had to agree to remove their structures if they became located on an active beach).

123. Justice Blackmun, at 505 U.S. at 1041–43, stressed this point in dissent, as well as the point that Lucas had never challenged the setback line under the original 1988 BMA; *see also* Justice Kennedy's concurrence at 505 U.S. at 1032.

124. Brett Bursey, *The Incredible Shrinking Coastal Agency* at http://www.scpronet.com/point/9609/p07.html (last modified Sept. 14, 1996).

125. Been, *supra* note 8, at 248–51.

ing and walls of gigantic two-and three-ton sandbags, though the Council disallowed the latter as armor in disguise.[126] The Council's successor, the Office of Ocean and Coastal Resource Management (OCRM), has with some exceptions continued to resist the ever-ongoing importunings for armor, and it has readjusted the baseline up to 150 feet shoreward just west of Beachwood East, Lucas' old street.

B. What Happened to the Property Rights Movement? Legal Developments, Pundits, and a Story about the "Political Failure" Theory of Takings

The later history of the property rights movement is a long and still ongoing story, but it might be best to begin with Lucas himself: the case opened a whole new career for him as a conservative spokesperson and organizer for property rights.[127] Some conservatives were not entirely happy with the *Lucas* decision, however; William Niskanen, the chairman of the conservative Cato Institute, thought that the case's legal impact would be very much limited by its peculiar facts, especially the factual finding that Lucas' lots had suffered the loss of all economic value. Lesser losses, he predicted (not incorrectly, as it turned out), might get the same old shuffle.[128] Richard Epstein too pronounced himself disappointed; he thought that the Court should have gone for the jugular and declared even partial losses to be takings.[129]

But aside from those crocodile tears, *Lucas* was an occasion for conservative glee. Among other things, the case fueled the clamor for a more general protection of private land rights against alleged environmental assaults. Responding to newly energized property-rights organizations, about half of the state legislatures passed state anti-takings legislation in the early and mid–1990s. Some of the new laws took a relatively mild form of exhortation or impact review, but several upped the ante on Scalia's language in *Lucas*, fixing some percentage loss of value that would count as a compensable event.[130] One of the most

---

126. *See, e.g.*, Lynne Langley, *Wild Dunes Braces for High Tides: Homeowners Hope a State Agency Will Approve a More Generous Erosion–Control Permit*, The Post and Courier (Charleston, S.C.), Oct. 26, 1995, at A13; Lynne Langley, *Six Landowners Sue State Over Erosion*, The Post and Courier (Charleston, S.C.), July 19, 1996, at B1 (reporting that the Lucas lot purchasers were a part of the original group suing to install beach protection devices including 3–ton sandbags, though they later dropped out).

127. *Green Machine*, *supra* note 7, at 256–57, 279–80.

128. William Niskanen, *A Line in the Sand?*, Regulation: THE CATO REVIEW OF BUS. & GOV'T, Summer 1992, at 9, *available at* http://www.cato.org/pubs/regulation/reg15n3–niskanen.html.

129. Richard A. Epstein, *Lucas v. South Carolina Coastal Council: A Tangled Web of Expectations*, 45 STAN. L. REV. 1369 (1993).

130. For summaries and analysis of state takings legislation, see F. Patrick Hubbard, *"Takings Reform" and the Process of State Legislative Change in the Context of a*

elaborate of the new statutes was Florida's, for which Lucas himself campaigned and could claim some credit, though he had no such luck in his native South Carolina.[131]

At the federal level, the high water mark for anti-takings legislation occurred when the Republicans took over both houses of Congress after the 1994 elections. Protection of private property was to be a part of their "Contract with America," and in 1995 several bills were drafted with this end in mind. The leading bills in both houses notched up the *Lucas* holding to require compensation for specified percentage drops in the value of the "affected portion" of regulated land, even though critics re-raised the objection that under such language *any* loss of value could be manipulated to count as a taking.[132] One interesting feature of the House bill was that it specifically focused on environmental land uses, that is, wetland regulations and the Endangered Species Act.

In the end, however, no federal property rights bill became law. One important group opposing federal takings legislation was the National League of Cities. Local governments may not have liked state or national takeovers of land use controls, but they did not like expansive federal takings doctrines either. They lobbied against this takings legislation, just has they submitted briefs against David Lucas' takings claims.

Modern social theory argues that certain events can "frame" a public debate, and it seems clear that the *Lucas* case helped to do this for property rights proponents.[133] It justified their complaints and gave them additional language in which to put forth their grievances, and it undoubtedly spurred much state "takings" legislation while it cowed would-be land regulators. That nothing came of the federal takings bills was perhaps foreshadowed by the hedging and sharp disagreements within *Lucas* itself. More importantly, the conflicts may have been still sharper because this was a *federal* forum, where a takings bill would have applied to national-scale environmental measures, and where the theoretical basis for extensive "takings" concerns is rather fraught, a point to which I shall return shortly.

"National Movement", 50 S.C. L. Rev. 93, 114–19 (1998); Kirk Emerson & Charles R. Wise, *Statutory Approaches to Regulatory Takings: State Property Rights Legislation Issues and Implications for Public Administration*, 57 Pub. Admin. Rev. 411 (1997). Interestingly, only eleven of the thirty-five coastal states passed such legislation through 1996. See Emerson & Wise, *supra*, at 413, 421.

131. Been, *supra* note 8, at 238.

132. Emerson & Wise, *supra* note 130, at 416–17; Carol M. Rose, *A Dozen Propositions on Private Property, Public Rights, and the New Takings Legislation*, 53 Wash. & Lee L. Rev. 265, 289–90 (1996).

133. *See, e.g.,* Mayer N. Zald, *Culture, Ideology, and Strategic Framing, in Comparative Perspectives on Social Movements: Political Opportunities, Mobilizing Structures, and Cultural Framings*, 261, 268 (Douglas McAdam et al. eds., 1996) (describing ways in which a dramatic event can "crystallize opinion" on political issues).

Meanwhile, the *Lucas* case energized environmentalists too, though in quite a different way. A number of quite aggressive academic responses hit the law journals soon after *Lucas*, blasting away at Scalia's opinion for ignoring the infamous denominator problem, or for misreading established takings jurisprudence and earlier common-law property principles. Damage control was also on the writers' minds, however; some even echoed the conservative Mr. Nikansen and argued that the underlying factual finding of a "total taking" was so idiosyncratic as to have little precedential value.[134]

One interesting version of damage control was the suggestion that perhaps some parts of a property owners' value might not really belong to the owner afer all. *Lucas'* beachfront location especially lent itself to this idea, because the coast is a notorious consumer of public subsidies. These include not just such general programs as roads and sewers, but also the highly specific programs like flood insurance and emergency assistance, programs through which the Isle of Palms itself has repeatedly fed itself at the public trough. David Lucas himself was a fan, saying that flood insurance was the key to beach development.[135] But if so, how might all this pork play out in an owner's title? In one of those happy agreements between environmentalists and fiscal conservatives, Congress itself has been trying for some time to plug up at least part of this well-known hole in the public purse.[136] But with respect to takings claims, the environmentalists' not-so-subtle hint is that some deduction for these subsidies might be warranted before saying that a beach regulation takes away all the owner's value.[137] Who created the value, anyway? Wasn't it the rest of us taxpayers, whether we liked it or not?

---

134. Of the many, many commentaries, see, e.g., Joseph Sax, *Property Rights and the Economy of Nature: Understanding Lucas v. South Carolina Coastal Council,* 45 Stan. L. Rev. 1433, 1436, 1446–49 (1993) (arguing that a complete loss of economic value rare, and that the case misunderstood dynamic nature of property law); Lazarus, *supra* note 72, at 1426–27 (same; rigid view of nuisance exception unstable); Louise A. Halper, *Why the Nuisance Knot Can't Undo the Takings Muddle,* 28 Ind. L. Rev. 329 (1995) (arguing that the common-law "background principles" in fact often deferred to legislatures with respect to nuisance definition, hence reference to those principles to limit legislatures is circular).

135. Been, *supra* note 8, at 254; *see also* FEMA National Flood Insurance Program, Loss Statistics, *available at* http://www.fema.gov/nfip/10400212.shtm#45 (last visited Feb. 5, 2005) (noting almost $62 million in flood emergency funds to Isle of Palms between 1978 and the end of 2002). Of the countrywide expenditures of $11.7 billion, the three highest state recipients were all coastal states, respectively Texas (approximately 2.6 billion), Louisiana (approximately 1.7 billion), and Florida (approximately 1.5 billion). *Id.*

136. *See* Elise Jones, *The Coastal Barrier Resources Act: A Common Cents Approach to Coastal Protection,* 21 Envt'l L. 1015 (1991) (describing the effects of the 1982 act and 1990 extension, denying federal subsidies to coastal areas designated as especially prone to hazards).

137. Marc R. Poirier, *Takings and Natural Hazards Policy: Public Choice on the Beachfront,* 46 RUTGERS L. REV 243 (1993). For an earlier critique of these subsidies, see

A somewhat similar line of damage-control inquiry has been picked up more by the courts than by Congress. What exactly is "inherent in the owner's title"? Specifically, might the old public trust idea be one of those inherit limitations? Readers will recall that the public trust is a jurisprudential concept that dates back to Roman times, and that has bobbed about somewhat uncertainly through Anglo–American law thereafter. The "trust" supposedly reserves for public use the seacoast below the mean high tide line, originally for purposes of navigation and fishing; but a post–1970 revival of public trust jurisprudence suggested wider spaces and purposes.[138] In the *Nollan* case, even Justice Scalia himself toyed with something like a public right to a view in the beach.[139] But *Lucas* set off yet another wave of interest in the trust, as a kind of rebuttal to takings claims. Might the public trust be a limitation inherent in beach owners' title? Some scholars pounced on the idea,[140] and as it turned out, some courts agreed with them, including South Carolina's.

Indeed, the hoary traditions of public trust ownership became a kind of doctrinal ace-in-the-hole for South Carolina's beachfront management. As mentioned earlier, although the 1990 BMA amendments gave ground to beachfront home construction, the Council resisted most hard armor on the beach, and it placed the risk of storm destruction on the owners who insisted on building anyway. Beachfront owners bitterly complained that unless they could install hard control devices (or at least giant sandbags) their properties would be lost to the sea, and thus "taken" by the state's policy. But Judge Larry Patterson, the very trial judge who had decided in Lucas' favor in 1989, in 1996 decided against their new claims. He now said that the prohibition on beach armoring was a limitation inherent in the owners' title.[141] In a more major case,

Oliver A. Houck, *Rising Water: The National Flood Insurance Program and Louisiana*, 60. Tul L. Rev. 61 (1985).

138. The modern revival and extension of the public trust doctrine is generally attributed to Joseph L. Sax's article, *The Public Trust Doctrine in Natural Resource Law: Effective Judicial Intervention*, 68 Mich. L. Rev. 471 (1970). For responses and reactions to Sax's controversial work, see Carol M. Rose, *Joseph Sax and the Idea of the Public Trust*, 25 Ecol. L. Q. 351 (1998).

139. *Nollan*, 483 U.S. at 835–37.

140. *See, e.g.,* Jack H. Archer et al., *The Public Trust Doctrine and the Management of America's Coasts* (1994); Paul Sarahan, *Wetlands Protection Post–Lucas: Implications of the Public Trust Doctrine on Takings Analysis*, 13 Va. Envtl. L.J. 537 (1994); Hope M. Babcock, *Has the U.S. Supreme Court Finally Drained the Swamp of Takings Jurisprudence?: The Impact of Lucas v. South Carolina Coastal Council on Wetlands and Coastal Barrier Beaches*, 19 Harv. Envtl. L. Rev. 1, 36–67 (1995).

141. Been, *supra* note 8, at 239; Lynne Langley, *Owners Wait for Decision on Erosion*, The Post and Courier (Charleston, S.C.), July 23, 1996, at B1; Lynne Langley, *Wild Dunes Sandbag Injunction Denied*, The Post and Courier (Charleston, S.C.), Aug. 21, 1996, at B1; *see also* Lynne Langley, *Panel Sacks Sandbag Request*, The Post and Courier

McQueen v. South Carolina Coastal Council, a tidelands owner claimed a taking when he was denied permission to build bulkheads to keep the water from his property. The South Carolina Supreme Court held that the property was within the state's public trust authority and thus a limitation was inherent in an owner's title in South Carolina. On this issue the U.S. Supreme Court denied certiorari.[142] The public's property, it appeared, has become a doctrinal limit "inherent in title."

To return to the federalism issue: from a theoretical perspective, one of the more curious aspects of *Lucas* and the *post-Lucas* property rights developments has been their studied inattentiveness to questions of federalism because these are questions central to the "political failure" theory of takings. The longstanding and oft-repeated political failure theory focuses particularly on local governments, which are thought to be especially likely to single out and pick on minority property owners. Why? Because, it is said, unlike the larger state and federal legislatures, local governments have fewer issues and smaller numbers of participants, and thus fewer occasions for shifting the composition of majorities. Hence local governments are said to be more apt to engage in what James Madison called the "factional oppression" of small numbers of vulnerable owners, who have no opportunity to protect their interests by joining majorities.[143]

No one seemed to pay the slightest attention to this political-failure theory, with its federalism ramifications, at the time that Congress brought forth anti-takings bills in the mid–1990s, bills that would have applied *Lucas*-like constraints to federal legislation, not local acts. At least one highly relevant court has been similarly oblivious: the Federal Circuit, an Article I court that among other things hears appeals of claims against the United States. In the 1980s, bolstered by the Reagan administration's conservative appointments, the Federal Circuit began to apply the Supreme Court's increasingly stringent takings doctrine, not to local issues, which were outside its jurisdiction, but to Federal regulatory authority. In the wake of *Lucas*, no court was more enthusiastic than the Federal Circuit in applying tougher takings doctrine; the

---

(Charleston, S.C.), Sept. 12, 1998, at B1 (discussing the administrative ruling against Wild Dunes' owners' request for giant sandbags).

142. McQueen v. South Carolina Coastal Council, 580 S.E.2d 116 (S.C. 2003), *cert. denied,* 540 U.S. 982 (2003). The case had earlier been before the U.S. Supreme Court, but had been sent back for further findings by the South Carolina Supreme Court.

143. For a description and a critique of these political failure theories, see Carol M. Rose, *Takings, Federalism, Norms,* 105 Yale L. J. 1121, 1126–27, 1131–39 (1996) (reviewing William A. Fischel, *Regulatory Takings: Law, Economics, and Politics* (1995)). My own view is that the political failure theory has never been very persuasive; at least in the American federal structure, there are a number of safeguards built into local government, though they are not the same as state or national ones. *Id.; see also* Rose, *supra* note 39, at 886–87 (1983).

targets once again were environmental land use limitations, particularly wetlands regulation, where the Federal Circuit attempted to award a multimillion dollar judgment to one takings claimant.[144] The court took a particularly conservative position on the perennial "denominator question," finding that property was taken in cases where the losses were to all appearances only partial.[145] That is to say, the Federal Circuit was ready to apply a higher standard to national regulation than the Supreme Court did to state and local regulations.[146]

Thus both the victorious Republican Congress and the Federal Circuit at best ignored and at worst contradicted the "political failure" theory of takings doctrine, with its focus on local factional oppression. On that theory, legislation coming from Congress, with its large districts and opportunities for shifting coalitions, ought to be immunized from such problems (though it might have others). But the property-rights afficionados seemed not to care at all. In fact, these blithe inconsistencies only illustrate the embarrassment that the Supreme Court itself has set for the local-political-failure theory of takings. Among other things, it is rather hard to imagine that the well-connected David Lucas would have been subject to any political failure at all, or particularly that he would have been unable to have his views heard by sympathetic South Carolina legislators. Aside from that, while several important Supreme Court takings cases of the 1980s and 1990s concerned local governments, it would be easy to argue that the most important cases of all were *Nollan* and especially *Lucas*, concerning *state* coastal zone management, that is, legislation passed by presumably less faction-ridden larger legislatures.

The Supreme Court withdrew some distance from *Lucas* in two subsequent environmental land use cases, both concerning state or state-regional waterfront legislation. In both, the Court indicated that it would not be easy to show a total taking, and where there was no total taking, the Court would return to the multi-factoral decision pattern outlined in *Penn Central*.[147] Perhaps the Justices thought that states might deserve a greater degree of deference after all. But if they thought that, they weren't saying so, leaving political-failure theorists with the task of executing some painfully fancy footwork.[148]

---

144. Michael C. Blumm, *The End of Environmental Law? Libertarian Property, Natural Law, and the Just Compensation Clause in the Federal Circuit*, 25 Envtl. L. 171, 177–78 (1995) (discussing early phases of the Florida Rock case); *see also* Kendall & Lord, *supra* note 43, at 558–61, 566–71.

145. Florida Rock Indus., Inc. v. United States, 18 F.3d 1560, 1568–73 (Fed. Cir. 1994); Loveladies Harbor, Inc. v. United States, 28 F.3d 1171 (Fed. Cir. 1994).

146. Blumm, *supra* note 144, at 172–73, 196.

147. Palazzolo v. Rhode Island, 533 U.S. 606, 631–32 (2001); Tahoe–Sierra Pres. Council, Inc. v. Tahoe Regional Planning Agency, 535 U.S. 302 (2002).

148. Rose, *supra* note 143, at 1141 (describing some of this footwork).

In fact, *any* law that engages larger environmental policy is likely to be passed at the state or federal level, not the local level. Why, then, are so many takings claims directed at environmental land use controls, and why are these claims considered seriously? At least on the standard theory of local political failure, environmental controls, as the products of large legislatures, should more or less be above the takings fray. But they are not, suggesting one of two possibilities: first, that something is amiss with these environmental land use takings claims, or second, that something is amiss with the political failure theory. And so, just as *Lucas* opened up a yawning gap in the cost-internalization theory of takings, so did it also blow a hole in the political-failure theory. Which leaves us with the question, just what *is* the theory of takings after *Lucas*?

C. What's Left of Takings Theory? Equality? No, Transition Management

Given the tattered condition in which *Lucas* left both the cost-internalization and the political-failure theories, only one of the three major takings theories is left over. That is the much more traditional idea of equality or fairness: that particular owners should not have to bear special burdens not shared by others.

But unfortunately, environmental initiatives illustrate the frailty of the equality/fairness version of takings, too, and *Lucas* is once again an example. Environmental resources typically have some threshold below which use is not harmful, but beyond which marginal costs rise not just additively but exponentially. Bodies of water, for example, can tolerate some organic materials, but over a threshold, each increment of additional waste is not just additively but exponentially more damaging to wildlife, vegetation, and water quality. The smoke from an old-fashioned house furnace or two will dissipate without damage, but if you burn enough, you run the risk of a killer fog.[149]

Beachfront management is another clear example of this pattern of exponentially rising costs. A single revetment or seawall would have had little impact on South Carolina's beaches or their ability to replenish themselves; what threatened to become devastating was the accumulation of ever more armored structures, the pattern that Orrin Pilkey called New Jersification of the coast. It isn't just increasing numbers of slices off the salami; it's that each next slice is fatter than the previous one.

As a practical matter, the ever-fattening salami slices very often map onto a temporal chronology: earlier increments of use of an environmental resource are likely to be less harmful than the later ones are, because

---

149. William Wise, *Killer Smog: The World's Worst Air Pollution Disaster* (1968) (describing role of household furnaces in deadly London smog of 1952).

the former did not yet pressure the carrying capacity of the resource. Besides that, the earlier uses are in effect stuck; it is often cheaper and more humane to regulate new uses than already-established ones. The old uses have already been built and capital has already been sunk, and it often costs more to retrofit the older structure than it does to build in greater constraints on newer development.

That is why a conventional notion of equality is inadequate with respect to environmental uses, including land uses. If early uses are relatively harmless, it would be pointless and overly intrusive to try to regulate them. But something has to be done when later uses slice far enough out on the salami. At that later point, it can be an invitation to environmental disaster to look around at pre-existing uses, and to say that new users should all receive the same old lax treatment, as Scalia suggested in *Lucas*.

All this is to say that at times of transition, environmental regulators often have good reasons to treat latecomers more rigorously than early users—at least for some period of time. A simple-minded version of the equality theory is simply untenable for a great range of environmental issues, including land use issues.

What we need is a different theory of takings altogether: that is, takings doctrine as a pragmatic tool in the management of regulatory transitions, as the need for constraints becomes more acute.[150] And in fact, this understanding of takings stares us in the face, from a century or more of land use management practice. Nineteenth-and early twentieth-century courts were perfectly willing to allow legislatures to tighten nuisance definitions as the environmental carrying capacity was pressured,[151] contrary to Scalia's depiction of common law nuisance as a static set of property rules. Early zoning applied to *new* land uses, while taking into account special hardships and making exemptions for so-called pre-existing nonconforming uses; it probably would have been considered a taking not to do so. The same idea is encapsulated in *Penn Central's* emphasis on takings compensation where regulation disrupts "investment-backed expectations."

Grandfathering for a limited time often acts as a rough substitute for compensation in the case where an owner has such investment-backed expectations. And to come back to *Lucas*, limited-time grandfathering was exactly what South Carolina hoped for in the gradual retreat policy of the 1988 BMA, where existing beach structures could remain

150. For a fuller development of this view, see Carol M. Rose, *Property and Expropriation: Themes and Variations in American Law*, 2000 Utah L. Rev. 1, 15–24 (2000).

151. *See, e.g.*, Hadacheck v. Sebastian, 239 U.S. 394 (1915); Reinman v. City of Little Rock, 237 U.S. 171 (1915). This point is thoroughly explored, using South Carolina sources, in Halper, *supra* note 134.

but could only be replaced within defined limits, in the hope that eventually all would decay and "retreat." There is no question that grandfathering has problems of its own; it may induce premature development or lead to foot-dragging about replacing obsolete equipment.[152] But it misses the point simply to use grandfathering as evidence of unequal treatment and hence a taking, as Scalia did in *Lucas*.

Even aside from grandfathering, takings compensation is certainly an important element in transition management. Among other things, appropriate compensation can take some of the heat out of needed regulatory initiatives, and can alleviate the sort of backlash that might undermine the initiative altogether. Aside from that, regulators do make errors. They do sometimes violate investment-backed expectations. They sometimes let the salami get sliced so far that in the case of the last slice, the expectation of equal treatment overwhelms the normal necessities of managing more strictly a diminishing resource. In such cases of sudden regulatory spikes, compensation is important in easing the transition. But it is a part of property law that transitions *do* occur, and property owners too need to adjust their expectations.

And in fact, they do. None of us expect to be able to drive our cars as fast as we like in a school zone, though at some point in the past, there were no speed limits. No New York City property owner thinks that she can keep pigs in the back of the building, though once, she could have. As Justice Kennedy observed in *Lucas*, takings law cannot take some pre-existing state of the law as the template against which to measure all future regulation; laws change as the world changes, and as they do, so do expectations about property.

VII. Retrospective: The Intersection of Land and Environment

Now is the time to return to the issue with which this chapter began: why land? Why does the Pacific Legal Foundation have a special ax to grind against the California Coastal Commission? Why is the Federal Wetlands Program a special target in the Federal Circuit? Why is the Endangered Species Act on the hit list of property rights proponents?

The *Lucas* case, for all the ambiguities of its history and theoretical basis, reminds us of the reason. As Scalia said, land is different. It is not different just because, as Scalia said, our law has protected land from regulation. much more than commercial matters. No, for environmentalism, land's most salient difference is that land is so much easier to "propertize," so much more recognizable as property, than are the

---

152. *See, e.g.*, David Dana, *Natural Preservation and the Race to Develop*, 143 U. Pa. L. Rev. 655, 684 (1995) (arguing that the nonretroactivity of nature preservation legislation invites premature development).

environmental resources that land uses so deeply affect. As persons who hold clearly demarked property—visible and tangible property, as Holmes noticed—landowners believe in their own entitlement with a vigor and sense of right that can easily overwhelm more general concerns about unowned environmental resources.

Lucas brilliantly illustrates this problem, something that might be called "imbalanced propertization." Imbalanced propertization explains why—as in *Lucas*—takings charges occur so often at the intersection of land and water. This is the quintessential location where an easily propertizable resource meets a much larger and more diffuse one, indeed where the land itself seems to liquify into moving sand, to the horror of its owner. What follows is the first jetty across the seemingly unowned beach, and then the next and the next; and by the time the public calls for more conservative building practices, owners are likely to view the old land practices as part of their landed entitlement, perhaps bolstered, as Scalia intimated, by the fact that no one ever called these practices nuisances before.

Imbalanced propertization also lurks behind some of the other more specific issues that critics raise about takings jurisprudence. Among these are the skewed cost/benefit calculations that threaten land regulation, where landowners count the costs to the penny but no one can really measure the diffuse unowned benefits of constraints. Among these issues too are the un-accounted-for subsidies to landowners, who lobby tenaciously for benefits to their property while the rest of us barely realize that we are footing the bill for someone else's flood insurance, or for that matter, for other landowners' agricultural subsidies, or for the poisoning of "pests" that later wind up on the endangered species list.[153]

But most of all, imbalanced propertization helps to explain the pattern of belated, narrow, and often ineffectual efforts to address even grossly inefficient environmental practices when those practices engage the very focused interests of landowners. This is not to say that environmental regulations on land are always well-conceived. But often they are, and legislators nevertheless are often hard put to generate the support that overcomes landowners' sharp attention to their own property. And even when legislators do succeed, the next stop may well be the courthouse.

There are a variety of responses to the set of issues that come from imbalanced propertization, responses that can sideline the bulldozer of

---

153. Been, *supra* note 8, at 254–55; J. B. Ruhl, *Farms, Their Environmental Harms, and Environmental Law*, 27 Ecology L. Q. 263, 324 n.342 (2000) (noting pattern of subsidizing crops with high chemical and erosion potential); June C. Edvenson, *Predator Control and Regulated Killing: A Biodiversity Analysis*, 13 U.C.L.A. J. Envtl. L. & Pol'y 31, 54–55 (1994) (describing poisoning programs).

takings litigation. A very important response is to meet property rights with property rights, and to note that property is often engaged on both sides of environmental land use controls, as at the beach, where other homeowners, businesses, taxpayers, and fishing interests are protected by restraints on individual owners' development. Indeed, the beach cases illustrate that although these environmental interests may be diffuse, there is a longstanding property tradition of "public rights" as well as private ones, and public rights or the public trust can be deployed in takings cases. Interestingly enough, there are similar traditions of public rights with respect to wildlife and fresh water, two other well-known diffuse environmental resources.

A broader response is to focus on cutting back subsidies, which are much harder for landowners to characterize as property rights. Still other responses look to different forms of compensation. These include using "windfalls" from public programs to pay for the "wipeouts" suffered by others, transferable rights regimes on an area-wide basis, as well as various forms of conservation easements, possibly in conjunction with eminent domain.[154] Still another response is to work on earlier planning and assessment over larger geographic areas, avoiding the "train wrecks"[155] that come with narrow and belated regulation, and that make claims of unequal treatment so much more salient. Modern environmentalist thinking is at work on all these techniques, to avoid the scenario where all the attention falls on the easily-propertized land, and little or none on the less-propertized environmental resources that touch and interact with it.[156]

A second reason why "land is different" strikes a kind of minor chord that has run through this chapter: the role of local governments in environmental land uses. In discussing a national land use bill long ago, Secretary of the Interior Rogers Morton made the point that land use is key to environmental control. But the common law of property in its wisdom has regarded each piece of land as unique. If the uses of land

---

154. For "windfalls," see *Windfalls for Wipeouts: Land Value Capture and Compensation* 31–71 (Donald G. Hagman & Dean J. Misczynski eds., 1978); more recently this idea is discussed in Abraham Bell & Gideon Parchomovsky, *Givings*, 111 Yale L.J. 547 (2001); for area-wide trading in a different land use context, see, e.g., Ruhl, *supra* note 153, at 342–43; for conservation easements at the beach, see James G. Titus, *Rising Seas, Coastal Erosion, and the Takings Clause: How to Save Wetlands and Beaches Without Hurting Property Owners*, 57 Md. L. Rev. 1279 (1998) (advocating "rolling easements").

155. "Train wrecks" are most associated with Secretary of the Interior Bruce Babbitt and his effort to avoid them through more careful advance planning. *See* John D. Leshy, *The Babbitt Legacy at the Department of the Interior: A Preliminary View*, 31 Envtl. L. 199, 215 (2001).

156. For these and some other strategies, see Carol M. Rose, *Property Rights and Responsibilities, in Thinking Ecologically: The Next Generation of Environmental Policy* 49, 56 (Marian R. Chertow & Daniel C. Esty eds., 1997)

have external effects on environmental resources—and obviously they do—then the control of land uses requires a particularly hands-on, lot-by-lot application of regulatory policy, and like it or not, that means engagement with local forms of regulation.

Clearly local governmental concerns have made themselves heard in environmental law, chiefly with respect to land use, and unfortunately often negatively. As we have seen, local governments resisted coastal zone management and substantially influenced its form. But the examples of local governmental foot-dragging are legion elsewhere, even outside the jurisprudence of takings. Land use controls are essential to cope with nonpoint sources of water pollution, yet nonpoint sources remain largely unregulated and unmanageable.[157] Land use management could much benefit automotive air pollution, yet in the face of local governmental and developer opposition, Congress dropped land use controls from the measures that states were required to consider in reducing air pollution.[158]

Some portion of local governmental concern over wider environmental regulation comes from the fear of lost control, and with that, lost revenue. But another way to understand this concern is to note the simple fact that local governmental participation is critically important in implementing environmental land use management, important even if the larger environmental policies cover much wider swaths. The very specificity of land means that standardized management solutions will not do. To control something like agricultural runoff, for example, management practices like lagoons, swales, vegetation and plowing techniques will have to be engaged; even if the affected area is as large as the Mississippi watershed, and even if sophisticated watershed trading regimes are put in place, the essential task of monitoring the trades will require hands-on local presence. The same could be said about controlling the vast number of small-scale nonpoint pollutants—both airborne and waterborne—that flow into the San Francisco Bay, or the Great Lakes, or the Chesapeake, or the Gulf of Mexico.

Here too, modern environmentalism is moving toward new solutions. As a number of scholars have pointed out, local governments are increasingly recognized for and engaged in land-related environmental initiatives.[159] Local governments themselves have become more environ-

---

157. Sarah Birkeland, *EPA's TMDL Program*, 28 Ecology L. Q. 297, 320–24 (2001) (describing the need for land use controls to control nonpoint sources; comparing pressures to weaken shoreline nonpoint source control to demise of indirect source review under the CAA).

158. Del Duca & Mansueto, *supra* note 36, at 1140, 1152–54.

159. *See* John R. Nolon, *Introduction: Considering the Trend Toward Local Environmental Law*, 20 Pace Envtl. L. Rev. 3 (2002) (describing articles in symposium issue).

mentally sophisticated, and state legislation has given them not only more environmental responsibilities, but also—like North Carolina's CAMA— a forum for comparing their respective needs.

To come back to *Lucas* and the pattern of environmental land use management at the beach, at least one historical pattern emerges when this story is seen in retrospect. The National Land Use debates and the CZMA revealed that the chief opponents to wider environmental land use regulation would be landed interests and local governments. In some of the legislation following the CMZA, legislators avoided this Scylla of resistance by narrowing the scope of the legislation to a thin geographic area. But in so doing, they steered straight toward the Charybdis of takings charges, where the few affected owners could claim that they were "singled out." Even more important, by confining the regulatory ambit so narrowly, they threatened to undercut their own environmental goals. Much of the same might be said about another embattled environmental land use control, the ESA, where the narrowness of the protected subject both raises charges of special burdens from private landed interests and undermines more comprehensive approaches to species protection.

There are plenty of theoretical doubts about takings doctrine, especially as enunciated in the *Lucas* case. But even without takings litigation, landowners and local governments, for good or ill, are still strategically situated to make trouble for environmental land use controls if they choose to do so, through political machinations and through the self-help of premature development. Thus even aside from its takings implications, the *Lucas* story is important because it suggests that in dealing with land uses in particular, environmentalists need to think through new strategies, strategies that among other things develop some of the responses mentioned above, and that do in fact contemplate compensation under appropriate circumstances. These strategies are needed in order to calm the most-affected landowners' sense of unequal burdens, to widen the responsibility for land uses, to find room for local governments, and most important of all, to allow for the steady enactment of environmental regulatory constraints as new needs arise, both through eminent domain and through what Holmes called "the police power in its proper sense."*

* I would like to thank Fred Bosselman and Mark Poirer, as well as Henry Frampton and the members of the Yale Environmental Law Association. Elizabeth Black provided invaluable research assistance.

*

9

Thomas W. Merrill

The Story of *SWANCC*: Federalism and the Politics of Locally Unwanted Land Uses

Introduction

All politics may not be local, but many environmental controversies can be understood only by examining their local roots. The dispute that gave rise to the Supreme Court's most important pronouncement about the scope of federal authority to regulate the environment was an intensely local one, involving the siting of a municipal garbage dump. A group of suburban communities wanted to use an abandoned gravel pit to dispose of their garbage; the community located nearest the site strenuously objected. Each side groped for any political or legal advantage it could obtain. The pro-dump communities won at the state regulatory and judicial level. The anti-dump community fought back, securing a veto of the site by the United States Army Corps of Engineers. The pro-dump communities countered by challenging the constitutional authority of the Army Corps to regulate the site. The result was a landmark decision, *Solid Waste Agency of Northern Cook County v. U.S. Army Corps of Engineers (SWANCC)*,[1] which interpreted the statutory authority of the Army Corps narrowly in light of concern that regulation of the site might exceed the constitutional power of the federal government.

The Supreme Court's decision in *SWANCC* is widely studied because of what it says—and what it may portend—about constitutional federalism in the context of environmental regulation. The story of *SWANCC* recounted here offers a different view of federalism, not as a formal doctrine of constitutional law but a bewildering complex of checking

---

1. 531 U.S. 159 (2001).

powers operating at all levels and branches of government. This story suggests that American federalism offers so many opportunities for one governmental actor to trump another that disputes about locally unwanted land uses can continue indefinitely, until one or both sides drop from exhaustion, or run out of money to pay the lawyers and consultants.

I.   *The Bartlett Balefill*

The roots of the *SWANCC* controversy lie in the early 1980s, when the municipal garbage disposal industry began to undergo a major transformation. The driving force behind this transformation was a shift in public attitudes about wastes buried in the ground. After the discovery of toxic chemicals seeping into the basements of homes at Love Canal in New York in the late 1970s, and the publicity surrounding the enactment of the Superfund Act in 1980, the public became much more aware of the perils of long-term waste disposal. Moreover, the public did not generally differentiate between "municipal solid waste" (the preferred euphemism for ordinary household garbage) and "hazardous waste" (the term used for toxic chemicals generated by industrial processes), perhaps because it was all too aware that ordinary household garbage often includes toxic materials.[2] As a consequence, garbage dumps came under increasingly strict regulatory oversight at all levels of government.

The result was to change fundamentally the way household waste is processed in this country. The garbage industry in 1980 was highly decentralized, characterized by large numbers public and private entities operating large numbers of dumps under regulatory standards that were uneven at best. In the next two decades, the industry was transformed into one dominated by a handful of corporate waste disposal firms operating out of a much smaller number of tightly-regulated mega-sites. Accompanying the consolidation in the industry was a shift in the location of sites. Virtually all new disposal sites today are located in rural areas outside the path of urban development. Perhaps the biggest adjustment associated with the change in the solid waste industry has been coming to terms with the higher costs of transporting garbage to these remote areas for burial.

While this transformation of the garbage disposal industry was taking place, many observers spoke with alarm about the country "running out" of solid waste disposal sites.[3] There was some basis for

---

2. *See* Carol Vinzant, *200 Protest Des Plaines Waste Site*, Chi. Trib., Jan. 20, 1992, at 3 (reporting estimates by rival advocates that domestic garbage includes between 0.1 and 7 percent toxic material).

3. *See, e.g.*, Senator Al Gore, *Earth in the Balance* 151 (1992) (stating that "the volume of garbage is now so high that we are running out of places to put it"); Issac

this inference in observable facts. Sites in urban areas were closing; there was intense public opposition to opening new sites near urban areas; and the total number of sites was falling rapidly.[4] These facts were interpreted against the backdrop of the vivid story of Mobro 4000, the New York City garbage barge that wandered up and down the east coast looking for someone who would take its load. But we now know the inference was mistaken. By 2000, when the makeover of the industry was essentially complete, total disposal capacity was growing rather than contracting.[5] Especially during the early years of the change, however, it was difficult to perceive what was happening. Not surprisingly, many local politicians became concerned about how their communities were going to dispose of their garbage in the years ahead.

Among the local politicians who had this reaction were the elected officials of the suburban municipalities of Cook County, Illinois, north of Chicago. These communities, especially the "Northshore" suburbs along Lake Michigan, are among the wealthiest in the country, with high levels of education and civic participation. Throughout the area, residents are generally supportive of environmental protection laws, and see themselves as good environmental citizens.

Beginning in 1958, thirty-some suburbs north and northwest of Chicago banded together to address common problems through an entity called the Northwest Municipal Conference. In 1982, the Conference began a study of how its member communities were going to dispose of solid waste in the years ahead. The first fruit of this study was a plan to open a new disposal site in a Cook County Forest Preserve District, but the idea was dropped when the District enacted an ordinance barring such uses of its land.[6]

Late in 1985, the Conference announced a new plan. It had acquired options to purchase a large tract of land (totaling 533 acres) at the far west end of Cook County near the Village of Bartlett. The tract in fact straddled Cook and Kane Counties, with 410 acres in Cook and 123 in Kane. The Bartlett tract had a number of attractions. There was an

---

Asimov & Frederik Pohl, *Our Angry Earth* 144 (1991) (stating that "almost all the existing landfills are reaching their maximum capacity, and we are running out of places to put new ones").

4. *See* Editorial, *Burying Our Heads in the Garbage*, Chi. Trib., Oct. 28, 1987, at 18 (stating that in the last 17 years "the state has suffered a decline in landfills from 1,200 to 146, and in incinerators from 10 to 1. There have been no new landfills since 1981, no incinerators since 1970.").

5. Environmental Protection Agency, Municipal Solid Waste in the United States: 2000 Facts and Figures (June 2002), *available at* http://www.epa.gov/epaoswer/non-hw/muncpl/pubs/report–00.pdf.

6. Department of the Army, Permit Evaluation and Decision Document, Solid Waste Agency of Northern Cook County, Jan. 30, 1991, at 7.

abandoned gravel pit on the site, which meant it had already been excavated in significant part. The closest residence was a mile away. The nearest populated area—a mobile home park—was 1¼ miles away. The vacant land surrounding the site was zoned for industrial use. There were only two significant drawbacks. The site was forty miles away from the Northshore suburbs, and hence would increase transportation costs relative to a site more centrally-located in the county. And it was located above a glacial aquifer, the Newark Aquifer, which serves as a source of drinking water for many communities in the Fox River Valley.

As events would soon reveal, the Bartlett tract also had political advantages. A controversial 1981 Illinois law required that any new solid waste disposal site had to obtain permission to operate from both the Illinois Environmental Protection Agency and the relevant political subdivision having jurisdiction over the site.[7] Although the tract identified by the Conference was near the towns of Bartlett, Elgin, South Elgin, and Wayne, it was in an unincorporated area. Thus, if Bartlett, the closest community and a member of the Conference, could not be induced to annex the site and grant the required approval, the Conference could seek approval from Cook County, where the influential communities who made up the Conference would be able to assert their considerable political muscle to help assure a favorable outcome.

Identification of the Bartlett site was part of a larger plan for dealing with solid waste, which the elected politicians who lead the Conference regarded as a progressive one. One key component was a commitment on the part of the member communities to mandate recycling by their residents.[8] In Evanston, for example (where I lived at the time), the City required that yard waste, newspapers, and metal and plastic containers be separated at curbside by residents, and these materials were collected for recycling by the City separately from other garbage. Eventually, the member communities achieved an impressive 40 percent reduction in waste volume through these recycling efforts.[9]

Additional details about the Conference waste disposal plan revealed that it was generally well conceived from an environmental engineering standpoint. Municipal waste which was not recycled was to be collected by each municipality and delivered to one of two (eventually three) transfer stations. There, it would be compressed into large 1½ ton bales before being transported to the new fill site near Bartlett. The baling

7. 415 Ill. Comp. Stat. 5/39(c) (2002). *See* Thomas M. Burton, *Tough Law on New Landfills Helps Trash Problems Pile Up*, Chi. Trib., Dec. 23, 1987, at 1.

8. *See* Shiela H. Schultz, *Balefill a Vital Part of Waste Solution*, Chi. Trib., Nov. 4, 1989, at 12.

9. Rogers Worthington, *Suburban Recycling May be Near a Peak*, Chi. Trib., Mar. 6, 1997, at 1.

process would reduce waste volume and hence transportation costs. It would also prevent loose litter from flying off delivery trucks or blowing away from the disposal site. To underscore this design feature, and differentiate the project from an ordinary garbage dump, the Conference cleverly labeled the project a "balefill" rather than a landfill. The label stuck, and was adopted by the newspapers and courts throughout the controversy.

The disposal site itself was to be prepared using techniques developed for hazardous waste disposal sites. The bales would be stacked in six large cells, and the cells would be lined with clay, gravel and an impermeable synthetic liner. Underground pipes would collect any leachate that seeped through the bottom layer. The fill area would be built on an inward gradient, meaning the bottom of the cells would be below the top of the groundwater, which could create reverse pressure should one of the cells accidentally spring a leak. Monitoring wells would be built around the fill area to detect any escaping leachate, and the site included a buffer zone large enough so that seepage could be stopped before it migrated off site.[10] This buffer zone would be planted with trees and graded with a berm in order to conceal the site from surrounding properties. The site was expected to remain open for twenty years, after which it would be covered with prairie grass and would look more-or-less like it looked before the gravel pit was excavated. The Conference would set aside a $1 million fund to compensate neighbors for any losses in property values associated with the development of the site.

If the Northwest Municipal Conference thought its good intentions and careful planning would carry the day, it was badly mistaken. Hoping to score quick approval, the Conference offered Bartlett unspecified financial incentives to annex and approve the site. But the ensuing annexation hearings served only to crystallize local opposition to the project. A group of Bartlett residents formed an organization, initially called Balebusters but soon renamed Citizens Against the Balefill, which picketed the hearings and offered emotional testimony opposing the plan. After six months of contentious hearings, on August 7, 1986 the Bartlett Zoning Board denied the request for annexation by a vote of 7–3.[11]

Undeterred, the Conference shifted to Plan B, seeking a special use permit from the Cook County Zoning Board. Hearings commenced before the Zoning Board of Appeals in March, 1987. Balefill opponents turned out in force with protest signs and banners. The Village of Bartlett, responding to the intense local opposition, retained as counsel Myron

---

10. Dean Geroulis, *A Baleful Problem*, Chi. Trib., May 2, 1993, at 3.

11. *See* T.J. Rolando Jr., *The Case Against Bartlett Balefill*, Chi. Trib., Dec. 27, 1986, at 8.

Cherry, a well-known environmental activist. He and other lawyers for
the opponents proceeded to conduct guerrilla warfare over every procedural detail. The hearings lasted five months, the longest and most
contentious zoning hearing the Chairman of the Appeals Board could
remember in more than twenty-one years of service.

The outcome, however, was never in doubt. The Zoning Appeals
Board deliberated only ten minutes before unanimously recommending
approval of the balefill project.[12] The matter then went before the full
Cook Bounty Zoning Board for decision on the record compiled by the
Zoning Appeals Board. Acting with dispatch, the Board granted preliminary approval on November 16, 1987, by a vote of 14–2. Final approval
was conditioned on the Illinois EPA granting a development permit
within two years.

More than a year elapsed before the Conference filed for the required approval from the Illinois EPA. One reason for the delay may
have been that balefill opponents filed a petition with the Illinois
Pollution Control Board challenging the Board's action. This was denied,
on the ground that the decision was not final, which was followed by an
appeal to the Illinois Appellate Court, which also failed.[13] Another reason
may have been that the proponents of the balefill were busy creating a
new municipal joint-action agency to operate the transfer stations and
the disposal site. The new agency, named the Solid Waste Agency of
Northern Cook County (SWANCC), needed time to obtain financing
commitments from member communities.[14] In any event, it was not until
November 22, 1988, that the Conference, acting now as SWANCC,
submitted its application for a development permit with the Illinois EPA,
accompanied by six volumes of supporting evidence. To sweeten the
proposal, SWANCC added a "Good Neighbor" feature to the plan,
whereby it would contribute $1 million per year (as opposed to $1 million
in total, as under the original plan) to guarantee local property values
and drinking water.[15] Opponents filed their own supporting materials.
The Illinois EPA also conducted public hearings.

Six months later, on May 18, 1989, the Illinois EPA ruled that the
balefill project could not be approved in the form submitted. The agency
focused on the danger of groundwater contamination, finding, for example, that the site needed more monitoring wells, and should have been

12. Steve Johnson, *Controversial Landfill Near Elgin Passes Hurdle at Zoning
Board*, Chi. Trib., Oct. 22, 1987, at 3.

13. Stark v. Pollution Control Board, 532 N.E.2d 309 (Ill. App. Ct. 1988).

14. *See* Steve Johnson, *28 Suburbs to Ante Up for Balefill*, Chi. Trib., Mar. 16, 1988,
at 4.

15. Stevenson Swanson, *Balefill Plan to Guarantee Land Values*, Chi. Trib., Nov. 23,
1988, at 1.

lined with ten feet of compacted clay rather than three feet as called for in the proposal. SWANCC promptly declared these objections were "not insurmountable,"[16] and submitted a revised application designed to meet the agency's objections. On November 16, one day before the Cook County Board's conditional use permit was set to expire, the Illinois EPA granted the revised application.[17]

The next day, the four municipalities closest to the balefill site filed suit in Cook County Circuit Court, seeking to overturn this decision. A parallel action was launched in Kane County Circuit Court. State court review of the Illinois EPA action would drag on for six more years, eventually generating a decision of the Illinois Appellate Court consolidating the two cases, and a further decision of the Illinois Supreme Court.[18] On January 29, 1996, slightly more than ten years after the project had been announced, the Illinois Supreme Court denied all the challenges, eliminating the last state-law obstacle to opening the site.

II. Citizens Against the Balefill

Before turning to the federal phase of the controversy, it is instructive to take a closer look at the community of Bartlett, the opponents of the balefill project, and the nature of their objections. Bartlett was founded in 1873 as a railroad town thirty-one miles from the Chicago Loop. The town center includes a number of nineteenth century buildings, giving it some charm.[19] The surrounding area was initially dedicated exclusively to farming. But with the growth of Chicago as a major metropolis, certain types of extractive and industrial operations, such as gravel mining and cement plants, eventually arrived. Beginning in the 1980s, the outer fringes of sprawl were encroaching on Bartlett. The town experienced a dramatic growth spurt, surging from a population of 19,373 in 1990 to 36,706 in 2000. Residents have been and remain overwhelmingly white, with a small number describing themselves as Hispanic (5.5%).[20] Newcomers have been drawn by subdivisions of new homes, which seem to sprout from the cornfields overnight. The principal attractions they cite are the "affordability" of housing relative to older suburbs, a friendly, small-town atmosphere, and good transporta-

---

16. Stevenson Swanson, *Balefill Plan Rejected by Illinois EPA*, Chi. Trib., May 19, 1989, at 1.

17. Stevenson Swanson, *State OKs New Suburb Landfill; Opponents Call Action 'Unconscionable,' Vow Lawsuit*, Chi. Trib., Nov. 17, 1989, at 7.

18. City of Elgin v. County of Cook, 629 N.E.2d 86 (Ill. App. Ct. 1993), *aff'd in part, rev'd in part*, 660 N.E.2d 875 (Ill. 1995).

19. *See* Ilyce R. Glink, *Bartlett Eyes Its Next Century of Progress*, Chi. Trib., Apr. 1, 1989, at 15.

20. *See The Encyclopedia of Chicago* 1007 (James R. Grossman et al. eds, 2004).

tion connections to downtown Chicago (via commuter train) and O'Hare Airport.[21]

Opposition to the balefill project centered in Citizens Against the Balefill, a grass roots organization that appears to have formed spontaneously during the annexation hearings in 1986, and remained active until 2001. Membership in the group fluctuated in inverse proportion to the likelihood of success of the balefill, ranging from less than 100 to a peak of about 900 persons in 1988.[22] The leaders and presumably most of the members were local homeowners, although one gets the impression they were generally persons of modest means and education.

For example, Mary Byrne, the third president of the organization, was the daughter of an ironworker who grew up in Green Bay, Wisconsin. One profile stressed that she had little "formal education," and was initially too timid to speak in public. She became an environmental activist when she witnessed a neighbor club a woodchuck to death in a back yard. Byrne joined Citizens Against the Balefill because she feared the project, which was to be located ten minutes from her home, would destroy property values and leak poisons into the water supply.[23] Another profile said she had given up membership in a local women's club, writing a book, and composing poetry to devote herself to the anti-balefill cause, which became a consuming passion for sixteen years of her life.[24] In any event, Byrne unquestionably developed a flare for publicity, burning effigies of SWANCC and its regulatory supporters, and providing a steady stream of colorful quotations to reporters.

Throughout the state regulatory phase of the controversy, that is, up through 1989, balefill opponents advanced both environmental and equity arguments in opposition to the project. The environmental argument with by far the most traction was the threat of groundwater contamination. The rhetoric of balefill opponents on this point was often strident in the extreme. A resident from the nearby mobile home park testified that putting garbage above an aquifer was like removing the "pin from an ecological grenade."[25] John Stark, who was president of Citizens Against the Balefill before he was elected Bartlett Village

---

21. Phil Borchmann, *Anomaly; Bartlett Flourishes, Despite The Flaws*, Chi. Trib., Oct. 29, 1994, at 1.

22. Matthew Nickerson & Joseph Kirby, *Balefill Isn't Home Free in Bartlett*, Chi. Trib., July 7, 1992, at 1.

23. Matthew Nickerson, *Once Timid, She Now Roars to Save the Environment*, Chi. Trib., Jan. 25, 1993, at 2.

24. Sue Ter Maat, *Balefill Opponents Put Lives On Hold For Fight*, Chi. Daily Herald, Nov. 1, 2000, at 18.

25. Steve Johnson, *Neighbors Rail Against Balefill Plan*, Chi. Trib., June 25, 1987, at 1.

President in 1989, said he was worried that the landfill would make his town "another Chernobyl."[26]

Although groundwater contamination elicited the most emotional response, a generalized threat to property values was also consistently mentioned by balefill opponents.[27] Other environmental concerns, such as increased truck traffic, were occasionally cited. However, until the Army Corps of Engineers got into the picture, balefill opponents made virtually no mention of ecological concerns, such as the need to preserve the habitat of migratory birds. The gravel pit had been abandoned since 1950. It was surrounded by a fence, and upper surface areas were covered with a tangled forest of volunteer trees and brush. Consequently, few residents had ever actually visited the site, and it had little presence as a natural resource important to the community.

Although environmental objections were given primacy of place in public hearings, equity arguments came to the fore in more informal commentary by opponents, such as interviews with the press and letters to the editor. The principal equity argument was a simple claim of distributive justice: The rich and powerful should not be allowed to dump their garbage on those of more modest means and influence. One letter to the editor of the Chicago *Tribune*, for example, bridled at the paper's frequent use of the term NIMBY (not in my backyard) to describe landfill opponents, suggesting that SWANCC was an ANNME: Anywhere Not Near Me. "Such is the politics of waste," the author wrote. "Those who generate it want to get rid of it as cheaply as possible, and as far from them as possible. This means dumping on those poorer and less powerful than themselves ... "[28] When the Mayor of Wheeling wrote an op-ed touting the virtues of the project, another letter writer responded: "If the balefill is such a good idea, why didn't Ms. Schultz volunteer to have it placed in Wheeling?"[29] One can detect in these comments the feeling that there is something uniquely demeaning

---

26. Steve Johnson, *Suburb Chief Fears Landfill Could Spark 2D "Chernobyl,"* Chi. Trib., July 23, 1987 at 8.

27. Landfills can affect property values, although residents are probably prone to exaggerate the magnitude of the impact. One study indicates that relatively expensive residential property can lose up to 7.3% of its value if a landfill is located within several blocks. *See* Alan K. Reichert et al., *The Impact of Landfills on Residential Property Values,* 7 J. Real Estate Research 297 (1992). Impacts on rural land values, however, are virtually nonexistent. *Id.* SWANCC submitted expert testimony in the proceedings before the Army Corps of Engineers that the Bartlett balefill, because of its careful design, its large buffer zone, and its distance from existing housing, would have no negative impact on residential property values. The Corps accepted this testimony. *See* Department of the Army, Permit Evaluation and Decision Document, *supra* note 6, at 55.

28. Thomas Osran, *Landfill Protesters Unfairly Labeled,* Chi. Trib., Sept. 18, 1990, at 18.

29. Herb Fiedler, *"Dumped in Lap,"* Chi. Trib., Nov. 17, 1989, at 26.

about being asked to take the unwanted refuse of another community, particularly one perceived to be higher on the socio-economic scale.

Notwithstanding its penchant for generating publicity, Citizens Against the Balefill would never have gotten very far in its struggle without help. The group quickly found powerful allies, however, in the form of elected politicians from the immediate vicinity. Whatever these officials initially thought about the balefill project, they quickly learned what their constituents wanted. The key event here was probably the April, 1987 municipal elections in Cook County. Three trustees of Bartlett were standing for reelection, and were opposed by an informal slate of candidates led by John Stark, President of Citizens Against the Balefill, who "contended that the incumbents had not opposed the landfill vigorously enough."[30] The upshot was that two incumbents were defeated by anti-balefill candidates, and a third barely survived. Two years later, Stark was elected Bartlett's Village President. The message could hardly have been clearer: local voters expected elected officials to oppose the balefill with all means at their disposal.

The support of local politicians is critical in explaining how the contesting parties could sustain a sixteen-year war of attrition over the balefill, costing each side millions of dollars in legal and consulting fees. Basically, each side was able to call upon the taxing and borrowing power of local government to defray the costs of the marathon litigation. Stark, once elected Bartlett Village President, was able to tap into hundreds of thousands of taxpayer dollars to pay legal and consulting fees for fighting the balefill, at least until he faced a revolt in late 1991 from other Village Trustees over the mounting costs.[31] SWANCC, for its part, had independent authority to borrow monies secured by the fees it would charge member communities for garbage disposal services once its system became operational. Litigation and consulting fees could be capitalized as part of the costs of constructing the site, and these costs could be spread out over time and across twenty-three different communities, rendering the enormous expenditures on litigation largely invisible to ordinary budgetary processes of the suburban communities that had joined together to form SWANCC.

The balefill opponents found another, even more important ally among politicians elected from the immediate vicinity of the proposed

---

30. Steve Johnson & George Papajohn, *Status Quo Takes a Drubbing; Northwest Suburbs Shout, "Out With Old, In With New,"* Chi. Trib., Apr. 8, 1987, at 14.

31. At one point Village Trustees who were at odds with Village President Stark planned a referendum asking voters to approve a tax increase in order to cover Bartlett's mounting litigation costs, then estimated to be $600,000. *See* Matthew Nickerson, *Bartlett Now Sees No Need For Tax Hike to Fund Balefill Fight,* Chi. Trib., Jan. 10, 1992, at 3. The referendum was cancelled when Stark produced a consultant who told the Trustees, at a closed-door meeting, that success was close at hand. *Id.*

balefill. The congressman who represented the area was Dennis Hastert, the powerful Republican who was to shortly become Speaker of the House. It was Hastert, more than any one else, who equalized the dominating influence the wealthy SWANCC communities enjoyed at the county and state level. The chosen instrument Hastert was able to deploy to these ends was a federal administrative agency, the U.S. Army Corps of Engineers.

III.   The Army To The Rescue

For historical reasons, the Army Corps of Engineers is the federal body with primary responsibility for issuing "dredge and fill" permits under Section 404 of the Clean Water Act. Such a permit is required whenever someone proposes to discharge fill material into "navigable waters."[32] In the 1972 Amendments to the Clean Water Act, Congress stipulated that "navigable waters" means "waters of the United States."[33] This was deliberately vague, but the general understanding at the time was that "navigable waters" as defined would extend more broadly than the traditional definition of navigability—waters subject to the action of the tides or waters that are, had been, or could be made traversable by some kind of vessel.[34]

After initial hesitation, the Army Corps issued regulations expanding the definition of navigable waters to include tributaries of navigable waters and wetlands "adjacent" to navigable waters or their tributaries.[35] In *United States v. Riverside Bayview Homes, Inc.*,[36] the Supreme Court upheld this regulatory definition insofar as it applied to wetlands that are adjacent to navigable waters. In addition, the Army Corps regulations also asserted jurisdiction over any waters "the use, degradation or destruction of which could affect interstate or foreign commerce."[37] The preamble to a further revision and clarification of the regulations in 1986 stated that the category of waters affecting interstate commerce includes those which "are or could be used as habitat" by

---

32.   33 U.S.C. § 1344(a) (2000).

33.   Federal Water Pollution Control Act Amendments of 1972, tit. V, § 502, Pub. L. No. 92–500, 86 Stat. 886 (codified at 33 U.S.C. § 1362(7) (2000)).

34.   For an excellent analysis of the history of navigability as a jurisdictional concept, see Jennifer DeButts Cantrell, *For the Birds: The Statutory Limits of the Army Corps of Engineers' Authority Over Intrastate Waters After SWANCC*, 77 S. Cal. L. Rev. 1353 (2004).

35.   Permits for Activities in Navigable Waters or Ocean Waters, 40 Fed. Reg. 31,320 (July 25, 1975) (codified as amended at 33 C.F.R. §§ 328.3, 329.4 (2004)).

36.   474 U.S. 121 (1985).

37.   33 C.F.R. § 328.3(a)(3) (2004). Examples given in the regulations were waters used by interstate travelers for recreation purposes; waters from which fish are taken and sold in interstate commerce; and waters used for industrial purpose by industries in interstate commerce. *Id.* § 328.3(a)(3)(i)-(iii).

migratory birds that cross state lines or birds protected under migratory bird treaties.[38] Although commentary in a preamble is ordinarily not considered legally binding, this became known as the "Migratory Bird Rule," and was invoked from time to time by the Army Corps as justification for asserting jurisdiction over isolated waters and wetlands.

The prospect that the Bartlett balefill might require a dredge and fill permit arose in early 1986. As part of its due diligence, the Northwest Municipal Conference asked the Army Corps to confirm that the property it planned to acquire near Bartlett would not require a Section 404 permit. After sending an inspector to the site, the Corps responded that the tract contained no jurisdictional wetlands or waters under the regulations.[39] When the Conference acquired an option for additional land, the Corps reconfirmed this decision in 1987.[40] These initial inquiries and the Corp's perfunctory responses went unreported by the local newspapers, which otherwise covered the major events in the controversy quite thoroughly.

After the Corps clarified its regulations by adding the Migratory Bird Rule, however, the Illinois Nature Preserves Commission (a state agency) asked the Corps to reconsider its jurisdictional rulings. The commission claimed that it had observed four different species of migratory birds at the abandoned gravel pit, and hence that the Bartlett balefill was subject to Army Corps jurisdiction. On November 16, 1987, after further inspection of the site, the Corps agreed. The agency found that the gravel pit was periodically filled with standing pools of water, which were or could be used as a habitat by migratory birds. The Corps explained that its previous denial of jurisdiction "was based on the fact that the water areas did not meet the definition of a wetland or lakes, and not on the broader definition of 'waters of the United States.' "[41]

This fateful decision also elicited no recorded response from either the proponents or the opponents of the balefill controversy. In particular, there was no sign at the time that SWANCC questioned the

38. Final Rule for Regulatory Programs of the Corps of Engineers, 51 Fed. Reg. 41,206, 41,217 (Nov. 13, 1986).

39. Letter from James E. Evans, Regulatory Functions Branch, U.S. Army Corps of Engineers, Chicago District, to Daniel Dietzler, Patrick Engineering, Inc. (Apr. 17, 1986) (on file with author).

40. Letter from James E. Evans, Regulatory Functions Branch, U.S. Army Corps of Engineers, Chicago District, to Daniel P. Dietzler, Patrick Engineering, Inc. (Mar. 4, 1987) (on file with author).

41. Quoted in *Solid Waste Agency of N. Cook County v. U.S. Army Corps of Eng'rs*, 998 F. Supp. 946, 949 (N.D. Ill. 1998). The Army Corps subsequently clarified that it was asserting jurisdiction over the site as part of the "waters of the United States," not because it exhibited the characteristics of a wetland. Letter from Jess J. Franco, Regulatory Functions Branch, U.S. Army Corps of Engineers, Chicago District, to William F. Abolt, Solid Waste Agency of Northern Cook County (Mar. 23, 1989) (on file with author).

jurisdiction of the Army Corps over the site, at least not in comments to the press. The Corps had a record of granting 90% of applications to fill wetlands, perhaps after imposing some mitigation requirement. The Corps had agreed that the abandoned gravel pit was *not* a wetland, but only a "seasonal pool" subject to its jurisdiction because of the presence of migratory birds. SWANCC appeared to be confident that a Section 404 permit would eventually be forthcoming, perhaps after some further mitigation efforts on behalf of the birds. For their part, Citizens Against the Balefill and other vocal opponents of the project also initially paid little attention to the impending Section 404 permit process, apparently because they failed to appreciate its strategic potential as a way of blocking the balefill project.

That potential was soon revealed, however. Bartlett's representative in Congress, Dennis Hastert, was a man of considerable influence in Washington. Starting in 1988, well before the Section 404 permitting process surfaced in public commentary, Hastert initiated a series of interventions designed to underscore his strong opposition to the balefill project. Most of these interventions exploited the fact that the U.S. EPA has statutory authority to veto Section 404 permits issued by the Corps.[42] Hastert's opposition to the plan enjoyed the solid support of Valdas Adamkus, the longtime EPA regional administrator for the Chicago area. Adamkus was no political slouch himself; he would later resign his civil service position at EPA and return to his native Lithuania, where he was elected that country's President.

Hastert's first move was to attach a rider to an Army Corps appropriations bill enacted in 1988.[43] The rider required the Corps, before issuing any Section 404 permit at the Bartlett site, to review the adequacy of the Illinois EPA's assessment of the impact of the balefill on the Newark Aquifer that serves as the source of groundwater for area communities. The rider specifically required the Corps to consult with the U.S. EPA before completing its examination of the Illinois EPA's decision, and to issue a report to Congress with its conclusions.

The next year, before the Army Corps had completed the required assessment, Hastert wrote a letter to Lee Thomas, Administrator of the U.S. EPA, urging the agency to weigh in against the proposed balefill because of the threat to groundwater.[44] The EPA responded in the form

---

42. *See Bartlett Leader in Washington To Tell His Fears About Balefill*, Chi. Trib., July 20, 1990, at 4 (recounting meeting between Bartlett Village President Stark, Hastert, and U.S. EPA officials concerning "EPA's veto power over any decision by the Army Corps of Engineers").

43. Water Resources Development Act of 1988, Pub. L. No. 100–676, § 47(b), 102 Stat. 4012.

44. Stevenson Swanson, *Balefill Foes Will Try to Divide, Conquer*, Chi. Trib., May 22, 1989, at 2.

of a letter from Adamkus, which reported that the Chicago regional office had investigated the matter, and had concluded that the proposed balefill would leak into the aquifer that feeds the South Elgin municipal well. The letter stated that the EPA would therefore likely recommend that the Army Corps reject any Section 404 permit for the site.[45]

Then, in 1992, shortly before SWANCC submitted its second Section 404 permit application, Hastert announced his intention to introduce a bill to amend the Resource Conservation and Recovery Act to make it unlawful to locate a solid waste disposal site within 3,500 feet of a fen. Hastert justified the measure by saying that fens (marshes or moors) need protection since they support rare aquatic plants. Local opponents of the balefill gleefully noted that the Bartlett site was located 3,000 feet south of something called the Bluff Spring fen, and that the bill, if enacted, would "effectively cripple the project."[46] Although Hastert's fen-protection measure gathered some attention in the press, it is not clear that it was ever formally introduced.

The collective effect of these interventions is difficult to assess with any precision. At a minimum, as the *Tribune* subsequently remarked of the appropriations rider, they were "intended to put the corps under a spotlight."[47] Based on these interventions, Army Corps officials would have been aware that a powerful Washington politician was keenly interested in blocking the Bartlett balefill. This politician appeared to enjoy unwavering support of the regional EPA office, which raised the prospect of an EPA veto of any favorable decision. Under the circumstances, it is hardly surprising that the Army Corps became an implacable obstacle to the balefill project.

SWANCC had originally planned to submit its application to the Army Corps before the state permitting process was completed.[48] But the Corps took the position that it would not entertain any Section 404 application until Illinois EPA approval was secured.[49] As a result, the dispute did not enter the federal arena until 1990.

45. Stevenson Swanson, *Letter from EPA Official Casts Doubt on Balefill*, Chi. Trib., Dec. 2, 1988, at 2.

46. Nickerson & Kirby, *supra* note 22.

47. Stevenson Swanson, *Balefill Battle Enters Federal Arena*, Chi. Trib., Jan. 22, 1990, at 1.

48. *See* Steve Johnson, *Balefill Opponents Tell State Official Their Side*, Chi. Trib., Feb. 11, 1988, at 3 (quoting Conference official that application to the Corps was expected to be filed in June, and application to the state EPA was expected to be filed in August).

49. Letter from Jess J. Franco, Regulatory Functions Branch, U.S. Army Corps of Engineers, Chicago District, to William F. Abolt, Northwest Municipal Conference (Apr. 21, 1988) (on file with author).

Because the Army Corps based its jurisdiction on the Migratory Bird Rule, the parties naturally concentrated, at least in the initial round of Section 404 proceedings, on the impact of the project on migratory birds. SWANCC's 1,600–page submission acknowledged that many species of migratory birds used the site. Although none were listed as endangered or threatened under federal law, two—the veery and Cooper's hawk— were listed as endangered or threatened in Illinois. However, by far the most attention was devoted to a colony of blue herons found in one part of the gravel pit. SWANCC retained a team of naturalists to devise a way to protect the herons. They proposed moving the colony to an artificial nesting ground nearby, complete with wooden poles with arms and platforms placed on a man-made island.[50]

Bartlett countered with a report by another team of environmental consultants. Their report argued that the blue herons could not be successfully relocated, because large cottonwood trees had grown up around the site in the forty-five years since the gravel mine was abandoned, and such trees were vital to the heron colony.[51]

As the date for public hearings loomed, more official voices sounded off, offering conflicting messages. The Fish and Wildlife Service of the Department of the Interior issued a report declaring the mitigation plan for the blue heron and veery colonies "unacceptable."[52] The Chicago office of the U.S. EPA weighed in, on cue, with a strongly worded letter urging rejection. Speaking through the acting water division chief, the local office said it was concerned that the project would destroy vital wildlife habitat and could pose a long-term threat to underground water supplies. The agency also suggested that the member communities of SWANCC had not done enough to encourage recycling and composting of trash in order to reduce the amount of garbage that would go into the landfill.

Shortly thereafter, however, the Army Corps issued its report to Congress mandated by Hastert's 1988 appropriations rider. The report concluded that the balefill would pose "virtually no risk" to the Newark Aquifer underlying the site.[53] Remarkably, the report also indicated that it had been reviewed and approved by the national office of EPA.[54] Evidently, EPA's national office and Adamkus's Chicago office were not

---

50. Stevenson Swanson, *Balefill Plan Offers Herons A Sanctuary*, Chi. Trib., Feb. 9, 1990, at 3.

51. Stevenson Swanson, *Study Says Birds, Dump Don't Mix*, Chi. Trib., Feb. 1, 1990, at 6.

52. Stevenson Swanson, *Balefill Foes Say Politics Dictated Site*, Chi. Trib., May 30, 1990, at 2.

53. Department of the Army, Permit Evaluation and Decision, *supra* note 6, at 21.

54. *Id.*

operating on the same page, at least with respect to the threat the balefill posed to water quality. Hastert summoned the Army Corps officer in charge of the Bartlett hearings to Washington, and made plain his displeasure. According to an account of the meeting released by his staff, Hastert instructed the officer that "the report should have stressed that the site is not conducive for a balefill and that current plans are not good enough."[55]

After mulling the conflicting evidence and political signals for another six months, the Army Corps, on January 31, 1991, rejected SWANCC's application for a Section 404 permit. The Corps agreed with SWANCC that a solid waste facility was critically needed and that the project was well designed. Consistent with its report to Congress, the Corps specifically rejected the claim that the balefill posed a threat to the Newark Aquifer. Moreover, it found that "property values would not be adversely impacted by the project," and that "[t]he project's reasonably foreseeable benefits outweigh its foreseeable detriments." Nevertheless, the Corps found the plan would cause "unmitigatable" damage to woodlands and wetlands on the site. It also found that SWANCC had failed to demonstrate that alternative sites were not available that would avoid the need to fill "waters of the United States"; specifically, the Corps suggested that SWANCC should have investigated the possibility of acquiring multiple, smaller disposal sites.[56] Opponents were predictably jubilant.[57]

SWANCC debated whether to seek judicial review, but ultimately decided to revise and resubmit the plan with an aim to overcoming the Corps' objections to the loss of the migratory bird habitat. While consultants were working on the new plan, a moment of panic occurred when someone reported spotting a bald eagle at the site. Notwithstanding speculation that the sighting was an April Fool's joke, SWANCC rented an airplane and swooped back and forth over the site with a Fish and Wildlife Service agent in a futile search for the bird.[58]

The new plan was unveiled on September 8, 1992. The centerpiece was a promise by SWANCC to establish a new entity, called the Poplar Creek Environmental Trust, which would be endowed with $12.5 million to purchase an additional 250 acres of land to replace the habitat damaged by the balefill construction. The trust would also acquire a

55. Mike Comerford, *Balefill Showdown Seen at Hearing*, Chi. Trib., May 28, 1990, at 9.

56. Department of the Army, Permit Evaluation and Decision, *supra* note 6, at 55, 56, 61.

57. Stevenson Swanson, *Proposed Balefill Dealt Blow by Army Corps*, Chi. Trib., Feb. 1, 1991, at 1.

58. Christine Winter, *Is It An Eagle Or Is It Garbage?*, Chi. Trib., Apr. 3, 1992, at 1.

wildlife corridor eight miles in length, linking various existing forest preserves in northwest Cook county to the 250 acres and the other undeveloped land around the balefill site. The trust, which would be governed by an independent board, would be responsible for monitoring how SWANCC operated the site.

The original land acquisition for the Bartlett site had cost $5 million, and the completed project had been estimated to cost about $20 million. With the addition of the Poplar Creek Environmental Trust, along with the Good Neighbor fund and the extensive operational modifications of the site necessary to secure Illinois EPA approval, not to mention nearly a decade of nonstop litigation, the projected price tag for the project once construction was completed had now been pushed to $90 million.[59]

Jockeying for position proceeded apace. The opponents scored a victory when Adamkus, on behalf of the U.S. EPA, again weighed in with a letter recommending against granting the permit. He emphasized both the danger to wildlife and "a long-term threat to valuable ground water resources."[60] But SWANCC, assisted by an expensive Washington lobbyist, gained important allies too, persuading the Fish and Wildlife Service[61] and the Illinois Department of Conservation,[62] both of which had previously objected to the site on ecological grounds, to endorse its Environmental Trust mitigation plan, thus seemingly overcoming the principal reason the Army Corps had cited in denying its first application. Ominously, however, a Corps spokeswoman said the agency was "starting from scratch and all issues will be reviewed once more."[63]

By the time the record closed, the Corps had received 10,000 letters, comments, reports, and other submissions, including 4,000 "objection forms" handed out by an Assistant States' Attorney in Kane County, and 400 letters sent by sophomores from Naperville North High School as a class room assignment.[64] About one hundred people showed up at a public hearing conducted at a local college. SWANCC declined to present extensive oral testimony, leaving opponents to rant for eight hours about destruction of wildlife habitats, poisoning groundwater, and the avail-

---

59. Mathew Nickerson, *Agency Offers Trade To Win Balefill OK*, Chi. Trib., Sept. 9, 1992, at 1.

60. Sue Ellen Christian, *U.S. EPA Against Plan for Balefill*, Chi. Trib., Aug. 10, 1993, at 1.

61. Martha Russis, *2nd Round of Balefill Battle Set*, Chi. Trib., Sept. 28, 1993, at 1.

62. Martha Russis, *Opponents Hope Ground Water Will Sink Balefill*, Chi. Trib., May 6, 1993, at 2.

63. Russis, *supra* note 61.

64. Wayne Baker, *Balefill Opponents Flood Army Corps*, Chi. Trib., May 17, 1993, at 3.

ability of alternatives in the form of private landfills opening in more distant locations.[65]

While the Corps was pondering the record, Congressman John Porter, who represented much of the Northshore, convened a summit meeting between the Illinois Republican congressional delegation, EPA officials, SWANCC officials, and officials from Bartlett. Hastert attended the meeting "on behalf of his constituents to monitor what was being said," but denounced the gathering to the press as "improper." As he explained to one of the *Tribune*'s reporters, who detected no irony in the statement, "This is a move to put political pressure from the top down."[66]

On July 20, 1994, the Army Corps rejected the Section 404 application for a second time. Although the potential jeopardy to wildlife was mentioned in the decision, the primary reason for rejecting the application returned—once again—to the long-term threat to local water supplies. Specifically, the decision found that SWANCC had failed to show that it had set aside sufficient funds "to finance in perpetuity its required long term maintenance responsibilities" at the site needed to protect groundwater.[67] SWANCC complained, with considerable justification, that the Army Corps was a "moving target."[68] Two years earlier, the Corps had issued a report to Congress finding that the project posed no significant risk to groundwater, and had concluded the problem was wildlife habitat. After proposing to spend $12.5 million to mitigate the wildlife problem, the Corps now said the fatal flaw was the long-term threat to groundwater. SWANCC's only realistic option was to go to court.

IV. *The Navigable Waters of the United States*

SWANCC's lawsuit was filed in federal district court in the Northern District of Illinois on December 21, 1994. The agency argued, as expected, that the Army Corps had acted in an arbitrary and capricious fashion in rejecting its application on grounds previously found to be insubstantial. But for the first time in the controversy, SWANCC also argued that the Bartlett site was not part of the "navigable waters" of the United States, and hence it was beyond the jurisdiction of the Corps to regulate under the Clean Water Act. There is reason to believe that

---

65. Martha Russis, *Balefill's Foes Voice Water Fears*, Chi. Trib., Sept. 29, 1993, at 1.

66. Anne Hazard, *Rep. Hastert Blasts D.C. Meeting On Balefill*, Chi. Trib., May 6, 1994, at 4.

67. Department of the Army, Permit Evaluation and Decision Document, Solid Waste Agency of Northern Cook County, July 20, 1994, at 86–87.

68. Ted Gregory, *Bartlett Balefill Project Dealt 2nd Blow by Army*, Chi. Trib., July 22, 1994, at 1.

SWANCC was in fact putting all its chips on the jurisdictional argument. In late January, the agency allowed an option to purchase land for the Poplar Creek Environmental Trust to expire unexecuted.[69] And it moved to line up long-term waste disposal contracts with private waste companies, in the event the Corps decision should be upheld.[70]

At this point the languorous pace of the controversy slowed even further. The case was assigned to Judge Brian Duff, who refused to permit Bartlett and Citizens Against the Baleful to intervene, saying he did not want the case "bogged down" with "emotional arguments charging the balefill is an environmental hazard."[71] This resulted in an interlocutory appeal to the Seventh Circuit, which directed Judge Duff to consider permissive intervention.[72] Shortly thereafter, dogged by questions about his judicial temperament, Judge Duff resigned from the bench,[73] and the case was reassigned to Judge George Lindberg. All these distractions meant that more than three years elapsed before Judge Lindberg issued a thirty-four-page opinion affirming the Army Corps' jurisdiction.[74] In order to obtain a final judgment and secure an immediate right to appeal, SWANCC voluntarily dismissed its claim that the Corps' decision was arbitrary and capricious.[75] The decision generated relatively little publicity, perhaps because of the long delay, perhaps because it did not change what was then the status quo (no balefill).

SWANCC in fact seems by this point to have come to view the Bartlett project with less urgency. In its public statements, the agency continued to insist that Bartlett was a better solution to the garbage disposal problem than a long-term contract with a private disposal company. But such a contract was clearly an alternative if Bartlett did not work out. Still, having sunk some $20 million into the site, which was now effectively barred from any development by the terms of the Corps' order, SWANCC concluded it had little to lose by appealing the jurisdictional ruling.

---

69. Martha Russis, *Agency Seeking Balefill Considers Other Options*, Chi. Trib., Jan. 26, 1995, at 2.

70. Martha Russis, *Alternate Waste Plan Considered*, Chi. Trib., Feb. 9, 1995, at 2.

71. Martha Russis, *Balefill Foes Are Denied; Bartlett, Citizens Group Have No Say in Dump Lawsuit*, Chi. Trib., Sept. 8, 1995, at 1.

72. Solid Waste Agency of N. Cook County v. U.S. Army Corps of Eng'rs, 101 F.3d 503, 509 (7th Cir. 1996).

73. John Carpenter, *Landfill Plan Takes Long, Winding Road*, Chicago Sun–Times, Dec. 15, 1996, at 34.

74. Solid Waste Agency of N. Cook County v. U.S. Army Corps of Eng'rs, 998 F. Supp. 946 (N.D. Ill. 1998).

75. Jamie Sotonoff, *Focus Of Waste Agency Balefill Case Shifts To Army Corps Jurisdiction*, Chi. Daily Herald, Apr. 21, 1998, at 4.

Moreover, the argument against jurisdiction looked stronger than it had when the litigation had commenced in the district court. In *United States v. Lopez*,[76] the U.S. Supreme Court, for the first time in over forty years, had invalidated a federal statute as exceeding the scope of authority granted by the Commerce Clause. The Court stressed that regulation under the Commerce Clause must have some stopping point, and thus cannot upheld on the basis of a theory that would permit Congress to regulate everything within the traditional police power of the States.[77] Restating its precedents, the Court said that permissible Commerce Clause regulation will generally fall within one of three categories: (1) regulation of the channels of interstate commerce; (2) regulation of the instrumentalities of interstate commerce, or persons or things in interstate commerce; and (3) regulation of activities that, in the aggregate, substantially affect interstate commerce.[78]

Two years before *Lopez*, the Seventh Circuit had upheld the Army Corps' Migratory Bird Rule.[79] The court had recognized that wild birds flying across state lines are not "interstate commerce." But it had found that migratory birds, in the aggregate, have a substantial affect on interstate commerce, because of the large number of people who spend millions of dollars each year to hunt, trap, and observe such birds. SWANCC had reason to hope that the new, more restrictive conception of the commerce power in *Lopez* might cause the Seventh Circuit to reconsider this ruling.

The Seventh Circuit, however, was unmoved by the argument that *Lopez* rendered the Migratory Bird Rule suspect. The court reaffirmed its previous ruling that the Rule was constitutional under the substantial effects test. Writing for the court, Judge Diane Wood noted that 3.1 million Americans spend $1.3 billion per year to hunt birds, many of them crossing state lines to do so.[80] The court also gave short shrift to the argument that the Migratory Bird Rule exceeded the scope of authority conferred by the Clean Water Act. The court cited prior circuit authority for the proposition that Congress, by defining "navigable waters" to mean "the waters of the United States," had intended to assert jurisdiction to the fullest extent of the Commerce Clause.[81]

Attorney Myron Cherry acclaimed the decision—upholding the authority of a federal agency to veto a project approved by a county, a state

---

76.   514 U.S. 549 (1995).

77.   *Id.* at 556–58.

78.   *Id.* at 558–59.

79.   Hoffman Homes, Inc. v. EPA, 999 F.2d 256 (7th Cir. 1993).

80.   Solid Waste Agency of N. Cook County v. U.S. Army Corps of Eng'rs, 191 F.3d 845, 850 (7th Cir. 1999) (citing data for 1996).

81.   *Id.* at 851.

environmental agency, and a state supreme court—as "a great victory for local government."[82] Overall, however, the Seventh Circuit's decision generated even less publicity than the district court's ruling; the *Tribune* reported the decision in a short article on page six.[83]

As SWANCC pondered whether to seek further review by the U.S. Supreme Court, the Rehnquist Court's federalism revolution moved into high gear. *Lopez* was reaffirmed in *United States v. Morrison*,[84] which added the further twist that the intrastate effects which may be aggregated to establish a substantial effect on interstate commerce generally must involve *economic* activity.[85] Migratory birds landing on isolated waters and wetlands—whether they fly across interstate or international boundary lines to get there or not—are not in and of themselves a form of economic activity. Thus, it was hard to see how the Migratory Bird Rule could be justified under the substantial effects test, as clarified by *Morrison*. Not surprisingly given the direction of the decisional law, SWANCC put its money down for one more roll of the judicial dice. It was vindicated when the Court granted the agency's petition for certiorari late in the spring of 2000.[86]

The briefing in the Supreme Court confirmed that *Morrison* had rendered the Seventh Circuit's constitutional theory—that migratory birds are big business—problematic. The Solicitor General, representing the Army Corps, sought to defend the judgment by offering a new argument in support of the constitutional power of the Army Corps to regulate the Bartlett site: dumping garbage in the ground is a form of economic activity that, in the aggregate, clearly has a substantial effect on interstate commerce.[87] This neatly solved the problem of identifying a form of economic activity to aggregate, garbage dumping rather than birds coming and going. The only question was whether the Court would allow the executive branch to cite a branch of Commerce Clause authority that *could* have been relied upon by Congress as a basis for federal regulation, without regard to whether it was the branch of authority Congress *actually* relied upon.

In fact, by shifting the ground of constitutional defense in this manner, the Solicitor General's brief drew attention to the restrictive

---

82. Matt Arado, *Ruling Against Balefill Pleases Bartlett, But Fight May Not Be Over*, Chi. Daily Herald, Oct. 8, 1999, at 6.

83. Janan Hanna, *Court Rejects Push for Garbage Dump Near Bartlett*, Chi. Trib., Oct. 8, 1999, at 6.

84. 529 U.S. 598 (2000).

85. *Id.* at 610–11.

86. 529 U.S. 1129 (2000).

87. Brief for Federal Respondents at 43–47, *Solid Waste Agency of N. Cook County v. U.S. Army Corps of Eng'rs*, 531 U.S. 159 (2001) (No. 99–1178).

language of Section 404 of the Clean Water Act. Congress had invoked its authority over the "navigable waters of the United States," which seemed to connote its authority over one of the channels of interstate commerce. The Army Corps regulations, including the Migratory Bird Rule, went beyond the channels of interstate commerce and sought to justify regulation of waters having a substantial effect on interstate commerce. Unless the Court bought the argument that Congress intended to permit any form of regulation permissible under the Commerce Clause, notwithstanding the language referencing "navigable waters," the Solicitor General's argument exposed the Migratory Bird Rule to the challenge that it was inconsistent with the statute.

As the briefing unfolded, alarm bells began to go off within environmental circles.[88] The Commerce Clause is the constitutional foundation on which most of the Nation's environmental laws rest. If the Commerce Clause does not permit aggregation of noneconomic phenomena in order to determine whether some activity has a substantial effect on interstate commerce, then more than the Migratory Bird Rule could be in jeopardy. The Endangered Species Act seeks to preserve endangered species of plants and animals and the habitat of endangered animals, phenomena which are not themselves economic, even though they may have a substantial effect on interstate commerce. And the Clean Air Act seeks to regulate air quality, a state of being which is not itself economic, even if clean air has a substantial effect on interstate commerce. To many environmentalists, it appeared as if SWANCC was stubbornly persisting in its quest for vindication of its balefill plan, even at the price of putting a substantial chunk of the federal environmental laws at risk.

Thus it happened that on the eve of oral argument, a group of environmental leaders, fearing that the Court's decision "could lead to a disastrous ruling for the nation's environmental laws," launched a novel effort to get the parties to settle the case. Howard Learner, a leading Chicago-area environmentalist, spearheaded the effort. In a letter to SWANCC officials, he warned that the agency's constituents "have very strong environmental values" and would not want to be party to a decision that undermined those values. Learner further argued that the balefill was no longer necessary, "because the private sector seems to be meeting the Chicago area's waste-disposal needs."[89]

George Van Dusen, the Mayor of Skokie, responded on behalf of SWANCC. Describing himself as "an environmentalist and a 'child of the 60s,'" Van Dusen nevertheless dismissed the environmentalists' con-

---

88. *See, e.g.,* Richard Lazarus, *Three Grants of Cert Raise Uncertainty*, Envtl. Forum, July/Aug. 2000, at 10.

89. William Grady, *Groups Seek Settlement of Balefill Suit; Environmentalists Fear Effect on Laws*, Chi. Trib., Sept. 22, 2000, at 1.

cerns as unfounded. He wrote, "Contrary to your letter, the agency's case will have no impact on any federal environmental legislation." SWANCC was "looking for a very narrow ruling from the court," he said. Its argument was "not with the Clean Water Act but rather with the corps' decision to use the presence of migratory birds as a reason for applying the law to the balefill site." Learner responded that SWANCC might be seeking a narrow ruling, but the high Court tends to "do what the court wants to do."[90]

The *Tribune*, which up to that point had consistently supported SWANCC, now saw the danger in the path it was pursuing, and editorialized that it was time to end the "grudge match" over the balefill.[91] Van Dusen was unmoved. The claim that the Court's decision could overturn the Endangered Species Act and parts of the Clean Air and Clean Water Acts was "patently ridiculous" he wrote in a letter printed by the paper. "This is a federalism, not an environmental, case. . . . The issue presented in SWANCC's case involves the power of duly elected local officials to address the needs of their local communities without interference from the federal government."[92]

The environmental consortium led by Learner stepped up the pressure for a settlement, mailing 5,000 brochures to environmentalists in seven suburbs, urging them to lobby SWANCC officials to settle. But on the eve of oral argument, SWANCC again rejected the overture, asserting that "[t]here has been no credible offer to settle this case on the table to date."[93] While published reports focused on SWANCC's intransigence, national environmental groups were internally divided as well. With the matter fully briefed before the Supreme Court, some environmental groups believed that the case was a strong one in which to secure a reaffirmation of federal authority over isolated waters, and they too argued against any deal. In the end, both sides decided to stake everything on a ruling by the country's highest federal court on abstract points of constitutional law and statutory interpretation.

Oral argument took place on October 31, 2000. Several Justices seemed concerned that upholding the Army Corps' jurisdiction over the site could expand the federal government's role over local land use issues in a way that Congress had never intended. Justice Sandra Day O'Connor, always a critical vote in federalism cases, asked why Illinois could not adequately handle the matter. "Has Illinois shown no interest at all?" she queried. "Is this a situation where the state has turned its back

---

90. *Id.*

91. Editorial, *End the Landfill Grudge Match*, Chi. Trib., Sept. 30, 2000, at 22.

92. George Van Dusen, *Towns Deal with Solid Waste*, Chi. Trib., Oct. 10, 2000, at 14.

93. William Grady, *Landfill Accord Unlikely As Case Heads For Court*, Chi. Trib., Oct. 21, 2000, at 5.

and said, 'We don't care'?" Timothy Bishop, representing SWANCC, was quick to assure her that Illinois EPA had imposed "51 conditions" before allowing it to proceed, while Cook County had undertaken the "longest process it ever engaged in" before granting its approval.[94]

It took the Court little more than two months to deliver a knockout victory for SWANCC. Writing for a 5–4 majority, including Justice O'Connor, Chief Justice Rehnquist said that it was unnecessary to reach the constitutional issue. Whether or not Congress could have enacted the Migratory Bird Rule under its Commerce Clause authority, the Clean Water Act conferred jurisdiction only over the "navigable waters of the United States."[95] The Court reaffirmed its *Riverside Bayview* decision, including the proposition that Congress in 1972 intended "navigable waters" to encompass more than the classical understanding of that term.[96] But, the Court said, it would be improper to read "the term 'navigable waters' out of the statute."[97] Moreover, no deference was due to the Army Corps' interpretation of the statute, because that interpretation would raise a serious constitutional question, which was avoided by interpreting the statute as foreclosing the Migratory Bird Rule.

The holding was clear: the Migratory Bird Rule is unlawful. What was unclear was the exact identity of the "significant constitutional question" that was being avoided by this construction of the Act. The Court said the significant question was "the precise object or activity that, in the aggregate, substantially affects interstate commerce"; was it the presence of migratory birds on the site, as the Migratory Bird Rule seemed to suggest, or was it the landfilling of the site, as the Solicitor General had argued in his brief?[98] And why was identity of the object or activity a significant constitutional question?

Two possibilities are consistent with the Court's cryptic opinion. One possibility is that the Court was referring to the economic/noneconomic distinction of *Morrison*. Under that distinction, it would be constitutionally permissible to aggregate economic activity (like landfilling), but unconstitutional to aggregate noneconomic activity (like birds landing on isolated waters). If this is what the Court meant, then the Executive Branch could restore Army Corps jurisdiction over sites like the Bartlett balefill by changing the regulations to focus on commercial filling activity, rather than the presence of migratory birds.

---

94. Jan Crawford Greenburg, *U.S. Justices Hear Sides in Bartlett Landfill Case*, Chi. Trib., Nov. 1, 2000, at 1.

95. *Solid Waste Agency of N. Cook County*, 531 U.S. at 173–74.

96. *Id.* at 167–68.

97. *Id.* at 172.

98. *Id.* at 173.

Another possibility is that the Court was concerned about the constitutionality of upholding federal regulation of an activity based on one Commerce Clause theory (substantial effects), when Congress had invoked another Commerce Clause theory (channels of commerce). In other words, the problem was not the scope of congressional power, but whether that power had in fact been exercised. If this is what the Court meant, then only Congress could restore Army Corps jurisdiction over sites like the Bartlett balefill, by amending the Clean Water Act to assert the substantial effects test.

V. *The National Aftermath*

By avoiding a ruling on the constitutional question, and resting on statutory interpretation, *SWANCC* appeared to invite one or both of the political branches to speak more clearly about the scope of federal authority over decisions that effect the environmental quality of isolated waters. So far, however, neither Branch has acted, and they are unlikely to act in the foreseeable future. The failure of the political branches to respond means that the task of interpreting *SWANCC* has been left to the lower federal courts.

A. Congress

SWANCC seems to cry out for legislative action. The Court emphasized that the Clean Water Act, in its current form, invokes the authority of the federal government over "navigable waters." In effect, the Clean Water Act is grounded in the federal government's authority over the "channels of interstate commerce." This restrictive reading of the Act was underscored by the Court's refusal to sustain the Army Corps' jurisdiction under a "substantially affects commerce" rationale, as the Administration had urged. The obvious solution would appear to be for Congress to amend the Act to replace or supplement the exercise of the "channels" power with an express invocation of one or both of the other prongs of interstate commerce power recognized in *Lopez*—the "instrumentalities of commerce" power or the "substantially affects commerce" power.

Legislation was in fact introduced in both the 107th and 108th Congresses to amend the Clean Water Act by restoring the authority eliminated in *SWANCC*. The principal vehicle was the Clean Water Authority Restoration Act of 2002, and the nearly-identical Clean Water Authority Restoration Act of 2003.[99] These bills would have deleted the

---

99. *See* Clean Water Authority Restoration Act of 2003, S. 473, 108th Cong., 1st Sess. (2003); Clean Water Authority Restoration Act of 2003, H.R. 962, 108th Cong., 1st Sess. (2003); Clean Water Authority Restoration Act of 2002, S. 2780, 107th Cong., 2d Sess. (2002); Clean Water Authority Restoration Act of 2002, H.R. 5194, 107th Cong., 2d Sess. (2002).

word "navigable" from the jurisdictional language of the Clean Water
Act, and would have enacted into statutory law the Army Corps' pre-
SWANCC jurisdictional regulations, including the Migratory Bird Rule.[100]
This restoration of the status quo ante would have been reinforced with
various legislative findings about how isolated wetlands and waters have
an effect on interstate commerce.[101] The net effect, if the legislation had
been enacted, would have been to force the courts to confront the
constitutional question the Supreme Court avoided in *SWANCC*: whether the substantial effects branch of the Commerce Clause permits
Congress to regulate noneconomic activity—like isolated waters used as
landing strips by migratory birds—when Congress has made formal
findings that this has a substantial effect on interstate commerce.

In effect, the bills laid down the gauntlet, daring the Supreme Court
to enforce its dictum in *Morrison* that only economic activity, not
noneconomic activity, can be aggregated under the substantial effects
test. It is unclear why members of Congress supposedly eager to protect
the environment would relish such a showdown. A safer approach would
be to enact a statute based on the argument set forth in the government's brief in *SWANCC*: that Congress can regulate *economic* activity
like landfilling that results in the loss of isolated waters and wetlands.
Such a statute would almost surely be constitutional under the Court's
recent explications of the Commerce Clause, because it would target
economic rather than noneconomic activity. And it would probably cover
99% of the isolated waters and wetlands reached by the pre-*SWANCC*
regulations.

But for whatever reasons, the safe constitutional solution apparently
has no champion on the Hill. It scarcely matters. All observers agree that
legislation restoring the Army Corps' jurisdiction has little prospect of
being enacted in the closely divided and partisan atmosphere that has
characterized Congress in recent years.[102]

---

100. *See* S. 473, §§ 4–5; H.R. 962, §§ 4–5; Federal Jurisdiction of Navigable Waters
Under Clean Waters: Hearings Before the Subcomm. on Fisheries, Wildlife and Water of
the Senate Comm. on Env't and Public Works, 108th Cong., 1st Sess. (2003) (statement of
Richard Hamann, Associate in Law, University of Florida).

101. *See* S. 473, § 3(8)-(10) ("(8) The pollution or other degradation of waters of the
United States, individually and in the aggregate, has a substantial relation to and effect on
interstate commerce. (9) Protection of the waters of the United States, including intrastate
waters, is necessary to prevent significant harm to interstate commerce and sustain a
robust system of interstate commerce in the future. (10) Waters, including wetlands,
provide protection from flooding, and draining or filling wetlands and channelizing or
filling streams, including intrastate wetlands and streams, can cause or exacerbate flooding, placing a significant burden on interstate commerce.").

102. *See, e.g.,* David E. Kunz, *A River Runs Through It: An Analysis of the
Implications of Solid Waste Agency of Northern Cook County v. United States Army Corps
of Engineers on the Clean Water Act and Federal Environmental Law*, 9 Envtl. Law. 463,

In the absence of congressional action, state and local governments have begun to step into the breach, at least to some degree. Several states have enacted new legislation asserting authority over isolated wetlands.[103] In other states, Illinois for example, the state legislature has not acted, but many counties have adopted preservation measures. According to one report, Lake County quickly adopted regulations that mimicked the U.S. Army Corps regulations, except that they apply to all isolated wetlands. Kane and McHenry Counties followed suit; Du Page already had wetlands regulations on the books more stringent that the Army Corps program; Cook County is studying the matter.[104]

B. The Executive

Like all major judicial decisions, *SWANCC* contains ambiguities that require interpretation. The Court clearly invalidated the Migratory Bird Rule as exceeding the authority conferred by the Clean Water Act. The Court also clearly reaffirmed its holding in *Riverside Bayview*, that jurisdiction under the Act extends to wetlands that are "adjacent" to navigable waterways. Left undecided were other issues, such as whether other rationales for regulating wetlands based on a substantial effects test are permissible under the statute, or whether wetlands that are not "adjacent" to navigable waters may be regulated if they are nevertheless hydrologically connected to some tributary that flows into a body of navigable water.

SWANCC was decided in the waning days of the Clinton Administration. In an attempt to minimize the impact of the decision, the General Counsels of EPA and the Army Corps issued a joint memorandum shortly before inauguration day, interpreting *SWANCC* as invalidating only the Migratory Bird Rule, but not otherwise restricting federal authority.[105]

The Bush Administration proceeded cautiously in developing an approach to the issues raised by *SWANCC*. Nearly two years elapsed

---

485, 487 (2003) (describing H.R. 5194 "not receiv[ing] fanfare" and S. 2780 "not receiv[ing] much publicity or generat[ing] much support in Congress.").

103. Indiana, Ohio, South Carolina, and North Carolina have extended state water quality programs to include isolated wetlands. In June 2001, the Ohio General Assembly passed Substitute House Bill Number 231 (HB 231) to provide protection for isolated wetlands. On May 7, 2002, Wisconsin Governor Scott McCallum (R) signed into law Act 6, giving authority to the Wisconsin Department of Natural Resources to regulate the development of isolated wetlands.

104. John Keilman, *Counties Embrace Wetlands Protection; Changes Follow High Court Ruling*, Chi. Trib., Oct. 28, 2001, at 1.

105. Memorandum from Gary S. Guzy, General Counsel, U.S. Environmental Protection Agency & Robert M. Anderson, Chief Counsel, U.S. Army Corps of Engineers (Jan. 19, 2001), *available at* http://www.epa.gov/owow/wetlands/guidance/SWANCC/swancc-ogc.pdf.

before it did anything at all. Then, in January 2003, the Administration issued an Advance Notice of Proposed Rulemaking (ANPRM), along with a new guidance memorandum.[106] The ANPRM was noncommittal about the implications of *SWANCC*, indicating that new regulations delineating the scope of federal authority under the Clean Water Act would be proposed only after an initial round of public comment. The guidance memorandum, which was non-binding, reaffirmed federal jurisdiction over navigable waters and their adjacent wetlands, and "generally speaking" over tributary systems of navigable waters and their adjacent wetlands.[107] However, where jurisdiction could be based only on the substantial effects test (other than the Migratory Bird Rule invalidated in *SWANCC*), the guidance memorandum cautioned field staff that they should seek "project specific" approval from EPA headquarters before proceeding to assert federal authority.[108] By April 2003, when the time for comment under the ANPRM closed, the Administration had received over 133,000 comments, most of them critical.

The caution turned out to be well advised. On November 6, 2003, the *Los Angeles Times* leaked the information that the Bush Administration was about to release proposed jurisdictional rules.[109] According to the paper, the proposed rules would reaffirm federal authority over non-navigable tributaries of navigable waters and adjacent wetlands of those tributaries.[110] But the proposed rules would have deleted all remaining reliance on the substantial effects test, and would have otherwise limited federal authority to wetlands hydrologically connected to navigable waters.[111] The newspaper claimed that these modifications would "significantly narrow the scope of the Act, stripping many wetlands and streams of federal pollution controls and making them available to being filled for commercial development."[112]

The *L.A. Times* article unleashed editorials from around the country condemning the administration for seeking to "devastate" the federal

---

106. Advance Notice of Proposed Rulemaking on the Clean Water Act Regulatory Definition of "Waters of the United States", 68 Fed. Reg. 1991 (Jan. 15, 2003).

107. Advance Notice of Proposed Rulemaking on the Clean Water Act Regulatory Definition of "Waters of the United States", 68 Fed. Reg. at 1998.

108. Advance Notice of Proposed Rulemaking on the Clean Water Act Regulatory Definition of "Waters of the United States", 68 Fed. Reg. at 1997.

109. Elizabeth Shogren, *Rule Drafted that Would Dilute the Clean Water Act*, L.A. Times, Nov. 6, 2003, at A12.

110. *See* Robert R.M. Verchick, *Toward Normative Rules for Agency Interpretation: Defining Jurisdiction Under the Clean Water Act*, 55 Ala. L. Rev. 845, 871 n.158 (2004) (quoting draft proposed rule).

111. *Id.*

112. Shogren, *supra* note 109.

wetlands regulation program.[113] In the midst of the controversy, President Bush met with representatives of hunting and fishing organizations that favor wetlands preservation on December 12, 2003. Four days later, the White House raised the white flag. EPA issued a press release, reaffirming the Administration's commitment to " 'no net loss' of wetlands," and announcing that it had decided "not [to] issue a new rule on federal regulatory jurisdiction over isolated wetlands."[114] Executive revision of the jurisdictional regulations was dead for the foreseeable future.

C. The Courts

With Congress and the Executive paralyzed, the lower federal courts have been left to their own devices in trying to figure out what *SWANCC* means. It did not take long for a wide-ranging disagreement among these courts to emerge. The decisions can be arrayed along a spectrum. At one extreme stands the Fifth Circuit, which has held that after *SWANCC* the Clean Water Act applies only to navigable waters, wetlands immediately adjacent to navigable waters, and tributaries of navigable waters,[115] a position even more restrictive than that taken in the aborted Bush Administration regulations. An intermediate group of courts, which probably reflects the majority view, holds that the Act applies to navigable waters, adjacent wetlands, and any other body of water (including wetlands) hydrologically connected to navigable waters.[116] At the other extreme, a handful of district courts have held that *SWANCC* invalidated only the Migratory Bird Rule, leaving all other pre-*SWANCC* grounds for federal jurisdiction in place. Thus, these courts would uphold federal jurisdiction over navigable waters, adjacent wetlands, waters hydrologically connected to navigable waters, and waters found to substantially affect interstate commerce, for example because of industrial or recreational usage.[117]

The emerging split among the lower courts reveals how a decision like *SWANCC* can have wholly unanticipated consequences. One would expect post-*SWANCC* disagreement to center on whether the substantial

---

113. *See, e.g.,* Robert F. Kennedy, Jr., *The White House Plays Dirty with the Environment,* L.A. Times, Nov. 24, 2003, at B11; Editorial, *Safeguard 'Minor' Bodies of Water,* Atlanta Journal–Constitution, Dec. 8, 2003, at 12A; Bob Marshall, *Wetlands Change Would Devastate Ducks,* Times–Picayune (New Orleans), Nov. 9, 2003, at 12.

114. Quoted in Verchick, *supra* note 110, at 869.

115. *See* In re Needham, 354 F.3d 340 (5th Cir. 2003); Rice v. Harken Exploration Co., 250 F.3d 264 (5th Cir. 2001).

116. *See, e.g.,* United States v. Rapanos, 376 F.3d 629 (6th Cir. 2004); United States v. Deaton, 332 F.3d 698 (4th Cir. 2003); Headwaters, Inc. v. Talent Irrigation Dist., 243 F.3d 526 (9th Cir. 2001).

117. *See* Brace v. United States, 51 Fed. Cl. 649 (2002); United States v. Krilich, 152 F. Supp. 2d 983 (N.D. Ill. 2001).

effects test can be used to delineate the outer reaches of federal authority. This in fact was the focus of the efforts in Congress to overrule
SWANCC, and the central point of controversy in the Bush Administration's aborted rulemaking. But the lower courts have divided along a
different dimension: how far Congress's authority over navigable waters
can be extended, and in particular whether this authority can be extended to reach any body of water hydrologically connected to navigable
waters. Previously it had been unnecessary to decide how far the power
over "navigable waters" extends, because the Army Corps' regulations
included various substantial effects tests that provided an alternative
basis to reach most of these waters. Now, since most courts have
concluded that *SWANCC* rules out any substantial effects tests, the issue
about how far "navigable waters" can be stretched has come to the fore.
Assuming Congress and the Executive do not act to clear up the
confusion, the Supreme Court will presumably have to resolve this issue
in the not too distant future, given its importance to the scope of federal
authority.

VI. *The Aftermath in Bartlett*

The Supreme Court's decision in *SWANCC* appeared to lift the last
regulatory barrier to moving forward with the balefill. Final state
approval had been given in 1996, when the Illinois Supreme Court
rejected the last challenge to the site. The U.S. Supreme Court's decision
wiped out any federal regulatory jurisdiction over the site. But the
proverbial ink was barely dry on the *SWANCC* opinion before local
opponents of the balefill announced that they would fight on. Mary
Byrne, president of Citizens Against the Balefill, vowed "We're not going
to roll over and play dead."[118] Myron Cherry, Bartlett's environmental
lawyer, dismissed the Court's ruling as a "hypertechnicality," and said
"there are many avenues left open to us."[119] SWANCC officials, for their
part, announced that they were determined to see the project through.
But they sounded a qualified note, refusing to rule out the possibility of
doing "something else" with the land.[120]

In truth, much had changed in the decade of litigation over the
Army Corps' veto of the site. From SWANCC's perspective, the predictions of an impending landfill crisis in Illinois, still common at the
beginning of the decade, had failed to materialize. Illinois EPA had
steadily pushed back the "doomsday" date when the State was projected
to run out of landfill capacity, and it was now clear that private firms

---

118. Michael Higgins, *Despite Win, Balefill Isn't a Done Deal; Agency Could Decide to
Sell Bartlett Site*, Chi. Trib., Jan. 10, 2001, at 12.

119. Matt Arado, *Opponents Say Ruling Only a Setback*, Chi. Daily Herald, Jan. 10,
2001, at 9.

120. Higgins, *supra* note 118.

controlled ample capacity for several decades into the future.[121] Tipping fees, which had been predicted to rise dramatically, hovered at around $30 per ton, approximately the same level they had been a decade earlier. Unable to open the Bartlett site, SWANCC was disposing of its garbage at a Waste Management, Inc. landfill in Bristol, Wisconsin, under a long term contract running to 2015.

From the perspective of Bartlett residents, it was now clearer than ever that the highest and best use for the abandoned gravel pit was real estate development. By 2001, Bartlett was in the midst of a sustained real estate boom.[122] Indeed, after the district court decision upholding the authority of the Army Corps over the site, Bartlett had agreed to rezone some of the land within a mile of the SWANCC property for residential development. A developer had constructed a new subdivision called Westridge in this area, complete with an elementary school ironically-named Nature Ridge, and the properties had sold well.[123] (The residents who purchased these homes had not been deterred by the possibility that the balefill would be constructed, but they could now be counted on to add their strident voices to the chorus of opposition against any plan to complete the project.[124]) Even before the Court's decision, a real estate executive, apparently unaware of the status of the gravel pit as a habitat for migratory birds, expressed the view that the site should be filled in and devoted to residential development.[125] After the decision, a waste management consultant contacted by the *Tribune* opined that "operating a landfill near a high land value area is not going to be the highest value use of the land. They'd be better off selling the land to developers and sending the waste elsewhere, rather than spending all this money on a fancy balefill."[126]

In the wake of the *SWANCC* decision, balefill opponents quickly settled on a two-front strategy composed of carrots and sticks. The carrot part sought to build on the settlement discussions that had taken place on the threshold of oral argument in the Supreme Court. In

---

121. *See* Stevenson Swanson, *New Efforts Take The Edge Off Garbage Crisis*, Chi. Trib., Feb. 11, 1991, at 1.

122. The boom had been building for at least a decade. *See* Ilyce R. Glink, *Growth Spurt: Building Becomes Big in Bartlett*, Chi. Trib., Nov. 4, 1990, at 1; Ilyce R. Glink, *Bartlett Eyes Its Next Century of Progress*, Chi. Trib., Apr. 1, 1989, at 15.

123. Mick Zawislak, *No Longer On The Outskirts; Growth Has Caught Up To Site Of Proposed Trash Dump*, Chi. Daily Herald, May 30, 2000, at 1.

124. Ray Quintanilla, *A Mountain Out Of A Balefill*, Chi. Trib., Sept. 3, 1998, at 1 ("At the 500–home West Ridge subdivision, which is expected to grow by 136 homes in two years, residents remain adamantly opposed.").

125. Zawislak, *supra* note 123.

126. Michael Higgins, *Ruling Doesn't Bury Debate over Balefill; 15 Years Later, Question Remains: Is it Needed?*, Chi. Trib., Jan. 14, 2001, at 1.

particular, they sought to induce the state government, which was in the waning days of a spending binge brought on by the budget surpluses of the late 1990s, to purchase the site. Citizens Against the Balefill organized a letter writing campaign in an effort to persuade the Governor of Illinois, George Ryan, to condemn the Bartlett site and turn it into a state park.[127] This idea did not catch on, but Ryan was sufficiently impressed by the intensity of the campaign that he agreed to meet with Dennis Hastert, now Speaker of the House, to consider how to "make the controversial Bartlett balefill proposal go away for good."[128]

The stick part involved the possibility of new legislation by the Illinois legislature, one of the few political institutions that had not yet been heard from in the endless dispute. To this end, State Senator Doris Karpiel, a Carol Stream Republican and landfill opponent, introduced legislation in the State Senate providing that any unused Illinois EPA permit for a waste-disposal operation would expire after ten years. Since the Bartlett balefill had been approved in 1989, and it was now 2001, the legislation would have had the effect of stripping the project of its existing state operating authority, which would mean SWANCC would have to begin the state permitting process all over again. The bill was quickly passed by the Republican-controlled Senate, by a lopsided 55–2 vote.[129] SWANCC Chairman and Skokie Mayor George Van Dusen admitted he was caught off guard by these developments.[130]

In the House, which was controlled by Democrats, the bill was bottled up in committee. But after Dennis Hastert placed a call to House Speaker Michael Madigan, the bill was discharged from committee by one vote. Speculation swirled that Hastert had promised Madigan unspecified assistance in obtaining federal approval for an expansion of O'Hare Airport as a quid pro quo for help in killing off the balefill. Hastert's spokesman denounced this as "one of the craziest conspiracy theories I've heard in a long time." SWANCC's leaders were not pleased. " 'It stinks,' said Prospect Heights Mayor Ed Rotchford. 'It's Republicans screwing the Republicans. The residents in our communities got screwed.' "[131]

---

127. Sue Ter Maat, *Balefill Opponents Look to Governor for Help*, Chi. Daily Herald, Mar. 7, 2001, at 4.

128. John Patterson & Mick Zawislak, *New Political Muscle in Bartlett Balefill Battle; Ryan, Hastert Working Together to Find a Way to Stop It*, Chi. Daily Herald, Apr. 6, 2001, at 1.

129. Raoul V. Mowatt, *Bill Could Threaten Bartlett Balefill Plan; Senate Vote Might Lead to Big Setback*, Chi. Trib., Apr. 7, 2001, at 12.

130. Patterson & Zawislak, *supra* note 128.

131. John Patterson & John S. Sharp, *A Deal to Defeat the Balefill? Hastert Seeks Madigan's Help to Stop Landfill*, Chi. Daily Herald, May 4, 2001, at 1

The handwriting was now on the wall, and SWANCC moved quickly to secure the best deal it could under the circumstances. On August 9, 2001, Governor Ryan announced the outlines of a settlement. SWNACC would abandon the balefill plan. In return, the State of Illinois would purchase the core of the site where the gravel pit was located and turn it into a state forest preserve. The purchase price would be sufficiently high that, together with other land sales from the tract, SWANCC would be able to recover all costs incurred to date both in acquiring the site and seeking regulatory approvals, estimated to be $31 million.[132]

The *Chicago Tribune*, erstwhile cheerleader for the project, was not pleased by the prospect that Northshore politicians would escape from their ill-conceived venture, with taxpayers throughout the State picking up the tab for their folly:

> While the Cook towns kept shoveling their taxpayers' dollars down this hole, the landfill crisis of the 1970s faded. Against all sense, the Cook towns kept fighting, and their bills for legal costs and environmental studies grew and grew.... This is a plan born of bruised egos. It may stop the landfill. It may satisfy SWANCC. But essentially it would pour another $21 million of public funds into a hole in the ground so warring bureaucrats can all save face.[133]

The extent of the taxpayer bailout of SWANCC was never revealed, but it can be estimated. The State of Illinois purchased the abandoned gravel pit and surrounding perimeter, a total of 284 acres, for $21 million, or $74,000 per acre. The 123 acres in Kane County immediately west of this site were sold to Bluff City Materials, a local gravel mining company, for $2.7 million, or $22,000 per acre. Although land values are never exactly comparable, it would appear based on the prices for these two adjacent parcels that the State paid roughly $14–15 million in excess of the condemnation value of the tract. Meanwhile, SWANCC had little trouble selling the 126 acres to the east of the balefill site, which were originally to serve as a buffer zone, to private developers for more housing subdivisions.[134] The influx of cash allowed SWANCC to pay off its debt and reduce the fees it charged member communities for garbage disposal services, which translated into modest tax reductions for some residents.[135]

---

132. Michael Higgins, *Balefill Battle Winds Down; State Offer To Buy Bartlett Site May End 16–Year Feud*, Chi. Trib., Aug. 10, 2001, at 1.

133. Editorial, *Filling a Landfill With Cash*, Chi. Trib., June 11, 2001, at 12.

134. Sue Ter Maat, *Long Balefill Fight Comes to Happy End for Bartlett*, Chi. Daily Herald, Aug. 9, 2001, at 1.

135. Matt Arado, *Budget Boost Helps Salve Wounds From Demise Of 'Balefill'*, Chi. Daily Herald, Aug. 25, 2002, at 1.

Some of the greatest ironies of the whole saga are presented by the portion of the site in Kane County sold to Bluff City Materials. The company quickly "tore out many of the trees there before anyone even had time to react."[136] Then, in the summer of 2003, Bartlett granted approval to Bluff City to develop a room-and-pillar limestone mine beneath the site, together with a large "damaged-auto sales lot" on the surface and a liquid asphalt plant on an adjacent parcel.[137] Newspapers reported some concern among state officials that underground blasting in the mine would disrupt water flows to the nearby fen, and some concern among residents about increased truck traffic and asphalt odor.[138] But the proposal moved smoothly through the local land use review process, gaining approval of the Bartlett Planning Commission in June 2003, and of the Village Board shortly thereafter.[139]

There are several reasons that might explain why Bluff City's mining and asphalt operation was acceptable to Bartlett residents, whereas SWANCC's sanitary landfill was not. Bluff City, a local Bartlett firm, had operated gravel mines and cement plants in the area for years, and was regarded as a good corporate citizen. For example, in the same summer its request to open the limestone mine was pending, Bluff City donated equipment and employees to grade an abandoned gravel pit for use as a new "showpiece" Little League baseball field for the community.[140] The company also demonstrated good public relations skills, chartering planes on two occasions to take local officials (and the press) to visit a similar mine in Kentucky operated by a partner in the venture.[141] Finally, Bluff City made significant financial concessions to Bartlett, including a $500,000 "annexation fee," and a promise to pay $120,000 to $140,000 per year for thirty years "for the right to mine the land," in addition to ordinary property taxes.[142]

---

136. Eric Peterson, *How Group Won 16–year Balefill Battle*, Chi. Daily Herald, Sept. 23, 2002, at 13.

137. Tom O'Konowtiz & Kara Spak, *Tales of Two Cities*, Chi. Daily Herald, May 30, 2003, at 1.

138. *See* Sue Ter Maat, *With Thoughts on Home, Officials Visit Mine Again*, Chi. Daily Herald, Feb. 14, 2003, at 4 (noting effort by one area resident to mount a campaign against the project); Ted Gregory, *Bartlett Officials Praise Kentucky Mine; Similar Site Planned Locally*, Chi. Trib., Mar. 2, 2003, at 5L (noting concern by Illinois Nature Preserve Commission about possible disruption of water flow to fen).

139. Sue Ter Maat, *Bartlett Planners Back Proposal for Mining Operation*, Chi. Daily Herald, June 12, 2003, at 4.

140. Eileen O. Daday, *Bartlett's New Sports Park Honors Late Mayor*, Chi. Daily Herald, June 15, 2003, at 3. The Little League fields were named for Glen A. Koehler, the Village President who had been ousted by balefill opponent John Stark in 1989.

141. *See* Ter Maat, *supra* note 138; Gregory, *supra* note 138.

142. Sue Ter Maat, *supra* note 139.

Still, it is more than a little jarring that a town which fought so tenaciously for sixteen years to stop a government-operated balefill operation would acquiesce in a decision to use part of the same property for a limestone mine and asphalt refinery, with barely a whimper of opposition. While placing compressed bales of garbage in a carefully lined cell above an aquifer had been described as pulling a pin on an ecological grenade, only a few voices spoke out against a plan that called for daily discharges of dynamite above the same aquifer. And while a landfill was perceived to pose an unacceptable threat to residential property values, a potentially smelly asphalt plant was viewed with apparent equanimity.

Conclusion

The story of *SWANCC* raises many questions about the law and politics of locally unwanted land uses. Although these questions cannot all be enumerated here, let alone explored in any detail, a few deserve brief mention:

-What does the story tell us about the design of legal institutions that it took sixteen years and millions of dollars in legal and consulting fees to decide that a garbage dump should not be located in Bartlett, Illinois? The story suggests that local communities that desperately want to avoid becoming the home of a garbage dump will get their way in the end. Granting such communities a veto over siting decisions would allow this result to be reached much more quickly and at much less cost. Private waste disposal companies would then concentrate on locating disposal sites in communities willing to waive their veto rights, for a price. Although the Illinois statute giving local communities the right to veto landfill sites has been criticized for contributing to a landfill "crisis,"[143] the story suggests that the statute may in fact reflect a sensible policy. From this perspective, the problem that created the marathon litigation in *SWANCC* was that the site was located in an unincorporated area, which meant Bartlett did not have a statutory veto. This in turn suggests that the fatal misstep may have been Bartlett's decision to refuse to annex the site in 1986. If it had agreed to annexation, it could have exercised the veto power given by the Illinois statute. But perhaps because the balefill opponents did not trust their political leaders at that time, or were simply legally unsophisticated, the opponents fought against annexation, which denied them a veto.[144] They had to fight for sixteen years to get it back by other means.

---

143. *See* Burton, *supra* note 7.

144. Bartlett learned its lesson quickly. When another landfill project was proposed in 1988, the town quickly annexed the site and denied permission to build a landfill. *See* John Lucadamo, *Bartlett Puts Landfill Site Out Of Reach*, Chi. Trib., Feb. 12, 1988, at 1.

-What does the episode suggest about the wisdom of spreading alarm about the nation "running out" of landfill capacity? Many environmental groups and environmental regulators deliberately promoted the "running out" idea in the 1980s—however implausible it seems in retrospect, given the vast empty spaces in America—as a way to motivate people to recycle. In one sense, the strategy worked, witness the 40% reduction in waste volume achieved through recycling by Northshore communities. But it also had the effect of creating a dogged determination on the part of SWANCC officials to persist with the Bartlett balefill scheme, in the face of mounting evidence that commercial disposal sites were readily available in more rural areas. SWANCC's conviction that it had to act to secure disposal capacity somewhere in Cook County created great animosity between suburbs in the east and west parts of the county, generated enormous legal and consulting expenses that went for naught, and produced a Supreme Court decision restricting the authority of the federal government over isolated waters.

-What does the story tell us about the psychological forces that produce the NIMBY response? Most of the story seems straightforward: Bartlett residents feared that their water supply would be poisoned, and their property values undermined. But late in the story a discordant fact emerges: Real estate developers experienced little difficulty in selling homes in a new subdivision within a mile of the balefill site, notwithstanding legally mandated disclosure to prospective purchasers of the plans for the site, which was visible from the homes. And the final twist to the story, Bartlett's nonchalant approval of an limestone mine and asphalt refinery on the parcel immediately west of the abandoned gravel pit, casts further doubt on the notion that the fury over the site was simply a response to the risk of groundwater contamination or a threat to property values. All of which suggests that perhaps the social stigma attached to being the dumping ground for someone else's garbage may provide a better explanation for the passions the balefill project stirred. That is, the balefill may have touched a raw nerve because it represented a reminder to the striving lower-middle class residents of Bartlett that they were regarded as the economic and social inferiors of the upper-middle and upper class residents of the Northshore. The limestone mine and asphalt plant, whatever threat to groundwater and property values they might pose, did not have this connotation.

-Finally, what does the story tell us about the role of federalism in environmental law? The textbook picture of environmental federalism posits that state institutions should attend to local problems, while federal institutions attend to multi-jurisdictional problems. In our story, this line of division was little observed. The Army Corps of Engineers, a federal agency, got involved in the balefill controversy because of a multi-jurisdictional problem, preserving a habitat for migratory birds.

But it ultimately vetoed the project because of worries about protecting a groundwater aquifer, largely a local concern. The Supreme Court stripped the Corps of jurisdiction over the site, thereby restoring control to state institutions. But it did so in a way that left many waters and wetlands of multi-jurisdictional significance without any effective federal protection. Moreover, the partisans in the struggle over the Bartlett balefill drew no distinction between federal and state actors. What is most astonishing is the number and variety of political institutions the contesting parties were able to call upon: city, county, state agency, state judiciary, state legislature, state governor, federal agencies, Congress, and the federal judiciary. Our federal system of government gave them almost limitless opportunities to move back and forth between different levels and branches of government in response to their perceptions of where their tactical advantage lay. If the will to persist had not finally subsided, it is conceivable that they could still be fighting today.*

---

* Many thanks to Jodie Kirshner for her invaluable research assistance.

*

10

Christopher H. Schroeder

The Story of *American Trucking*: The Blockbuster Case that Misfired

Introduction

In *Whitman v. American Trucking Ass'ns (American Trucking)*,[1] business and industry petitioners made a frontal assault on a central feature of the Clean Air Act Amendments of 1970: they challenged the authority of the Environmental Protection Agency to set air quality standards for ubiquitous air pollutants. The immediate details of the litigation are themselves engaging, but the full story of *American Trucking* stretches back in time to the original enactment of those Amendments. It stretches back, actually, not just to those Amendments, but also to a whole body of laws Congress enacted in the late 1960s and into the 1970s known as the "new social legislation."

Political scientists ascribe the label "new social legislation" to these laws to distinguish them from the earlier New Deal wave of legislation that directly regulated businesses in the name of economic stability and growth.[2] An even better reason to consider these laws "new" is that many of them adopt a new regulatory philosophy. The new social

---

1. Whitman v. American Trucking Ass'ns, 531 U.S. 457 (2001). Disclosing my prior biases, I represented the Clean Air Trust in filing an amicus brief in the part of the case concerning whether the Clean Air Act allows consideration of costs in the setting of national ambient air quality standards. The amicus brief contended that the Act does not permit consideration of costs in the setting of such standards.

2. Richard A. Harris & Sidney N. Milkis, *The Politics of Regulatory Change: A Tale of Two Agencies* vii (2d ed. 1996) (providing that the new social legislation "involved the federal government directly in so-called quality of life issues such as safety in the workplace, affirmative action, pollution control, and consumer protection."); *see also* David Vogel, *The "New" Social Regulation in Historical and Comparative Perspective, in Regulation in Perspective* 155, 161–75 (Thomas K. McCraw ed., 1981) (chronicling the development of recent safety and environmental regulation).

legislation—and especially those parts of it dealing with environmental, health and safety issues—embraces a preventative or anticipatory approach to problem-solving. This approach contrasts with an approach based on common law principles, under which government intervention is unjustified until the existence of significant harm has been clearly demonstrated and the particular burdens to be placed on business and industry have been justified by the particular benefits to be achieved.

At first, the regulated community strongly resisted many of these new laws and sought to repeal them. While such efforts continue, the strategies employed by the regulated community toward these laws have also necessarily become more nuanced, because that community realizes that almost all of the goals of this legislation are highly prized by the American people. Being opposed to these goals is neither a good political nor a good business strategy.

Business and industry have shifted their point of attack away from the legislation's laudable goals—everyone is for clean air—and toward their lousy means—everyone is against government bureaucracy, waste, inefficiency and one-size-fits-all solutions. Accordingly, the legislation comes under attack for being inefficient, overly expensive and even counterproductive; for sacrificing jobs and competitiveness needlessly; for burying small businesses in paperwork; for relying on national bureaucrats rather than state and local governments or private organizations; for being driven by hysterical fears rather than real problems; and for being based on incompetent analysis using inferior science and inaccurate estimates of costs. The focus on means also seeks to convert a battle between villains and victims into a discussion among people who share the same goals, and ultimately to persuade citizens that there are great advantages to thinking about regulatory means in common law terms.

Litigation like *American Trucking* is ideally suited to play a significant role in this more indirect strategy. Indeed, the litigation arm of the strategy becomes increasingly important in light of the inability of business and industry coalitions to change the operative texts of many important statutes, as they so dramatically failed to do during the first years of the Gingrich Revolution.[3]

As *American Trucking* wended its way from the D.C. Circuit to the Supreme Court, it appeared as though business and industry interests might have found the blockbuster case, with the potential to exceed their greatest expectations of what litigation might accomplish. A successful attack on the ambient air quality provision under any legal theory would be of monumental importance all by itself if it would decrease the likelihood that these provisions would generate costly new anti-pollution

---

3. *See infra* text accompanying notes 44–45.

obligations. There are very few environmental regulatory actions whose national compliance costs are even remotely comparable to those triggered by new ambient standards.[4] Beyond this, some of the legal theories put into play in *American Trucking* would not only prevent specific regulatory decisions regarding ozone and particulate matter from going into effect; they would also transform the ambient air quality provisions of the Clean Air Act, one of the crystalline forms of preventative legislation, into the common law approach. Furthermore, if the regulated community could succeed here, the same legal theories would almost certainly ripple outwards to impact other aspects of national environmental law and policy as well. Thus there was a tremendous amount at stake in *American Trucking*.

This chapter presents the story of *American Trucking* from both its longer-and shorter-term perspectives. Part II takes up EPA's regulatory action and its initial reception in the D.C. Circuit. Part III traces the story of efforts by the regulated community to restore the preferred regulatory approach. Part IV picks up the story in the Supreme Court.

I. The D.C. Circuit

Ozone and particulate matter (PM) are two of the six pollutants that EPA regulates as "criteria" pollutants under the Clean Air Act. So named because the agency issues "Criteria Documents" for each of them, these pollutants are ubiquitous, produced by numerous sources and associated with significant adverse health effects.[5] When the EPA revised the standards for ozone and PM in 1997, it was reacting to substantial scientific evidence documenting those adverse effects. With respect to PM, epidemiological studies associated existing PM levels with perhaps as many as 60,000 premature deaths in the United States annually. Other studied linked ozone with respiratory problems in children, especially asthma, as well as bronchitis and congestive heart failure. EPA also reviewed evidence suggesting that these adverse health effects became less prevalent as the amount of these pollutants in the air was reduced, but the evidence did not affirmatively demonstrate that there was any level of exposure above zero where adverse health effects were entirely non existent.

The statutory provisions covering criteria pollutants are demanding and complex. EPA must set ambient standards that are "requisite to protect the public health," "allowing an adequate margin of safety."[6] This then triggers state obligations to write specific emissions limitations

---

4. There are also few regulatory changes that achieve even remotely comparable public health benefits.

5. EPA has recognized six criteria pollutants: oxides of nitrogen, sulfur dioxide, carbon monoxide, lead, ozone and particulate matter.

6. Clean Air Act § 109(b)(1), 42 U.S.C. § 7409(b)(1) (2000).

for stationary sources that will "achieve and maintain" those standards. The Act places states under tough deadlines to make those decisions and now contains additional federally imposed requirements for air sheds that are significantly out-of-compliance with the standards.

EPA had last revised the ozone standard in 1979. The statute mandates revisiting ambient standards every five years, and EPA's 1997 action came in response to environmental organization litigation to enforce that mandate. The agency announced a lowered requirement of .08 ppm averaged over an 8–hour period.[7] In the case of PM, the existing standard measured particles of ten microns or less in diameter, and imposed a 24–hour standard of 150 micrograms per cubic meter. These standards for so-called coarse particles were continued unchanged, but EPA also added tougher requirements for fine particles, those with diameters of 2.5 microns or less, because of mounting evidence that these fine particles are considerably more hazardous than the large ones in their ability to penetrate tissue in the lungs.

EPA examined all of the scientific studies relevant to the question of whether exposure to ozone or PM was associated with adverse health effects. It took into account "the nature and severity of the health effects involved, the size of the sensitive population(s) at risk, the types of health information available, and the kind and degree of uncertainties" presented by the existing science.[8] Such uncertainties are themselves ubiquitous in environmental standard setting at the levels that concern regulators. Thinking a substance to be clearly hazardous at some level of exposure is entirely consistent with uncertainty about how hazardous it is at much lower levels.

The statute does not instruct the administrator on how to combine all of these factors, nor does it define "public health" or "adverse health effect" or "adequate[] protect[ion]" or "margin of safety." When all of the science has been analyzed and all of the relevant considerations chronicled, EPA is necessarily required to add an element of additional judgment in order to come to a conclusion and take action under the statute; this is precisely what the statute contemplates.[9]

---

7. EPA typically does not adopt a single numerical standard but instead promulgates a "suite" of standards that may include several different averaging times, concentration levels, a statistical measure of compliance and, in the case of PM, a particle size. In the case of ozone, EPA moved from a 1–hour short-term standard to an 8–hour standard due to scientific findings suggesting the greater importance of the longer exposure time. A 1–hour, .12 ppm standard (the previous standard) corresponds roughly to an 8–hour, .09 ppm standard.

8. National Ambient Air Quality Standards for Ozone, 62 Fed. Reg. 38,856, 38,883 (July 18, 1997).

9. The EPA is to issue standards which "in the judgment of the Administrator ... are requisite to protect the public health," "allowing an adequate margin of safety." Clean Air Act § 109(b)(1), 42 U.S.C. § 7409(b)(1) (2000).

In reaching that judgment, EPA administrator Carol Browner took one possible source of supplementation off the table. The ambient air quality provisions did not permit the EPA to take into account the feasibility of meeting the standards, nor to weigh their compliance costs against the health and welfare benefits. Instead, EPA was to set standards solely on the basis of its understanding of the adverse health effects of exposure and on its judgment as to what level of exposure would adequately protect public health. That had been the consistent agency interpretation of the statute from the very beginning.[10] It had also been confirmed in an influential court of appeals decision in 1980, *Lead Industries Ass'n v. EPA*.[11] *Lead Industries* endorsed a preventative as opposed to a common law reading of the statute.[12] The D.C. Circuit subsequently affirmed *Lead Industries'* central holding at least three times, and the Supreme Court consistently denied certiorari.[13]

If such countervailing considerations as feasibility and cost are not to be taken into account, how then should the administrator determine when air quality is "adequate"? Whatever the answer to this question, one thing is clear: in answering it, the administrator will be filling in a detail, albeit a crucial detail, that Congress has not provided. As Carol Browner herself said when proposing the ozone and PM standards, "the question is not one of science, the real question is one of judgment."[14]

It was this exercise of judgment that business and industry attacked in *American Trucking*. Business and industry challengers consolidated into two main groups: Non–State Petitioners/Intervenors and Small Business Petitioners/Intervenors, each represented by seasoned litigators

---

10. EPA's first administrator, William Ruckelshaus, issued the first ambient air quality standards in 1971. National Primary and Secondary Ambient Air Quality Standards, 36 Fed. Reg. 8186 (Apr. 30, 1971). At that time, he stated that the "Clean Air Act ... does not permit any factors other than health to be taken into account ... " *Id.*

11. Lead Indus. Ass'n v. EPA, 647 F.2d 1130 (D.C. Cir.), *cert. denied*, 449 U.S. 1042 (1980).

12. *See* discussion *infra*, notes 35–39.

13. *See* Natural Res. Def. Council, Inc. v. EPA, 902 F.2d 962 (D.C. Cir. 1990), *vacated in part by* 921 F.2d 326 (D.C. Cir.), *cert. denied*, 498 U.S. 1082 (1991) (upholding 1987 PM standards); Natural Res. Def. Council, Inc. v. EPA, 824 F.2d 1146 (en banc) (D.C. Cir. 1987) (endorsing *Lead Industries* in case interpreting the hazardous air pollutants provision of the Clean Air Act); American Petroleum Inst. v. Costle, 665 F.2d 1176 (D.C. Cir. 1981), *cert denied*, 455 U.S. 1034 (1982) (upholding 1979 ozone standards).

14. Quoted in *Air Pollution: Agency Announces Proposals to Toughen Regulations for Ozone, Particulate Matter,* 27 Env't Rep. Cur. Dev. (BNA) 1571 (1996). Administrator Browner was not always so candid. Later, she is quoted as saying "I think it is not a question of judgment, I think it is a question of science." *Air Quality Standards: Science–Driven Ozone, PM Proposals will be Finished by July 19, EPA Says,* 27 Env't Rep. Cur. Dev. (BNA) 2068 (1997). The inconsistency is pointed out by Craig N. Oren, *Run Over By American Trucking, Part I: Can EPA Revive Its Air Quality Standards?*, 29 Envtl. L. Rep. 10653 (Envtl. L. Inst. 1999).

eager for an opportunity to take on the crucial premise that the Clean Air Act precluded the agency from considering costs when setting the ambient standards.[15] The non-State Petitioners challenged *Lead Indus-tries* by claiming that the decision had misinterpreted the Clean Air Act and also by arguing that revisions of ambient standards, as opposed to initial standard setting, were governed by different provisions. On a separate flank, the Small Business petitioners claimed that a recent statute, the Small Business Regulatory Enforcement Fairness Act of 1996 (SBREFA)[16] required EPA to consider regulatory alternatives less burdensome on small businesses.

Other challenges raised by petitioners could also be traced back to the common law model. In addition to a norm of weighing costs against benefits and acknowledging technological feasibility, the common law approach emphasizes the need for a convincing demonstration of harm. Business and industry challengers argued that the evidence in support of further tightening of the standards was simply inconclusive. Thus the quality of the administrative record as a factual matter also became a basis for challenging the rule. Together with the benefit-cost challenge, this attack on the "inclusive evidence" in the record nicely framed the major differences between the preventative and common law approaches.[17]

American Trucking drew a three-judge panel of Stephen Williams, Douglas Ginsburg and David Tatel. It was a powerhouse panel quite likely to give a sympathetic ear to the challenges brought by the regulated community. Stephen Williams had written widely on adminis-trative law both as a sitting judge and during the nearly twenty years he had been a professor of administrative law at the University of Colorado, before being appointed to the bench by President Reagan. Doug Gins-burg had briefly been President Reagan's nominee to the Supreme Court, after Judge Bork's nomination had been defeated by the Senate and before Nina Totenburg exposed Ginsburg's marijuana smoking with his students while teaching at the Harvard Law School. The third member of the panel, David Tatel, a recent appointee of President

---

15. Challenges were also lodged by a number of states and by several environmental organizations, including the American Lung Association and Environmental Defense. They urged that the revisions were too lax.

16. Pub. L. No. 104–12, Title II, 110 Stat. 864 (codified as amended in scattered sections of 5, 15, and 28 U.S.C.).

17. *American Trucking*, of course, was more than a vehicle for litigating regulatory philosophy. As already indicated, there is a lot at stake when any ambient standard is revised, and so the challengers had a strong interest in prevailing on any theory at all, whether or not the theory fit into the larger business and industry agenda or was statute- or fact-specific. Accordingly, business and industry petitioners made other statutory and factual arguments, some of them applicable to one ambient revision but not the other. For a more comprehensive summary of the issues raised, *see* Oren, *supra* note 14.

Clinton, could be expected to be more receptive to agency arguments in defense of a preventative rule aimed at protecting the public health.

The panel decision ran true to form, giving business petitioners a significant legal victory and remanding the standards to the EPA for further consideration. Somewhat surprisingly, however, the broadest legal defect found by the panel was that the *Environmental Protection Agency* had violated the nondelegation doctrine:

> Although the factors EPA uses in determining the degree of public health concern associated with different levels of ozone and PM are reasonable, EPA appears to have articulated no "intelligible principle" to channel its application of these factors; nor is one apparent from the statute.... Here it is as though Congress commanded EPA to select "big guys," and EPA announced that it would evaluate candidates based on height and weight, but revealed no cut-off point. The announcement, though sensible in what it does say, is fatally incomplete. The reasonable person responds, "How tall? How heavy?"[18]

In a graduate seminar, someone might here pipe up to say that this argument commits a category mistake. The nondelegation doctrine is a constitutional doctrine applicable to the *Congress*, not to the administrative agencies. The doctrine prohibits the Congress from giving away its legislative power by enacting laws to be implemented by others without giving those others an intelligible principle to apply. It has also never been a terribly powerful doctrine, seldom invoked successfully, and never in this way. Only twice has the Court used it to invalidate a law.[19] At other times, the Court has invoked the doctrine more modestly, combining it with the canon of statutory construction that statutes should be construed to avoid constitutional infirmities, to construe statutes narrowly to avoid a potential nondelegation problem.[20] Never, however, has the Supreme Court held that an *administrative agency* violates the nondelegation doctrine when it fails to develop its own intelligible principle pursuant to a statute that lacks one.

This novel aspect of the opinion was made even more intriguing because the argument had scarcely been briefed by the parties. Although Judge Williams credits the Small Business Petitioners with arguing the point,[21] in fact their merits brief devotes less than one page to it in a

---

18. American Trucking Ass'ns v. EPA, 175 F.3d 1027, 1034 (D.C. Cir. 1999).

19. A.L.A. Schechter Poultry Corp. v. United States, 295 U.S. 495 (1935) and Panama Refining Co. v. Ryan, 293 U.S. 388 (1935).

20. See the discussion of *Industrial Union Dep't, AFL–CIO v. American Petroleum Inst.*, 448 U.S. 607 (1980), *infra* note 24.

21. *American Trucking Ass'ns*, 175 F.3d at 1034 (noting that these petitioners argued that "EPA has construed §§ 108 & 109 of the Clean Air Act so loosely as to render them unconstitutional delegations of legislative power").

thirty-page filing.[22] In that abbreviated discussion, they cite only two cases. One is *Industrial Union Department, AFL–CIO v. American Petroleum Institute (Benzene)*,[23] but Justice Stevens' plurality opinion for the Supreme Court in that case merely invokes nondelegation in one of the traditional ways, as the basis for construing the OSHAct to restrict OSHA's discretion more than the administrator had thought that it did.[24] Judge Williams' opinion, in contrast, does not construe the Clean Air Act in any specific way to narrow it; rather it finds that the agency has itself violated the doctrine by failing to narrow the statute by supplementing it with an intelligible principle of its own.

The second citation was to *International Union, UAW v. OSHA*, 938 F.2d 1310 (D.C. Cir. 1991) (*Lockout/Tagout I*),[25] and this does a better job explaining the doctrine's provenance, albeit in an entirely self-referential way. *Lockout/Tagout I* is a prior decision by none other than Judge Williams himself. The decision's greatest notoriety comes from its peroration on the virtues of benefit-cost analysis. The virtue of benefit-cost analysis warranted such attention that Judge Williams authored an unusual concurrence with his own opinion for the panel to explain how benefit-cost analysis was nothing more than common sense. He traced its pedigree back to Ben Franklin's "prudential algebra," which Franklin had described to a friend as a process for making difficult decisions. The way he did it, Franklin wrote, was to divide a piece of paper in half, and then list the pros on one side and the cons on the other. Once that was done, the decision was easier.

In the immediate context of *Lockout/Tagout I*, the praise of benefit cost analysis supported Williams' conclusion that the most sensible way to construe the operative phrase "reasonably necessary and appropriate" in the OSHAct was to call for benefit-cost analysis. Read more generously, though, it anticipates being able to interpret a wide range of statutory

---

22.   Brief of Small Business Petitioners and Intervenors at 20–21, *American Trucking Ass'ns* (No. 97–1441 and consolidated cases).

23.   Industrial Union Dep't, AFL–CIO, 448 U.S. 607 (1980). The case is commonly referred to as the *Benzene* decision, because it involved OSHA's proposed regulation on the amount of benzene to which workers could be exposed. *Benzene's* story is told in Chapter 5 of this volume.

24.   *Id.* at 646 (adopting a construction of the OSHAct requiring OSHA to make a determination that existing exposures to a toxic agent posed a "significant risk," because otherwise "the statute would make such a 'sweeping delegation of legislative power' that it might be unconstitutional under the Court's reasoning") in *A.L.A. Schechter Poultry Corp. v. United States*, 295 U.S. 495, 539 (1935) and *Panama Refining Co. v. Ryan*, 293 U.S. 388 (1935).

25.   938 F.2d 1310 (D.C. Cir. 1991). The case is called this because it dealt with OSHA regulations proscribing when businesses had to protect workers from dangerous equipment by the use of locks rather than simply tagging the equipment to alert workers that it is dangerous.

phrases as calling for benefit-cost analysis, perhaps even all statutory phrases that do not explicitly prohibit benefit-cost analysis. It does for benefit-cost analysis what *A House is a House for Me* does for houses.[26]

In its rulemaking, OSHA had concluded that the pertinent statutory provisions established a significant risk/feasibility regulatory regime, meaning that once OSHA had found the presence of a significant risk in the workplace it could regulate up to the point of technological and economic feasibility, but that it also had the discretion to stop short of that point as well. Judge Williams found this unfettered discretion invalid under the nondelegation doctrine, and remanded to the agency for it to try again, after providing advice that a benefit-cost approach to regulation would certainly be a valid alternative.

Despite the nondelegation rhetoric, *Lockout/Tagout I* could also be read as a more garden variety statutory interpretation opinion, in which the D.C. Circuit was simply rejecting a particular interpretation put forward by the agency. *American Trucking* presented a more elaborate version of the argument, and made it clear that Judge Williams had something distinctive in mind: he sought to use the doctrine as a device to extract a more articulated explanation from the agency as to why it chose one particular numerical standard for ozone and PM rather than some other number. In his view, only such an articulated explanation would provide the intelligible principle that was lacking from the statute itself.

Although the petitioners were pleased to benefit from Judge Williams' extension of nondelegation theory from *Lockout/Tagout I* to *American Trucking*, they would have much preferred Judge Williams to have carried forward the *A House is a House for Me* theme of *Lockout/Tagout I*, and to have read the Clean Air Act to permit or compel benefit-cost analysis. Here they were disappointed. *American Trucking* rejected each of the various arguments petitioners had advanced either to undermine *Lead Industries* or to argue that it did not apply.[27] Judge

---

26. The book's illustrations and text develop ever less obvious examples of houses and things that live in them, such as a husk being a house for an ear of corn, and a throat being a house for a hum:

And once you get started in thinking this way,

It seems that whatever you see

Is either a house or it lives in a house,

And a house is a house for me!

Mary Ann Hoberman, *A House is a House for Me* (Betty Fraser illus., Puffin Books 1978).

27. *American Trucking Ass'ns*, 175 F.3d at 1040–41. As for the application of SBREFA's requirement that the EPA must minimize the impact of its rule on small business—the major argument put forward by the Small Business Petitioners for distinguishing *Lead Industries*—the D.C. Circuit agreed with the EPA's contention that SBRE-

Williams seems to have concluded that *Lead Industries* was too firmly established as the law of the Circuit.[28]

Despite this adherence to *Lead Industries*, Judge Williams' opinion was not entirely unhelpful on the benefit-cost point. In much the same way as he had in *Lockout/Tagout I*, Judge Williams took notice of the fact that benefit-cost analysis certainly would be a very sensible way to supply the ambient provisions with an intelligible principle. Committing the agency to set the standards at the point at which the line charting decreasing benefits crosses the line charting increasing costs in principle defines a point that could serve as a "determinate, binding standard[]" that would resolve the nondelegation problem.[29] That point also is normatively reasonable from the perspective of the common law approach;[30] indeed, it may be the only normatively reasonable point from that perspective. Judge Williams thus lays out the basic contours of an argument that challengers would use in the Supreme Court.

American Trucking provided an even more important boost to the benefit-cost argument, because it virtually guaranteed petitioners a hearing in the Supreme Court. Their own stand-alone application would most likely have been rejected as not cert-worthy. Not only was there no circuit split,[31] but the Court had also already declined nearly identical requests three times previously, including in *Lead Industries* itself.[32]

FA was inapplicable to its ambient air standard setting. SBREFA applies only to federal actions that will have a significant impact on small business, and under the statutory scheme it is the state measures implementing the new standards that will cause such impacts, not the federal standards all by themselves. So SBREFA was simply inapplicable to the EPA's rulemaking. *Id.* at 1055–45.

28. He and the other panelists may have been particularly influenced by *Natural Res. Def. Council, Inc. v. EPA*, 824 F.2d 1146 (D.C. Cir. 1987) (en banc). This case involved a challenge under the hazardous air pollutants provision of the Clean Air Act, which was then indistinguishable from the ambient provisions in addressing whether costs were to be considered in standard setting. The earlier panel decision in the case, authored by Judge Bork, had called *Lead Industries* into question, but the *en banc* court had endorsed *Lead Industries*. Subsequently, Congress had amended the hazardous air pollutants provisions to back off from a health-effects only form of regulation, but had left the ambient provisions unchanged. Congressional inaction is always a slippery reed, but this, too, may have had some influence on the *American Trucking* panel.

29. *American Trucking Ass'ns*, 175 F.3d at 1038.

30. See *Lockout/Tagout I's* discussion of how "reasonableness" can be given a benefit-cost connotation that is consistent with the common law definition of negligence. *Int'l Union, UAW v. OSHA*, 938 F.2d at 1319.

31. The D.C. Circuit has exclusive venue for hearing such challenges. *See infra* text accompanying notes 51–53.

32. *See* Natural Res. Def. Council, Inc. v. EPA, 902 F.2d 962 (D.C. Cir. 1990), *vacated in part by* 921 F.2d 326 (D.C. Cir.), *cert. denied*, 498 U.S. 1082 (1991); American Petroleum Inst. v. Costle, 665 F.2d 1176 (D.C. Cir. 1981), *cert. denied*, 455 U.S. 1034 (1982); Lead Indus. Ass'n v. EPA, 647 F.2d 1130 (D.C. Cir.), *cert. denied*, 449 U.S. 1042 (1980).

Now, however, the United States was virtually compelled to appeal the nondelegation holding due to the far reaching ramifications of Judge Williams' novel theory. Once the government appealed, Judge Williams' opinion then supplied the template for the petitioners to argue that the *Lead Industries* holding was so closely implicated by the nondelegation issue that it became fair game for the Supreme Court. If benefit-cost analysis was actually contemplated by the Clean Air Act, the nondelegation problem perceived by Williams went away. Law of the circuit might constrain the D.C. Circuit; in the Supreme Court the question would be one of first impression.

Small Business Petitioners followed the belt-and-suspenders strategy of not relying exclusively on logical connection to get the costs issue before the Court. They also took the fairly unusual step of filing a conditional cross-petition for a writ of certiorari. Reversing the D.C. Circuit on its adherence to *Lead Industries* would permit the Court to avoid "the constitutional nondelegation issue on which EPA focuses."[33]

II. The Larger Battleground

A. The Shift in Regulatory Philosophy

Although Congress had addressed air quality issues as recently as the 1967 Air Quality Act, it revisited the issue in 1970 and enacted changes that were radical departures from earlier federal efforts. The 1970 Amendments were hard hitting, aggressive and expensive. They took a "stick to the states" to prod them into action and imposed very substantial costs on the private sector.[34] Although elements of the law have been characterized as merely "symbolic," that label clearly does not apply to the law as a whole.[35] Nothing evidences the non-symbolic character of the Clean Air Act Amendments of 1970 better than its price tag. The law has become "one of the most costly pieces of regulatory legislation in history,"[36] costing the private sector—primarily business and industry—$523 billion between 1970 and 1990.[37]

---

33. Conditional Cross–Petition for Writ of Certiorari at 1, *American Trucking Ass'ns* (No. 99–1426).

34. *See* Union Elec. Co. v. EPA, 427 U.S. 246, 249 (1976).

35. John P. Dwyer, *The Pathology of Symbolic Legislation*, 17 Ecology L.Q. 233 (1990).

36. Kenneth Chilton & Ronald Pennoyer, *"Making the Clean Air Act More Cost Effective"*, Working Paper (St. Louis: Center for the Study of American Business, Sept. 1981), *quoted in* David Vogel, *A Case Study of Clean Air Legislation 1967–1981, in The Impact of the Modern Corporation* 309, 314 (Betty Bock et al. eds., 1984).

37. Environmental Protection Agency, *The Benefits and Costs of the Clean Air Act, 1970–1990* ES–2 (Oct. 1997), *available at* http://www.epa.gov/air/sect812/copy.html. The ambient provisions have also achieved health benefits; the monetary value of these benefits

The 1970 Clean Air Act Amendments exemplify the preventative approach to environmental quality. Prevention has four important elements. *First*, the public has a legitimate claim to an environment free, to the maximum extent possible, from significant health risks associated with pollution and other human-generated stressors. *Second*, government appropriately can act in the public's interest in a preventative or anticipatory manner, once there is a reasonable basis to believe that harm may occur, but in advance of any harm actually occurring. *Third*, technological innovation ought to be stimulated to achieve whatever advances are necessary to achieve the goals of a clean and safe environment while also enabling satisfactory economic growth and prosperity. *Fourth*, implementing these principles requires a sense of urgency.

The preventative approach departs sharply from traditional assumptions, which up to this time largely mirrored those that governed common law tort litigation, as they had developed over the centuries.[38] Under the principles of common law tort, corrective action typically waits for a convincing showing that harm was being caused, or was substantially likely to be caused. Even when harm is shown, deciding whether or not to regulate frequently entails evaluating whether the benefits of action outweigh the costs of compliance.[39]

Not only were these common law principles dominant in the policy community, common law litigation itself was the major legal response to issues of environmental hazards until the latter part of the twentieth century. When health-protective legislation or local ordinances were enacted, it was deficiencies in the common law litigation system, not in its underlying substantive principles, that provided the reason for the supplemental legislation. Litigation was and is a poor instrument when harms are diffuse or their sources numerous, or when technological innovation is required for adequate abatement. In such cases, regulation might step in. That legislation, however, like common law suits, was predicated on well-proven existing hazards whose sources could be identified. Likewise, regulation would typically demand only what was

---

is calculated to be greatly in excess of those costs. The report provides that the total monetized benefits of the Clean Air Act between 1970 and 1990 ranges from 5.6 to 49.4 trillion dollars, with a central estimate of 22.2 trillion dollars. *Id.* at ES–8.

38. The core principles of tort are, of course, contested territory. This paragraph means to describe those principles that business and industry interests have embraced. While these principles amount to a plausible interpretation of common law tort principles, it is by no means the only possible interpretation. The debate over whether the principles identified here with common law tort do in fact constitute the best reconstruction of evolving common law principles is beyond the scope of this chapter.

39. This analysis is akin to the traditional "balance of the equities" that a court, sitting equity, undertakes in considering whether an injunction should issue to remedy a legal violation. See Boomer v. Atlantic Cement Co., 26 N.Y.2d 219, 257 N.E.2d 870, 309 N.Y.S.2d 312 (1970) (discussed in Chapter 1).

within current technological capabilities, and would provide for a "reasonable time" for compliance. Where technology was perceived to be inadequate, federal legislation sometimes went beyond the common law by calling for additional research, but this came via public research monies, and not by ordering the regulated community to produce technology that did not currently exist.[40]

All of this changed in a hurry in the late sixties and early seventies.[41] In a remarkably short number of years, the Congress populated the United States Code with legislation addressing environmental problems that embodied significant elements of the preventative paradigm while rejecting key elements of the common law paradigm.[42] The ambient air quality provisions are one of the flagships for this approach.

B. Meat Axes vs. Scalpels

Explaining the apparently sudden attractiveness of the preventative paradigm would take us too far afield from our story,[43] which is much

---

40. One reason for this, of course, was that research funding was acceptable to industry whereas mandated compliance with technological goals was not.

41. The two contrasting philosophies were not lost on those involved in the legislative battles of the time. Commenting on the relative success of coal industry lobbyists in shaping the 1967 Air Quality Act, a spokesperson for the National Coal Association put it this way:

> NCA ... set to work to convince Congress that whatever it did about controlling air pollution must be reasonable, practical, and economically feasible.... As a result of these activities and others, the coal industry and allies seem to be making progress in the face of overzealous demands for instant clean air.

Quoted in Richard H. K. Vietor, *Environmental Politics and the Coal Coalition* 148 (1980). Later, business and industry would attack the new legislation for demanding the impossible, regulating in the face of uncertainties, and failing to balance costs and benefits.

42. *See, e.g.,* Mary Graham, *The Morning After Earth Day* 4 (1999) (explaining that "in the four years beginning in 1969, almost overnight in political terms, congressional action transformed what had been mainly state and local housekeeping chores into a national campaign to protect the environment. Legislation created new public participation in major government and private decisions, new notions of federalism, and new government power over big business."). Graham's book stresses social and political considerations that distinguish the new legislation rather than the new regulatory philosophy. Instead, it highlights elements of the new legislation's regulatory approach that this chapter largely ignores, such as its notions of federalism, the enhanced role of citizen participation, and its skepticism toward bureaucracy.

43. It seems evident that public attitudes toward public health and the environment were changing profoundly in the years leading up to the late sixties, so that getting at the causes of those changes ought to play an important role in any explanation. *See, e.g.,* Richard J. Lazarus, *The Making of Environmental Law* 47–66 (2004). A complete explanation combines some understanding of why the diffuse public interest was so effectively represented in the legislative chambers as well as why the ordinarily strong interests of business and industry were unequipped to counter that broad interest. For work that seeks to explain the strong public interest, *see, e.g.,* Daniel Farber, *Politics and Procedure in*

more closely tied to what happened after this legislation passed. However remarkable it was that they came into being, the core features of the preventative laws enacted in the late sixties and early seventies have proven remarkably resilient over time, resisting many efforts to revise them.

A significant difficulty business and industry have always confronted in the legislative arena stems from the fact that the American public highly values the lofty goals embodied in the early environmental legislation. Any thoroughgoing switch from prevention back to the common law necessarily entails abandoning those goals, notwithstanding protests that the switch is only about better means to the same ends. Whenever legislative efforts have been popularly understood as rollbacks of those goals, the protests have been loud enough to get the attention of elected officials.

This reality was brought home to the deregulation minded 104th Congress, the spearhead of the Gingrich Revolution. Its reform efforts ran aground when the public became aware that the casualties of deregulation would include the preventative goals they valued.[44] After a quick retreat on regulatory reform helped the Republicans retain the House by a narrow margin, Senator John McCain offered a post-mortem in a New York Times op-ed. By showing themselves "too eager to swing the meat ax of repeal when the scalpel of reform is what's needed," House Republicans, McCain argued, had succeeded in making their stewardship of the environment "the voter's number-one concern about continued Republican leadership of Congress."[45]

Environmental Law, 8 J. L. Econ. & Organ. 59, 66 (1992); E. Donald Elliott, Bruck A. Ackerman and John C. Millian, *Toward A Theory of Statutory Evolution: The Federalization of Environmental Law*, 1 J. L. Econ. & Organ. 313 (1985); Christopher H. Schroeder, *The Political Origins of Modern Environmental Law: Rational Choice vs Republican Moment–Explanations for Environmental Law*, 1969–73, 9 Duke Env. L. & Policy Rev. 29, (1998). For work explaining business and industry's relative ineffectiveness, see David Vogel, *Fluctuating Fortunes—The Political Power of Business in America* (1999).

44. For the story of how the environmental community and the EPA helped generate public opposition to the regulatory reform initiatives, see Thomas O. McGarity, *Deflecting the Assault: How EPA Survived a "Disorganized Revolution" by "Reinventing" Itself a Bit*, 31 Envtl. L. Rep. 11249 (Envtl. L. Inst. 2001).

45. John McCain, Editorial, *Nature is Not a Liberal Plot*, N.Y. Times, Nov. 22, 1996, at A31. These lessons of the 104th Congress might have been anticipated had the flirtation with radical statutory change early in President Reagan's first term been recalled to mind. In the early eighties, Lou Harris, the AP–NBC News and the New York Times–CBS News had conducted polling that depicted the dangers of overhauling environmental legislation so as to weaken its standards. Harris found that fully eighty percent of Americans wanted no weakening of the Clean Air Act and the New York Times–CBS News poll found that two-thirds of them wanted air laws "as tough as they are now" even if "some factories might have to close." These and similar findings led Harris to counsel Republicans to "[W]atch out. [Voters] will have your hide if you [weaken the air laws.]" *Congress Begins*

The nearly sacrosanct status of the core features of environmental laws like the Clean Air Act strongly reinforces the importance of having a litigation strategy. As a much more subtle instrument of legal change, litigation presents several advantages over legislative victories. Whatever may be the unpopular consequences of successful litigation, responsibility for them can be laid off on the court that rendered the decision or on the enacting Congress. The benefits from litigation also accrue without demanding that business' champions in Congress directly take on the environmental sacred cows. Finally, litigation victory can also prove very durable in comparison even to legislative success and certainly compared to any particular agency decision, and a litigation victory can have ramifications far beyond the particular suit or statute being litigated. This durability value can hardly be over-emphasized in times of sharp political division over environmental policy. Under these circumstances, which have prevailed since the Reagan presidency, each side has the ability to block the other's legislative initiatives, so that whichever side enjoys the benefit of the statutory status quo enjoys a tremendous advantage.[46]

Success with the litigation scalpel did not come easily at first. In the early years after the enactment of preventative legislation some influential members of the federal bench seemed to appreciate the paradigm-shifting nature of the legislation, and its importance.[47] Consequently, the 1960s and 1970s gave birth to landmark decisions that reflected a heightened sense of environmental awareness, several of which are represented in this volume.[48] In a number of important cases, business argued that the regulatory authority established under the new laws ought to be interpreted in light of the paradigm of common law standards and "reasonableness," only to be told that the statutes that Congress had enacted were properly viewed under the new paradigm of prevention and anticipation. The appellate courts became protectors and defenders of the new paradigm, often using judicial review to ensure that

---

Rewrite of Clean Air Act, 37 Cong. Q. Almanac 505, 512 (1981). "[C]lean air," he continued, "happens to be one of the sacred cows of the American people." *Id.*

46. The Court's recent narrowing reinterpretation of the scope of the Clean Water Act in *SWANCC* illustrates this point. It will prove impossible for supporters of the broader interpretation to enact corrective legislation any time soon. *SWANCC's* story is told in Chapter 9 of this volume.

47. Judges Harold Leventhal and David Bazelon of the D.C. Circuit are frequently cited as originators of hard look review; other prominent judges, including Carl McGowan and J. Skelly Wright of the D.C. Circuit and James Oakes of the Second Circuit, also authored important hard look and reasoned decisionmaking opinions.

48. See U.S. EPA v. Reserve Mining Co., 514 F.2d 492 (8th Cir. 1975) (en banc) (discussed in Chapter 2); Calvert Cliffs' Coordinating Comm., Inc. v. U.S. Atomic Energy Comm'n, 449 F.2d 1109 (D.C. Cir. 1971) (discussed in Chapter 3).

administrative agencies took the new paradigm seriously.[49] As Judge
Skelly Wright famously wrote, the courts' "duty, in short, is to see that
important legislative purposes, heralded in the halls of Congress, are not
lost or misdirected in the vast hallways of the federal bureaucracy."[50]

The D.C. Circuit and other courts of appeals in the country were not
always in accord on the interpretation of the new statutes and some,
such as the Fifth Circuit, soon acquired a reputation for being more
sympathetic to business arguments.[51] Whenever business interests could
litigate in circuits other than the D.C. Circuit, they preferred to do so.[52]
More favorable venues could not assist business interests, however, if
they could not get to them, and often they could not.[53] The Clean Air
Act, for example, restricted judicial review of EPA air rules with nation
applicability—such as the national ambient air quality standards—to the
D.C. Circuit. For that reason, business and industry were forced to
litigate challenges to EPA's air quality rules in the relatively inhospita-
ble D.C. Circuit.

Thus it was that *Lead Industries* came to be filed in the D.C.
Circuit, and during the era in which that Circuit's protection of preventive legislation was running strong. There, petitioners contended that
EPA had failed to consider the economic and technological feasibility of
attaining the standards, relying instead on an estimation of the health
effects of lead exposure alone. The court of appeals rejected the argument that EPA must consider costs as being "totally without merit." In
the court's view, "the statute and its legislative history make clear that

---

49. For discussion of the attitudes of federal appellate judges regarding environmental litigation in the 1970s and 1980s, see Robert Glicksman & Christopher H. Schroeder,
EPA and the Courts: Twenty Years of Law and Politics, 54 Law & Contemp. Probs. 249
(1991).

50. *Calvert Cliffs' Coordinating Comm., Inc.*, 449 F.2d at 1111. See Chapter 3 of this
volume.

51. *See, e.g.*, Thomas O. McGarity, *Multi-Party Forum Shopping for Appellate Review
of Administrative Action*, 129 U. Pa. L. Rev. 302, 312 n.42 (1980) ("[R]umor has it that on
environmental questions the District of Columbia Circuit and First Circuit generally tend
to favor the agency, while the Fourth and Fifth Circuits are generally more 'pro-
business.'").

52. *Id.*

53. Even the more hospitable venues did not always produce the results business
preferred. In *Union Electric*, 427 U.S. at 246, for instance, the Supreme Court rejected a
utility company's argument that the EPA was required to consider technological and
economic feasibility in deciding whether to approve a state plan implementing the NAAQS.
In the *"Cotton Dust"* decision, *American Textile Mfrs. Inst., Inc. v. Donovan*, 452 U.S. 490
(1981), also, the Court rejected business arguments that setting standards under the
OSHAct required benefit-cost analysis. Overall though, business interests fared better in
the Supreme Court than they did in the D.C. Circuit. *Compare* Richard J. Lazarus,
Restoring What's Environmental about Environmental Law in the Supreme Court, 47
U.C.L.A. L. Rev. 703 (2000), *with* Glicksman & Schroeder, *supra* note 49.

economic considerations play no part in the promulgation of ambient air quality standards under Section 109."[54]

All the while that business and industry were making poor headway against the preventative approach, they were still honing the scalpel, if you will, by continuing to develop the intellectual and public policy case for the common law approach. While there is no single canonical statement of the regulated community's preferred approach, a short book published by the Business Roundtable articulates the major points. Entitled *Toward Smarter Regulation*, it identifies "twelve tenets of rational regulation." Five of these are directly relevant to how individual standards such as the ambient air quality standards are set:

1. *Risk-Based Priorities*: Resources should be committed to where the greatest risks can be reduced at the least cost.

2. *Risk Assessment and Risk Management*: A clear distinction should be drawn between the objective process of identifying (assessing) risk and the policy decisions about how to manage those risks.

3. *Sound Science*: Agency decisionmaking should be grounded on the most advanced scientific knowledge currently available, using "best estimates," not worst-case estimates of risk.

4. *Benefit-Cost Analysis*: Agencies should use benefit-cost analysis to determine whether or not a proposal should be considered for adoption. They should also choose the most cost-effective regulatory option.

5. *Market Incentives and Performance Standards*: Market-oriented solutions and performance standards should be preferred over command-and-control regulation.[55]

Each of these "tenets" touts a separate aspect of the scalpel of regulatory reform. None of them argues for dirtier air or worsened environmental conditions. They appeal to things that most Americans value or trust, such as science and scientists, whom Americans tend to

---

54. *Lead Indus. Ass'n*, 647 F.2d at 1148. *Lead Industries* was equally significant in upholding the EPA's authority to regulate on the basis of "subclinical effect[s]," effects that could be detected through testing, but which did not manifest themselves in any significant impairment of bodily function or disease. This enabled the EPA to regulate down to lower levels of exposure than would have been possible had the law required demonstrated showings of harm as a necessary condition to regulation. Together the health-based standard and the use of subclinical effects capture essential characteristics of the preventative or precautionary approach. *Id.* at 1156–59.

55. The Business Roundtable, *Toward Smarter Regulation* i-ii (1994). The other seven tenets addresses issues of Productivity, Wages and Economic Growth; Coordination Among and Within Agencies; Openness; Periodic Review; Federalism; Paperwork Burdens; and Regulatory Budget. *Id.* at iii-v.

hold in high regard as credible, especially compared to the suspicion with which they view government bureaucrats. Americans tend to believe that the results of scientific research are accurate and objective.[56] They also believe in the power of science to uncover true phenomena and separate these from things that are not true. Thus the idea that there should be a scientific justification for regulatory action strikes many people as a sensible and non-threatening requirement. Both the "sound science" principle and the "risk assessment/risk management" allow technical and scientific expertise to dominate the regulatory process.[57]

Of all of these regulatory principles, the benefit-cost principle is the Holy Grail of regulatory reform for business and industry, because it serves as the proximate justification or motivation for the others. For instance, benefit-cost analysis contemplates a quantitative risk assessment and such risk assessments contemplate the best science available. While cost-effectiveness is not strictly required by benefit-cost analysis, maximizing the benefit-cost ratio is an inviting goal. Market-oriented approaches to regulation are more congenial to the benefit-cost mindset than command-and-control approaches.[58]

As the 1970s drew to a close, business and industry advocacy of these principles was beginning to register some successes.[59] Some of the moral edge was beginning to wear off objections to the use of benefit-cost

---

56. *See, e.g.*, National Science Board, *Science and Engineering Indicators—2000* 8-1, 8-13 (describing public trust in scientists and medical researchers), *available at* http://www.nsf.gov/sbe/srs/seind00/pdf/c8/c08.pdf (last visited Feb. 10, 2005); Cary Coglianese & Gary E. Marchant, *Shifting Sands: The Limits of Science in Setting Risk Standards*, 152 U. Pa. L. Rev. 1255, 1264–66 (2004) (describing the confidence the public places in science).

57. Tenet 1, "risk based priorities," which plays a less immediate role in any particular rulemaking, also draws on science in a manner similar to tenet 3.

58. There is a problem with benefit-cost analysis, however: Opinion research shows that the public doesn't understand it and when some of its more controversial features are explained to them, like placing a monetary value on human life or discounting, they don't like them. The struggle over regulatory philosophy has always been a two-front war, with the discourse used in policy-elite conversations often quite different than the public discourse used by business and industry to defend their actions.

59. Business and industry have deployed a larger number of strategies to assist in developing a popular base of support for their regulatory philosophy than we can explore in this chapter. They fund think tanks and give grants to scholars to develop the theoretical arguments necessary to support benefit-cost analysis and sound science proposals. They have established research organizations and funded others to do the risk assessments and benefit cost analyses that are key elements in their ideal of rational regulation, and to critique the science being relied upon by agencies. They have also worked to undermine the effectiveness of environmental organizations, to split environmental coalitions where possible, to urge inquiries into the tax exempt status of some and to discredit the work of individual scientists when that work supports more stringent regulation. For a picture of the larger strategic efforts put forth by business and industry to seek to rebound from their earlier defeats, see Richard Lazarus, *The Making of Environmental Law* 94–97 (2004).

analyses for health and safety legislation.[60] Business and industry interests also began to improve their success rate in the courts. This came about in significant part because Republican Presidents Nixon, Ford, Reagan and Bush were making judicial nominations for all but four years during the twenty-year period between 1968 and 1992. Statistically, judges appointed by Republican presidents are more favorably disposed toward business and industry interests in environmental litigation than are Democratically appointed judges.[61]

Notwithstanding the increased confidence with which business and industry interests brought challenges to environmental statutes in the lower courts, their ambition continues to be a Supreme Court embrace of their regulatory tenets. The Court had never taken the walk to the green-side that the lower courts had.[62] Furthermore, in the *Benzene* litigation business and industry had caught a sense of what victory in the Court could mean. Although their arguments that the OSHAct embodied a benefit-cost test received only Justice Powell's vote in *Benzene*, and were later to be rejected by the court in the *Cotton Dust* case,[63] Justice Stevens' plurality decision showed everyone what a profound effect a Supreme Court decision could have on reinforcing regulatory principles, as well as how creative the justices could be with a statute. On the basis of statutory language that did not self-evidently bear this interpretation, *Benzene* found that OSHA had an obligation to make a prior determination of significant risk before lowering a standard for workplace toxics. Although the plurality opinion claims it was not imposing a "mathematical straitjacket" on the agency, in fact that requirement had the effect of helping to guarantee the rapid development of quantitative risk assessment in virtually all health standard

60. *See, e.g.*, Federal Regulation and Regulatory Reform, Report of the Subcomm. on Oversight and Investigations of the House Comm. on Interstate and Foreign Commerce, H.R. Rep. No. 95–134, at 515 (1976) ("The limitations on the usefulness of benefit/cost analysis in the context of health, safety, and environmental regulatory decisionmaking are so severe that they militate against its use altogether."). As President Carter and every subsequent President called for benefit-cost analysis of major rules—primarily as a way to monitor agency action—the charge of immorality was muted. For a recent critical assessment of the role of benefit-cost analysis in health and safety standard setting see Lisa Heinzerling & Frank Ackerman, *Priceless* (2004).

61. Richard Revesz, *Environmental Regulation, Ideology and the D.C. Circuit*, 83 Va. L. Rev. 1717 (1997); Christopher H. Schroeder & Robert L. Glicksman, *Chevron, State Farm and EPA in the Courts of Appeals During the 1990s*, 31 Envt'l L. Reptr 10371 (2001).

62. There were notable tensions between the Supreme Court and the D.C. Circuit during the 1970s, with the higher court issuing some sharp rebukes of some decisions from the appellate court. *See, e.g.*, Chevron U.S.A., Inc. v. Natural Res. Def. Council, Inc., 467 U.S. 837 (1984) (discussed in Chapter 6); Vermont Yankee Nuclear Power Corp. v. Natural Res. Def. Council, Inc., 435 U.S. 519 (1978).

63. *American Textile Mfrs. Inst., Inc.*, 452 U.S. at 490.

setting.[64]

In the years after *Benzene*, the Supreme Court added justices who have expressed even stronger skepticism toward environmental legislation than the plurality or Justice Powell had in *Benzene*. Thus, there was some optimism—and on the other side, a considerable nervousness—that *American Trucking* could be the case to cement benefit-cost analysis into regulatory practice, much as *Benzene* had had the practical effect of compelling quantitative risk assessment.

III. The Supreme Court Argument and Decision

The Court granted both the government's petition and the American Trucking Association's (ATA's) cross-petition and then set the cases down for consecutive argument on November 7, 2000.[65] Among other things, this meant that challengers would have an hour of argument time, instead of the usual thirty minutes. A Supreme Court argument carries significant prestige even among seasoned litigators (or perhaps especially among them), and the availability of additional argument time might have been anticipated to ease the problem of choosing who was to do the oral argument. There had been two major groups of business and industry petitioners below, and so each group might anticipate taking one of the two cases, one arguing the nondelegation issue, and the other the costs issue. It ended up, however, that the entire argument was done by Ed Warren of Kirkland & Ellis; Warren was assisted by Professor Charles Fried of the Harvard Law School and a former Solicitor General, on the brief. At a meeting of the parties called by the Chamber of Commerce, several seasoned Supreme Court advocates had urged that a single voice would be more effective than splitting the argument, and Warren, who was representing both the Chamber and ATA in the litigation, had gotten the nod from the group.

A single advocate certainly had advantages, especially if challengers intended to push the argument presented in their cross-petition that there was a nearly seamless connection between the nondelegation problem and the alleged mistake made by the *Lead Industries* decision on the costs issue. In that event, the parties could expect questioning during either argument to range across both issues, notwithstanding the formal division. This would mean that an advocate prepared on one issue only would be faced with either trying to defer questions on the other

---

64. *See, e.g.*, John F. Martonik et al., *The History of OSHA's Asbestos Rulemakings and Some Distinctive Approaches That They Introduced for Regulating Occupational Exposure to Toxic Substances*, 62 AIHA J. 208, 213 (2001) (opining that "quantitative assessment of risk was a result of the Supreme Court's 1980 benzene decision requiring OSHA to perform such an analysis when appropriate data are available").

65. This section is based in part on conversations with some of the litigators involved in the case, including Ed Warren, Bill Pedersen, Boyden Gray and Seth Waxman.

issue to his colleague or else risking an inadequate answer of his own. Either course of action would not fare well with the active inquisitors on the Supreme Court bench.

The availability of additional briefing space in the coordinated cases presented business and industry with a number of strategic decisions not faced by the government, whose strategy was comparatively straightforward. The government would challenge Judge Williams' nondelegation theory head on as unprecedented and unjustifiable. The challenge would be backed by a body of precedent finding an "intelligible principle" in laws no more precise than the ambient air quality provisions. The government would also defend *Lead Industries* as correctly decided, and would be backed by thirty years of consistent agency interpretation, multiple D.C. Circuit decisions, the text and structure of the statute and the considered view of nearly every scholar who had ever studied the issue.

In contrast, business and industry faced tougher choices. They had to decide how much they wanted to tie their theory of the case to Judge Williams' novel approach. Whatever its virtues, that theory remained a distinctly awkward application of what had been understood for two centuries as a constraint on the Congress, not on the Executive. It was also a doctrine that the Court had shown little inclination to use. Shoring up Williams' theory would take considerable effort, so perhaps they should attempt to defend the ruling on more traditional grounds.[66]

On the other hand, shying away from nondelegation entirely posed difficulties. Cases like *Benzene, SWANCC* and others taught that the Court could occasionally be persuaded to adopt an otherwise unorthodox reading of a statute to avoid a constitutional problem and—in *Benzene* and *SWANCC*—specifically to avoid a nondelegation problem. Business and industry knew that they might well need any interpretive leverage the nondelegation concern might provide in pursuit of their main objective.

Business and industry challengers also had to decide just how to attack *Lead Industries*. They had used a scattershot approach in the appellate courts, with multiple arguments not all of which were logically

---

66. One such alternative ground was suggested by the *American Lung Ass'n* decision. American Lung Ass'n v. EPA, 134 F.3d 388 (D.C. Cir. 1998). There, the D.C. Circuit had remanded an EPA decision not to revise the sulfur dioxide ambient standard on the ground that the agency had not engaged in "reasoned decision-making." *Id.* at 392. The court concluded that EPA had inadequately explained why 180,000 to 395,000 annual incidents of asthmatics suffering temporary adverse effects were not a "public health" problem that the Clean Air Act required EPA to address by lowering the standard. *Id.* The same themes that Judge Williams had woven into a nondelegation ruling might be used in a similar way here.

related to one another.[67] At various times and in various briefs, challengers argued that the Clean Air Act *permitted* consideration of costs, that it *required* consideration of costs and that it required a *Benzene*-like prior finding of significant risk at existing levels followed by a showing of demonstrable health improvements by lowering the levels.[68] At various times and in various briefs, the statutory basis for reading costs into the statute had been supplied by the term "public health," the term "margin of safety," the term "criteria," and by the reference to "appropriate" revisions of existing standards. Arguments based on these different texts did not lead to entirely congruent interpretations. A more consolidated approach was called for in briefing the case to the Supreme Court.

One decision the challengers did not face was whether to frame the argument in terms of the major tenets of the common law approach: the separation of risk assessment from risk management, the need for conclusive evidence of harm based on sound science, the obligation to balance costs and benefits, and the importance of risk-based priority setting to avoid waste.[69] By now, these tenets had become ingrained in the minds of advocates for the regulated community, and, of course, promoting the linchpin benefit-cost principle was what the case was all about. It would be difficult to imagine how challengers could argue a regulatory case without these tenets being presupposed. In the course of attacking EPA's decisionmaking, challengers pointed out how EPA had violated each of the tenets.

These were complex choices, but at least the cross-petitioners would not be battling alone. *American Trucking* generated an enormous number of amicus briefs, probably an unprecedented number in the annals of commercial litigation. While the United States had its amici, the vast preponderance of them filed on industry's side. General Electric retained Professor Laurence Tribe, renowned liberal constitutional scholar and frequent Supreme Court advocate, to file amicus briefs in both cases. In the nondelegation case, GE's brief made the most sustained and intellectually intriguing argument of all the submitted briefs. (At the same time, it presaged the choice cross-petitioners would eventually also make, choosing not to defend Williams' brand of nondelegation, but to urge instead the reinvigoration of the traditional use of nondelegation, which

---

67. *See supra* text accompanying notes 15–17.

68. *See, e.g.,* Conditional Cross–Petition for Writ of Certiorari at 22–26, *American Trucking Ass'ns* (No. 99–1426) (setting forth these as arguments, "among others," that challengers "will likely present should *certiorari* be granted").

69. *See supra* text accompanying notes 55–58. The only significant tenet that played no role in the briefing was the preference for market-or incentive-based regulation. Because the issue at hand was purely how the target air quality level should be set and not how it should be achieved, the question of whether to prefer command-and-control or market-based means of achieving it did not arise.

if applied would render the Clean Air Act unconstitutional.[70]) In the costs brief, GE urged a generalization of *Lockout/Tagout I*, raising Williams' inclination to see benefit-cost analysis in every statute to the status of a canon of statutory construction in which it would indeed be found in every statute unless Congress had clearly stated the contrary.

Other amicus briefs hammered away at nearly every aspect of the smarter regulation agenda, but of course stressing that the use of benefit cost analysis was essential to rational regulation. Robert Litan of the Brookings Institute, a think tank with a liberal reputation, wrote a brief for a lengthy list of economists, including many Nobel Laureates and chairs of the President's Council of Economic Advisors from both Democratic and Republican administrations. It extolled benefit-cost analysis and urged its universal deployment in regulatory proceedings. Numerous law professors and other regulatory policy scholars submitted a brief detailing how science alone cannot answer risk management questions, and then advocating benefit-cost analysis as the right tool for that job. Accountants, agricultural firms, chemical companies, electronics and computer firms, steel and aluminum firms, states, trade associations, senators and representatives and think tanks all weighed in on the side of their business and industry colleagues.

ATA itself eventually made its own strategic choices. As for Judge Williams' nondelegation theory, the challengers abandoned it. The opening sentence of the ATA/Chamber brief on nondelegation states that "Lead Industries spawned the nondelegation holding below."[71] Implicitly characterizing *Lead Industries* as a mistake, the sentence signals that the overarching objective of the challengers was indeed to dislodge *Lead Industries*. Referring to the "nondelegation holding below," rather than the "nondelegation problem," also anticipates distancing the brief and argument from that holding. The challengers thus signaled that they were giving up the prospect of achieving some far ranging holding requiring *agencies* to articulate "determinate, binding standards" to cabin whatever discretion the Congress had assigned to it, in order to concentrate on their prime objective. Instead, the brief depicts the lower court as trapped in a dilemma of the D.C. Circuit's own creation, facing the choice of rejecting *Lead Industries* which *stare decisis* principles counseled against, or else finding some other constraint on the unfet-

---

70. General Electric's brief linked its argument to the Court's recent reinvigoration of other structural features of the Constitution, such as its invalidation of the legislative veto and the line item veto and its restrictions on Congress' Commerce Clause authority, arguing that a reinvigorated nondelegation doctrine was cut from the same cloth. Brief of Amicus Curiae The General Electric Co., *American Trucking Ass'ns* (No. 99–1257).

71. Brief of Respondents American Trucking Associations, Chamber of Commerce of the U.S., et al. at 7, *American Trucking Ass'ns* (No. 99–1257) [hereinafter ATA Nondelegation Br.].

tered discretion the *Lead Industries* holding gave to EPA. In the brief, the latter problem of unfettered discretion is presented as the traditional nondelegation problem, and one that has been created entirely by an erroneous statutory interpretation. Just get the statute right—see that it entails weighing costs against benefits—and the statute thereby has an intelligible principle.

Driving this point home further, Mr. Warren's opening at oral argument began in exactly the same place as his opening brief. In response to the first question from the bench, Mr. Warren replied that "we are not saying that this statute does not provide an intelligible principle [as Judge Williams' had concluded] ... [W]e are saying that it is the *Lead Industries* line of cases that created the delegation problem here."[72]

Relying on the traditional formulation of nondelegation avoided the need to persuade the Court that Judge Williams had actually unearthed a portion of the nondelegation doctrine hidden for the past 220 years, but the traditional formulation created its own problems for cross-petitioners' argument. The "intelligible principle" standard, unlike Judge Williams' call for a "determinate ... standard," is an extremely forgiving one. The justices had a difficult time finding the nondelegation problem in the statutory language, which was studded with more discrete requirements than were statutes providing for "just and reasonable rates" or for regulation according to "the public convenience and necessity." If these latter statutes passed nondelegation muster, it was not clear what the delegation problem here was. Nondelegation would provide some purchase here only if the Court reinvigorated the nondelegation doctrine's traditional use, as GE had urged in its brief. The Court showed no inclination in that direction.

The response challengers offered at oral argument as to why the Clean Air Act was constitutionally defective was to say that nondelegation required there to be *countervailing* factors that the agency must consider, factors that suggested reasons not to regulate more strictly. In pushing against more stringent regulation, the argument seemed to be, these factors would become stronger as the ambient levels being considered moved lower and lower, and would provide a reason to stop at some point. Such countervailing factors would be supplied if the agency considered compliance costs or feasibility. Furthermore, it was not even necessary to commit the agency to any specific method for weighing costs. What simply was required was a consideration of the pros and cons. The image invoked to explain what challengers had in mind came

---

72. Oral Argument Transcript at 21–22, *American Trucking Ass'ns* (No. 99–1257) [hereinafter Nondelegation Tr.].

directly from Judge Williams. It was the idea of Ben Franklin's prudential algebra from *Lockout/Tagout I.*[73]

Questions from the justices at oral argument intimated that this argument did not persuade them, because it did not seem to cure the supposed problem. The complaint against the EPA's earlier decisionmaking was not that it lacked factors to consider; it was that the agency had not explained how the factors should be combined to produce a standard. Adding more factors, even countervailing ones, did not alleviate that problem. Countervailing factors are "just as indeterminate," offered Justice Scalia. "It seems to me it's not enough to have other factors on the other side. If you're going to bring more certainty to this statute, you need more determinative factors, not just more factors."[74] When Justice Breyer expressed identical concerns, the argument seemed in trouble from both ends of the bench.[75]

Of course, formal benefit-cost analysis would be determinative in the sense required. In choosing to articulate benefit-cost weighing in the much looser language of the prudential algebra, the challengers may have been hoping for an outcome similar to *Benzene*. The plurality there had ruled that OSHA must make a finding of significant risk, but had also insisted that this did not put a "mathematical straitjacket" on the agency. Notwithstanding that disclaimer, the opinion had supplied strong impetus for quantitative risk assessment requirements throughout the federal bureaucracy.[76] A ruling that agencies must employ Mr. Franklin's prudential algebra might well be expected to morph into formal benefit-cost analysis in the same way. The weakness of that approach here was that the softer form of weighing pros and cons did not seem to lessen the agency's discretion sufficiently to justify finding the EPA's interpretation unconstitutional.

This left the statutory argument to stand on its own. After a fair amount of discussion among the challengers' team of lawyers, the cross petition had anchored the costs argument in the requirement that EPA must protect the "public health." Both the brief and the argument

---

73. *See* ATA Nondelegation Br., *supra* note 71, at 6; Oral Argument Transcript at 11, *American Trucking Ass'ns* (No. 99–1426) [hereinafter Costs Tr.] (arguing that "[w]e are not talking about econometrics ... we're talking about what Ben Franklin called prudential algebra. Put one side of the column pros. One side of the column cons.... What we're talking about is a common sense weighing of competing considerations in a systematic way.").

74. Nondelegation Tr., *supra* note 72, at 32.

75. *Id.* at 33 ("Then what you're saying is that if you have 50 countervailing factors you may get a more informed judgment. I agree with you on that, but I now suffer from Justice Scalia's question. That is, I agree with that. I don't see how it's one wit more determinative whether you have 50 factors informing your judgment or one, or two.").

76. *See supra* text accompanying notes 63–64; Chapter 5 of this volume.

stressed that "public health ... is a discipline which examines health questions in terms of protecting the public with explicit reliance on cost/benefit considerations."[77] The justices were not persuaded here, either. To them, the object of the infinitive in the phrase "requisite to protect the public health" was distinct from the discipline practiced by public health professionals. More to the point, the idea that public health as used in the statute referred to the public's physical health made much more sense of Section 109, and the idea that costs were not part of the ambient standard setting process made much more sense of the text and structure of the entire Act.

While the questioning of the challengers' efforts to infuse costs into the statute through the term "public health" indicated much skepticism, the oral argument on the costs issue certainly vindicated the decision for a single advocate, because the nondelegation issue continued to be a major focus in the second argument, as it was in the first. Throughout the briefing, opinions and argument in the case so far, challengers had emphasized the need to rein in the unfettered discretion that the *Lead Industries* interpretation of the statute supposedly gave EPA. This is what reading costs into the statute was supposed to accomplish. A similar concern about a federal agency ranging widely across the entire U.S. economy with broad powers had been a clear influence on the plurality in *Benzene*, and challengers were hoping for a similar effect here. In the second argument, challengers were put to the proof: "[Y]ou say you don't know how we can live with this kind of a regime [in which costs are ignored]," asked Chief Justice Rehnquist. "Well, we have lived with it for 20 years."[78] With this, challengers were caught in a vise: on the one hand the Court did not seem persuaded that the prudential algebra proposed by challengers was any more intelligible than the method EPA was currently using, while on the other hand they did not see the method EPA was currently using to present the problem of unfettered discretion challengers alleged.

In the end, yoking the costs issue to an appeal on nondelegation may have proven more beneficial to the government's case and harmful to the challengers' than anyone would have supposed. It certainly served challengers' purposes of getting the question before the Court, but the oral arguments suggest that challengers' arguments on costs were greatly overshadowed by the Court's interest in nondelegation, and often it was a interest in—and skepticism toward—nondelegation in the strong sense of supposedly demanding "determinate standards." In this writer's opinion, there were no sufficiently strong statutory arguments available

---

77. Costs Tr., *supra* note 73, at 8.

78. *Id.* at 20.

to challengers on the costs question, but what arguments there were seemed almost drowned out by the nondelegation discussion.

After the argument, the government lawyers were entitled to some cautious optimism. For their part, the challengers' lawyers were discouraged. When it came down, the Court's opinion was unanimous. Justice Scalia's opinion for the Court reversed on the nondelegation point and upheld the interpretation of the statute put forth in *Lead Industries*. In a left-handed complement to the concerted efforts of the challengers and their amici, the Court observed on the costs issue that "[w]ere it not for the hundreds of pages of briefing respondents have submitted on the issue, one would have thought it fairly clear that this text does not permit the EPA to consider costs in setting the standards."[79] The Williams approach to nondelegation and the traditional nondelegation challenge to the statute were dispatched as well. Williams' idea that the doctrine requires the agency to supply an intelligible principle where it is otherwise lacking was cut off at its source:

> The idea that an agency can cure an unconstitutionally standardless delegation of power by declining to exercise some of that power seems to us internally contradictory. The very choice of which portion of the power to exercise—that is to say, the prescription of the standard that Congress had omitted—would *itself* be an exercise of the forbidden legislative authority.[80]

The statute itself then was found to fit comfortably within existing Court precedent as containing a sufficiently intelligible principle.[81]

Conclusion

After this sound defeat, the challengers' assault on the Clean Air Act's ambient air quality standards and their efforts to insert benefit-cost analysis into the statute petered out. On remand, the EPA's rulemaking survived a final challenge on the ground that it had not engaged in reasoned decisionmaking, a challenge the Court had treated as not yet before it.[82]

So when the dust settled, the preventative structure of the Clean Air Act was left unaffected by the *American Trucking* litigation. This will hardly be the end of the efforts of business and industry to impress common law principles onto preventative statutes when ever the opportunity presents itself, but it may well be the end of the attack on the ambient air quality standards. Over the years, those standards have been

79. *American Trucking Ass'ns*, 531 U.S. at 465.

80. *Id.* at 473.

81. *Id.* at 474.

82. American Trucking Ass'ns, Inc. v. EPA, 283 F.3d 355 (D.C. Cir. 2002).

ratcheted down to quite low levels and it is not clear that nationally uniform standards can go much lower. Increasingly, both the regulated community and the regulators are coming to see regulatory pressure coming from other places than the national ambient standards, whether they be pre-construction review of new sources, restrictions driven by regional air quality concerns rather than national standards, or from entirely new directions such as global warming-related or energy-related regulation.

That said, so long as preventative statutes remain on the books, the clash of the two paradigms will continue, because business and industry are just as firmly committed to the one as the environmental laws are to the other. Nor does *American Trucking* suggest that future efforts will fail. The Court did not so much endorse the preventative model as it expressed its willingness to uphold that model if Congress has been sufficiently explicit in enacting it. Not all of the statutes are as explicit has the Clean Air Act. Additionally, what Congress can create it can also amend, so the legislative scalpel will continue to be wielded by business and industry as well. *American Trucking* is a landmark chapter but it is not the end of the story.*

---

* I would like to thank Justin Coon and Lauren Donner Chait, Duke Law Class of 2006, for excellent research assistance.

Contributors to
Environmental Law Stories

John S. Applegate is Associate Dean for Academic Affairs and Walter W. Foskett Professor of Law at Indiana University School of Law–Bloomington. His scholarship and teaching in environmental law have focused on the regulation of toxic and radioactive chemicals, and he is the co-author of the casebook, *The Regulation of Toxic Substances and Hazardous Wastes*. Since 1993, he has served in several capacities as an advisor to the U.S. Department of Energy on the environmental consequences of nuclear weapons production, including chairing a citizens advisory board at the Fernald site in Ohio and membership on National Academy of Sciences committees. He is a scholar member of the Center for Progressive Regulation. Before joining the Indiana faculty, Professor Applegate was the James B. Helmer, Jr., Professor of Law at the University of Cincinnati College of Law, an associate with Covington & Burling in Washington, D.C., and a law clerk to Hon. Edward S. Smith of the U.S. Court of Appeals for the Federal Circuit. He holds a B.A. from Haverford College and a J.D. from Harvard Law School.

William A. Buzbee is Professor of Law at Emory Law School and Director of the Emory Environmental and Natural Resources Law Program. He is the author of numerous articles, book chapters and reports on environmental law, constitutional law and administrative law, with a particular focus on issues of regulatory federalism. Among his recent related publications are *Unidimensional Federalism: Power and Prospective in Commerce Clause Litigation*; *Commons: A Theory of Regulatory Gaps*; and *Standing and the Statutory Universe*. He is a founding Member Scholar of the Center for Progressive Regulation and the Vice President of the Georgia Center for Law in the Public Interest. Professor Buzbee received his J.D. from Columbia Law School and his B.A. from Amherst College. Between law school and joining Emory's faculty, he clerked for United States District Court Judge Jose A. Cabranes, was an attorney-fellow at the Natural Resources Defense Council, and did environmental, land use and litigation work for the New York City law firm, Patterson Belknap Webb and Tyler.

Holly Doremus is Professor of Law and Chancellor's Fellow at the University of California, Davis, and a Member Scholar of the Center for Progressive Regulation. She also teaches in the Ecology graduate program at UC Davis. She received her B.S. in biology from Trinity College (Hartford, CT), Ph.D. in plant physiology from Cornell University, and

J.D. from the University of California, Berkeley (Boalt Hall). After law school, she clerked for Judge Diarmuid O'Scannlain of the United States Court of Appeals for the Ninth Circuit, and practiced municipal and land use law in Corvallis, Oregon, before joining the faculty at UC Davis She has written extensively about endangered species and biodiversity protection, as well as about the intersection of science and natural resources policy. Illustrative articles include *Science, Judgment, and Controversy in Natural Resource Regulation*; *The Purposes, Effects, and Future of the Endangered Species Act's Best Available Science Mandate*; and *Biodiversity and the Challenge of Saving the Ordinary*.

Daniel A. Farber is Sho Sato Professor of Law and the Director of the Environmental Law Program at the University of California at Berkeley. He received a B.A. in philosophy with high honors in 1971 and an M.A. in sociology in 1972, both from the University of Illinois. In 1975 he earned his J.D. from the University of Illinois, where he was a member of the Order of the Coif, editor in chief of the *University of Illinois Law Review,* a Harno Scholar and class valedictorian. After graduating, Professor Farber clerked for Judge Philip W. Tone of the Seventh Circuit and for Justice John Paul Stevens of the U.S. Supreme Court. He then practiced law with Sidley & Austin before joining the faculty of the University of Illinois Law School in 1978. In 1981 he became a member of the University of Minnesota Law School faculty. During his years there he became the first Henry J. Fletcher Professor of Law in 1987, served as a visiting professor at Stanford Law School, Harvard Law School and the University of Chicago Law School, and was named McKnight Presidential Professor of Public Law in 2000. Professor Farber's books include *Eco-Pragmatism: Making Sensible Environmental Decisions in an Uncertain World* (1999), and *Environmental Law in a Nutshell*. He has also written many articles on environmental and constitutional law as well as about contracts, jurisprudence and legislation.

Jody Freeman is Professor of Law at Harvard Law School, where she teaches environmental law and administrative law. She was previously on the UCLA faculty. She holds a B.A. from UCLA, LL.B. from Stanford, LL.M. from the University of Toronto and S.J.D. from Harvard. Her scholarship in administrative law focuses generally on public-private collaboration in governance, and her work in environmental law focuses on questions of institutional design. She co-authors a casebook in environmental law. Her article *The Congressional Competition to Control Delegated Power* (with DeShazo) was selected as one of the top ten articles of the year by the Land Use and Environmental Law Review; *The Private Role in Public Governance* received the annual scholarship award from the American Bar Association's Section on Administrative

Law and Regulatory Practice for the best article on administrative law; *Extending Public Law Norms Through Privatization* was published in the Harvard Law Review in 2003.

Oliver A Houck is Professor of Law at Tulane University and directs its environmental law program. He is a graduate of Harvard College and Georgetown Law Center, with three intervening years in the U.S. military. He served as an Assistant United States Attorney for the District of Columbia, then as General Counsel of the National Wildlife Federation, also in Washington, before joining the faculty of Tulane. He has published more than thirty books and law review articles on environmental, constitutional, administrative and tax law.

Richard J. Lazarus is a Professor of Law at Georgetown University where he also serves as Faculty Director of the Supreme Court Institute. He is a graduate of the University of Illinois and Harvard Law School. He served as an attorney in the Environment and Natural Resources Division and as an Assistant to the Solicitor General of the United States Department of Justice. He was previously on the law school faculties of Indiana University, Bloomington and Washington University in St. Louis and has been a visiting professor at Northwestern University, University of Texas and Harvard law schools. His primary areas of legal scholarship are environmental and natural resources law, with particular emphasis on constitutional law and the Supreme Court. He recently published a book on the history of U.S. environmental law, *The Making of Environmental Law* (University of Chicago Press 2004). Professor Lazarus has represented the United States, state and local governments, and environmental groups in the United States Supreme Court in 37 cases decided on the merits.

Thomas O. McGarity holds the W. James Kronzer Chair in Trial and Appellate Advocacy at the University of Texas School of Law. He has taught environmental law, administrative law and torts at Texas since 1980. Prior to that he taught at the University of Kansas School of Law. After clerking for Judge William E. Doyle of the Tenth Circuit, Professor McGarity served as an attorney-advisor in the Office of General Counsel of the Environmental Protection Agency in Washington, D.C. Professor McGarity has written widely in the areas of environmental law and administrative law. He has written two books on federal regulation, *Reinventing Rationality* (1991) and *Workers at Risk* (1993) (with Sidney Shapiro). Professor McGarity is President of the Center for Progressive Regulation.

Thomas W. Merrill is the Charles Keller Beekman Professor at Columbia Law School, where he has served since 2003. He previously taught at Northwestern University School of Law, and served as Deputy Solicitor General in the Department of Justice (1987–1990). He has undergraduate degrees from Grinnell College and Oxford University, where he studied as a Rhodes Scholar, and a law degree from the University of Chicago. He clerked on the D.C. Circuit (for Chief Judge David Bazelon) and the U.S. Supreme Court (for Justice Harry Blackmun). Professor Merrill divides his scholarly energies between property, administrative law, and environmental law. He is the author of *Property:Takings* (Foundation Press 2002)(with David Dana), and of numerous articles, including *Rethinking Article I, Section 1*, 104 Colum. L. Rev. 2097 (2004); *The Origins of the American Public Trust Doctrine*, 71 U. Chi. L. Rev. 799 (2004) (with Joseph Kearney), *Agency Rules with the Force of Law*, 116 Harv. L. Rev. 467 (2002) (with Kathryn Watts); *The Landscape of Constitutional Property*, 86 Va. L. Rev 885 (2000); and *Golden Rules for Transboundary Pollution*, 46 Duke L.J. 931 (1997). He is a member of the American Academy of Arts and Social Sciences.

Carol M. Rose is the Gordon Bradford Tweedy Professor of Law and Organization at Yale Law School and Lohse Visiting Professor at the University of Arizona. She has degrees from Antioch College (B.A. Philosophy), the University of Chicago (MA Political Science, J.D. Law), and Cornell University (Ph.D. History). Professor Rose's research focuses on history and theory of property, and on the relationships between property and environmental law. Her writings include two books, *Property and Persuasion* (1994), and *Perspectives on Property Law* (2002, with R.C. Ellickson and B. A. Ackerman), and numerous articles on expropriation, traditional and modern property regimes, environmental law, environmental ethics, and natural resource law. She is a member of the American Academy of Arts and Sciences and is on the Board of Editors of the Foundation Press.

Christopher H. Schroeder is Charles S. Murphy Professor of Law and Professor of Public Policy Studies, Director of the Program in Public Law at Duke University. Schroeder received his B.A. from Princeton University, M. Div. from Yale University, and his J.D. degree from University of California, Berkeley (Boalt Hall). He has served as deputy assistant attorney general in the Office of Legal Counsel, U.S. Department of Justice, and in 1996–97 was the acting assistant attorney general in charge of that office. In 1992–93, he was chief counsel to the Senate Judiciary Committee. In addition to a range of environmental law topics, his scholarship includes work on constitutional law and democratic theory, Congress, risk regulation and theory, and tort. He co-authors *Environmental Regulation: Law, Science and Policy* (5th Edition forthcoming 2005) (with R. Percival, A. Miller & J. Leape) and co-edited *The New Progressive Agenda for Health Safety and the Environment* (2005) (with R. Steinzor). He serves as vice president of the Center for Progressive Regulation. Recent articles include *Foreword: Conservative and Progressive Legal Orders*, 67 Law & Contemporary Problems 1 (2004);

Priests, Prophets and Pragmatists, 87 Minnesota Law Review 1065 (2003); *Environmental Law, Congress and the Court's New Federalism Doctrine,*78 Indiana Law Review 413 (2003); *Military Commissions and the War on Terrorism* 29 Litigation 28 (Fall 2002); *Deliberative Democracy's Attempt to Replace Politics with Law*, 65 Law & Contemporary Problems 95 (2002); *Lost in the Translation: What Environmental Regulation Does That Tort Cannot Duplicate*, 41 Washburn L.J. 583 (2002).

Dan Tarlock is a Distinguished Professor of Law at the Chicago-Kent College of Law. He holds an A.B. and LL.B. from Stanford University. Professor Tarlock was a participant at the 1969 Conservation Foundation Arlie House Conference which helped to launch environmental law, and has taught environmental law, international environmental law, water law and related seminars since 1966. From 1969–1982, he was a member of the faculty at Indiana University, Bloomington and has visited at several law schools including the universities of Chicago, Hawaii, Kansas, and Michigan. Professor Tarlock has published over 100 articles on environmental, water and land use law. His books include *Environmental Protection: Law and Policy* (4th ed. 2003) (with F. Anderson, R. Glicksman, D. Markell, D. Mandelker) and *Water Resources Management* (5th ed 2002) (with Professor J. Corbridge and D. Getches). Professor Tarlock has served on some twenty National Research Council/National Academy of Sciences committees studying the environmental risks of pesticides and the protection and recovery of stressed aquatic ecosystems, including a study of the restoration of the Missouri River ecosystem, published as The Missouri River Ecosystem: Exploring the Prospects for Recovery (2002). In 2004, he was designated a National Associate of the National Academies of Science, Engineering and Medicine for his service to the National Research Council and the National Academy of Sciences.

†